International Series in Operations Research & Management Science

Volume 168

For further volumes:
http://www.springer.com/series/6161

Randolph Hall
Editor

Handbook of Healthcare System Scheduling

Springer

Randolph Hall
Epstein Department of Industrial and Systems Engineering
Viterbi School of Engineering
University of Southern California
McClintock Ave. 3715
Los Angeles, CA 90089-0193
USA
e-mail: rwhall@usc.edu

ISSN 0884-8289
ISBN 978-1-4614-1733-0 e-ISBN 978-1-4614-1734-7
DOI 10.1007/978-1-4614-1734-7
Springer New York Heidelberg Dordrecht London

Library of Congress Control Number: 2011940036

Printed on acid-free paper

Springer is part of Springer Science+Business Media (www.springer.com)

Preface

Provision of high quality and affordable health care is one of the greatest challenges facing the nations of the world. Growing elderly populations are straining the budgets of developed countries, such as the United States. Meanwhile, many third world countries face constant hardship in the form of low life expectancy and high infant mortality due to harsh environmental conditions, poor water quality, scarce medical resources, and risky and violent behavior. To solve the twin problems of human health and economic health, health care systems must become more efficient at delivering care and preventing disease.

This book is dedicated to improving the efficiency of health care by improving the scheduling of health care resources (such as doctors, nurses, and medical equipment) to meet patient needs. Building from operations research and industrial engineering, the authors address the complexities of healthcare scheduling in contexts ranging from ambulatory clinics to out-patient procedure centers to surgical theaters. All of the chapters demonstrate the importance of applying resources in accordance to anticipated needs, and making adjustments as needs change. In particular, the authors demonstrate how forecasting, queueing models, stochastic process models, and mathematical programming can improve nurse scheduling, bed management, appointment setting, and many other healthcare processes.

It is our hope that the knowledge and techniques presented in this book will help make quality healthcare accessible to more people. Industrial engineering and operations research are ready to contribute to improving health care around the globe.

Contents

Contributors

Bjorn Berg Edward P. Fitts Department of Industrial and Systems Engineering, North Carolina State University, Raleigh, NC 27695, USA, e-mail: bpberg@ncsu.edu

Richard J. Boucherie Stochastic Operations Research and Center for Healthcare Operations Improvement and Research, University of Twente, 217, 7500 AE, Enschede, The Netherlands, e-mail: r.j.boucherie@utwente.nl

Nebil Buyurgan Department of Industrial Engineering, University of Arkansas, Fayetteville, AR 72701, USA, e-mail: nebilb@uark.edu

Murray J. Cote Department of Health Policy and Management, Texas A&M Health Science Center, Houston, USA, e-mail: cote@srph.tamhsc.edu

Brian T. Denton Edward P. Fitts Department of Industrial and Systems Engineering, North Carolina State University, Raleigh, NC 27695, USA, e-mail: bdenton@ncsu.edu

Diwakar Gupta University of Minnesota, 111 Church Street S. E., Minneapolis, MN 55455, USA, e-mail: guptad@me.umn.edu

Randolph Hall Epstein Department of Industrial and Systems Engineering, University of Southern California, Los Angeles, CA 900089-0193, USA, e-mail: rwhall@usc.edu

Erwin W. Hans Center for Healthcare Operations Improvement and Research, Department of Operational Methods for Production and Logistics, University of Twente, Enschede, The Netherlands, e-mail: e.w.hans@utwente.nl

Markvan Houdenhoven Haga Ziekenhuis, Den Haag, The Netherlands

Peter J. H. Hulshof Center for Healthcare Operations Improvement and Research, Department of Operational Methods for Production and Logistics, University of Twente, Enschede, The Netherlands and Reinier de Graaf Groep, Delft, The Netherlands

Laleh Kardar University of Houston, Houston, USA, e-mail: lkardar@uh.edu

Gino J. Lim Department of Industrial Engineering, University of Houston, 4800 Calhoun Road, Houston, TX 77204, USA, e-mail: ginolim@uh.edu

Ashlea Bennett Milburn University of Arkansas, Fayetteville, AR 72701, USA, e-mail: ashlea@uark.edu

Arezou Mobasher University of Houston, Houston, USA, e-mail: amobasher@uh.edu

Edward Pohl Department of Industrial Engineering, University of Arkansas, Fayetteville, AR 72701, USA, e-mail: epohl@uark.edu

Manuel D. Rossetti Department of Industrial Engineering, University of Arkansas, Fayetteville, AR 72701, USA, e-mail: rossetti@uark.edu

Pieter Stepaniak Econometric Institute Erasmus University Rotterdam, Rotterdam, The Netherlands, e-mail: stepaniak@casema.nl

Martin Utley Clinical Operational Research Unit, University College, London, UK, e-mail: m.utley@ucl.ac.uk

Peter T. Vanberkel Center for Healthcare Operations Improvement and Research, Department of Operational Methods for Production and Logistics, University of Twente, Enschede, The Netherlands, e-mail: p.t.vanberkel@utwente.nl

Ronald van der Velden Econometric Institute Erasmus University Rotterdam Rotterdam, The Netherlands

Wen-Ya Wang University of Minnesota, 111 Church Street S. E., Minneapolis, MN 55455, USA, e-mail: wenya@ie.umn.edu

Dave Worthington Department of Management Science, Lancaster University Management School, Lancashire, UK, e-mail: d.worthington@lancaster.ac.uk

Maartje E. Zonderland Division I, Leiden University Medical Center, Postbox 9600, 2300 RC, Leiden, The Netherlands; Stochastic Operations Research and Center for Healthcare Operations Improvement and Research, University of Twente, Postbox 217, 7500 AE Enschede, The Netherlands, e-mail: m.e.zonderland@utwente.nl

Chapter 1
Matching Healthcare Resources to Patient Needs

Randolph Hall

Abstract Healthcare scheduling entails matching health care resources (providers, rooms, equipment, supplies, organs, devices and instruments) to patient needs, when and where they need them. Effective scheduling reduces waste, reduces patient waiting and improves health outcomes. Scheduling methods rely on operations research techniques, including forecasting, mathematical modeling and optimization, queue models and stochastic processes. These techniques are used in many ways, including setting appointments, scheduling staff, planning surgeries and managing the flow of patients through health care systems.

1.1 Introduction

Most people have been frustrated by the experience of waiting to see a doctor. We have sat in crowded rooms surrounded by other frustrated patients; we have waited for appointments that had to be booked months in advance; we have lain on examination tables anticipating when the doctor will step through the door. And, as we have waited, we have undoubtedly wondered: why? Why is it that waiting is so pervasive when we seek health care, and why is it so much more common than when we receive other types of service?

Patient delay can be traced in part to economics. Societies believe that quality health care is important for all people—akin to a "right"—and therefore find ways to minimize costs charged to patients, whether through subsidized service,

R. Hall (✉)
Epstein Department of Industrial and Systems Engineering,
Viterbi School of Engineering, University of Southern California,
McClintock Ave. 3715, Los Angeles, CA 90089-0193, USA
e-mail: rwhall@usc.edu

R. Hall (ed.), *Handbook of Healthcare System Scheduling*,
International Series in Operations Research & Management Science 168,
DOI: 10.1007/978-1-4614-1734-7_1,

regulated prices or government-provided free care. But in doing so, we have removed the ability of markets to match supply and demand through competitive pricing. There may be insufficient health professionals, or insufficient professionals of particular specialties. Or patients may seek more care than they truly need because it is so inexpensive. Or providers may have no incentive to expand capacity to serve groups of patients who are unable to pay full costs.

Economics alone, however, does not fully explain patient waits. Culture also plays a part. In most nations, doctors are among the elite. They are highly educated, intelligent and well paid. Moreover, patients become attached to their own care providers and do not readily switch to others when they experience poor service. Put these factors together, and we see that patients often believe that they are the lucky ones when they are so privileged to see their own doctors (not the other way around, that the doctors are privileged to have patients as customers). Patients simply do not have high expectations for quality of service in many places because they are resigned to accept waiting for health care.

Economics and culture are two parts of the story. The third, and the focus of this book, is the efficiency by which health care is managed and delivered. Waiting is the consequence of a mismatch between the needs for service and the availability of resources to provide that service. This mismatch might be the result of having too little of needed resources, or perhaps because the needs themselves are excessive. But it is just as likely that resources and needs have not been adequately synchronized with each other. Perhaps there are sufficient doctors, but they are working in places where the demands are not so great, or at times of day when the needs are not as strong. Perhaps operating or procedure rooms are underutilized because of gaps in time created by patient, or doctor, cancelations. Or maybe in-patient rooms are left vacant while patients are left on gurneys in the emergency department, simply because cleaning crews have not been scheduled or patient transport is unavailable.

It is no simple task to match resources to needs in health care. Providing a medical procedure to a patient often entails sequences of tasks performed by different individuals in combination with equipment, supplies and specialized work spaces. Sometimes the patient must move from place to place within or among buildings to complete the care, and other times multiple specialists must come to the patient to provide needed services. At each stage of care, waiting may ensue; is a challenge to ensure that "patient flow" will be smooth from one step to the next.

Moreover, the time required to deliver a particular procedure tends to be more variable than in other systems, such as manufacturing, where each part may be processed in more or less the same time as the next. While health care can surely be more standardized than it is, patients are not all the same. Whether it is their genetic make-up, environment from which they come, demographic characteristics (such as age, language and mobility), particular symptoms that they exhibit or their own health behavior, patient care must always be individualized to some degree. Beyond this, the presentation of patients for service is inherently variable because health conditions can emerge at random due to injury or illness, and because patients do not always show up on-time. Uncertainty, thus, creates a "wild card" for the best planned schedules.

Also, unlike manufacturing, health care usually requires the presence of the customer (i.e., the patient), often within a stressful or uncomfortable environment. It is not like dropping off shirts at the dry cleaner and waiting several days for them to come back. For health care, patients usually cannot leave until the job is done, making waiting that much more costly. But the consequences of waiting go beyond simple loss of time. The patient may experience pain, or conditions might worsen. For some diseases, death may result if not treated with sufficient speed. In emergency rooms, complications may occur when patients become frustrated with long waits and leave without being seen, or leave against medical advice.

Unfortunately, many care givers usually lack the skills to systematically improve service by creating schedules that better match resources to patient needs. health care today operates on the foundation of its historical roots, that of individual doctors serving patients from their private practices. The person in charge of the office is typically the doctor, someone with no managerial or engineering training. Even in larger clinics or health centers, it is uncommon to have someone with an advanced analytical education, such as operations research or industrial engineering, even though a large center may be a multi-billion dollar enterprise, much larger than a typical manufacturer. Looking at the national level, the industry of health care in America tends toward decentralization, rarely operating at a larger scale than regional networks. Only recently have organizations like Geisinger Health System developed ways to effectively standardize care and shown the benefits in improved efficiency, quality and outcomes.

1.2 Defining Patient Needs

The intent of this book is to offer a foundation from which skilled professionals can improve the delivery of health care through improved scheduling—that of matching health care resources with needs in time and place. Each chapter is written by an expert on a particular aspect of health care scheduling, and each chapter demonstrates how analytical methods arising from operations research can be used to produce schedules that reduce waiting, reduce idle time or improve health outcomes. From the patient perspective, we seek to ensure that their needs are met, such as:

Preferences to be served by particular individuals: These may be the people who have seen the patient in the past, or perhaps individuals who by recommendation or reputation are preferred by patients for their situation. A patient may also prefer providers who speak their own language, are the same gender, have comforting manners or understand his or her culture. One doctor does not easily substitute for the next given the close relationship that often develops with their patients.

Preferences to be Seen at a Particular Place: A location or provider may be preferred because of proximity to home or work; because it is a part of the patient's insurance network; because it offers a collection of integrated services; or because of good experiences in the past. Some centers are affiliated with the patient's own faith group. Others may provide an environment that reduces the stress of doctor visits.

Desire to be Seen at a Particular Time: A visit for care must fit within the complete set of activities (including work, school, childcare, etc.) in a patient's day, leading to preferences for visits at particular times. However, preferences are also driven by the urgency of the patient's condition, which may compel the patient to seek a same day appointment or drop in unscheduled for urgent or emergency care.

Medical Needs: Symptoms and diagnosed conditions motivate patients to seek particular types of care, sometimes from a primary care doctor, nurse practitioner or pharmacist, and other times from specialists. Preventive care—such as annual physicals, vaccinations or asymptomatic screenings—constitutes a modest portion of the demands for health care. Most care is driven by illness or injury, or symptoms thereof. However, the need for care is also affected by the availability and quality of prior care. Undiagnosed or untreated prior conditions, or the absence of preventive care, can lead to more severe future complications.

Medical Professional Opinion: Doctors, nurses and other medical professionals have the ability to create their own demand. This could be through routine scheduling of a follow-up visit. Or it could be the referral to another doctor for specialized care. It could be visits required for the management of chronic conditions. Or it could be scheduling a particular surgery at a particular hospital. In these and other examples, the demand for future care results, to a significant degree, from the professional opinion of the people who provide the care.

Coverage and Fees: Although health care is often subsidized by government or employer provided insurance, patients typically do pay a portion of their costs through varying "co-pays". Also, different providers charge different amounts, and different types of services bear different costs (e.g., care delivered in emergency departments is typically more expensive than care delivered in urgent clinics). These fees vary depending on whether the provider is inside or outside the patient's insurance network. And, the uninsured (or under insured) may only have access to care through particular providers.

1.3 Defining Healthcare Resources

All these factors—preferences for providers, place or time; medical need and professional opinion; and fees as well—affect the demands or needs for health care. Care is provided through the provision of resources that meet these needs, resources that include:

Doctors and other health professionals: Most aspects of care demand contact from health care professionals, and therefore availability of people drives most scheduling in health care. In some cases, the schedule represents appointments for specific patients to see specific doctors at specific times. In other cases, the schedule represents the assignment of particular people to work shifts with set start and end times. In other cases, the schedule represents the assignment of an operating room to a particular surgeon for a block of time. In all of these examples, the schedule focuses on the people providing care.

Rooms: The places where care is delivered are also scheduled and assigned, to both patients and providers. These include rooms for examinations, procedures, surgeries, diagnostics and tests and recuperation. Each of these types may be further specialized. For instance, hospital wards may be separated into intensive care, telemetry, isolation, recovery from anesthesia and so on. On the other hand, a hospital may opt to equip its rooms to accommodate virtually any type of condition. Rooms also reflect the needs of their facilities, anywhere from a private practice, to a specialized clinic, an academic health center or perhaps a rehabilitation hospital.

Equipment: Equipment is either permanently, or temporarily, assigned to each room to support the services that take place therein. When permanent, the room takes on the specialization offered by the equipment—for instance a place for conducting Magnetic Resonance Imaging (MRI) examinations or kidney dialysis. In other places, equipment may be portable (for instance a moveable x-ray machine), perhaps enabling the patient to stay put and allowing the equipment to move from room to room instead. Some equipment may reside in the homes of patients receiving care for a chronic condition, either temporarily or permanently.

Supplies: These are the expendable items that are consumed in the delivery of care. For instance, medications, bandages, protective garments, needles and blood are all expendable in the course of providing care. Supplies are stored in stock rooms or warehouses and made available as needed to serve medical needs. Scheduling is required for the transport of supplies and determination of stocking levels as well as planning their production.

Implantable devices and organs: Certain medical procedures require the implantation of an artificial device (e.g., a hip or knee replacement or a pacemaker) or a human organ (e.g., a kidney, liver or heart). The procedure cannot take place without the device or organ, and therefore surgery must be synchronized with their availability. In the case of transplants, scheduling includes matching particular organs (which become available at random) to particular patients, including the rapid transport of the organ to where it is needed.

Instruments: These items support medical procedures, diagnoses and other aspects of care, ranging from thermometers, to meters, and surgical instruments. Instruments are sometimes reusable, in which case they must be sterilized between patients, but are sometimes discarded after use.

For all of these examples of health care resources, the challenge is to synchronize availability with the needs for care, so that just the right amount and type are available when the patient needs them, thus minimizing both wastage and inconvenience (or harm) to patients.

1.4 Issues and Options for Scheduling Healthcare Resources

The keys to good scheduling in health care are data, analytics, systems, software, culture and management. **Data** combines with **analytics** to track historical trends, and forecast the future, answering questions like:

- How long will a particular procedure take for a given patient, with a given doctor, on a particular day?
- How many patients can we expect to present for care in an emergency department on a given day of the week, time of day and time of year?
- How will the demand for appointments depend on the prevalence of influenza, given the time of year and cases seen to date?
- What is the projected future need to care for a patient of a particular age, weight and blood glucose level, who has been diagnosed for type 2 diabetes?
- How likely is it that a particular patient will be a no-show for a scheduled appointment, made a set number of weeks in advance?
- What is the incidence of complications when care is delayed or foregone?

In all of these examples, the need is to maximize the precision by which health care is delivered to match demonstrated patterns of need.

Analytics, combined with **systems**, are also critical in the construction of schedules. Analytics provide the capability to optimize a schedule of a given type against defined objectives related to the cost of offering service, the quality of the service provided and health outcomes, while also meeting defined constraints. In surgery, the underlying system may be one of block scheduling, where particular times and rooms are reserved for specific doctors or specialties. Patients may then be assigned to dates based on the criteria defined by each surgeon. Within the context of such a system, computer algorithms may be used to optimally assign blocks to particular surgeons and to fill surgical appointment slots. As illustrated in this example, the analytics enable the schedule to be optimized within the context of the system created by the medical professionals or hospital administration. Analytics include algorithms for optimizing integer programs, stochastic process models representing patterns of patient and provider behavior and queueing models that predict the occurrence of delay as a function of supply and demand.

Data, **systems** and **analytics** come together within software, which is the enabling tool to support the implementation of a schedule and accompanying analytics. The software provides interfaces to: schedulers who set appointments and assign resources; doctors who may wish to input preferences and constraints; patients, who sometimes book their own appointments and management who monitor and control performance as well as allocate resources. The software can also support the automated acquisition and recording of data. And software can provide a tool for communication among and between departments, so that the arrival of patients and resources can be anticipated with greater accuracy.

The **culture** represents the collective ethos of staff and patients participating in the healthcare environment, and particularly how they might respond to the scheduling system and interact with its software. Scheduling is only successful when those involved respect the outcomes—that it is important to follow the schedule, serve patients on-time, arrive on-time, show up to work when needed and so on. Good schedules cannot overcome a weak culture, but they can help a strong culture become even better.

Last, effective **management** is an important driver for successful scheduling. Those in a position of leadership need to convey the need for efficiency and service, and translate those needs into the reward structure: as a component of annual compensation, a factor in raises, and an element in hiring new employees. Relative Value Units (RVUs) are one tool that management can use to measure physician productivity (converting assignments into a uniform measure of work), and can help balance capacity with patient needs. Management must also be the role model for the entire organization. For instance, doctors cannot be expected to keep to their schedules if the leadership does not do the same.

Thus, data, analytics, systems, software, culture and management come together in successful scheduling. Yet there are still more options.

- Should an "open access" model be adopted, easing the process of scheduling same day appointments for urgent conditions with one's one primary care doctor?
- Can electronic health records be leveraged, making it easier for alternate doctors to step in when the primary doctor is unavailable?
- How much discretion should a surgeon have for setting surgical times, based on their own experience and understanding of the cases, rather than following a data-driven approach?
- To what degree should appointments be "over booked", and how should this be done, in expectation that some appointments will be canceled?

While the methods of operations research can be used to help answer these questions, there are no universal truths. Each situation (system, patient population, etc.) must be carefully analyzed to see what works best within the context of good scheduling methods.

1.5 Book Organization

The remaining 11 chapters of this book address separate aspects of health care scheduling, beginning with more strategic issues and moving toward more detailed operational questions.

1 **Capacity Planning**: Through queuing models, this chapter illustrates how randomness creates the need for surplus capacity to accommodate uncontrollable fluctuations, how that level of surplus capacity can be calculated, and how pooling resources can reduce the requirement for surplus capacity.
2 **Nurse Scheduling**: Presents the mathematical programing formulations for the creation of nurse schedules, both for wards and for operating rooms. The chapter shows how multiple objectives, representing such factors as cost of shift preferences, can be represented in scheduling models.
3 **Patient Appointments in Ambulatory Care**: Describes systems for setting outpatient appointments in two stages, first establishing the clinic profile (dividing days into appointment slots) and second booking patient appointments.
4 **Operating Theatre Planning and Scheduling**: Defines the operating theatre as a driver for hospital activity, developing planning models for scheduling elective procedures within a hierarchical structure.
5 **Appointment Planning and Scheduling in Outpatient Procedure Centers**: Provides systems for setting appointments for specialized procedure facilities, such as outpatient surgery or specialized diagnostics, for which cases are less complex than in inpatient surgery.
6 **Human and Artificial Scheduling System for Operating Rooms**: Focuses on scheduling cases within surgical rooms, and in particular the need for incorporating the knowledge of human schedulers within systems for setting surgical schedules, accounting for delays and cancelations while seeking to keep operating rooms from completing their delay schedules too early or too late.
7 **Bed Management and Control**: Examines the role of the inpatient bed as a key resource that defines the flow of patients through a hospital, and the relationship of bed management to intake and discharge.
8 **Queuing Networks in Healthcare Systems**: Provides an analytical queueing framework to represent the interaction between different stages of services within a complex network of care, identifying bottlenecks that inhibit patient flows through the system.
9 **Medical Supply Logistics**: Addresses scheduling of supplies and managing inventories to support the delivery of care and the needs to coordinate the flow of these items with patient demands. Management of blood supply is used as an illustration.
10 **Operations Research Applications in Home Health Care**: Provides models for managing the movement and timing of nurses and other health professionals, serving patients in their own homes, along with the provisioning of needed resources in patient homes.
11 **A Framework for Healthcare Planning and Control**: Concluding the book, the final chapter provides an integrative framework for health care system scheduling, based on four management areas (medical planning, resource capacity planning and financial planning) implemented within a four level hierarchy (strategic, offline operational, online operational and tactical).

Collectively, the book's 12 chapters provide a state-of-the-art review of models and methods for scheduling the delivery of patient care.

1.6 Closing Thoughts

Health and longevity are nearly universal aspirations. Despite dramatic improvements in health in the industrialized world, some countries have experienced little gain in life expectancy over the last century. Poor water quality, risky behaviors, infectious disease, violence and weak health care systems all contribute to shortened lives in third world countries, which sometime fall below half that of the industrialized world. Healthcare scheduling alone cannot correct disparities as huge as these, but can help make care accessible to more people.

Just as health outcomes vary from country to country, so does the cost of health care–without always producing concomitant improvements in health outcomes. America has suffered a terrible fate in that its cost of care is far larger than other countries, whereas its life expectancy is not. Many people simply lack access to basic preventive care. Improvements in the delivery of care, and in particular the application of analytic methods arising from operations research, can help correct this type of economic disparity.

We should strive for systems that ensure that our doctors are not just well trained and provide good individualized care. We should expect that our health care providers contribute to a well-coordinated system that delivers care with great efficiency and quality, at reasonable cost, matching the resources for care to where (and when) they are needed most. As is the focus of this book, striving for efficiency in care through good scheduling is good for health.

Chapter 2
Capacity Planning

Martin Utley and Dave Worthington

Abstract In this chapter, we discuss some of the modeling methods available for use by health care organizations in determining the level of resources to make available for the delivery of a service or a set of services. We focus mainly on the insights available from different forms of queuing model but discuss also the role of simulation modeling. We then outline the challenges faced in populating capacity planning models with appropriate parameter estimates before closing with some remarks on the non-technical, cultural barriers to effective capacity planning.

2.1 Introduction

Scheduling in health care is often concerned with matching the demand for a service to the resources available to provide that service. At its simplest, this might involve scheduling for an outpatient clinic's patients who have identical and wholly predictable needs that can be met by a single clinician. Toward the other end of the spectrum is the composition of surgical theatre lists that balance the clinical urgency of the candidate patients and administrative wait time targets, account for heterogeneous, stochastic operating times and the prospect of emergency cases and enable targets to be met regarding theatre utilization, overtime and elective cancelation rates.

M. Utley (✉)
Clinical Operational Research Unit, University College London, London, UK
e-mail: m.utley@ucl.ac.uk

D. Worthington
Department of Management Science, Lancaster University Management School, Lancashire, UK
e-mail: d.worthington@lancaster.ac.uk

R. Hall (ed.), *Handbook of Healthcare System Scheduling*,
International Series in Operations Research & Management Science 168,
DOI: 10.1007/978-1-4614-1734-7_2,

Other chapters in this book set out Operations Research (OR) methods that can be used to foster efficient scheduling in health care, a major intellectual and organizational challenge and an area where OR has a considerable amount to offer. The pressure for efficient scheduling within health care stems from the fact that, in virtually all health care contexts, there are limits on the resources available to deliver services. Where resources are abundant to the point of excess, scheduling does not arise as a problem. Also, where resources are not at all adequate, the benefits of efficient scheduling can be marginal—system performance being determined by the lack of resources, however efficiently they are used. Given these considerations, it is fair to say that efficient and effective scheduling becomes a priority once there is a reasonable balance between the demands on a service and the resources available.

In this chapter, we focus on modeling methods for capacity planning, the process by which organizations determine the broad level of resources they make available for the delivery of a service or a set of services. Specifically we define capacity planning to be "deciding on the amount of beds, staff, consulting rooms, equipment, etc. sufficient to enable an organization to meet demand for one or more packages of care while achieving specified service standards".

Section 2.2 considers modeling approaches based on estimating the "unfettered demand" for resources associated with delivering a service, by which we mean the amount of each resource that would be used in a specified period of time if there were no constraints on any resource at any point in the system. Typically, this demand is the result of stochastic processes and, while the expected demand is a useful quantity for organizations to know, the intrinsic variability in this quantity is also of considerable importance when planning capacity.

Estimating unfettered demand is often amenable to intuitive, analytical techniques which can be quite insightful, and this aspect is emphasized. We introduce the notion of reserve capacity and the tension that variability introduces between the efficient use of resources and service standards based on accommodating a target proportion of requests for service. This leads to the central notion that, to estimate capacity requirements, you need to estimate or know demand, variability in demand and the desired service standards.

While modeling unfettered demand gives useful insights about capacity requirements, it cannot explicitly account for the impact that having finite resources available will have on the performance of a system. In Sect. 2.3 we introduce models designed to incorporate finite resource levels and their consequences more directly. Here there is scope for generating insights using analytical queueing models, but often simulation models are required for a detailed picture.

In Sect. 2.4 we discuss some of the issues that confront modelers and organizations when trying to populate capacity planning models with parameter estimates, with particular focus on the use of historical data. In Sect. 2.5 we give some closing remarks, touching on the potential role of simple "rule of thumb" approaches to capacity planning and some of the cultural and managerial challenges to ensuring that the benefits of careful capacity planning are realized. We do not attempt to provide an expert view here, but rather to flag to modelers some of the non-technical issues to be aware of.

2.2 Estimating Unfettered Demand Using Analytical Models

In Sect. 2.2.2, we consider capacity requirements in terms of the number of staffed beds that should be made available for the delivery of an inpatient service. Of course for some health services, capacity might be considered primarily in terms of the theatre time allocated to a specialty, the number of appointments a clinic offers or the number of CT-scanners available. Modeling the requirements for these and other key resources can be approached by applying similar techniques to those outlined here. Also, in many cases, the models outlined in Sect. 2.2.2 can be augmented to give a way of simultaneously estimating the capacity requirements for a range of different resources associated with the same service. First, we consider briefly the problem of estimating the overall number of patients to anticipate.

2.2.1 Estimating the Number of Patients to Cater For

How to model the number of patients that a service should be designed to cater for depends on the nature of the service and the nature of the health economy. For conditions such as cancer or heart disease and in societies that aspire to universal access to care for such conditions, models to forecast future patient numbers may be based on demographic projections for a particular catchment area, allied with fixed or projected age-specific incidence and prevalence rates. The number of patients to cater for may also be based on considerations of what makes a financially viable or successful service and also, in some settings, considerations of market share. Whatever benefits accrue when different institutions compete (either explicitly or implicitly) for patients, competition introduces additional uncertainty in terms of patient numbers. In general, additional uncertainty increases capacity requirements across a health economy, particularly in systems looking to guarantee patient choice over provider. This is not a problem, so long as it is recognized that many health care costs are driven by having the capacity in place to treat patients (staff, equipment, etc.) rather than by actually treating them.

In a context where plans are being made to increase access to a service that is not widely available (as has been the case for, say, the expansion of bariatric surgery services in some countries) it may not be feasible to attempt to meet the full demand for the service. Here, the number of patients to cater for may be driven and limited by the number of specialist staff available. In this context, capacity planning may be concerned with identifying the level of other resources to provide in order to ensure that efficient use can be made of scarce specialist skills while meeting service standards for those patients who do gain access to the service.

2.2.2 Demand Associated with Known Level of Patient Numbers

Having made an attempt to estimate the overall number of patients per year (for example) that might be expected to access or seek to access a service, there comes the task of translating this into the day-to-day or shift-to-shift demand for key resources. In this section we illustrate the extent to which variability in arrivals and variability in the resources used in the management of individual patients influence the capacity required to cater for a given number of patients, ensuring that a given proportion of requests for service can be met (other service standards are considered in later sections).

Starting from the simplest case, we present models that incorporate different sources of uncertainty and variability, using the illustrative context of an intensive care unit that admits patients following surgery. These models are discrete in time in that arrivals to the unit all happen at integer time units (assumed here to be days but potentially staff-shifts or hours) and patients stay on the unit for an integer number of time units prior to discharge.

Model 1. Suppose first that, each and every day, N patients are operated upon and each requires a bed in the intensive care unit for exactly L days. The demand for beds in this instance will be constant and equal to $N \times L$. Supplying $N \times L$ staffed beds will allow all demand to be met with certainty. Supplying less than $N \times L$ staffed beds would render the planned surgical program infeasible.

Model 2. If, as is typical, length of stay is variable, there will be inevitable variation in demand. Gallivan et al. (2002) developed a simple model to illustrate the variation in demand introduced by variation in length of stay. Suppose that N patients are admitted on a particular day and that the probability of a patient remaining on the unit for at least i days is p_i. The distribution of bed demand from this tranche of arrivals, j days after they arrived, is given by the binomial distribution with N trials each of probability p_i. Extending this, if N such patients are admitted each and every day the probability of n beds being required on a given day is given by the coefficient of s^n in the polynomial.

$$Q(s) = \prod_{i=0}^{\infty} [(1 - p_i) + p_i s]^N \tag{2.1}$$

where s is a dummy variable between 0 and 1. The product in Eq. 2.1 is over a series of binomial expansions, each of which represents the bed demand associated with a single day's admissions.

Figure 2.1 shows the impact of a degree of variability in length of stay (top left hand corner of figure) on the distribution of demand (bottom right). Despite the fact that, in this example, over 80% of patients stay just one day, the long tail on the length of stay distribution results in demand occasionally being three or more staffed beds above the average demand of 8–9. In this instance, the model can be used to estimate that, in order for capacity to be sufficient to meet demand on 95%

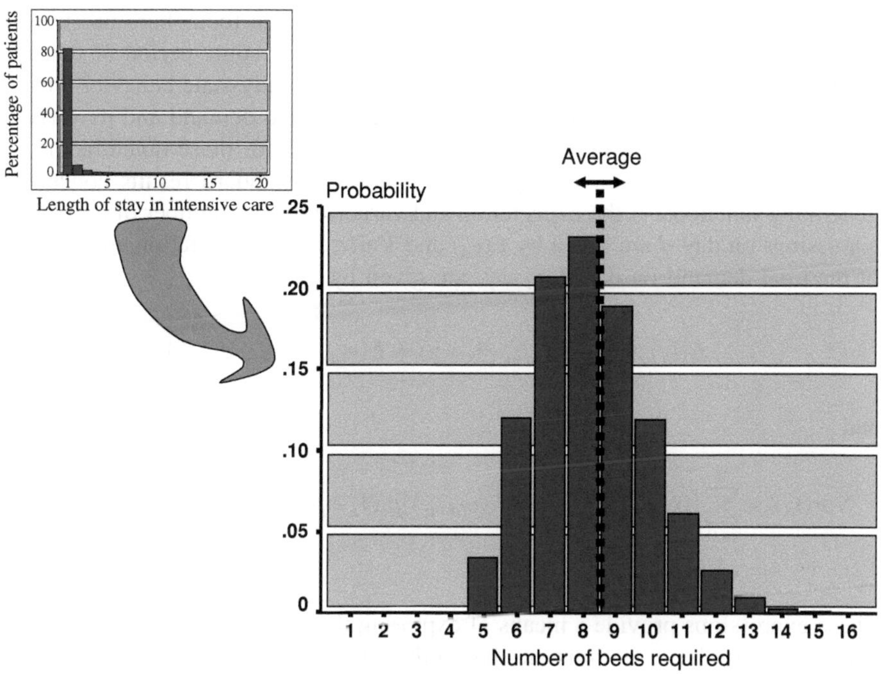

Fig. 2.1 The impact of variability in length of stay on bed demand

of days, the capacity provided should be about 30% above the expected daily demand. This illustrates the main use of models of unfettered demand: that of gauging the proportion of time that a system would be overloaded if capacity was in fact finite and set to a particular value.

Model 3. The model described above can be extended to incorporate numerous additional sources of variability and complexity (Utley et al. 2003). Suppose that any given surgical patient does not attend for surgery with probability v . Suppose further that the number of planned surgical patients is not constant but, on the dth day of the period of interest, is given by N_d. Suppose further still that, in addition to the post-operative patients, there is a probability q_{ed} of there being e emergency admissions to the unit on the dth day of the period of interest.

In this case, the probability of n beds being required on the dth day of operation is given by the coefficient of s^n in the polynomial.

$$Q_d(s) = \prod_{i=0}^{d}\left[[v + (1-v)((1-p_i) + p_i s)]^{N_{(d-i)}} \sum_{e=0}^{\infty} q_{e(d-i)}((1-p_i) + p_i s)^e\right] \tag{2.2}$$

Again, simple binomial expansions form the building blocks of this expression. Equation 2.2 gives the transient result for the full distribution of demand for a unit that is empty prior to the first day of operation. With the focus here on strategic capacity planning, it is worth considering demand after some period M that represents a maximum length of stay, before which any steady-state behavior will not emerge. Also, it can be useful to work with the expected demand and its variance rather than the full distribution. Obtaining expressions for these quantities is relatively straightforward, involving the application of standard results concerning generating functions. If the expectation and variance for the number of emergency admissions on day d are given by $E(e_d)$ and $\mathrm{Var}(e_d)$, the expectation and variance of the total demand on day d, t_d say, are given by

$$E(t_d) = \sum_{i=0}^{M} (N_{(d-i)}(1-v) + E(e_{(d-i)}))p_i \quad d \geq \mathrm{M} \tag{2.3}$$

and

$$\begin{aligned}\mathrm{Var}(t_d) = \sum_{i=0}^{M} \big[& (N_{(d-i)}(1-v) + E(e_{(d-i)}))p_i(1-p_i) + p_i^2(N_{(d-i)}v(1-v) \\ & + \mathrm{Var}(e_{(d-i)}))\big] \quad d \geq \mathrm{M}.\end{aligned} \tag{2.4}$$

These expressions provide a means of exploring the impact of different sources of variability on the variations in day-to-day demand and, hence, the capacity required to meet demand to a certain standard.

It is possible within such a modeling framework to estimate capacity requirements for a system incorporating different streams of patients with different length of stay and attendance characteristics and cyclic or otherwise varying patterns of planned and emergency admissions (Utley et al. 2003; Gallivan and Utley 2005). As an aside, the linear form of Eq. 2.2 in terms of the number of patients planned for admission on a particular day introduces the potential for using integer programming techniques to determine schedules of cyclic planned admission that smooth out demand over the cycle (Gallivan and Utley 2005).

In terms of strategic capacity planning, the key insight obtained from such models is that the greater the variability in a system, the greater the capacity required to meet a given service standard on availability or timely access to the service. Another insight is that, given that the variance in demand is (given reasonable assumptions around the variance of emergency admissions) linear in terms of overall patient numbers, there are economies of scale in capacity planning. Essentially, the reserve capacity (as expressed as a proportion of expected demand) required to meet a service standard diminishes with increasing mean demand. In designing services, there can be a tension here between ring-fencing capacity for particular patient groups (to reduce variability) and the economies of scale suggested by having larger pools of capacity. These models can be used effectively to explore the potential trade-offs (in terms of capacity requirements) between smaller pools of capacity dedicated to more homogeneous patient groups versus larger pools of capacity with more heterogeneous case-mix (see for example Utley et al. 2008).

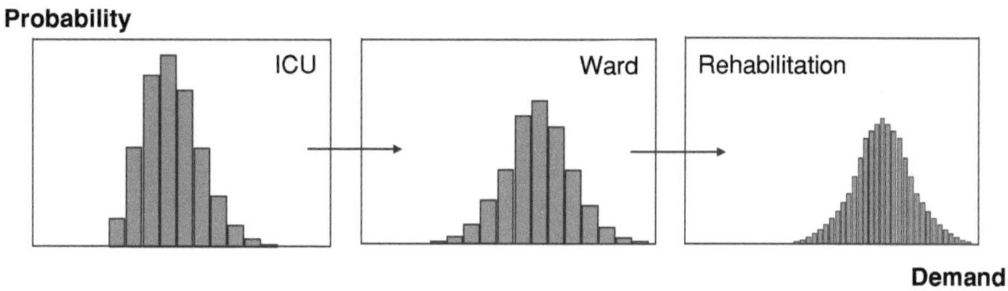

Fig. 2.2 Estimating demand across a number of clinical environments

Similar approaches can also be developed to estimate unfettered demand along a chain of clinical environments or, more generically, for the occupancy of states within any unfettered multi-state system that can be characterized with a simple tree structure (Utley et al. 2009). Such models can be used in capacity planning across environments (either within a single institution or across different institutions), for example to balance provision of acute and rehabilitation services as illustrated in Fig. 2.2.

The appeal of using estimates of unfettered demand in capacity planning lies in the simplicity of the approach and the ability to obtain an impression of the capacity required in order for a system to operate reasonably smoothly. In the next section we examine some of the intrinsic limitations that come with this approach and outline some of the other modeling approaches available.

2.3 Capacity Planning Using Queueing Models

2.3.1 Preamble

The models described in Sect. 2.2 can be used to estimate how often additional resources, above some notional level, would be called upon to meet all demand, or conversely how much resource to provide in order for provision to be adequate roughly 80, 90 or 95% of the time.

At a more detailed level of capacity planning we may need to consider how in practice any demand exceeding the agreed level of capacity would be managed. Is there some spare resource from a neighboring service or from a staffing agency that can be called upon when required? Does the excess demand simply get turned away, for instance referrals for intensive care diverted to another provider? If so, simple modifications of the previous models are possible to improve their accuracy. Does excess demand build up in a queue as with hospital waiting lists or outpatient waiting rooms? If so queueing models which reflect this aspect can be used to analyze and understand the impact of capacity constraints on system performance.

Two major types of queueing models are described in this section, which we will refer to as (i) analytical and (ii) simulation models. Analytical models are typically represented by formulae, which means that they are usually easy to apply (e.g. using a spreadsheet), and often provide valuable insights. Simulation models often require specialist software and are designed to allow the generation and evaluation of 'what if …' scenarios and produce quasi-empirical results rather than direct insights. However they are much more adaptable than analytical models and hence, with sufficient work, can be used to produce more accurate predictions of system behavior. The main components and basic behavior of queueing models are introduced in Sect. 2.3.2. Analytical queueing models together with capacity planning insights that they provide are described in Sect. 2.3.3. Section 2.3.4 outlines the potential value of simulation-based queueing models in this context.

2.3.2 Queueing Models in General

Before introducing analytical and simulation queueing models further we start by considering their common characteristics. The key characteristics of a queueing system are a 'service' that takes a period of time to deliver, the 'servers' who deliver the service and 'customers' who demand the service. When customers arrive to find all the servers busy they wait in a queue until a server becomes available. In a health care capacity planning context there are many examples of queueing systems, including outpatient clinics, emergency rooms, waiting lists for elective surgery, telephone advice lines, emergency ambulances, etc.

While in these situations models of unfettered demand give a good starting point for capacity planning, it is often necessary to consider the impact of queueing more precisely to characterize the relationship between capacity and system performance, particularly when providing substantial reserve capacity is not an option. The key components of the analysis of queuing systems are the arrival process (of customers), the service process, the number of servers (the capacity) and the queueing regime. We consider each briefly.

Arrival Process

Almost all analytical queueing models and many simulation models assume that arrivals occur 'at random', or equivalently as a 'Poisson process'. This is often a good representation of reality, especially if arrivals result from a large population within which individuals have a small probability of demanding the service under consideration. Exceptions to this sort of arrival process occur when arrivals are controlled in some manner, e.g. they are given appointments or grouped before arrival, which is where scheduling can have a big impact.

Even in such instances, the level of referrals for a service month-to-month can often be treated as the result of a Poisson process.
A Poisson process is defined by its underlying arrival rate. If the underlying rate is constant it is often denoted by λ; when it varies over time with known peaks and troughs it is referred to as time-dependent and is denoted by $\lambda(t)$. Note that even when the arrival rate is constant, the number of arrivals in a fixed period of time varies stochastically. For example, if arrivals occur as a Poisson process with mean rate of 5 per hour, the number of arrivals in one hour will have a Poisson distribution with mean 5.

Servers

In the capacity planning context, the 'servers' will often relate to the resources that are being planned. So, for example, the beds might be the servers when planning the size of an Intensive Care Unit (ICU), or the staff on duty might be the servers in an Accident and Emergency (A&E) department. However, the question should always be asked about whether the key resource has been identified. In the ICU setting the ability to treat patients is often limited by the number of staff available rather than the number of beds, and in A&E the bottleneck might sometimes be the number of cubicles rather than the number of staff. Often it makes sense to model capacity requirements for a number of resources.

Service Process

The service process refers to the length of time that the server needs to deliver the service. In an ICU where beds are the key resource, the patient's length of stay is the service process of interest from the capacity planning perspective. In the A&E setting, where patients are often managed using different resources (e.g. staff) as they progress, there are a number of service processes, e.g. initial assessment, X-ray, blood tests, final assessment and treatment.

Queueing Regime

Once patients have arrived in a queueing system the 'queueing regime' describes the way in which they are selected from the queue. For many capacity planning decisions the queueing regime is immaterial, and it can often be assumed that the regime is simply first-in-first-out (FIFO) which puts no restriction on the choice of modeling method.

In addition to these common components of queueing systems, the behavior that they exhibit also has some common features. For example consider a simple,

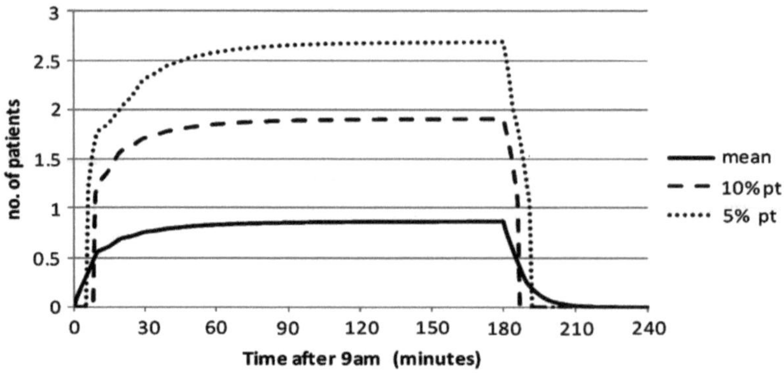

Fig. 2.3 Important features of real queueing systems

single-server outpatient clinic which nominally runs from 9 a.m. to 12 noon and in which 18 patients are given appointments, one every 10 min from 9 a.m. to 11:50 a.m. However, some arrive early, some arrive late and some do not arrive, with the overall effect that they arrive as a Poisson process with an underlying rate of 5 per hour between 9 a.m. and 12 noon. While appointments are every 10 min, consultations are typically shorter, with an average of 6 min. However, the consultation times vary, with a standard deviation of 4 min, so that quite often a consultation takes longer than the allotted 10 min. Using a suitable queueing model (see Brahami and Worthington 1991) for details, Fig. 2.3 graphs the average number of patients in the clinic over the planned duration of the clinic and beyond.

- First we note how the performance is *time-dependent*:
  - Early in the clinic all three performance measures indicate lower levels of congestion than later in the clinic, e.g. after 15 min the mean number of patients in the clinic is 0.61, whereas after 30 min it is 0.75 and after 120 min the mean has grown to 0.85;
  - Also, once patients have stopped arriving, i.e. after 180 min, the levels of congestion then decay away over the next few minutes.
- Between 90 and 180 min the congestion levels stay fairly constant. During this period of time the system has achieved its *steady state*, and indeed it would stay in steady state thereafter for as long as the underlying arrival and service rates do not change.
- However, whether it is in a time-dependent phase or a steady-state phase, the *behavior is stochastic*, i.e. the level of congestion needs to be described by a probability distribution to give understanding to the range of queue lengths, etc., that could be observed at any point of time.

In terms of capacity planning, this form of model could be used to explore the capacity required in the clinic waiting room.

2.3.3 Some Analytical Queueing Models for Capacity Planning

Single-Server Queues

A very useful and insightful queueing model is the Pollaczek-Khintchine formulae which are easy to use formulae for the mean number in the queue $E(q)$ (i.e. excluding anyone in service) and mean number in the system $E(Q)$ (i.e., including anyone in service or in queue) for single-server queues at steady-state in which arrivals occur as a Poisson process at constant rate λ and service times are described solely in terms of their mean ($1/\mu$) and coefficient of variation (CoV = standard deviation/mean).

$$E(q) = \frac{(\lambda/\mu)^2(1 + \text{CoV}^2)}{2(1 - \lambda/\mu)} \tag{2.5}$$

$$E(Q) = \frac{\lambda}{\mu} + \frac{(\lambda/\mu)^2(1 + \text{CoV}^2)}{2(1 - \lambda/\mu)} \tag{2.6}$$

For example, as the exponential distribution has CoV = 1, if service time is exponential with mean = $1/\mu$, then the equation for $E(Q)$ simplifies to the well known equation:

$$E(Q) = \frac{\lambda/\mu}{(1 - \lambda/\mu)} \tag{2.7}$$

Applying any of these formulae is very straightforward. For example, applying Eq. 2.6 to our outpatient clinic example, where $\lambda = 5$ patients per hour (ph), $\mu = 10$ph and CoV = 4/6 = 2/3, gives:

$$E(Q) = 0.5 + \frac{(0.5)^2(1 + 4/9)}{2(1 - 0.5)} = \frac{31}{36} = 0.861 \tag{2.8}$$

More importantly the formulae also provide important insights into the drivers of congestion, i.e. the drivers of poor performance. Furthermore while these particular formulae are only true for single-server systems, other formulae and further empirical work have shown that the same insights extend to many more queueing situations.

Insights

(i) The arrival rate (λ) and the service rate (μ) only occur as the ratio λ/μ. Thus only the ratio of arrival rate to service capacity is important. This ratio, which is generalized for systems with S servers to $\lambda/S\mu$, is referred to as traffic intensity, and is often denoted by ρ.

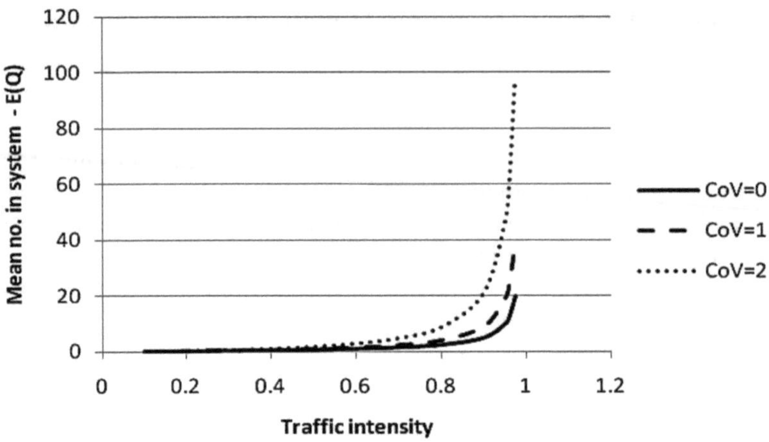

Fig. 2.4 The impact of traffic intensity on congestion

(ii) Simple experimentation with the formulae shows that whatever the value of CoV, the level of congestion grows with ρ, and that it grows increasingly quickly as ρ approaches 1.0; see for example Fig. 2.4 for the cases of CoV $= 0$, 1 and 2. In terms of capacity planning, this clearly indicates that attempting to achieve high traffic intensity (which equates to high server utilization) is unwise.

(iii) Formula (2.5) also clearly implies (and Fig. 2.4 shows some examples) that for any fixed value of ρ, the level of congestion depends on the CoV of service time, with greater variability (i.e., CoV) leading to higher congestion levels. Further theoretical and empirical work has shown that this insight also applies for multi-server systems.

(iv) A slightly different, but very important, insight that emerges from Eq. 2.5 is that ρ and CoV are the only drivers of this particular measure of congestion. This means that the same result would be obtained for any service time distributions which matched each other in mean and standard deviation. Although this finding is not the case for multiple servers or other performance measures for single-server systems, empirical work shows that service time mean and CoV are key drivers of performance in many other queueing systems.

Multi-server Queues

The main easy-to-use formulae for multi-server queues hold for the steady-state behavior of S server queues with a Poisson arrival process with underlying rate λ, and exponential service times with mean $1/\mu$. In this case the steady-state distribution of number in the system $\{P_n$: $n = 0, 1, 2,\ldots\}$ is given by:

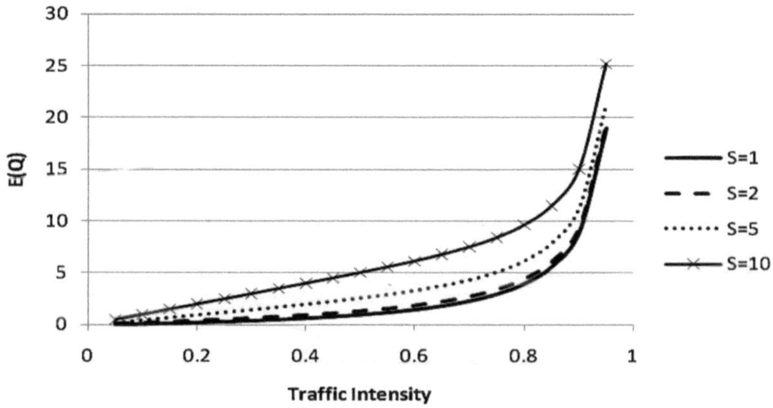

Fig. 2.5 Impact of S and traffic intensity on $E(Q)$

$$P_0 = \left[\sum_{1=0}^{S-1} \frac{(\lambda/\mu)^i}{i!} + \frac{(\lambda/\mu)^S}{S!} \frac{S\mu}{S\mu - \lambda} \right]^{-1};$$

$$P_n = \begin{cases} \dfrac{(\lambda/\mu)^n}{n!} P_0 \text{ for } n \leq S \\ \\ \dfrac{(\lambda/\mu)^n}{S! \quad S^{n-S}} P_0 \text{ for } > S \end{cases} \tag{2.9}$$

Furthermore the mean number in the system and the mean number in the queue are given by:

$$E(Q) = \lambda/\mu + \frac{(\lambda/\mu)^S \lambda\mu}{(S-1)! \ (S\mu - \lambda)^2} P_0 \tag{2.10}$$

$$E(q) = \frac{(\lambda/\mu)^S \lambda\mu}{(S-1)! \ (S\mu - \lambda)^2} P_0 \tag{2.11}$$

Insights Continued

(v) Subtraction of formula (2.11) from formula (2.10) shows that the mean number of customers in service, and hence also the mean number of servers who are busy, is simply λ/μ (or $S\rho$); and this result applies to the steady-state behavior of all queueing systems for which λ and μ are well defined.

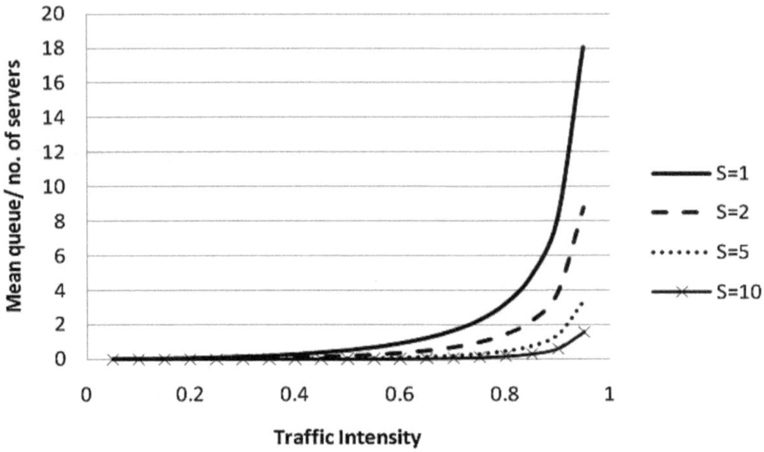

Fig. 2.6 Economies of scale in queueing systems

(vi) Simple experimentation with formula (2.10) supports the insight noted earlier that for any value of *S*, traffic intensity $\lambda/S\mu$ is a major driver of congestion. See for example Fig. 2.5, which plots E(Q) versus traffic intensity for various values of *S*.

(vii) Redrawing Fig. 2.5 with its y-axis now showing mean number in the queue per server results in Fig. 2.6, which highlights the sorts of economies of scale that can be achieved by pooling resources of (for example) a number of single-server systems into one multi-server system. We see in Fig. 2.6, for example, when traffic intensity is 0.8 in a single-server system the mean queue length per server is 3.20, whereas in 2, 5 and 10 server systems it is respectively 1.42, 0.44 and 0.16.

Waiting Times and Queueing Times

While number in the system and number in the queue are both important measures of congestion, customers will be much more interested in 'time in the system' (i.e. waiting time) and 'time in the queue' (i.e. queueing time). Except for the special case of exponential service times (see for example Gross and Harris 1985), the distributions of these two performances measures are very difficult to obtain analytically. However, thanks to Little (1961), their mean values ($E(W)$ = mean waiting time, $E(w)$ = mean queueing time) are very easy to obtain. In particular:

$$E(W) = E(Q)/\lambda \tag{2.12}$$

and

$$E(w) = E(W) - 1/\mu \tag{2.13}$$

This very strong relationship to $E(Q)$ means that *all the previous insights* related to $E(Q)$ also carry over to $E(W)$ and $E(w)$.

Networks of Queues

Many real queueing systems involve more than one service operation, and hence can be represented by either a sequence of queues or a network of queues (see Chap. 9). The key analytical model in this area is described in Jackson (1957, 1963), extending works of RRP Jackson (1954). It essentially says that under certain conditions a network of queues can be modeled as if they were independent queues, with arrival rates to each queue calculated from the aggregate arrival rate to that queue from both outside and inside the network. In particular, if a network of queues has:

- K different services (numbered $i = 1, 2,\ldots,K$);
- Customers can also arrive from outside the network to service i, as a Poisson process, at rate λ_i;
- Service i has an exponential distribution, with mean $^{1}/\mu_i$;
- Service i has S_i servers;
- Having received service i, customers proceed to service j with probability q_{ij}, or leave the network altogether with probability r_i (thus $q_{i1} + q_{i2} +\cdots q_{iK} + r_i = 1$) and these probabilities are independent of the state of the network and the history of the customers.

In this case the overall arrival rate to service i, say α_i, is given formally by:

$$\alpha_i = \lambda_i + \sum_{k=1}^{K} \alpha_k q_{ki} \quad \text{for } i = 1, 2, \ldots, K$$

and steady-state will then exist if $^{\alpha_i}/_{S_i\mu_i} < 1$ for each service i. In this case, steady-state behavior of system i is obtained using the multi-server queueing formulae (2.9), (2.10) and (2.11) presented earlier (with arrival rate $= \alpha_i$, mean service time $= {}^{1}/\mu_i$, and S_i servers), and it can be treated as if it is independent of the rest of the network. Clearly this analytical model again provides easy-to-use formulae which can be implemented in a spreadsheet, although the nature of the assumptions means that any results will be approximate at best. However these can be obtained quite quickly, can be valuable in producing at least an initial assessment of a problem, and will on occasions be accurate enough for practical purposes.

Furthermore the close links between these network results and the previous single-node results at least suggest that many of the previous insights will carry over to networks of queues.

Time-Dependent Queueing Models

In Sect. 2.2, we outlined a time-dependent model for unfettered demand but there are very few easy-to-use analytical models for the time-dependent behavior of fettered queueing systems despite their obvious importance in practice. Here we introduce one such approach and use it to provide insights into the time-dependent behavior of queueing systems. We also flag up important situations where the approach does not work and discuss how this can impact on the insights.

There are some queueing systems with time-dependent arrival rates $\lambda(t)$ in which the rate of change of arrival rate relative to the throughput of the system is sufficiently slow that the system more or less achieves the steady state associated with any arrival rate instantaneously. In these cases system behavior can be approximated by a pointwise stationary approximation (PSA). This implies that the behavior at any time t_0 is simply approximated by the steady-state behavior of the equivalent constant arrival rate system, with fixed arrival rate $\lambda(t_0)$.

The implication of this approximation is that *whenever the PSA is appropriate, all the insights previously identified as associated with steady-state behavior continue to hold.*

However there are many important time-dependent queues in health care for which this approach will not work well, and hence for which the insights will not necessarily hold. For example, for the outpatient clinics modeled previously in Fig. 2.3, the PSA would predict that the mean number of patients in the clinic immediately jump to their steady-state values at 9 a.m., and immediately drop back to zero at 12 noon. Figure 2.3 shows how the queue size can be expected to lag substantially behind the response predicted by the PSA. In cases where it is important to reflect this lagged behavior (for instance in determining staffing requirements over the course of a day in an emergency room), simulation models are often used.

2.3.4 Simulation-Based Queueing Models

As noted earlier, simulation models often require specialist software and are used in 'what if…' mode to produce quasi-empirical results rather than direct insights. However they are much more adaptable than analytical models and hence with sufficient work are capable of producing more accurate results.

One of the earliest queue modeling studies in health care was by Bailey (1952), who used manual simulation experiments to investigate the queueing process occurring in hospital outpatient departments. He came to the conclusion that "a substantial amount of the patients' waiting time may be eliminated without appreciably affecting the consultant."

Using simple simulation analyses of the clinic bottleneck (i.e. the consultation with the doctor) he revealed a number of characteristics of the clinics, including:

- Disproportionate patient waiting time compared to actual consultation time;
- An over-riding consideration to the requirement that the consultant is kept fully occupied;
- A large amount of room (which is often in short supply) just for those waiting.

These insights about the running of outpatient clinics have in fact proven to hold good in many subsequent studies, with simple recommendations such as ensuring that doctors arrive in time for the start of a clinic, and giving patients appointment times that ensure a reasonable balance between the time that patients will wait and the chance that the doctor is idle. See for example Worthington et al. (2005) for one of a number of reviews of such work.

Since that time there have been many studies using simulation-based queueing models to address a wide range of health care capacity planning issues. These have been reviewed on a number of occasions and from various perspectives. Jun et al. (1999) review about 30 years of research, identifying work that focuses on allocation of resources (including bed, room and staff sizing and planning). Fletcher and Worthington (2009) concentrate on simulation modeling of emergency flows of patients, categorizing models under the following areas of hospital activity: A&E, bed management, surgery, intensive care, diagnostics and whole systems models. Günal and Pidd (2010) have a wider remit and use the categories: A&E, inpatients, outpatients, other hospital units and whole systems. Both papers note the very limited amount of work on whole systems models. Brailsford et al. (2009) have an even more ambitious remit and apply a very structured process to review a stratified sample of simulation and other modeling approaches in health care.

The potential of simulation-based models to provide 'what if' analyses of many health care capacity planning issues is clear. However this approach needs to be viewed with care. The record of application of models reviewed in these various surveys is not high, and their flexibility can easily tempt the modeler to pursue an unnecessarily complex model. As suggested by Proudlove et al. (2007) in health care modeling, a combination of simplicity and supportive presentation is more important than aiming at a complex and detailed representation.

2.4 Populating Capacity Planning Models

The models outlined in the previous sections vary in terms of the amount of data or parameter estimates required for their use. These range from having to know mean arrival rates and resource use/service time per patient to knowing or estimating seasonal patterns of arrival, full distributions of service times and resource use and transfer rates between different environments for different sub-groups of the patient population.

For this reason, in addition to the strengths and weaknesses of alternative modeling approaches for capacity planning set out above, the level of information or data available to populate a model is an important consideration in adopting a modeling approach. As demonstrated in Sects. 2.2 and 2.3 it is clear that in planning capacity for a service, it is important to have estimates for the expected referral or arrival rate, the variability in arrivals, the mean use per patient of the key resources considered and the variability in this use from patient to patient. In instances where a network of environments or services are associated with delivering care for the patient population concerned, the anticipated flows between each service might be required, or at the very least an estimate of how many times (on average) a patient uses each service in the network during an episode of care.

Although not a parameter required in order to run many of the models discussed, an understanding of the desired service standards is essential for using models to inform capacity plans. These might be expressed as maximum cancelation rates for elective patients, or average waiting times or queue sizes for an outpatient clinic.

Typically, those planning a new service will have limited data from which to work and there may be considerable uncertainty in terms of model parameters. In these circumstances, the additional insights of complex models above what can be obtained from simpler models may be limited, or rather the relevance and credibility of these insights may be undermined by doubts as to whether the calibration of the model is sufficiently robust.

Planners looking to estimate future capacity requirements for an existing service are in a better position to estimate parameters but face difficulties of a different nature. The existence of reliable local data concerning the current operation and performance of a system can lead to planners and modelers using these data as direct estimates for model parameters. However, typically an organization will have data on, say, the number of patients admitted to a service rather than the actual demand for admission, since records may not be kept of patients turned away/diverted to another provider or of those who, seeing the queue in a walk-in center, decide not to join the queue. As another example, bed capacity models require estimates concerning clinically necessary length of stay, whereas historical data on length of stay will include any delays to discharging or transferring a patient caused by a shortage of capacity at another point in the system and perhaps instances where discharge was expedited due to pressure to admit an urgent case. Being aware of these potential limitations of historical data is important (particularly if one aim of the capacity planning exercise is to improve rather than simply scale up or scale down a service) since they are often linked to historical capacity provision and the service standards accepted in the past. Essentially, if one is not careful when interpreting data as model input, one risks carrying forward undesirable features of past system performance.

Another issue in calibrating capacity planning models is that changing capacity may influence the demands made of a service. For services where it is known or likely that there is latent, unmet demand or the prospect of genuine supply-induced demand, historical referral or arrival rates should clearly be used with particular care. The influence of increased capacity on referral rates can be modeled explicitly using dynamic models in which referrer behavior is influenced by, for example, waiting times. Another approach is to simply explore scenarios where referral/arrival rates are increased above and beyond any demographic trends to account for latent demand.

If one of the motivations or likely consequences of the capacity planning exercise concerned is to widen (or restrict) access to a service, it should also be recognized that case-mix (in terms of the severity of patients and resource use per patient) may change.

2.5 Final Thoughts

As indicated in the earlier sections of this chapter, it is possible to build capacity planning models that are highly complex and that incorporate the fine detail of a system as well as the key drivers to system performance. It is perhaps worth reflecting that, although additional complexity and detail in models can add value and in some circumstances will be warranted, there can be diminishing returns in terms of the utility of model output as models get more and more complex, take longer to develop and require more parameter estimates, etc. Indeed, there is an argument that, rather than use or configure explicit capacity planning models each time they undertake a capacity planning exercise, it might sometimes be just as beneficial for organizations to adopt a set of capacity planning rules based on the cumulative experience of capacity modeling of various forms. Such rules might include pooling resources wherever this is consistent with good clinical management, planning on the basis of working at bed utilization of 85%, with lower targets for smaller environments and services where instant access is imperative. Another rule might be to accept lower utilization of relatively cheap resources (for instance portering) where shortages hinder access to or the efficient use of very expensive or scarce resources.

Service configuration or reconfiguration that is informed by the considerations outlined in this chapter should achieve the aim of establishing a reasonable balance between demand and capacity, providing a basis for effective and efficient scheduling to enhance performance.

That said, planning is never enough and the right operational culture is required for the balance of capacity provided across a system to be associated with the performance anticipated from models. Reserve capacity will not have the desired effect on system performance in an organization where the flow of patients is only stimulated by the push of new arrivals at the front door. Proactive discharge planning and a pull through the system must be maintained somehow even when the system seems to be running smoothly. Having appropriate financial arrangements in place helps but ultimately this is a challenge for leadership within health care organizations.

In some health systems, the shift in working culture between the world as it is and the world as Operations Researchers would like it to be is vast and modelers, in their work, should be mindful of the barrier that this represents. The challenge of getting managers and clinicians who have spent their lives working at capacity to realize that an idle porter, a few empty beds downstream and a nurse spending half a day doing some online training because they are not needed on the ward are good things is one that goes way beyond the technical challenges of building and using models.

References

Bailey NTJ (1952) A study of queues and appointment systems in hospital out-patient departments, with special reference to waiting-times. J Roy Stat Soc Ser B 14:185–199

Brahimi M, Worthington D (1991) Queueing models for out-patient appointment systems: a case study. J Oper Res Soc 42:733–746

Brailsford SC, Harper PR, Patel B, Pitt M (2009) An analysis of the academic literature on simulation and modelling in health care. J Simul 3:130–140

Fletcher A, Worthington D (2009) What is a 'generic' hospital model?—A comparison of 'generic' and 'specific' hospital models of emergency flow patients. Health Care Manage Sci 12:374–391

Gallivan S, Utley M (2005) Modelling admissions booking of elective in-patients into a treatment centre. Inst Math Appl J Manage Math 16:305–315

Gallivan S et al (2002) Booked inpatient admissions and hospital capacity: mathematical modelling study. BMJ 324:280–282

Gross D, Harris CM (1985) Fundamentals of queueing theory, 2nd edn. Wiley, New York

Günal MM, Pidd M (2010) Discrete event simulation for performance modelling in health care: a review of the literature. J Simul 4:42–51

Jackson RRP (1954) Queueing systems with phase-type service. Oper Res Quart 5:109–120

Jackson JR (1957) Networks of waiting lines. Oper Res 5:518–521

Jackson JR (1963) Jobshop-like queueing systems. Manage Sci 10:131–142

Jun J, Jacobson S, Swisher J (1999) Application of discrete-event simulation in health care clinics: a survey. J Oper Res Soc 50:109–123

Little JDC (1961) A proof for the queueing formula $L = \lambda W$. Oper Res 9:383–387

Proudlove NC, Black S, Fletcher A (2007) OR and the challenge to improve the NHS: modelling for insight and improvement in in-patient flows. J Oper Res Soc 58:145–158

Utley M, Gallivan S, Treasure T, Valencia O (2003) Analytical methods for calculating the capacity required to operate an effective booked admissions policy for elective inpatient services. Health Care Manage Sci 6:97–104

Utley M, Jit M, Gallivan S (2008) Restructuring routine elective services to reduce overall capacity requirements within a local health economy. Health Care Manage Sci 11:240–247

Worthington DJ, Goulsbra R, Rankin J (2005) Scheduling appointments in outpatient clinics. In: Vissers J, Beech R (eds) Health operations management. Routledge, London, pp 223–248

Chapter 3
Nurse Scheduling

Gino J. Lim, Arezou Mobasher, Laleh Kardar and Murray J. Cote

3.1 Introduction

The cost of health care is increasing dramatically every year in the United States. For instance, according to the Towers Perrin healthcare survey, healthcare costs increased an average of 6% in 2008 compared to 2007 (Perrin 2008). Cost of developing new technologies and treatments, rising personnel income, America's aging population, and a relatively increased demand for health care are some of the reasons for this rapid growth. The Centers for Medicare and Medicaid Services estimated that by 2018, the cost of health care will be more than 4.3 trillion dollars, which is 20.3% of the total GDP (Foundation 2009). Over 50% of healthcare costs are for hospital resources, physicians and clinical services, as shown in Fig. 3.1.

One of the main concerns in many healthcare systems is to provide high quality services at lower costs to patients. People deserve to get the care that they need. The care should be patient centered and efficient in a safe and timely manner without wasting resources. For this purpose, inefficiencies and variabilities in the

Gino J. Lim (✉)
Department of Industrial Engineering, University of Houston,
4800 Calhoun Road, Houston, TX 77204, USA
e-mail: ginolim@uh.edu

A. Mobasher
University of Houston, Houston, TX, USA
e-mail: amobasher@uh.edu

L. Kardar
University of Houston, Houston, TX, USA
e-mail: lkardar@uh.edu

Murray J. Cote
Department of Health Policy and Management,
Texas A&M Health Science Center, College Station, TX, USA
e-mail: cote@srph.tamhsc.edu

R. Hall (ed.), *Handbook of Healthcare System Scheduling*,
International Series in Operations Research & Management Science 168,
DOI: 10.1007/978-1-4614-1734-7_3,

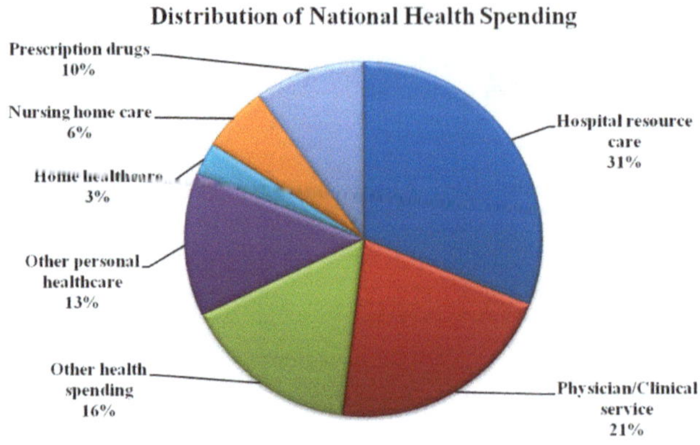

Fig. 3.1 Distribution of national spending (Foundation 2009)

usage of resources should be identified; proper activities should be introduced and suitable solution methods should be provided. Operations Research techniques are useful to provide optimal or efficient schedules to improve different aspects of healthcare systems, such as resource utilization, hospital patient flow, medical supply chain, staff scheduling and medical decision-making, to name a few, resulting in cost reductions. In this chapter, we focus on nurse scheduling.

Nurse shortage is a problem worldwide (Ulrich et al. 2002). Not having enough skilled nurses in clinical settings has caused a significant negative impact on patient outcomes, including mortality (Aiken et al. 2002). Under this epidemic of nurse shortage, hospital administrators and nurse managers are in dire need to optimally utilize and retain currently available nurses without jeopardizing their job satisfaction. When one schedules nursing staff, it is known that considering their shift preferences can increase job satisfaction, which leads to savings in labor costs due to reduced nurse turnover and other issues, such as retention rates, patient safety, and healthcare quality (Bester et al. 2007; Blythe et al. 2005; Cheng et al. 1997; Chiaramonte and Chiaramonte 2008). Therefore, it is essential to develop nurse scheduling tools that will optimally utilize and retain currently available nurses. Scheduling nurses to meet a hospital's daily demand and satisfy staffing policies, such as those dictated by a union contract and regulations mandating specific nurse-to-patient ratios, is an extremely complex task to perform. Confounding this environment is the fact that the nurses are non homogeneous with respect to their skill set, experience, employment type (e.g., part time versus full time, and nurse availability). Furthermore, the demand for nurses varies in accordance with patient census. Because some of these objectives may conflict with each other, nurse scheduling must be carefully done to capture appropriate tradeoffs among different objectives.

Assigning each available nurse to the right place at the right time is a major concern among many healthcare organizations. Well-designed schedules can generate an efficient work plan that should be able to precede restrictions and variabilities and have a predefined solution for addressing those constraints and expectations. However, it can be an extremely difficult task to develop a schedule that is robust against all constraints and variabilities in real-world problems. There are some inherently common rules in all hospital staffing that can be applied to most departments of a hospital, except for operating suites. Operating suites are considered to be the living heart of the hospital, and provide the largest amount of revenue for the hospital (Belien and Demeulemeester 2008). Since there is an increasing demand for surgeries caused by an aging population (Cardoen et al. 2010) and most operating suites face nurse shortages, it is essential for managers to develop suitable and effective scheduling plans for operating suites. Similarly, operating suites have nurse and shift restrictions along with regulatory and union requirements to schedule their nurses. However, specific limitations and the importance of surgery procedures that are associated with the patient's life can affect nurse scheduling procedures. For instance, nurses must not leave an operating room to take a break unless the surgery is finished or someone else is available to relieve them.

Consequently, we divide nurse scheduling problem into two categories: Nurse Scheduling Problem in a General Clinic and Nurse Scheduling Problem in an Operating Suite.

3.2 Nurse Scheduling Problems

In this section, two nurse scheduling problems are discussed: nurse scheduling problem in a general clinic and nurse scheduling problem in an operating suite. For each nurse scheduling problem, the attributes that are required to develop efficient nurse scheduling models are explained.

3.2.1 Nurse Scheduling Problem in a General Clinic

A general clinic is an area in a hospital or some other healthcare organization that provides healthcare services to patients with similar needs. These services are provided by healthcare professionals such as physicians and nurses, who have been trained in that specialty. Different attributes of a general clinic can be discussed as follows:

Patients. Patients can be divided into two groups: inpatients and outpatients. An outpatient is a patient who is not hospitalized overnight but needs to visit the department to receive medical attention, care, or treatment. On the other hand, an inpatient needs to stay in the hospital overnight or for an indecisive amount of time. Patient workload can be defined to be more than simply a care unit's census. Rather, patient workload is viewed as a factor for the care unit's case mix for a given shift. If the case mix is high, there will be a correspondingly high workload placed on nurses and, in turn, patient workload will be high. In effect, a high patient workload implies a higher workload for the nurses. Similarly, if the case mix is low, there will be low workload for the nurses. For example, if a patient comes for an MRI, he may need to receive a preliminary examination, a dye injection, and the MRI procedure. Therefore, this patient requires three different services, which can be considered as three separate workloads.

Nurse Categories in a General Clinic. A nurse is a healthcare professional who provides medical care and treatment to patients as prescribed by physicians. Note that, nurse practitioners are excluded as they may operate independently in some situations. Nurses, one of the largest human resources in a hospital, can be classified into different groups. Based on the number of working hours, nurses can be categorized as full time and part time (contracted and staff nurses). A full time nurse typically works 40 hours a week while part time nurses work based on their weekly contracted work hours. Also, nurses can be categorized into different grades based on their skill levels, experience, education, knowledge, and certificates. Nurses are distinguished from each other by their area of specialty. Therefore, each patient can receive medical care from nurses who can provide specific treatments. Different nurses with the same specialty area can do the same task at varying time durations based on their skill levels and experiences. If patient workload is less than nursing capacity, there will be idle nurses. However, this is not common in many clinics due to nurse shortages. In the case of shortages, many schedulers consider downgrading in which higher skilled nurses are assigned to shifts that lower skilled nurses are capable of performing. However, the reverse is not true.

Shift Limitations. Providing patients with medical attention is an every day task. Therefore, a general clinic should make sure that there are available nurses at all times responding to the patient workload. On the other hand, nurses are not allowed to work more than their scheduled daily work hours. So there should be nurses assigned to multiple consecutive shifts per day.

3.2.2 Nurse Scheduling Problem in an Operating Suite

An operating suite is an area in a hospital or other healthcare organization which provides surgical procedures and consists of several operating rooms (OR). An operating room is designed to perform different types of surgeries; however, some rooms are equipped for special treatment needs such as robotic rooms that have different robots or brain surgery rooms that provide MRI during surgery. Services in an OR are provided by surgeons, nurses, and anesthesia professionals who have been trained for different specialties. Different attributes of an operating suite can be discussed as follows:

Surgery Specialty. Surgery is a medical operation, using instruments and techniques on a patient to treat or improve a disease or injury. Each operating suite in a hospital can provide different surgery specialty services. For instance, in a cancer center, there can be surgery specialties such as neurosurgery, plastic surgery, head and neck surgery, to name a few.

Surgery Procedure Complexity. Each surgery can have different procedure complexities. Each procedure in a surgery can be classified as easy, moderate, or complex.

Surgery Case. We define a *surgery case* as a series of surgery operations with different surgery specialties and procedure complexities that should be performed on one patient in one operating room in a scheduled day. Many surgery cases may require multiple operations performed by different surgeons in different times in one OR. Each surgery case should be scheduled in advance, unless it is an emergency situation. Therefore, surgery specialties, procedure complexity, required equipments, nurses types, and surgery case duration are often known beforehand. Surgery duration can be defined as the time that is required to finish a surgery case starting from transferring the patient to the operating room (patient-in time), proceeding by performing the surgery (surgery time) and finishing by moving the patient out of the operating room (patient-out time). Also, each surgery has a nurse demand, which is the number of different nurses required for each surgery case at each time period to do different roles with various specialties.

Nurse Categories in an Operating Suite. An OR nurse is a healthcare professional who provides technical and medical help to the surgeon during a surgery and to the patient before and after surgery. Also, nurses can be categorized by different types based on their skill level, experience, education, knowledge, and certification. Some attributes of nurses in an operating suite are as follows:

- Nurse role: Nurses can have different roles during a surgery based on their skill level. The most recognized roles in surgeries are *circulation* and *scrub*. Both roles are essential during a surgery to provide smooth surgery operation on a patient.
- Nurse specialty: Different nurses can work on different specialties based on their skill levels and certifications.
- Nurse procedure competency: Not all nurses can support surgeries with complex procedures. Nurses can handle surgery procedure complexities based on their skill level and experience. They can work on simple, moderate, or complex procedures. Nurses who have enough experience to work on more complex procedures can also work on easier procedures.

Shift Limitations. Generally, operating suites have various predefined shifts during a working day. All nurses upon their hiring will be assigned to these established shifts based on their contracts. Each shift has its own regulations and limitations, such as break and lunch hours, overtime rules, and nurse availability.

Variability. Operating rooms are associated with many variabilities, such as human behavior, surgery time, and nurse availability. An excessively complicated model will be the result of considering all these variabilities.

3.2.3 Problem Statement

We introduced two different nurse scheduling problems (NSP): nurse scheduling problem in a general clinic and nurse scheduling problem in an operating suite. For both problems, the purpose is to develop a decision-making tool that assigns nurses to the right place at the right time to do the right job. Researchers may develop different nurse scheduling tools for each NSP by finding proper answers for the following questions.

- What input parameters are available or should be provided for each NSP?
- What are the goals associated with each NSP?
- What limitations and constraints should be considered in each NSP?
- What are the proposed methods for each NSP?
- What will be the outcome of each NSP?

The problem in a general clinic is to develop a decision-making tool that assigns nurses to shifts based on nurse preference and patient workload requirements. It is assumed that decision makers have complete information about the number of available skilled nurses, different categories of nurse skill level, nurse shift preference, patient workload types, patient workload durations, and working contract options. Therefore, the purpose is to develop nurse scheduling tools that consider different goals, such as minimizing costs, patient dissatisfaction, and nurse idle time and overtime, and maximizing nurse job satisfaction by incorporating nurse preferences. The problem to optimize in an operating suite is similar to the nurse scheduling problem in a general clinic. The main goal is to assign nurses to surgery cases in each shift by incorporating nurse specialty, nurse availability, role abilities, and surgery case requirements in optimization models. The purpose is to develop nurse scheduling tools that consider different goals, such as minimizing nurse overtime, idle time, and delays during the day; and maximizing surgery case demand satisfaction.

3.3 A Review of Optimization Applications and Methods

Nurse scheduling is a complex and time-consuming task that has a daily effect on hospital staffing. Developing mathematical or heuristic approaches that can easily provide solutions can efficiently improve the time and effort required for scheduling. These solution algorithms can provide more balanced and practical schedules as well as improve staff satisfaction.

Massive amounts of work to introduce models and solution algorithms for the nurse scheduling problem have been done recently. In this section, the literature on nurse scheduling problem is categorized into two main sections. The first provides models and solution algorithms for the general nurse scheduling problem and the second into emphasizes on the nurse scheduling problem in an operating suite.

Several nurse scheduling models are introduced, decision variables and constraints are expressed and solution algorithms are discussed for each nurse scheduling problem.

3.3.1 Nurse Scheduling Problem in a General Clinic

Given the significance of healthcare scheduling and the severity of the problem, a great deal of work has recently been directed toward the nurse scheduling problem.

Primary Nurse Scheduling Problems

Fries (1976) presented a bibliography of early methods for personnel rostering in healthcare institutions. Many of those early approaches relied on manual procedures, following a set of arbitrary rules. They are too restricted to be directly applicable to problems faced in modern hospitals. The large size of clinics as well as many limitations, such as shift and regulatory limitations, consecutivity requirements, different types of treatment needs, are some of the main challenges that should be considered nowadays. Burke et al. (2004) mentioned that one of the first optimization models in nurse scheduling was introduced by Warner and Prawda (1972). The main contribution of this model was its emphasis on maintaining the integral and capacity constraints of the nurse scheduling problem. A mixed-integer quadratic programming formulation was presented to calculate the number of nurses from a certain skill category to undertake a number of shifts per day. Three non-overlapping shift types of 8 hours each are used. The objective function aimed at minimizing the difference between a given lower limit for the number of nurses and the variables. The minimum staffing requirements should consider the possibility of replacing personnel members with different skills as well as the organization's established standards. We describe the model's decision variables, model formulation, and the proposed solution method as follows.

Decision Variables

The parameters for this problem defined as: $R = R_{\text{int}}$ denote a demand for nursing care services matrix; $U = U_{\text{imnt}}$ denote an allocation of nursing time matrix; Q_{imnt}, for $i \in I, m, n \in N$ and $t \in T$, is the ratio at which a nurse of skill class m is able to substitute for a nurse of skill class n on ward i during shift t; W_{int} is the relative seriousness of a deviation between R_{int} and X_{int}; B_n is the number of nurse-shifts of type n nurse that are available to be scheduled over $i \in I$ and $t \in T$; and A_{int} is the percentage of the nursing personnel requirement of skill class n nurse that must be provided on ward i during shift t.

Let $X = X_{\text{int}}$ be an allocation of the nurses matrix, which is considered as the decision variables.

Optimization Model

$$\text{Min } C(U|R) = \sum_{i \in I} \sum_{n \in N} \sum_{t \in T} W_{\text{int}} (R_{\text{int}} - \sum_{m} Q_{\text{imnt}} U_{\text{imnt}}) \tag{3.1}$$

$$\sum_{p} U_{\text{inpt}} - X_{\text{int}} \leq 0, \qquad \forall i \in I, n \in N, t \in T \tag{3.2}$$

$$\sum_{i \in I} \sum_{t \in T} X_{\text{int}} \leq B_n, \qquad \forall n \in N \tag{3.3}$$

$$X_{\text{int}} \geq A_{\text{int}} R_{\text{int}}, \qquad \forall i \in I, n \in N, t \in T \tag{3.4}$$

$$X_{\text{int}} \leq R_{\text{int}} + e_{\text{int}}, \qquad \forall i \in I, n \in N, t \in T, e_{\text{int}} \geq 0 \tag{3.5}$$

$$X_{\text{int}} \text{ integer}, \qquad \forall i \in I, n \in N, t \in T \tag{3.6}$$

$$U_{\text{imnt}} \geq 0, \qquad \forall i \in I, m, n \in N, t \in T \tag{3.7}$$

Constraints (3.2) ensure that the total number of nurses with skill class n assigned as any skill class $p \in N$ cannot exceed the total number of skill class n nurses assigned during scheduling. Also resource capacity is included as a constraint in Eq. 3.3 and B_n is defined as the number of nurse-shifts of type n nurse which are available to be scheduled over $i \in I$ and $t \in T$. The next constraint (3.4) is developed based on the assumption that there exists some minimum amount of nursing care services of each skill class that must be provided in order to maintain minimum professional standards of care. The last constraint limits the amount of substitution of nursing tasks among skill classes, where $e_{\text{int}} \geq 0$ is a given scalar that establishes upper bounds on the feasible range of applying the substitution ratios Q_{imnt}.

Solution Method

The problem was decomposed by a primal resource-directive approach into a multiple-choice programming master problem, with quadratic programming sub-problems. Initial results suggested that a linear programming formulation, with a post-optimal feasibility search scheme, may be substituted for the multiple-choice master problem.

Burke et al. (2004) mentioned that this early approach could not consider the current needs of hospitals. Also there was no possibility of including personal preferences in this model. All the nurses were anonymous. An excess of nursing supply for a particular skill category could absorb the shortage of other skills. A drawback of the approach was that an accurate forecast of personnel demand could not be trustworthy for a period longer than 4 days.

Single-Objective Nurse Scheduling Problems

The articles by Cheang et al. (2003) and Burke et al. (2004) are two of the most comprehensive surveys in nurse scheduling and rostering problems. Burke et al. (2004) described a general nurse scheduling and rostering problem, and evaluated various models and solution approaches found in more than 140 articles and PhD dissertations. Some of these papers can be found in (Aickelin and Dowsland 2004; Berrada et al. 1996; Dowsland 1998; Miller et al. 1976). Integer programming (IP) has been widely used for solving the NSP problem (Aickelin and Dowsland 2004; Aickelin and Li 2007; Aickelin and White, 2004; Aickelin et al. 2007; Bai et al. 2010; Bard and Purnomo 2005; 2007; Li and Aickelin 2003; Ogulata et al. 2008; Purnomo and Bard 2006). Most of the proposed optimization models deal with a single objective function. Minimizing costs and maximizing nurse preferences are the two most common objectives introduced in the literature.

Cost as an Objective Function

The cost of assigning nurses to each shift is one of every hospital's main concerns. Typically, the total cost includes salary, benefits, and any other extra expenses that the hospital must be responsible for hiring nurses.

Bai et al. (2010) developed a pattern-based optimization model to minimize the penalty cost of assigning different nurses to different shift patterns. The contribution of this paper is the presentation of a robust hybrid algorithm for the nurse rostering problem. The hybrid algorithm is, in fact, very flexible and can be readily adapted to many other constrained optimization problems. This problem was motivated by a real nurse rostering problem faced by a large U.K. hospital. The formulation employed in this model represents a generic nurse rostering problem and has been used in several other studies. The problem is to make weekly schedules for about 30 nurses. Each day's schedule consists of a day shift and a night shift. For each shift, a feasible solution has to assign sufficient nurses to cover the actual demands, which are subject to changes throughout the week. Two practical constraints have made this problem particularly challenging. First, nurses have three different grades. A higher grade nurse can cover the demand for a lower grade nurse but not vice versa. Second, there are some part-time nurses who can only work a certain number of hours each week and may also not be able to work on certain shifts. The schedule should also be able to satisfy "day-off" requests by nurses. It should also spread some unpopular shifts (e.g., night and weekend shifts) among nurses for fairness.

Decision Variables

Given a number of nurses (n) with each nurse having a grade among the range from 1 to g, let G_r be the set of nurses with grades r or higher, R_{kr} the minimal demand of nurses of grade r for shift k, and F_i the set of feasible shift pattern for nurse i. Set $a_{jk} = 1$ if pattern k covers shift j and 0 otherwise. Let p_{ij} be the penalty cost of nurse i working on pattern j.

The decision variables are defined as x_{ij} such that x_{ij} is 1 if nurse i works on pattern j and 0, otherwise.

Optimization Model

The model is as follows:

$$\text{Min}\, f = \sum_{i=1}^{n} \sum_{j \in F_i} p_{ij} x_{ij} \tag{3.8}$$

$$\sum_{j \in F_i} x_{ij} = 1, \qquad \forall i \in \{1, \cdots, n\} \tag{3.9}$$

$$\sum_{i \in G_r} \sum_{j \in F_i} a_{jk} x_{ij} \geq R_{kr}, \qquad \forall k, r \tag{3.10}$$

Constraints (3.9) ensure that each nurse must work on exactly one specific shift pattern. Also, it is important to make sure that there are sufficient nurses to cover each shift at each grade (3.10). The objective, shown in Eq. 3.8, is to minimize the total penalty cost of assigning nurses to different patterns. Several methods have been used to tackle the constraints (3.10), which make the solution search space severely constrained.

Solution Method

Evolutionary algorithms are inspired from the natural evolution and selection principle of "survival of the fittest." For an optimization problem, a solution is usually encoded in a specially designed string. A population of individuals is maintained and evolves from one generation to another through some genetic operations and a selection method until some stopping criteria are met. Penalty functions are commonly used to transform the constrained optimization problem into an unconstrained one by introducing a penalty term into the objective function to penalize constraint violations. Let X be the vector of decision variables and $f(X)$ be the original objective function. The transformed objective function $\phi(X)$ is then presented in the form of

$$\phi(X) = f(X) + \lambda\varphi(g_\pi(X)); \quad \pi \in \Pi \tag{3.11}$$

where λ is the associated penalty coefficient and $\varphi(g_\pi(X))$ is the function that measures the severity of violations of the following constraints

$$g_\pi(X) \geq 0; \quad \pi \in \Pi \tag{3.12}$$

In the case of the nurse rostering problem addressed in this paper, the following function was used to measure the violation of the covering constraints (3.10).

$$\varphi(g_\pi(X)) = \sum_{k=1}^{14}\sum_{r=1}^{g}\left\{\max\left\{0, R_{kr} - \sum_{i\in G_r}\sum_{j\in F_i} a_{jk}x_{ij}\right\}\right\} \tag{3.13}$$

Another type of constraint handling method is stochastic ranking. The underlying idea is to "fuzzify" the common ranking criteria by introducing a ranking probability P_f. The ranking can be obtained by a procedure similar to a stochastic version of the bubble-sort algorithm with N sweeps. In this method, the ranking is based on an objective function only if all the individuals are feasible. Otherwise, the ranking is stochastic. Denote by P_w the probability of an individual winning a comparison with an adjacent individual.

$$P_w = P_{fw}P_f + P_{\varphi w}(1 - P_f) \tag{3.14}$$

where P_{fw} and $P_{\varphi w}$ are, respectively, the probability of the individual winning according to the objective function and the penalty function. By fixing the number of sweeps n and by adjusting the probability P_f, the dominance of the objective function f and the penalty function φ[10] can be balanced. The number of sweeps is fixed to $N = S$. When $P_f < 0.5$, the ranking is mainly dominated by the objective function f and $P_f > 0.5$ means the ranking favors smaller penalty function values φ. Since the ultimate purpose is to search for the best feasible solution, the parameter should be set to $P_f < 0.5$. Finally, a hybrid algorithm was developed to solve the problem. The hybrid algorithm combines a genetic algorithm and a simulated annealing hyper heuristic (SAHH). In this algorithm, a stochastic ranking method was used to improve the constraint handling capability of the genetic algorithm while an SAHH procedure was incorporated in order to locate local optima more efficiently. The hybrid algorithm is developed based on a total of nine simple low-level heuristics. Here is the complete list of these heuristics.

Heuristic 1: Change the shift-pattern of a random nurse to another random feasible shift-pattern.
Heuristic 2: Similar to Heuristic 1, except the acceptance criteria is "1st improving φ value."
Heuristic 3: Same as Heuristic 1 but "1st improving φ and not deteriorating f."
Heuristic 4: Same as Heuristic 1 but "1st improving f."
Heuristic 5: Same as Heuristic 1 but "1st improving f and not deteriorating φ."
Heuristic 6: Switch the shift-pattern type (i.e., from day to night and vice versa) of a random nurse if the solution is unbalanced.

Heuristic 7: This heuristic tries to generate a balanced solution by switching the shift-pattern type [i.e., change a day shift-pattern with a night one if night shift(s) is unbalanced and vice versa. If both days and nights are not balanced, swap the shift patterns of two nurses who are working on different shift-pattern types].
Heuristic 8: This heuristic tries to find the first move that improves f by changing the shift pattern of a random nurse and assign the abandoned shift pattern to another nurse.
Heuristic 9: Same as Heuristic 8 but "1st improving f without worsening φ."

Compared with genetic algorithms that use penalty function methods as a constraint handling approach, the stochastic ranking method has demonstrated better performance with regard to feasibility. To improve the solution quality in terms of the objective function value, an SAHH algorithm was hybridized with the genetic algorithm. Experimental results have demonstrated the high-performance and consistency by this hybrid approach when compared with the genetic algorithm with stochastic ranking and the simulated annealing alone.

Nurse Preferences as an Objective Function

Fulltime nurses are vital components in hospital operations. However, nursing shortages has been an issue worldwide. This is due to lack of trained nurses and low job satisfaction, to name a few factors (Ulrich et al. 2002). Many approaches have been developed to address this issue, such as the score card approach to adopt nurse preferences on shift assignment (Bard and Purnomo 2005) and the auction approach (Chiaramonte and Chiaramonte 2008; Koeppel 2004). In the score card approach, each nurse is given a sheet of upcoming empty shift assignments. Based on their personal preference, the nurse is asked to assign penalty scores in such a way that a smaller penalty should be assigned to a preferred shift while a higher penalty should be given to an undesirable shift. Some master schedulers may share this round of schedule preferences among nurses and resolve some conflicting shifts that no one wants to take or everyone wants to take.

Purnomo and Bard (2006) proposed a new integer programming model for cyclic preference scheduling and hourly workers. The objective of cyclic scheduling is to generate a set of rosters that minimizes the number of uncovered shifts, while in the preference scheduling the objective is to minimize a "dissatisfaction" cost associated with violations of soft constraints. The problem combines elements of both cyclic and preference approaches and includes five different shift types. The first three divide the day evenly into non-overlapping periods of 8 hours each and are referred to as day (D), evening (E), and night (N). The remaining two divide the day into 12 hour, non-overlapping periods and are called a.m. and p.m. The objective function aims to minimize the weighted sum of preference violations and the cost of covering gaps with outside nurses.

Decision Variables

The parameters for this problem are defined as: r_a denotes penalty assigned to a roster that has a violation; h_t denotes length of shift t (hours); M_t is a large number representing the cost of an outside nurse for shift t; H_i is number of hours nurse i is contracted to work every 2 weeks; $LD_{dt}(UD_{dt})$ is lower (upper) demand requirement for shift t and day d; D_t^{maxon} presents maximum number of consecutive days that nurse i is permitted to work; $W_i^{\max}$ presents number of weekend shifts nurse i must work every 2 weeks; $V_{\max}$ denotes maximum number of violations allowed for each nurse; $TR_{\max}$ denotes maximum number of transitions from one shift type to another on consecutive days allowed in 14 days; and $O_{dt}^{\max}$ presents maximum number of outside nurses that can be assigned to shift t on day d.

The decision variables for the problem are: x_{idt} is 1 if nurse i works in shift t on day d, and 0 otherwise; w_{im} is 1 if nurse i works on weekend m, and 0 otherwise; $v_{i\alpha}$ is 1 if nurse i has α violations, and 0 otherwise; b_{id} is 1 if nurse $i \in N_R$ works in shift t_1 on day d and shift t_2 on day d+1, and 0 otherwise. Let $p_{id} = 1$ when nurse i has a 0–1–0 pattern that starts on day d, and 0 otherwise, and $q_{id} = 1$ when nurse i has a 1–0–1 pattern that starts on day d, and 0 otherwise. Let y_{dt} denote the number of outside nurses assigned to shift t on day d and s_{dt} present excess number of nurses assigned to shift t on day d.

Optimization Model

$$\theta_{ip} = \text{Min} \sum_{i \in N} \sum_{a=1}^{V_{\max}} r_a v_{ia} + \sum_{d \in D} \sum_{t \in T} M_t y_{dt}, \tag{3.15}$$

$$\sum_{i \in N} x_{idt} - s_{dt} + y_{dt} = LD_{dt}, \qquad \forall d \in D, t \in T \tag{3.16}$$

$$\sum_{d \in D} x_{idt} \geq P_{it}, \qquad \forall i \in N_R, t \in T_i \tag{3.17}$$

$$\sum_{d \in D} \sum_{t \in T_i} h_t x_{idt} = H_i, \qquad \forall i \in N \tag{3.18}$$

$$\sum_{t \in T_i} x_{idt} \leq 1, \qquad \forall i \in N, d \in D \tag{3.19}$$

$$x_{idt_2} + x_{i,d+1,t_1} \leq 1, \qquad \forall i \in N_{BB}, d \in D \tag{3.20}$$

$$\sum_{l=d}^{d+D_i^{\text{maxon}}} \sum_{t \in T_i} x_{ilt} \leq D_i^{\text{maxon}}, \qquad \forall i \in N, d \in D \tag{3.21}$$

$$\sum_{d \in D_w} \sum_{t \in T_i} x_{idt} = W_i^{\max} w_{im}, \qquad \forall i \in N, m \in W \tag{3.22}$$

$$\sum_{m \in W} w_{im} = 1, \qquad \forall i \in N \tag{3.23}$$

$$\sum_{t \in T_i} x_{idt} + \left(1 - \sum_{t \in T_i} x_{i,d+1,t}\right) + \sum_{t \in T_i} x_{i,d+2,t} + p_{id} \geq 1, \qquad \forall i \in N, d \in D \tag{3.24}$$

$$\left(1 - \sum_{t \in T_i} x_{idt}\right) + \sum_{t \in T_i} x_{i,d+1,t} + \left(1 - \sum_{t \in T_i} x_{i,d+2,t}\right) + q_{id} \geq 1, \qquad \forall i \in N, d \in D \tag{3.25}$$

$$1 - x_{idt_\alpha} + 1 - x_{i,d+1,t_\beta} + b_{id} \geq 1, \qquad \forall d \in D, \alpha \neq \beta \tag{3.26}$$

$$\sum_{d \in D} b_{id} \leq TR_{\max}, \qquad \forall i \in N_R \tag{3.27}$$

$$\sum_{d \in D} (p_{id} + q_{id} + b_{id}) = \sum_{a=1}^{V_{\max}} a v_{ia}, \qquad \forall i \in N \tag{3.28}$$

$$\sum_{a=1}^{V_{max}} v_{ia} \leq 1, \qquad \forall i \in N \tag{3.29}$$

$$0 \leq s_{dt} \leq UD_{dt} - LD_{dt}, 0 \leq y_{dt} \leq O_{dt}^{\max}, \qquad \forall t, d \tag{3.30}$$

$$b_{id}, p_{id}, q_{id} \geq 0, \forall i, t, d; \quad v_{ia} \in \{0,1\}, \forall i, a; \quad w_{im} \in \{0,1\}, \forall i, m \tag{3.31}$$

$$x_{idt} \in \{0,1\}, \forall i, t, d, \quad \text{where } x_{i,14+l,t} \equiv x_{ilt}, l = 1, \ldots, D_i^{\text{maxon}} \tag{3.32}$$

There are two sets of constraints. Constraints (3.16–3.23) are hard constraints and the rest are soft constraints. Constraints (3.16) correspond to the demand requirement for each shift $t \in T$ on day $d \in D$. These constraints, along with constraints (3.30) show that the number of nurses assigned to shift t must be at least LD_{dt}, and no more than UD_{dt}. Constraints (3.17) guarantee that for all $i \in N_R$ at least P_{it} shifts of type t are assigned every 2 weeks. Equations (3.18) state that the total number of hours assigned to nurse i must be equal to the number of hours H_i that she is obligated to work every 2 weeks contractually. Constraints (3.19) restrict a nurse to at most one shift assignment within 24 hours. Constraints (3.20) rule out back-to-back shifts. Constraints (3.21) ensure that the work stretch of nurse i is not more than D_i^{maxon} days in any time window of $D_i^{\text{maxon}} + 1$ consecutive days. Together, constraints (3.22) and (3.23) require that nurse i works exactly $W_i^{\max}$ weekend days every 2 weeks. Constraints (3.24–3.29) determine the quality of the schedules. The undesirable patterns including $0-1-0$ and $1-0-1$ are counted by the variable p_{id} and the summation $\sum_{d \in D} p_{id} + q_{id}$ in constraints (3.24) and (3.25) respectively. Constraints (3.26) detect a shift transition that nurse i may have during consecutive days. The maximum number of permitted transitions is given by $TR_{\max}$ in (3.27). Constraints (3.28–3.29), count the number of preference violations and determine which penalty coefficient r_a will be in effect, respectively. Finally the bounds in constraints (3.30), on the y_{dt} and s_{dt} variables limit the amount of under-and over coverage, respectively, for each shift on each day.

Solution Method

A branch-and-price algorithm was developed for solving the problem. An IP-based neighborhood search heuristic was proposed, which always found the best solutions and enabled the algorithm to converge in a matter of minutes in most cases. The problem was decomposed and two approaches were investigated to modify branching rules in the construction of the search tree, one based on the master problem variables and the other on subproblem variables. It can be shown that the former was more suited for instances with a large number of nurses and profiles, while the latter was more efficient for small- and medium-sized problems. A unique feature of the formulation is that the master problem contains integer rather than binary variables.

Multi-Objective Nurse Scheduling Problems

Although many researchers have focused on only one objective function to model nurse scheduling problems, NSP is truly a multiple objective optimization problem (Burke et al. 2010; Maenhout and Vanhoucke 2010; Parr and Thompson 2007). There can be many goals in scheduling nurses such as minimizing the nurse assignment cost, maximizing nurse job satisfaction, or any other goals that the hospital has due to different sets in terms of scheduling nurses. Some of these may have conflicts of interests. Maenhout and Vanhoucke (2010) presented a branch and price algorithm for solving a multi-objective nurse scheduling problem incorporating some penalty scores associated with scheduling inefficiencies. Other relevant nurse scheduling papers can be found in (Azaiez and Al Sharif 2005; Jaumard et al. 1998).

Hadwan and Ayob (2010) proposed a greedy constructive heuristic algorithm based on the idea of generating the most required shift patterns to solve the nurses' rostering problem that arises in University Kebangsaan Malaysia Medical Centre (UKMMC), Malaysia. This work aims to ensure the availability of enough nurses by giving them fair consideration during the rostering period. The complexity of the solution search space was reduced by generating all the allowed two-day and three-day shift patterns to build up the roster. Due to different sets of soft constraints, they proposed a weighted method approach to model the problem different from other objectives in the literature. The objective function aimed to minimize the total penalty cost that occurs due to the violations of soft constraints.

Decision Variables

The parameters and indexes for this problem are: I denotes the set of nurses available; I_s denotes the set of senior nurses $I_s \subset I$; D denotes the set of days; G denotes the set of grades; W presents the set of weights; S presents the set of shifts. The possible shifts are considered as: morning, evening, night, and day off. These four shifts are respectively represented by the set $S = \{1,2,3,4\}$. P presents the set of possible night patterns; d is the dth day where $d \in D$; s is the sth shift where $s \in S$; w is the wth weight where $w \in W$; p is the pth possible pattern where $p \in P$; R_{ds} denotes the demand for day d on shift s; d_p denotes the starting date for pattern p.

The decision variables are defined as: X_{ids} is 1 if nurse i works on day d shift s, and 0 otherwise; and Y_{pi} is 1 if pattern p is worked by nurse i, and 0 otherwise.

Optimization Model

$$\begin{aligned} \text{Min } & w_1 \sum_{i \in I} (d1_i^+ + d1_i^-) + w_2 \sum_{i \in I} d2_i^+ \\ & + w_3 \sum_{i \in I} \sum_{d \in D} d3_{id}^- + w_4 \sum_{i \in I} \sum_{d \in D} d4_{id}^- + w_5 \sum_{p \in P} d5_p^+ \end{aligned} \tag{3.33}$$

Subject to:

$$\sum_{i \in I} X_{id(1)} \geq R_{d(1)}, \qquad \forall d \in D \tag{3.34}$$

$$\sum_{i \in I} X_{id(2)} \geq R_{d(2)}, \qquad \forall d \in D \tag{3.35}$$

$$\sum_{i \in I} X_{id(3)} \geq R_{d(3)}, \qquad \forall d \in D \tag{3.36}$$

$$\sum_{s \in S} X_{ids} = 1, \qquad \forall i \in I, d \in D \tag{3.37}$$

$$\sum_{i \in I_s} X_{ids} \geq 1, \qquad \forall d \in D, s = 1 \ldots 3 \tag{3.38}$$

$$\begin{aligned} & X_{id(4)} + X_{i(d+1)(1)} + X_{i(d+1)(2)} + X_{i(d+1)(3)} + X_{i(d+2)(4)} \leq 2, \quad \forall i \in I, \\ & d = 1 \ldots |D| - 2 \end{aligned} \tag{3.39}$$

$$\sum_{d\in D}\sum_{s\in S-\{4\}} X_{ids} \leq 12, \qquad \forall i \in I \tag{3.40}$$

$$\sum_{d\in D}\sum_{s\in S-\{4\}} X_{ids} \geq 10, \qquad \forall i \in I \tag{3.41}$$

$$X_{id4} + X_{i(d+1)4} + X_{i(d+2)4} + X_{i(d+3)4} + X_{i(d+4)4} \geq 1, \qquad \forall i \in I, \quad d = 1\ldots|D| - 4 \tag{3.42}$$

$$\sum_{i\in I} Y_{pi} = 1, \qquad p \in P \tag{3.43}$$

$$\sum_{p\in P} Y_{pi} \leq 1, \qquad i \in I \tag{3.44}$$

$$\sum_{i\in I} Y_{pi}\left(\sum_{l=0}^{l=3} X_{i(d_p+l)(3)} + \sum_{l=4}^{l=5} X_{i(d_p+l)(4)}\right) = 6, \quad p = 1\ldots 9 \tag{3.45}$$

$$\sum_{i\in I} Y_{pi}(X_{id_p3} + X_{i(d_p+1)3}) = 2, \qquad p = 10, 11 \tag{3.46}$$

$$\sum_{d\in D} X_{id4} \geq 2, \qquad \forall i \in I \tag{3.47}$$

$$\sum_{d\in D}\sum_{s\in S-\{4\}} X_{ids} + (d1_i^+ - d1_i^-) = 11, \qquad \forall i \in I \tag{3.48}$$

$$X_{i(6)(4)} + X_{(i)(7)(4)} + X_{i(13)(4)} + X_{i(14)(4)} + (d2_i^+ - d2_i^-) = 1, \qquad \forall i \in I \tag{3.49}$$

$$X_{id(1)} + X_{i(d+1)(2)} + (d3_{id}^+ - d3_{id}^-) = 1, \qquad \forall i \in I, \quad d = 1\ldots|D| - 1 \tag{3.50}$$

$$X_{id(2)} + X_{i(d+1)(1)} + (d4_{id}^+ - d4_{id}^-) = 1, \qquad \forall i \in I, \quad d = 1\ldots|D| - 1 \tag{3.51}$$

$$\left(\sum_{i\in I}[Y_{pi} \times (X_{i(7)(2)} + X_{i(7)(4)})]\right) + (d5_p^+ - d5_p^-) = 1, \quad p \in \{1,2,3\} \tag{3.52}$$

$$\left(\sum_{i\in I}[Y_{pi} \times (X_{i(11)(2)} + X_{i(11)(4)})]\right) + (d5_p^+ - d5_p^-) = 1, \quad p \in \{4,5,6\} \tag{3.53}$$

Constraints (3.34–3.47) represent the hard constraints. Constraints (3.34, 3.35 and 3.36) ensure that the demand is fulfilled at all times, while, constraints (3.37) state that each nurse is working one shift a day at the most. In addition, constraints (3.38) assign at least one senior nurse for each shift. Furthermore, constraints (3.39) ensure not to give an isolated working day. Next, constraints (3.40) ensure that the maximum number of working days during the whole rostering period is

12 days. However, constraints (3.41) ensure that the minimum number of working days during the whole rostering period is not more than 10 days. Meanwhile constraints (3.42) ensure the maximum number of consecutive working days is 4 days. Then, (3.43, 3.44, 3.45 and 3.46) ensure that the patterns are covered exactly with one nurse for each. Constraints (3.47) state that each nurse is subject to having at least 2 days off during the roster period, which is 14 days.

Constraints (3.48–3.53) represent soft constraints. Constraints (3.48) are to give a fair number of working days and days off to all of the nurses, which is the average between the maximum and minimum working days. Constraints (3.49) ensure that each nurse has at least one day off in the weekend during the roster period. Constraints (3.50) and (3.51) attempt to give stable shifts, either consecutive morning or evening. Constraints (3.52) and (3.53) attempt to give either a day off or an evening shift after the days off that followed the night shift. The objective function in the problem concerns minimizing the total penalty that occurs due to the violations of soft constraints. In order to incorporate the soft constraints in the rostering model, our goals are: $d1_i^-$ ($d1_i^+$) is the amount of negative (positive) deviations from goal 1 (Minimizing the violation of (3.48)) for nurse i. Both positive and negative deviations are penalized. $d2_i^-$ ($d2_i^+$) is the amount of negative (positive) deviation from goal 2 (Minimizing the violation of (3.49)) for nurse i. Negative deviations are penalized. $d3_i^-$ ($d3_i^+$) is the amount of negative (positive) deviation from goal 3 (Minimizing the violation of (3.50)) for day d and nurse i. Negative deviations are penalized. $d4_i^-$($d4_i^+$) is the amount of negative (positive) deviation from goal 4 (Minimizing the violation of (3.51)) for day d and nurse i. Negative deviations are penalized. $d5_i^-$($d5_i^+$) is the amount of negative (positive) deviation from goal 5 (Minimizing the violation of (3.52) and (3.53)) for day d and nurse i. Positive deviations are penalized.

Solution Method

In order to solve NRP, a modified shift patterns approach was proposed, followed by a simulated annealing algorithm to generate a good quality roster. Generally, the approach was divided into three main stages: (1) Initialize the problem by reducing search space and generating valid shifts sequence patterns; (2) Construct feasible or near feasible initial solution; and (3) Optimize the initial solution that was constructed in the previous two stages to get the optimal or near optimal solution. It can be shown that the proposed approach is capable of accommodating all the hard and soft constraints experienced by the rostering system at UKMMC.

Constraint-Based and Heuristic-Oriented Nurse Scheduling Problems

Many researchers have used mathematical programming to find optimal solutions for nurse scheduling problems. However, due to the large size it is extremely difficult to solve the problems optimally when many hard and soft constraints are involved. To tackle this challenge, some researchers have restricted the problem dimensions and developed simplified models. However, this leads to solutions that are not applicable to real hospitals. Therefore other researchers attempt to focus on heuristic approaches that provide good feasible solutions in a reasonable amount of time for NSP (Bai et al. 2010; Burke et al. 2010; He and Qu 2009; Sundaramoorthi et al. 2009).

We describe a hybrid model of integer programming and variable neighborhood search (VNS) for highly constrained nurse scheduling problems developed by Burke et al. (2010). They partitioned the constraint sets in such a way that those with lower complexity and higher importance have more priority to be included in the subproblem solved using IP.

Decision Variables

The parameters for this problem are defined as: I denotes the set of nurses available; J denotes the set of indices of the last day of each week within the scheduling period; and K presents the set of shift types 1(early), 2(day), 3(late), 4(night). $I_t|t \in \{1, 2, 3\}$ denotes the subset of nurses that work 20, 32, 36 hours per week respectively; k' presents the set of undesirable shift type succession $\{(2, 1), (3, 1), (3, 2), (1, 4)\}$; d_{jk} is the coverage requirement of shift type k on day $j \in \{1, \ldots, 7|J|\}$; m_i is the maximum number of working days for nurse i; n_1 and n_2 are the maximum number of consecutive night shifts and working days, respectively; c_k is the desirable upper bound of consecutive assignments of shift type k; g_t and h_t are upper and lower bounds of weekly working days for the tth subset of nurses.

The decision variables are presented as: x_{ijk} is 1 if nurse i is assigned to shift type k in day j, and 0 otherwise.

Optimization Model

$$\text{Min}G(x) = [g_1(x), g_2(x), g_3(x), g_4(x), g_5(x), g_6(x), g_7(x), g_8(x)], \tag{3.54}$$

Subject to:

$$\sum_{i \in I} x_{ijk} = d_{jk}, \qquad \forall j \in \{1, \ldots, 7|J|\}, k \in \mathscr{K} \tag{3.55}$$

$$\sum_{k \in K} x_{ijk} \leq 1, \qquad \forall i \in I, j \in \{1, \ldots, 7|J|\} \tag{3.56}$$

$$\sum_{j=1}^{7|J|} \sum_{k \in K} x_{ijk} \leq m_i, \qquad \forall i \in I \tag{3.57}$$

$$\sum_{j\in J}\sum_{k\in K} x_{ijk} \leq 3, \qquad \forall i \in I \tag{3.58}$$

$$\sum_{j=1}^{7|J|} x_{ij4} \leq 3, \qquad \forall i \in I \tag{3.59}$$

$$x_{i(j-1)4} - x_{ij4} + x_{i(j+1)4} \geq 0 \qquad \forall i \in I,\ j \in \{2,\ldots,7|J|-1\} \tag{3.60}$$

$$x_{i(j-1)4} - \sum_{k=1}^{3} x_{ijk} + \sum_{k=1}^{3} x_{i(j+1)k} \leq 1, \qquad \forall i \in I,\ j \in \{2,\ldots,7|J|-1\} \tag{3.61}$$

$$x_{i(j-1)4} + \sum_{k=1}^{3} x_{ijk} - \sum_{k=1}^{3} x_{i(j+1)k} \leq 1, \qquad \forall i \in I,\ j \in \{2,\ldots,7|J|-1\} \tag{3.62}$$

$$x_{i(j-1)4} + \sum_{k=1}^{3} x_{ijk} + \sum_{k=1}^{3} x_{i(j+1)k} \leq 2, \qquad \forall i \in I,\ j \in \{2,\ldots,7|J|-1\} \tag{3.63}$$

$$\sum_{j=r}^{r+n_1} x_{ij4} \leq n_1, \qquad \forall i \in I,\ r \in \{1,\ldots,7|J|-n_1\} \tag{3.64}$$

$$\sum_{j=r}^{r+n_2}\sum_{k\in K} x_{ijk} \leq n_2, \qquad \forall i \in I,\ r \in \{1,\ldots,7|J|-n_2\} \tag{3.65}$$

$$x_{16(j)3} = 0, \qquad \forall j \in \{1,\ldots,7|J|\} \tag{3.66}$$

$$\sum_{k\in K}[x_{i(j-1)k} - x_{ijk}] + s^1_{ij} - s^2_{ij} = 0, \qquad \forall i \in I,\ j \in J \tag{3.67}$$

$$\sum_{k\in K}[x_{i(j-1)k} - x_{ijk} + x_{i(j+1)k}] + s^3_{ij} \geq 0, \qquad \forall i \in I,\ j \in \{2,\ldots,7|J|-1\} \tag{3.68}$$

$$\sum_{k\in K}[x_{i(j-1)k} - x_{ijk} + x_{i(j+1)k}] - s^4_{ij} \leq 1, \qquad \forall i \in I,\ j \in \{2,\ldots,7|J|-1\} \tag{3.69}$$

$$\sum_{j=r}^{r+3} x_{ijk} - s^5_{irk} \leq c_k, \qquad \forall i \in I,\ r \in \{1,\ldots,7|J|-3\},\ k \in \{1,3\} \tag{3.70}$$

$$x_{i(j-1)k} - x_{ijk} + x_{i(j+1)k} + s^6_{ijk} \geq 0, \qquad \forall i \in I,\ j \in \{2,\ldots,7|J|-1\},\ k \in \{1,3\} \tag{3.71}$$

$$\sum_{j=7w-6}^{7w}\sum_{k\in K} x_{ijk} - s^7_{tiw} \leq g_t, \qquad \forall t \in \{1,2,3\},\ i \in I_t,\ w \in \{1,\ldots,|J|\} \tag{3.72}$$

$$\sum_{j=7w-6}^{7w} \sum_{k \in K} x_{ijk} + s_{tiw}^{8} \geq h_t, \qquad \forall t \in \{1,2,3\},\ i \in I_t,\ w \in \{1,\ldots,|J|\} \tag{3.73}$$

$$\sum_{j=r}^{r+3} \sum_{k \in K} x_{ijk} - s_{ir}^{9} \leq 3, \qquad \forall i \in I_1,\ r \in \{1,\ldots,7|J|-3\} \tag{3.74}$$

$$x_{ijk_1} + x_{i(j+1)k_2} - s_{ijk'}^{10} \leq 2, \qquad \forall i \in I,\ j \in \{1,\ldots,7|J|-1\},\ k' = (k_1,k_2) \in K' \tag{3.75}$$

Where

$$g_1(x) = \sum_{i \in I} \sum_{j \in J} (s_{ij}^{1} + s_{ij}^{2}), \tag{3.76}$$

$$g_2(x) = \sum_{i \in I} \sum_{j=2}^{7|J|-1} s_{ij}^{3}, \tag{3.77}$$

$$g_3(x) = \sum_{i \in I} \sum_{j=2}^{7|J|-1} s_{ij}^{4}, \tag{3.78}$$

$$g_4(x) = \sum_{i \in I} \sum_{r=1}^{7|J|-3} \sum_{k \in \{1,3\}} s_{ijk}^{5}, \tag{3.79}$$

$$g_5(x) = \sum_{i \in I} \sum_{j=2}^{7|J|-1} \sum_{k' \in \{1,3\}} s_{ijk'}^{6}, \tag{3.80}$$

$$g_6(x) = \sum_{t=1}^{3} \sum_{i \in I_t} \sum_{w=1}^{|J|} (s_{tiw}^{7} + s_{tiw}^{8}), \tag{3.81}$$

$$g_7(x) = \sum_{i \in I_1} \sum_{r=1}^{7|J|-3} s_{ir}^{9}, \tag{3.82}$$

$$g_8(x) = \sum_{i \in I} \sum_{j=1}^{7|J|-1} \sum_{k' \in K'} s_{ijk'}^{10}. \tag{3.83}$$

The problem has hard and soft constraints. Constraints (3.55–3.66) are hard constraints. Constraints (3.55) correspond to the daily requirement of each shift type. Constraints (3.56) restrict a nurse to at most one shift assignment for each day. Constraints (3.57), (3.58), and (3.59) are related to the maximum number of total working days, on-duty weekends, and night shifts during the scheduling period, respectively. Constraints (3.60) guarantee no standalone night shift. Three sub-constraints (3.61–3.63) state a minimum of two free days after a series of night shifts. Constraints (3.64) and (3.65) correspond to the maximum number of consecutive night shifts and working days, respectively. Constraints (3.66) ensure there are no late shifts for one particular nurse.

The problem has the following additional soft constraints and the objective is to satisfy them as much as possible. Constraints (3.67) ensure nurses work either no shifts or two shifts in weekends. Constraints (3.68) guarantee that there is no standalone shift (i.e., a single day between 2 days off). Constraints (3.69) are related to the minimum number of free days after a series of shifts. Constraints (3.70) and (3.72) correspond to the maximum/minimum number of consecutive assignments of shifts, weekly working days respectively. Constriants (3.74) restrict the number of consecutive working days for part-time nurses to its maximum number, and finally constraints (3.75) rule out certain shift-type successions.

Solution Method

The advantages of both the IP and the VNS for global optimization are combined. First, IP is used to solve the subproblem including the full set of hard constraints and a subset of soft constraints. Then, a VNS with the neighborhood of swapping blocks of shifts is used to make the improvement on the IP's resulting solution, mainly from the aspects of satisfying the excluded constraints from the preceding IP model. It is claimed that the proposed hybrid model was able to handle all the requirements and constraints of nurse rostering in complex hospital environments.

3.3.2 Nurse Scheduling Problem in an Operating Suite

Cardoen et al. (2010) have provided a comprehensive overview of recent operational research method developments on operating room planning and scheduling. They evaluated multiple domains related to problem settings, performance measures, solution methods, and uncertainty considerations. Established upon the survey, many researchers have ventured either to develop patient-room scheduling models or to propose improvement methods associated with performance measures. Many researchers have tried to optimally utilize surgery scheduling to find the best surgery-room assignments, surgery-physician assignments, and surgery-block time assignments (Cardoen 2010; Dexter et al. 1999, 2010a, b; Fei et al. 2009; Feia et al. 2008; Lamiri et al. 2008; Ozkarahan 2000).

Most of the literature in operating room scheduling focuses on either providing the optimal allocation of surgeries to operating rooms, surgeries to available time intervals, and surgeries to physicians or to find the best possible surgery sequencing with minimum costs and variabilities. However, there is little literature

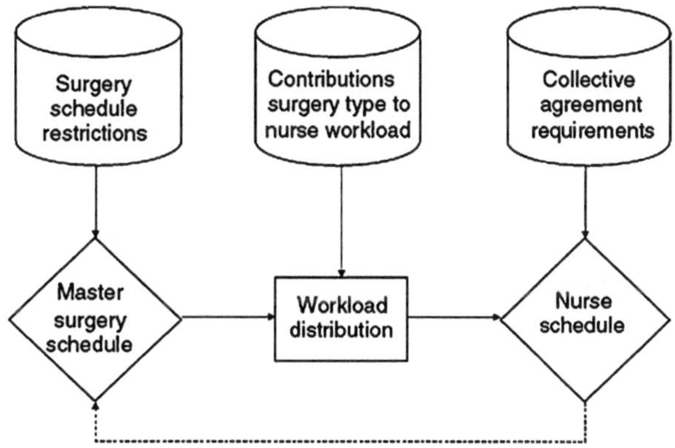

Fig. 3.2 Schematic overview of the general idea

in operating room scheduling that considers the effect of nurse assignments to surgeries and their vital influence on surgery performance.

Integrated Operating Room Scheduling

Belien and Demeulemeester (2008) have developed an integrated nurse and surgery scheduling problem using IP. A schematic overview of the general idea is presented in Fig. 3.2.

The input for the nurse scheduling process consists of the restrictions implied on the individual nurse roster lines on the one hand and the workload distribution over time on the other hand. Individual roster line was developed that can be viewed as a sequence of days on and days off, where each day on contains a single shift identified by a label such as day, evening, or night. A set covering model was developed for this problem. The workload distribution itself is determined by the master surgery schedule introduced as workload model. In order to be able to deduce the workload from the surgery schedule one also has to know the workload contributions of each specific type of surgery. Finally an integrated nurse scheduling model was presented to satisfy nurse preferences as well as surgery block assignments. They showed how the column generation technique approach can easily cope with their model extension. They showed that by means of a large number of computational experiments an idea of the cost saving opportunities and required solution times was provided.

Initial Optimization Model

This nurse scheduling problem consists of generating a configuration of individual schedules over a given time horizon. The configuration of nurse schedules is generated so as to fulfill collective agreement requirements and the hospital staffing demand coverage while minimizing the salary cost.

Decision Variables

If j is the set of feasible roster lines j, and i is the set of demand periods i; $d_i \in R^+ \forall i \in I$ denotes the required number of nurses scheduled during period i. Also a_{ij} is 1 if roster line j contains an active shift during period i and 0 otherwise.

The integer decision variable $x_j \forall j \in J$ indicates the number of individual nurses that are scheduled by roster line j.

Optimization Model

The nurse scheduling problem (NSP) can now be stated as follows:

$$\text{Minimize} \sum_{j \in J} x_j \tag{3.84}$$

$$\sum_{j \in J} a_{ij} x_j \geq d_i, \tag{3.85}$$

$$x_j \in \{0, 1, 2, \cdots\} \qquad \forall j \in J. \tag{3.86}$$

Coverage constraints imply how many nurses of appropriate skills have to be scheduled for each demand period.

Workload Optimization Model

In the NSP, the right-hand side values of the coverage constraints were considered to be fixed. However, instead of assuming the demand values to be fixed, a general NSP was developed considering that demand values should be dependent on the number and type of patients undergoing surgery in the hospital at each moment. By manipulating the master surgery schedule hospital management can create a number of different workload distributions, further referred to as workload patterns.

Decision Variables

k denotes the set of possible workload patterns that could be generated by modifying the surgery schedule. These were obtained by enumerating all possible ways of assigning operating blocks to the different surgeons, subject to surgery demand and to capacity restrictions. Each workload pattern k is described by a number of periodic demands $d_{ik} \in \{0, 1, 2, \cdots\} \forall i \in I$.

Decision variable z_k was defined as 1 if the surgery schedule that corresponds to workload k was chosen, and 0 otherwise.

Optimization Model

The problem was stated as follows:

$$\text{Minimize} \sum_{j \in J} x_j \tag{3.87}$$

$$\sum_{j \in J} a_{ij} x_j \geq \sum k \in K d_{ik} z_k, \tag{3.88}$$

$$\sum_{k \in K} z_k = 1, \tag{3.89}$$

$$x_j \in \{0, 1, 2, \cdots\} \qquad \forall j \in J, \tag{3.90}$$

$$z_k \in \{0, 1\} \qquad \forall k \in K. \tag{3.91}$$

Coverage constraints imply how many nurses of appropriate skills have to be scheduled for each demand period and which workload patterns should be assigned to them.

Final Optimization Model

A new workload pattern can be obtained by building a new surgery schedule. In the application, a new surgery schedule was built by solving an integer program. To find a new workload pattern with minimal reduced cost given the current set of roster lines and workload patterns, the objective function minimizes the dual price vector of the demand constraints (3.88) multiplied by the new demands. Two types of constraints should be considered. Surgery demand constraints determine how many blocks must be preserved for each surgeon. Capacity constraints ensure that the number of blocks assigned during each period do not exceed the available capacity.

Decision Variables

y_{rt} ($\forall r \in R$ and $t \in T$) is the number of blocks assigned to surgeon r in period t where t represents the set of active periods and r the set of surgeons. It is assumed that q_r was the number of blocks required by each surgeon r, and b_t is the maximal number of blocks available in period t. $w_{rti} \in R^+$ denotes the contribution to the workload of demand period i of assigning one block to surgeon r in period t.

Optimization Model

The integer program to construct a new surgery schedule (and at the same time price out a new workload pattern k) is developed as follows:

$$\text{Minimize} \sum_{i \in I} \pi_i d_{ik} \tag{3.92}$$

$$\sum_{t \in T} y_{rt} = q_r, \tag{3.93}$$

$$\sum_{r \in R} y_{rt} \leq b_t, \tag{3.94}$$

$$\sum_{r \in R} \sum_{t \in T} w_{rti} y_{rt} \leq d_{ik}, \tag{3.95}$$

$$y_{rt} \in \{0, 1, 2, \cdots, \min q_r, b_r\} \quad \forall r \in R, \quad \forall t \in T, \tag{3.96}$$

$$d_{ik} \in \{0, 1, 2, \cdots\} \qquad \forall i \in I. \tag{3.97}$$

The first set of constraints implies that each surgeon obtains the number of required blocks. Also, it is essential to ensure that the number of blocks assigned does not exceed the available number of blocks in each period. Finally, d_{ik} values are assigned to the appropriate integer values.

Solution Method

The column generation method is utilized to solve the model. The column generation technique can easily cope with their model extension. The approach involves the solution of two types of pricing problems, the first one is solved with a standard dynamic programming approach using recursion, the second one by means of a state-of-the-art mixed integer programming optimizer. A constraint branching scheme is proposed to drive the solution into integrality with respect to the workload patterns while the integrality of the roster lines is left out of the scope of the paper. They also calculate, through a large number of computational experiments, cost savings and required solution times.

The schematic overview of the branch-and-price to solve the models is presented in Fig. 3.3.

The results show that, first of all, column generation is a good technique to deal with the extra problem dimension of modifying surgery schedules. Second, the results from the integrated approach can be used to quantify the shares of the two sources of waste: waste due to the workforce surplus per shift and waste due to the inflexibility of roster lines. Third, unlike the NSP, the GNSP turns out to become harder to solve when the collective agreement requirements are more strict. They indicated that considerable savings could be achieved by using this approach to build nurse and surgery schedules.

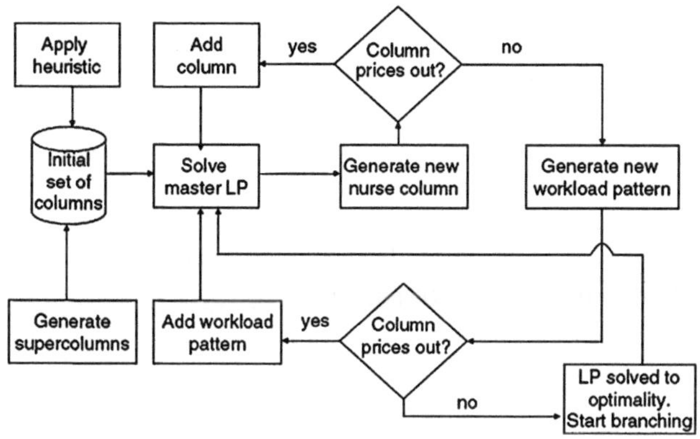

Fig. 3.3 Schematic overview of the GNSP branch-and-price algorithm

Nurse Scheduling in an Operating Suite Problem

Mobasher and Lim (2011) focus on the nurse scheduling problem in an operating suite by developing nurse scheduling optimization models for an actual operating suite in Texas, USA. A multi-objective integer programming nurse scheduling model in an operating suite is introduced that considers different aspects of the scheduling problem such as demand satisfaction, idle time and over times and job changes. The model called "Nurse Assignment Model", assigns nurses to different surgery cases based on their specialties and competency levels. Different heuristics are applied to develop solution methods for the multi-objective nurse assignment model. Real data are gathered from a cancer center in Texas and used to show the efficiency of the optimization models and solution methods.

The objective is to determine which nurses should be assigned to each surgery case. It is essential to provide schedules with minimum overtime, non-consecutivity, and changes during surgery procedures as well as maximum demand satisfaction.

Decison variables

Several input parameters were used for this modeling. These parameters can provide enough information about each nurse and surgery case.

P^1_{is} = 1, if If nurse $i \in \mathscr{I}$ is working in shift $s \in \mathscr{S}$; 0, otherwise.
P^2_{ikqp} = 1, if nurse $i \in \mathscr{I}$ can do role $k \in \mathscr{K}$ in specialty $q \in \mathscr{Q}$ with competency level $p \in \mathscr{P}$; 0, otherwise.

P^3_{it}= 1, if nurse $i \in \mathscr{I}$ has job level $t \in \mathscr{T}$; 0, otherwise.
P^4_{cj}= 1, if case $c \in \mathscr{C}$ is scheduled to happen in OR $j \in \mathscr{J}$; 0, otherwise.
P^5_{cqph}= 1, if case $c \in \mathscr{C}$ needs specialty $q \in \mathscr{Q}$ with procedure complexity $p \in \mathscr{P}$ in time interval $h \in \mathscr{H}$; 0, otherwise.
P^6_{ckh}= Required number of nurses for case $c \in \mathscr{C}$, who can do role $k \in \mathscr{K}$ in time interval $h \in \mathscr{H}$.
P^7_{ch}= 1, if case $c \in \mathscr{C}$ is in progress during time interval $h \in \mathscr{H}$; 0, otherwise.
P^8_{c}= Case $c \in \mathscr{C}$ duration (lenght of surgery).
P^9_{sh}= 1, if shift $s \in \mathscr{S}$ contains time interval $h \in \mathscr{H}$ as regular working hours; 0, otherwise.
P^{10}_{sh}= 1, if shift $s \in \mathscr{S}$ contains time interval $h \in \mathscr{H}$ as authorized overtime hours; 0, otherwise.

Decision variables were defined as y_{ickh} is 1, if nurse $i \in \mathscr{I}$ works on case $c \in \mathscr{C}$ at time $h \in \mathscr{H}$ doing role $k \in \mathscr{K}$, and 0, otherwise.

Optimization Model

Constraints

The constraints introduced for this integer programming model are as follows.

$$\sum_{c\in\mathscr{C}}\sum_{k\in\mathscr{K}} y_{ickh} \leq 1, \qquad i \in \mathscr{I}, h \in \mathscr{H}, \tag{3.98}$$

$$y_{ickh} \leq \sum_{s\in S} (P^1_{is} \times (P^9_{sh} + P^{10}_{sh})), \qquad i \in \mathscr{I}, c \in \mathscr{C}, k \in \mathscr{K}, h \in \mathscr{H}, \tag{3.99}$$

$$\sum_{c\in\mathscr{C}}\sum_{k\in\mathscr{K}}\sum_{h\in\mathscr{H}} y_{ickh} \leq \sum_{s\in\mathscr{S}}\sum_{h\in\mathscr{H}} (P^1_{is} \times (P^9_{sh} + P^{10}_{sh})), \qquad i \in \mathscr{I}, \tag{3.100}$$

$$y_{ickh} \leq P^7_{ch} \times \left(\sum_{q\in\mathscr{Q},\, p\in\mathscr{P}} \sum P^5_{cqph} \times P^2_{ikqp} \right), \qquad i \in \mathscr{I}, c \in \mathscr{C}, k \in \mathscr{K}, h \in \mathscr{H}, \tag{3.101}$$

$$\sum_{i\in\mathscr{I}} y_{ickh} \geq P^7_{ch}, \qquad c \in \mathscr{C}, k \in \mathscr{K}, h \in \mathscr{H}, \tag{3.102}$$

$$\sum_{h\in\mathscr{H}} y_{ickh} \leq M \times d^2_{ick}, \qquad \forall i \in \mathscr{I}, c \in \mathscr{C}, k \in \mathscr{K}, \tag{3.103}$$

$$\sum_{k\in\mathscr{K}} d^2_{ick} \leq 1, \qquad \forall i \in \mathscr{I}, c \in \mathscr{C}, \tag{3.104}$$

$$\sum_{i\in\mathscr{I}}\sum_{c\in\mathscr{C}}\sum_{k\in\mathscr{K}}\sum_{h\in\mathscr{H}}\sum_{t=1}y_{ickh}\times P^3_{it}\geq\alpha(\sum_{i\in\mathscr{I}}\sum_{c\in\mathscr{C}}\sum_{k\in\mathscr{K}}\sum_{h\in\mathscr{H}}\sum_{t\in\mathscr{T}}y_{ickh}\times P^3_{it}), \quad (3.105)$$

$$\sum_{i\in\mathscr{I}}\sum_{c\in\mathscr{C}}\sum_{k\in\mathscr{K}}\sum_{h\in\mathscr{H}}\sum_{t=2}y_{ickh}\times P^3_{it}\leq(1-\alpha)(\sum_{i\in\mathscr{I}}\sum_{c\in\mathscr{C}}\sum_{k\in\mathscr{K}}\sum_{h\in\mathscr{H}}\sum_{t\in\mathscr{T}}y_{ickh}\times P^3_{it}), \quad (3.106)$$

$$\sum_{i\in\mathscr{I}}y_{ickh}+de_{ckh}\geq P^6_{ckh}\times P^7_{ch}, \qquad \forall c\in\mathscr{C},k\in\mathscr{K},h\in\mathscr{H} \quad (3.107)$$

$$\text{DEM}\geq\sum_{h\in\mathscr{H}}de_{ckh}, \qquad \forall c\in\mathscr{C},k\in\mathscr{K} \quad (3.108)$$

$$\sum_{k\in\mathscr{K},c\in\mathscr{C},h\in\mathscr{H}}y_{ickh}\times P^4_{cj}\leq M\cdot X_{ij} \qquad \forall i\in\mathscr{I},j\in\mathscr{J} \quad (3.109)$$

$$\sum_{j\in\mathscr{J}}X_{ij}\leq XX, \qquad \forall i\in\mathscr{I} \quad (3.110)$$

$$\sum_{s\in\mathscr{S}}P^1_{is}\cdot P^{10}_{sh}\times(\sum_{c\in\mathscr{C},k\in\mathscr{K}}y_{ickh}+\sum_{s\in\mathscr{S}}P^1_{is}\times P^{10}_{sh}-d^4_{ih})\leq\sum_{s\in\mathscr{S}}P^1_{is}\cdot P^{10}_{sh}, \quad \forall i\in\mathscr{I},h\in\mathscr{H} \quad (3.111)$$

$$P^1_{is}\times(P^9_{s(h+1)}+P^{10}_{s(h+1)})\times|\sum_{\substack{c\in\mathscr{C}\\k\in\mathscr{K}}}y_{ick(h+1)}\times-\sum_{\substack{c\in\mathscr{C}\\k\in\mathscr{K}}}y_{ickh}|\leq d^7_{ih}, \qquad \forall i\in\mathscr{I},h\in\mathscr{H} \quad (3.112)$$

$$\text{DMs}\geq\sum_{h\in\mathscr{H}}d^7_{ih}, \qquad \forall i\in\mathscr{I} \quad (3.113)$$

$$\text{DMf}\geq\sum_{h\in\mathscr{H}}d^4_{ih}, \qquad \forall i\in\mathscr{I} \quad (3.114)$$

$$\sum_{k\in\mathscr{K},h\in\mathscr{H}}y_{ickh}-\sum_{h\in\mathscr{H}}P^7_{ch}+cd_{ic}+M\cdot(1-nc_{ic})\geq 0, \qquad \forall i\in\mathscr{I},c\in\mathscr{C} \quad (3.115)$$

$$\sum_{k\in\mathscr{K},h\in\mathscr{H}}y_{ickh}\leq M\cdot nc_{ic}, \qquad \forall i\in\mathscr{I},c\in\mathscr{C} \quad (3.116)$$

$$\sum_{c\in\mathscr{C}}nc_{ic}\leq nct, \qquad \forall i\in\mathscr{I} \quad (3.117)$$

$$\sum_{c\in\mathscr{C}}cd_{ic}\leq cdt. \qquad \forall i\in\mathscr{I} \quad (3.118)$$

The constraints were divided into two sets: hard and soft constraints. Shift limitations, nurse skill level, staffing ratio, and case requirements belong to hard constraints, to name a few. Although some nurses have sufficient skill levels to work on different roles, they cannot be assigned to do different jobs at the same time. Therefore, each nurse should be assigned to one case doing one specific role in each time interval. This constraint is shown in (3.98). Constraints (3.99) and (3.100) make sure that nurses will be assigned to the cases that are in progress during their shift hours. Also, the total working hours of a nurse in each day should be less than her total regular and overtime working hours. Each nurse is allowed to work at most 4 hours overtime and 8 or 10 hours regular time.

Constraints (3.101) and (3.102) show that a nurse can be assigned to a case if she has sufficient skills to handle the case specialty requirements. In addition, the nurse should have sufficient competency to deal with case procedure complexities. Also, a nurse should be assigned to the surgery case at time interval h if the case is in progress at that time interval.

Besides, at any time, the total ratio of RN/Scrub techs assignments should be $\alpha/(1-\alpha)$ during the day based on the current hiring plans of most hospitals. Different ratios can be used for different hospitals. This limitation is demonstrated by constraints (3.105) and (3.106).

Finally, it is not acceptable to assign nurses to do different jobs in one specific surgery. For this purpose, a binary decision variable d^2_{ick} is introduced which takes value 1 when a nurse i is assigned to case c to do job k. This decision variable is demonstrated in constraint (3.103). Constraints (3.104) make sure that the maximum number of times that a nurse will be assigned to perform on different roles during a surgery duration is at most one.

Soft Constraints can be violated to some extent. Each deviation in a soft constraint is defined as a decision variable. Surgery demand for each case at each time interval should be satisfied. Therefore, if the case is in progress during time interval h, the required number of nurses for each role should be assigned to the case unless we do not have enough nurses to satisfy all demand at the time. To handle this shortage, we define two integer deviation variables called de_{ckh} and DEM, which are the missing number of nurses that should have been assigned to the surgery case if there were enough nurses available for case c to do role k at time interval h and maximum demand shortages for each case c, respectively. By minimizing DEM, we ensure that surgery demand for each case will be satisfied to the greatest extent. The constraints related to the de_{ckh} and DEM deviations are shown in Eqs. 3.107 and 3.108.

It is preferred to assign nurses to work continuously during their shift hours and perform on the same role for the whole surgery duration rather than moving around between different cases to do different jobs. To minimize these movements, we introduce a binary deviation variable d^7_{ih} and an integer deviation variable DMs in constraints (3.112) and (3.113). By minimizing DMs, we ensure that the maximum number of times that nurses will work non-consecutively will be reduced and nurses will work sequentially as much as possible without too many idle assignments until nurse shift working hours are finished.

Constraints (3.109) and (3.110) demonstrate the preference for assigning nurses to work continuously on one operating room for their working day rather than moving around between different rooms. To minimize these movements, we introduce two binary deviation variables X_{ij} and XX. By minimizing XX, we ensure that the maximum number of ORs that a nurse will be assigned to work on is reduced as much as possible.

We prefer to not have schedules with nurses who are assigned to overtime hours. To minimize these assignments, we define a binary deviation variable called d_{ih}^4 and an integer deviation variable called DMf. The d_{ih}^4 will obtain value 1 if a nurse is assigned to overtime hours. Constraints (3.111) show the overtime deviations. By minimizing DMf shown in constraint (3.114), we ensure that the maximum number of times that a nurse is assigned to overtime hours is reduced and the nurses will not be assigned to overtime hours unless it is a necessity.

Constraints (3.115), (3.116), (3.117), and (3.118), with deviations nc_{ic}, cd_{ic}, *nct*, and *cdt*, make sure that if a nurse is assigned to a surgery case, she will stay for the whole surgery duration, unless there is need for that nurse due to nurse shortages. Also, by minimizing the max number of cases that a nurse can work on, we will make sure that nurses will not move between different cases continuously.

Objective Function

Considering all the deviations explained previously, a multi-objective function is developed for NAM to minimize these deviations.

$$\text{Min DEM},\ \text{Min DMf},\ \text{Min DMs},\ \text{Min XX},\ \text{Min nct},\ \text{Min cdt} \tag{3.119}$$

This objective function ensures that the maximum deviations for each goal (worst case results) will be minimized for all nurses and all surgery cases

Solution Method

Since the Nurse Assignment Model introduced in this paper has multiple objectives, a Solution Pool Method (SPM) is presented. This solution method utilizes the idea of solution pools to generate alternate feasible solutions for each deviation in the objective function (3.119). Obtaining information about alternate good feasible solutions can be a useful tool in cases where a mixed integer multiobjective problem is developed. Although it may be computationally complicated to solve a multi-objective model considering all deviations simultaneously, it may be easier to use the solution pool feature in order to find alternate good feasible solutions for each deviation. The solution pool feature generates and stores multiple solutions to the mixed integer programming (MIP) model for each deviation and then chooses the solution among these optimal solutions that have the smallest deviations. The solution pool-based method has three steps. In the first step, a single objective optimization model is developed for each deviation containing all hard constraints and soft constraints related to the current deviation. In the second step, the solution pool approach is applied to generate alternate good feasible solutions (with the absolute gap of less than 0.01) for each single objective model developed in Step 1. For each generated solution, a cumulative weighted index is obtained. It is assumed that a predetermined importance weight for each deviation was in hand. The decision maker can provide the appropriate weights associated with each goal based on operating suite regulations and policies. Finally, in Step 3, the comparison indexes can be compared and the best solution introduced for NAM. Numerical results indicated that this model can provide more efficient and reliable nurse schedules for operating suites.

3.4 Summary

The growing shortage of nurses continues to hamper the effective delivery of health care. Not having enough skilled nurses in clinical settings can cause a significant negative impact on nurse retention rates, patient safety, and healthcare quality. Due to the nurse shortages, hospital managers are in dire need to optimally utilize and retain current available nurses without jeopardizing their job satisfaction.

Assigning each available nurse to the right place at the right time to do the right job is a major concern for healthcare organizations. As the types of services and treatments offered by such organizations increase so do the skill requirements of their staff. In this chapter different nurse scheduling problems were introduced and optimization models and solution approaches that have been introduced in the literature have been demonstrated. These models and solution methods further assuage our ability to generate efficient daily schedules, the main objective of this chapter.

3.5 Future Directions

Although there is a vast amount of literature in NSP, not many of the optimization models have addressed the impact of patient workload in nurse scheduling problems.

Healthcare organizations nowadays are dealing with many uncertainties such as nurse shortages, call-ins, cancellations, and workload uncertainty. Therefore, it is essential for researchers to consider these uncertainties in their models and develop more simple, easy to understand solution methods that can tackle variabilities with more time efficient approaches.

References

Aickelin U, Dowsland K (2004) An indirect genetic algorithm for a nurse scheduling problem. Comput Oper Res 31(5):761–778

Aickelin U, Li J (2007) An estimation of distribution algorithm for nurse scheduling. Ann Oper Res 155:289–309

Aickelin U, White P (2004) Building better nurse scheduling algorithms. Ann Oper Res 128:159–177

Aickelin U, Burke E, Li J (2007) An estimation of distribution algorithm with intelligent local search for rule-based nurse rostering. J Oper Res Soc 58(12):1574–1585

Aiken L, Clarke S, Sloane D, Sochalski J, Silber J (2002) Hospital nurse staffing and patient mortality, nurse burnout, and job dissatisfaction. J Am Med Assoc 288(16):1987–1993

Azaiez M, Al Sharif S (2005) A 0-1 goal programming model for nurse scheduling. Comput Oper Res 32:491–507

Bai R, Burke E, Kendall G, Li J, McCollum G (2010) A hybrid evolutionary approach to the nurse rostering problem. IEEE Trans Evol Comput 14(4):580–590, ISSN 1089-778X

Bard J, Purnomo H (2005) Preference scheduling for nurses using column generation. Eur J Oper Res 164:510–534

Bard J, Purnomo H (2007) Cyclic preference scheduling of nurses using a Lagrangian-based heuristic. J Sched 10:5–23

Belien J, Demeulemeester E (2008) A branch-and-price approach for integrating nurse and surgery scheduling. Eur J Oper Res 189:652–668

Berrada I, Ferland J, Michelon P (1996) A multi-objective approach to nurse scheduling with both hard and soft constraints. Socio Econ Plan Sci 30(3):183–193

Bester M, Nieuwoudt I, Van Vuuren J (2007) Finding good nurse duty schedules: a case study. J Sched 10(6):387–405

Blythe J, Baumann A, Zeytinoglu I, Denton M, Higgins A (2005) Full-time or part-time work in nursing: preferences, tradeoffs and choices. Healthc Q 8(3):69–77

Burke E, De Causmaecker P, Van Landeghem H (2004) The state of the art of nurse rostering. J Sched 7(6):441–499

Burke E, Li J, Qu R (2010) A hybrid model of integer programming and variable neighborhood search for highly-constrained nurse rostering problems. Eur J Oper Res 203(2):484–493 ISSN 0377-2217

Cardoen B (2010) Operating room planning and scheduling: solving a surgical case sequencing problem. Q J Oper Res 8(1):101–104

Cardoen B, Demeulemeester E, Belien J (2010) Operating room planning and scheduling: a literature review. Eur J Oper Res 201(3):921–932

Cheang B, Li H, Lim A, Rodrigues B (2003) Nurse rostering problems-A bibliographic survey. Eur J Oper Res 151(3):447–460 ISSN 03772217

Cheng B, Lee J, Wu J (1997) A constraint-based nurse rostering system using a redundant modeling approach. Inf Technol Biomed 1(1):44–54

Chiaramonte M, Chiaramonte L (2008) An agent-based nurse rostering system under minimal staffing conditions. Int J Prod Econ 114(2):697–713

Dexter F, Macario A, Traub R, Hopwood M, Lubarsky D (1999) An operating room scheduling strategy to maximize the use of operating room block time: computer simulation of patient scheduling and survey of patients preferences for surgical waiting time. Econ Health Syst Res 89(1):7

Dexter F, Dexter E, Ledolter J (2010a) Influence of procedure classification on process variability and parameter uncertainty of surgical case durations. Anesth Analg 110(4):1155

Dexter F, Wachtel R, Epstein R, Ledolter J, Todd M (2010b) Analysis of operating room allocations to optimize scheduling of specialty rotations for anesthesia trainees. Anesth Analg 111(2):520

Dowsland K (1998) Nurse scheduling with tabu search and strategic oscillation. Eur J Oper Res 106(2-3):393–407

Fei H, Chu C, Meskens N (2009) Solving a tactical operating room planning problem by a column-generation-based heuristic procedure with four criteria. Ann Oper Res 166(1):91–108

Feia H, Chub C, Meskensa N, Artiba A (2008) Solving surgical cases assignment problem by a branch-and-price approach. J Prod Econ 112(1):96–108

Foundation KF (2009) Trends in health care costs and spending. Health Aff 22(1):154

Fries B (1976) Bibliography of operations research in health-care systems. Oper Res 24(5):801–14

Hadwan M, Ayob M (2010) A constructive shift patterns approach with simulated annealing for nurse rostering problem. Information Technology (ITSim), 2010 International Symposium 1:1–6

He F, Qu R (2009) A constraint-directed local search approach to nurse rostering problems. In: Sixth international workshop on local search techniques in constraint satisfaction

Jaumard B, Semet F, Vovor T (1998) A generalized linear programming model for nurse scheduling. Eur J Oper Res 107:1–18

Koeppel D (2004) Nurses bid with their pay in auctions for extra work. The New York Times

Lamiri M, Xie X, Dolgui A, Grimaud F (2008) A stochastic model for operating room planning with elective and emergency demand for surgery. Eur J Oper Res 185(3):1026–1037

Li J, Aickelin U (2003) A bayesian optimization algorithm for the nurse scheduling problem. In: Evolutionary computation, 2003. CEC '03. The 2003 congress on 3:2149–2156, Dec 2003

Maenhout B, Vanhoucke M (2010) Branching strategies in a branch-and-price approach for a multiple objective nurse scheduling problem. J Sched 13(1):77–93 ISSN 10946136

Miller H, Pierskalla W, Rath G (1976) Nurse scheduling using mathematical programming. Oper Res 24(5):857–870

Mobasher A, Lim G (2011) Nurse scheduling problem in an operating suite. In: IERC 2011 Proceedings

Ogulata S, Koyuncu M, Karakas E (2008) Personnel and patient scheduling in the high demanded hospital services. J Med Syst 32(3):221–228

Ozkarahan I (2000) Allocation of surgeries to operating rooms by goal programing. J Med Syst 24(6):339–378

Parr D, Thompson JM (2007) Solving the multi-objective nurse scheduling problem with a weighted cost function. Ann Oper Res 155(1):279–288

Perrin T (2008) 2008 Health Care Cost Survey. Towers Perrin, New York, pp 28

Purnomo H, Bard J (2006) Cyclic preference scheduling for nurses using branch and price. Nav Res Logist 54:200–220

Sundaramoorthi D, Chen V, Rosenberger J, Kim S, Buckley-Behan D (2009) A data-integrated simulation model to evaluate nurse-patient assignments. Health Care Manag Sci 12(3):252–268

Ulrich C, Wallen G, Grady C, Foley M, Rosenstein A, Rabetoy C, Miller B (2002) The nursing shortage and the quality of care. New Engl J Med 347(14):1118–1119

Warner D, Prawda J (1972) A mathematical programming model for scheduling nursing personnel in a hospital. Manag Sci 19(4):411–422

Chapter 4
Patient Appointments in Ambulatory Care

Diwakar Gupta and Wen-Ya Wang

Abstract Outpatient appointment system design is a complex problem because it involves multiple stakeholders, sequential booking process, random arrivals, no-shows, varying degrees of urgency of different patients' needs, service time variability, and patient and provider preferences. Clinics use a two-step process to manage appointments. In the first step, which we refer to as the *clinic profile setup problem*, service providers' daily clinic time is divided into appointment slots. In the second step, which we refer to as the *appointment booking problem*, physicians' offices decide which available slots to book for each incoming request for an appointment. In this chapter, we present formulations of mathematical models of key problems in the area of appointment system design. We also discuss the challenges and complexities of solving such problems. In addition, summaries of prior research, particularly advanced models related to the examples shown in this chapter are also presented.

4.1 Introduction

According to a national survey, there were an estimated 994.3 million ambulatory patient visits to office-based non-federally employed physicians in the US in 2007 (Hsiao et al. 2010). This is equivalent to an average of about 3.36 visits per person per year (Hsiao et al. 2010). Office visits can be further divided into three main

D. Gupta (✉) · W.-Y. Wang
University of Minnesota, 111 Church Street S. E., Minneapolis, MN 55455, USA
e-mail: guptad@me.umn.edu

W.-Y. Wang
e-mail: wenya@ie.umn.edu

R. Hall (ed.), *Handbook of Healthcare System Scheduling*,
International Series in Operations Research & Management Science 168,
DOI: 10.1007/978-1-4614-1734-7_4,

categories: primary-care including physicians specializing in internal medicine, pediatrics, obstetrics and gynecology (58 percent), other medical specialists[1] (22.2%) and surgical specialists (19.2%). The vast majority of office visits are planned, i.e. patients contact the physicians' offices in advance to book an appointment. Increasingly, appointments are managed via a computerized appointment scheduling (AS) system. Many electronic medical record (EMR) systems include AS modules.

Office-based medical services are a significant part of the overall delivery of health care and the utilization of such services is increasing, which is in part because of the aging of the US population (Hsiao et al. 2010). For these reasons, the problem of designing appointment systems has attracted significant attention in the Operations research (OR) literature. Recent surveys of relevant OR literature can be found in Cayirli et al. (2003) and Gupta et al. (2008).

Appointments are normally booked one at a time. At the time of booking appointments, physicians' offices do not have complete information about the number, sequence, urgency, and service requirements of future appointment requests. Therefore, clinics use a two-step process to manage appointments. In the first step, which we refer to as the *clinic profile setup problem*, service providers' daily clinic time is divided into appointment slots. In the second step, which we refer to as the *appointment booking problem*, physicians' offices decide which available slots to book for each incoming request for an appointment. AS design issues relating to both these steps are discussed in this chapter.

Ambulatory care appointment slots are typically of equal length. However, different appointments may be assigned a different number of discrete slots, depending on the service time requirements of the patient. For example, in the primary-care setting, a standard slot is appropriate for the vast majority of routine appointments, but physical exams and in-office procedures may require multiple slots (or an appointment slot with a different length). Similarly, many physicians require that appointment systems book more than one appointment slot for new-patient appointments. There are a whole host of other factors that affect both the clinic profile setup and the appointment booking decisions. Examples of factors that have been studied in the literature include demand for physicians' slots, physicians' willingness to work overtime, no-show rates, service time variability, and patients' preferences (see for example Denton and Gupta 2003; Gupta and Wang 2008; Ho and Lau 1992; LaGanga and Lawrence 2007; Robinson and Chen 2003; Weiss 1990). This chapter investigates how mathematical models could help improve AS design in the presence of such factors.

Appointment systems for office visits allow multiple types of appointments. In fact, there are multiple appointment classification schemes. We list commonly encountered examples of appointment categories below.

---

[1] Patients seeking the services of these and surgical specialists usually need a referral for their first appointment. In contrast, patients may book appointments with physicians belonging to the primary-care category without a referral.

1. New versus established patient appointments.
2. Diagnosis-specific versus non-specific (called office visit) appointments.
3. Acute versus follow-up appointments.
4. Urgent (also called same-day) versus advance-book appointments.
5. Provider specific versus non-specific appointments.
6. One-to-one versus one-to-many or many-to-one (group) appointments.

The above-mentioned typology has arisen because dividing appointments into categories helps clinics and physicians better manage their capacity. For example, many physicians prefer to book multiple slots for new patients (because a new-patient chart needs to be created) and for certain diagnosis-specific appointments (e.g. physical exams and in-office procedures).

Providers' (i.e. physicians, physician's assistants and nurse practitioners) workloads in the primary-care setting are often described in terms of their panel sizes. A panel is a group of patients for whom the same provider is the preferred service provider. The panel provider is also called the preferred care provider (PCP). A subset of new patients who have an office visit with a provider may choose that provider as their PCP, which increases the provider's panel and workload. For this reason, providers place caps on both the total panel size and the number of new-patient appointments available to manage their workloads. Panel sizes are less meaningful in a specialty care setting as a measure of workload. It is common in such settings to use the ratio of established to new patients that the practice serves to compare workloads.

The distinction between acute and follow-up appointments is important because acute requests arrive at random (e.g. as a result of a flare-up of a chronic condition) whereas providers determine follow-up visit frequency based on medical guidelines, personal preferences, and appointment backlogs in their practices. Because urgent or same-day appointment requests arise from patients who perceive their medical needs to be urgent, providers need to make sure that sufficient number of appointment slots are available to meet the demand for such appointments.

Office-based appointments with doctors, nurse practitioners, and physician's assistants are typically provider specific. Provider non-specific appointments tend to be appointments with laboratory technicians in which patients supply medical specimens (e.g. blood draws), or appointments for diagnostic imaging (e.g. X-ray, MRI, and CT Scan) and radiation therapy. In such cases, the patient can be served by any one of a group of qualified service providers.

The last remaining classification scheme described above is based on how many providers or patients are simultaneously needed or served in each appointment. Most office-visit appointments are one-to-one appointments between a patient and a specific service provider. However, some appointments involve multiple providers. Examples include appointments requiring an interpreter, nurse or physician assistant, or appointments with a team of consultants for complicated diagnoses. Multiple providers may be present (though not medically necessary) in certain situations, e.g. when residents assist experienced physicians during the course of their training. Appointments with multiple providers usually take longer and physicians' offices or clinics may use multiple slots to book such appointments. Many-to-one (group) appointments are usually appointments with therapists and nutrition and wellness coaches. Group appointments are not to be confused with the practice of block booking in which several patients are given the same appointment time. In a block booking setting, several patients arrive at the same time but they are served sequentially and individually.

The survey in Hsiao et al. (2010) also reports that 83% of visits were to practices that were either owned by a physician or a group of physicians and that the percentage of physicians who practiced in independent, solo, or small-group practices has declined in recent years.[2] In contrast, the percentage practicing in large practices has increased. These trends suggest that models addressing issues of AS design must be scalable to include multiple physician practices. Larger practices often include a variety of diagnostic and laboratory services. This introduces further complexity in AS design. Furthermore, in such settings primary-care providers order more labs/imaging in addition to tests that the patients' specialists order, which can lead to more waste and inconvenience to patients (e.g. unnecessary blood draws and extra travel time).

Next, we list typical problems arising in each step of the AS design. The purpose of this chapter is to present formulations of mathematical models and insights from the use of these models pertaining to a subset of the problems described below.

4.1.1 The Clinic Profile Setup Problem

1. How much capacity should a clinic have? When should it add capacity? Capacity can be increased either by asking some part-time providers to increase their working hours, or by hiring more providers.
2. What is the optimal panel size for each physician?
3. What is the optimal unit appointment length? How many appointment slots should be assigned to each new patient or diagnosis-specific appointment?
4. How many appointments should a clinic overbook for each service provider? Which strategy should a clinic use to accommodate excess demand—e.g. double or triple book versus uniformly shorter appointment slots?
5. How much capacity should the clinic target to have open at the start of each day to serve urgent (or same-day) demand?

The difference between the two overbooking strategies mentioned above can be explained as follows. In the former strategy of multiple bookings, if all appointments take a fixed amount of time equal to the appointment length and patients either arrive on time or no-show, then only the overbooked patients experience in-office waiting. That is, the first patient booked into each slot who shows up is

[2] Percent of visits to solo practices declined from about 39% in 1997 to about 31% in 2007.

served at the designated appointment time. In contrast, in the latter strategy, under the same circumstances described above, every patient except the first patient of the day may experience some waiting because the service provider is allotted less time than needed for each service.

4.1.2 The Appointment Booking Problem

1. Given a clinic profile, which appointment slot among the acceptable set of appointment slots revealed by the patients should a clinic book? The set of acceptable appointment slots is specified by a desired date for the appointment, time blocks when the patient can visit the clinic, and service providers that are acceptable to the patient at the indicated times.
2. How should a clinic manage follow-up appointments? This includes determining answers to a variety of questions. For example, what should be the inter-visit times for follow-up appointments? Which appointments should require an in-person contact with the service provider and which appointments should be e-visits? An e-visit is an appointment in which the patient measures and reports certain types of data (e.g. vital statistics) and communication with the provider occurs via telephone, Internet, or some other remote communication device.
3. When should the clinic book a follow-up appointment? Choices include booking the follow-up visit at the time when the patient completes an earlier visit, or notifying the patient at a later date to contact the clinic to book a follow-up appointment.

A model of the appointment booking process must accommodate different booking preferences of different patients. These preferences are not static and typically change over time. For example, some patients may be willing to see any available doctor to minimize their wait for an appointment, whereas some other patients may prefer to wait until a slot becomes available with their PCPs (thereby preserving continuity). Some patients are able to visit the clinic only within a short time window because of job-related constraints or personal schedules, whereas others can be quite flexible (Jennings et al. 2005; Olowokure et al. 2006). Time and physician preferences may change over time because of changes in work schedule, marital status, and family size. Appointment booking procedures must strive to match patients with their PCPs. This ensures continuity of care (Doescher et al. 2004), and allows physicians to provide more value-added services to their patients (O'Hare et al. 2004). Matching patients with their PCPs and offering them a convenient appointment time can also decrease the number of no-shows (Barron 1980; Carlson 2002; Simth and Yawn 1994).

AS design is a complex problem because it involves multiple stakeholders, sequential booking process, random arrivals, no-shows, varying degrees of urgency of different patients' needs, service time variability, and patient and provider preferences. The presence of multiple stakeholders leads to multiple criteria optimization problems. For example, clinic managers care about revenue, and patient and staff satisfaction. They worry about their clinic's scores on patient satisfaction surveys because high scores help them attract new patients and insurers (i.e. to achieve the preferred-provider-organization status with more insurance providers). Service providers care about remuneration, work schedules, overtime, and patient matching and satisfaction. By patient matching, we mean service providers' ability to see patients in their own panel. Providers' remuneration schemes vary across clinics. Three types of schemes are commonly found: salary basis, productivity basis, and guaranteed minimum payments with productivity based incentives. Provider productivity is commonly measured in terms of relative value units of the work they perform in each patient encounter (see Johnson and Newton 2002 for details). Remuneration schemes affect providers' willingness to work overtime and support overbooking. The latter approach is often used to counter the effect of missed opportunities on account of patient no-shows and cancelations.

As stated before, the purpose of this chapter is to present formulations of mathematical models of several key problems in the area of AS design. The chapter also discusses methods for solving selected models to shine light on the challenges and underlying complexities of the problems. In addition, summaries of prior research, particularly advanced models related to the examples shown in this chapter are also presented. We conclude the chapter with comments on future directions and implications for practitioners.

4.2 Data

As mentioned in the Introduction section, clinics increasingly rely on computerized appointment scheduling systems to monitor and improve utilization of their service providers' capacity. The existence of electronic appointment records makes it possible for researchers to obtain de-identified data and analyze it to learn how to improve AS design in the future. In this section, we present results of basic analysis of these type of data, which we obtained from three health systems.

The three health systems represent a diverse set of health care organizations. Our first data set, which we refer to as data set A, comes from a federally qualified health care facility with three departments—medical, dental, and mental health. Many patients seen in this facility do not have insurance. The second data set, which we call data set B, comes from a large health system with many primary-care and specialty clinics as well as multiple hospitals. This health system caters primarily to insured population. The third data set, which we call data set C, comes from a full-service network of systems. This network provides complete range of health services to all eligible patients. From a systems perspective, A is an open system, B is semi closed, and C is more or less a completely closed system. This means that patients who visit system A often visit other health care facilities and do not receive all of their health care services from that system. System B is able to offer more comprehensive services, but needs to refer its patients to specialists who are not a part of the system for certain types of services. System C is able to provide a full range of services and patients go outside the system for medical services only at times when the system becomes overly congested.

Data from system A is further divided into two parts: A1 refers to data prior to the implementation of an EMR system and A2 to similar data after such implementation. The reason for keeping this data into two separate pieces is that the names of the departments changed during the EMR implementation. There were 14,465 appointment records in A1, 18,480 in A2, 2,005,333 in B, and 312,764 in C. The key pieces of data we obtained were time stamps of the date/time when patients contacted the health system for an appointment and date/time stamp of the appointment. We also had information on whether the appointment was successful, canceled or no-show. Finally, we had de-identified information on the primary encounter providers, clinic types, and each patient's PCP. Note that our data did not have actual service times. Archival databases sometimes have information on the amount of service providers' time allotted for each appointment, but we have not encountered a system that has information on actual service times.

From the data we calculated appointment lead times—the differences between the date/time of the appointment and the date/time when each patient contacted the clinic to book that appointment. Appointment lead times should not be negative. We removed appointments that had negative lead times because we could not be sure of their accuracy. We also dropped records with other types of errors, such as missing data fields. In one data set, we also had a record of desired date—the date when a patient desired to be seen by a service provider. From desired dates, we were able to calculate patient wait times—the differences between actual appointment dates and the corresponding desired dates. Note that patient wait times can be negative. This happens when upon revealing a preference for a particular date, a patient thereafter takes an earlier appointment based on availability. A summary of basic performance metrics of interest to AS design is presented in Table 4.1. In this table, all summary statistics pertain only to valid appointment records i.e. records that remained after dropping those with errors and/or missing values, and N/A indicates situations in which data were not available to calculate certain performance metrics.

We also analyzed no-shows in detail in an effort to identify factors that are correlated with no-shows. Such factors can be used to predict no-show rates and might be useful in mitigating the negative effects of no-shows. Specifically, we examined factors that can be classified as either group characteristics, individual characteristics, or appointment characteristics. Among group characteristics, we analyzed

1. PCP ID,
2. age category,
3. insurance category, and
4. clinic type.

Table 4.1 Summary of performance metrics

	A1	A2	B	C
Time span	6 months	4 months	12 months	1 month
Valid appointments	11,541	17,647	1,601,080	82,547
Patients	4,366	5,626	457,187	39,884
Clinics	7	3	70	1,833
Providers	53	90	1,350	1,713
Average lead time[a]	19.20	23.90	13.20	39.06
95% CI[b] Avg lead time	[18.79, 19.61]	[23.50, 24.30]	[13.17, 13.23]	[38.70, 39.42]
Average wait time[c]	N/A	N/A	N/A	2.28
Same day appointments	3,635 (25.13%)	3,341 (18.93%)	738,840 (36.93%)	11,652 (11.71%)
PCP match rate	N/A	N/A	47.06%	49.92%
No-shows	2,535 (17.64%)	3,925 (22.24%)	79,137 (3.96%)	5,916 (5.94%)
Cancellations	2,827 (19.68%)	N/A	399,710 (20%)	27,960 (28.10%)
Late cancellations[d]	N/A	N/A	N/A	11,011 (11.07%)
Cancellations rebooked	95 (0.66%)	N/A	199,439 (10%)	N/A

[a] Appointment lead time is the difference in days between the date/time of the appointment and the date/time when the patient called to book

[b] CI is short for confidence interval

[c] Each patient's waiting time is the difference in days between the actual date of appointment and the desired date. Wait times can be negative when patients book appointments before their desired dates

[d] Late cancellations are those appointments that were cancelled within 24 h of the appointment date/time. Such appointments are treated as no-shows in statistical analyses

Among individual characteristics, we analyzed

1. distance from clinic, and
2. history of no-shows.

Finally, among appointment characteristics, we analyzed

1. urgency—same-day vs. advance book,
2. continuity—PCP matched vs. mismatched, and
3. appointment lead time.

We report statistically significant findings of correlation between no-shows and the factors mentioned above. In the interest of brevity, p-values are often omitted. However, when in this section we report statistically significant correlation and do not mention p-values, the corresponding p-values were less than or equal to 0.0001 in all cases. Note that significant correlation does not imply causation. However, a finding of significant correlation helps to identify those factors that may be used as predictors of appointment-keeping behavior.

All four group characteristics were correlated with no-show rates. In particular, no-show rates were significantly different for different PCP IDs. Age category information, defined in 5-year increments, was available only for data set B. In that case, we found that patients in age categories 20–24 and 25–29 were more likely to be no-shows than other age categories. Insurance information was available only

Table 4.2 No-shows and insurance status

	Commercial	Government	Self-pay
No-show rate (%)	4.34	6.37	7.5
Appointment records	1,130,876	462,447	7,757

Table 4.3 No-shows and the history of no-shows

	Without no-show history (% no-shows, n[a])	With no-show history (% no-shows, n)
A1	17.50%, 2,805	27.73%, 1,107
A2	15.90%, 3,585	27.17%, 2,142
B	4.12%, 470,569	11.62%, 67,201
C[b]	16.91%, 20,527	30.87%, 7,468

[a] n = Number of appointment records
[b] In this case, the percentages are the sum of no-shows and late cancellations

in data set B. We categorized patients into three types based on insurance status: government sponsored insurance, commercial insurance, and self-pay. We found that patients covered by commercial insurance plans had the smallest no-show rates, followed by government sponsored plans, and then self-pay patients. A summary of these results is shown in Table 4.2. No-show rates also differed significantly by clinic, but we did not find a pattern. Therefore, those results are not reported here.

Among individual characteristics information about distance from clinic was available only in data set B. Distance from clinic and no-show rates were not correlated in a statistically significant manner. We also found that history of no-shows was an important predictor of no-show behavior at the individual level for all three health systems. In order to test the correlation between history of no-shows and future no-shows, we divided the four data sets into two parts. The first part contained about 2/3 of all encounters and the second part contained about 1/3. We then identified patients whose records included no-shows in the first part. This allowed us to compare patient records in the second 1/3 of the data sets by history of no-shows. The results are summarized in Table 4.3 below.

Among appointment characteristics, we found that the urgency of the visit and PCP match were correlated with lower no-show rates in a statistically significant manner. However, after same-day appointments were excluded, higher appointment lead times were not correlated with higher no-show rates. For urgency of visits and PCP match, we present our results in Tables 4.4 and 4.5 below.

To investigate the relationship between no-shows and appointment lead times, we constructed a logistic regression model with $\log\left(\frac{\alpha}{1-\alpha}\right) = \beta_0 + \beta_1 L$, where α is the show rate and L is the lead time. Only appointments that had appointment lead time of 2 days or more were considered in this logistic regression. Results are shown in Table 4.6. Observe that the estimated value of β_1 for data sets A1, A2, and B is slightly negative, suggesting that higher lead times are associated with higher show rates. The value of β_1 is slightly positive for data set C, which may be because in this case no-show rate includes late cancelations as well.

Table 4.4 No-shows and the urgency of appointments

	Urgent (same day) (% no shows, n^a)	Non-urgent (% no shows, n)
A1	9.75%, 3,240	26.73%, 8,301
A2	9.79%, 3,341	25.15%, 14,306
B	2.29%, 663,976	6.82%, 937,104
C[b]	13.74%, 11,652	21.62%, 70,895

[a] n = Number of appointment records
[b] In this case, the percentages are the sum of no-shows and late cancellations

Table 4.5 No-shows and the PCP match

	Matched (%, n^a)	Mismatched (%, n)
A1	N/A	N/A
A2	N/A	N/A
B	3.61%, 550,974	6.34%, 619,687
C[b]	14.29%, 10,906	21.74%, 10,937

a n = Number of appointment records
[b] In this case, the percentages are the sum of no-shows and late cancellations

Table 4.6 No-shows and the appointment lead times

	n^a	β_1	p-value
A1	8,301	−0.00288	0.0034
A2	14,306	−0.00679	<0.0001
B	937,104	−0.00271	<0.0001
C[b]	70,895	0.00108	<0.0001

[a] n = Number of appointment records
[b] In this case, the sum of no-shows and late cancellations is treated as no-show rate

4.3 Key Problems, Formulations and Prior Research

In this section, we present model formulations for several key problems encountered in AS design. For each problem, we also describe how previous studies have contributed to developing solutions.

4.3.1 Clinic Capacity

From time to time, a clinic manager needs to ascertain if the clinic capacity is a good match with the demand. Inadequate capacity can increase patient wait times, and cause patients to seek services at other clinics in the health system or even outside the health system. In this section, we explore two models that can be used to guide clinic capacity decisions. Capacity decisions are important because it can take several weeks and sometimes months to attract a new provider.

Models needed to calculate requisite capacity can quickly become complicated because there are time of day, day of week, and time of year seasonal patterns of demand. Seasonal effects may cause the clinic to be fully booked on some weekdays, but relatively lightly booked on other days. Similarly, load imbalances are common, which means that some providers in a clinic may have large backlogs whereas others may have plenty of open slots. The first-pass models presented in this chapter do not consider seasonality and provider workload imbalances. More complex models that do consider such factors are discussed later in this chapter.

The first model assumes that patients wait in a virtual queue until it is their turn to be seen by a physician. This model ignores patients' preferences for a particular physician and a particular date/time of appointment. It is suitable only as a rough-cut capacity planning tool. Let λ be the average arrival rate, μ the average service rate, and C_a^2 and C_s^2 denote, respectively, the squared coefficients of variation of inter-arrival and service times. We will comment on how clinic managers may estimate these parameters from data shortly after presenting the model. Let $\rho = \lambda/\mu$ denote the capacity utilization. Then, a commonly used approximation for the mean waiting is (Buzacott et al. 1993)

$$E[W] = \left(\frac{\rho^2(1+C_s^2)}{1+\rho^2 C_s^2}\right)\left(\frac{C_a^2+\rho^2 C_s^2}{2\lambda(1-\rho)}\right).$$

This approximation works well so long as C_a^2 is not too large (less than 2). When *E[W]* approaches or exceeds a competitive threshold (e.g. 5 days for primary-care clinics), clinic managers may consider adding more capacity.

Mean and variance of inter-arrival times can be estimated by examining the time between appointment requests. For this purpose, clinics should ignore time elapsed when the clinic and call center operations are shut down. The term C_a^2 is the ratio of the variance and the square of the mean inter-arrival times. Service time related parameters can be calculated as follows. Suppose a fraction f_i of all appointments have scheduled appointment length of s_i and suppose there are m different scheduled appointment lengths, then $E[S] = (1/\mu) = \sum_{i=1}^m f_i s_i$, $\mathrm{Var}(S) = \sum_{i=1}^m f_i (E[S] - s_i)^2$, and $C_s^2 = \mathrm{Var}(S)/E[S]^2$.

The next model accounts for the fact that each patient requests a particular date for his or her appointment when he or she calls for an appointment. It is assumed that if the desired date is not available, a patient will book the next available appointment date after the desired date. The model is a discrete time model, where a unit of time is a day. We are interested in ascertaining the required clinic capacity per unit time, denoted by κ. Assignment of appointment to requests that arise occur at the start of each time period in the order of desired date, i.e. patients who request an earlier desired date are given appointments earlier. These requests,

D_1, D_2, …, D_n, are, respectively, for the current period,[3] two periods ahead, and so on, up to n periods ahead, where n is the booking horizon. Let $q = (q_1, q_2, \ldots, q_n)$ denote the state of the clinic's bookings at the start of an arbitrary period, and let π_t denote the cost of making a patient wait t days after the desired date. We assume that if the total demand exceeds the available capacity in the remainder of the booking horizon, then this demand is lost, incurring a cost π_L.

In order to calculate the patient waiting cost, we need to determine $x_{i,j}$ the number of patients who request a desired date i, but are booked on date $j > i$. This can be found by using the following recursive relationships.

$$x_{1,1} = \min[\kappa - q_1, d_1]$$

$$x_{1,j} = \min\left[\kappa - q_j), \left(d_1 - \sum_{\ell=1}^{j-1} x_{1,\ell}\right)^+\right], \quad j = 2, \ldots, n$$

$$x_{1,n+1} = d_1 - \sum_{j=1}^{n} x_{1,j}.$$

For $i \geq 2$, we have

$$x_{i,i} = \min\left[\left(\kappa - q_i - \sum_{\ell=1}^{i-1} x_{\ell,i}\right)^+, d_i\right]$$

$$x_{i,j} = \min\left[\left(\kappa - q_j - \sum_{\ell=1}^{i-1} x_{\ell,j}\right)^+, \left(d_i - \sum_{\ell=i}^{j-1} x_{i,\ell}\right)^+\right], \quad j = 2, \ldots, n$$

$$x_{i,n+1} = d_i - \sum_{j=i}^{n} x_{i,j}.$$

The waiting cost incurred by the clinic when booking state is q and realized demand is d can be calculated as follows:

$$w(q, d) = \sum_{i=1}^{n} \sum_{t=1}^{n-i} \pi_t x_{i,i+t} + \pi_L \sum_{i=1}^{n} x_{i,n+1}.$$

The clinic's per period cost associated with a state q can be written as

$$c(q) = E[W(q, D)] + c\kappa,$$

where c is the unit cost of provider's capacity. Starting with an initial state $q^{(0)} = (0, \ldots, 0)$, the clinic's problem is to minimize its expected discounted cost over the infinite horizon. Let α^t denote the discount rate in period t. Then, the clinic's problem can be written as follows:

---

[3] Note that the current period is indexed 1.

$$\min_{\{\kappa \geq 0\}} \left(\sum_{t=0}^{\infty} \alpha^t \{ E[W(q^{(t)}, D^{(t)})] + c\kappa \} \right), \tag{4.1}$$

where $q_i^{(t+1)} = q_{i+1}^{(t)} + \sum_{\ell=1}^{i} x_{\ell,i+1}^{(t)}$, for $i = 1, \ldots, n-1$, and $q_n^{(t+1)} = 0$. A variety of methods for solving stochastic dynamic programs can be brought to bear on the problem of evaluating the above cost function (see, for example, Puterman 1994 for details) for each value of κ. In the OR literature, researchers typically focus on identifying structural properties of an optimal policy, which helps to either fully or partially characterize an optimal choice of κ. We believe such investigations and extensions of the model presented above can be beneficial for addressing clinic capacity optimization problems.

In the remainder of this section, we comment on the literature that pertains to the problem of clinic capacity determination. Upon using a systematic approach to identify relevant literature, we found only a handful of papers on this topic. Some studies, e.g. (Clague et al. 1997 and Elkhuizen et al. 2007), use simulation models to evaluate clinic capacity decisions based on certain performance metrics (e.g. patient backlog and waiting time). Some other papers do not present approaches to calculate required clinic capacity, but are relevant because they evaluate the impact of capacity on performance. For example, Foster et al. (2010) discuss the use of queueing models to evaluate the decision of adding inpatient beds to a service. The performance metrics are average wait for admission and probability of waiting. Kaplan and Johri (2000) model the patient flow in a system where the demand for drug abuse treatment greatly exceeds available supply. The model calculates the capacity needed to achieve "treatment on demand" and the amount of time required to eliminate treatment queues. Schoenmeyr et al. (2009) develop a queueing model to predict operational dynamics of operating and recovery rooms as functions of the number of recovery beds, surgery case volume, recovery time, and other parameters.

A few papers discuss the impact of clinic size, where size refers to the volume of demand rather than capacity, on patient outcomes. We consider these papers to be relevant as well because volume of demand and capacity are usually strongly correlated. We discuss two examples in this chapter that contain conflicting findings in terms of the effect of clinic size. Plantinga et al. (2009) evaluate the correlation between clinic size (number of peritoneal dialysis (PD) patients treated at a clinic) and patient outcomes. The study finds that PD patients treated at larger clinics have better outcomes in terms of technique failure and cardiovascular morbidity. Mandel et al. (2003) investigate the impact of clinic size (measured by number of monthly patient visits) on patient satisfaction. They find that clinic size is negatively correlated with patient satisfaction.

Gupta and Wang (2008) use their model, which considers same-day and advance-book demand, physician workload imbalances, and patient preferences, in simulation experiments to estimate clinic capacity requirements and conclude that because of patients' preferences certain appointment requests do not translate into actual appointments. Therefore, clinics do not need to add capacity until the appointment request rate exceeds capacity by 5–10%, depending on the cost of dealing with excess same-day demand and the extent to which patient preferences are strict.

4.3.2 Physician Panel Size

As mentioned earlier, health systems typically ask patients to designate one primary-care provider as their preferred provider, or PCP. A panel is a group of patients who choose the same provider as their PCP. Ensuring that patients have appointments with their PCPs can improve continuity of care and clinic revenues (O'Hare et al. 2004). We also observed in Sect. 4.2 that no-show rates were smaller among appointments in which patients were matched with their PCPs. In this section, we address the problem of determining panel sizes in the primary-care setting. Throughout this section, the providers are referred to as PCPs, which includes physicians and mid-level providers such as physician's assistants and nurse practitioners, all of whom serve as PCPs.

Panel sizes are often used to benchmark providers' workloads. This practice has some drawbacks because workload is affected not only by the size of a provider's panel, but also by its composition, i.e. age and gender distribution, and health status of patients in the panel. Notwithstanding the difficulties that may arise when heterogeneous panels are compared in terms of their size, panel sizes are a metric of significant interest to primary-care clinics. Many clinics use information on panel sizes to predict demand and adjust capacity. When panels become too large, patient wait times go up and PCP match suffers, not only for the provider who has a large panel but also for other providers who end up serving urgent and semi-urgent demand of the former provider. For all of the reasons mentioned above, it is important for providers to choose their panel sizes carefully.

In what follows, we begin by describing a fluid model. Then, we summarize recent papers that discuss the determination of PCP panel sizes with the help of quantitative models. Suppose a PCP needs help to decide how many patients she should have in her panel. We denote the desired number of patients by P. The PCP has a capacity of κ office visits per day. For example, if she works 8 hours every day and appointments are 20 min long, then $\kappa = 24$. At any moment in time, a subset P_A of patients are not under direct care and a subset $P_F = P - P_A$ are undergoing follow-up care. The subset P_F also includes patients with chronic conditions who need to be monitored at regular intervals. Each inactive patient in the subset P_A may become active at any time because of an acute episode. Let r_A be the average incidence rate of acute requests per day per patient. Also, let k_F denote the average number of times each follow-up patient requires office visit appointments before returning to the group P_A of inactive patients. Physicians can typically choose an inter-visit time for follow-up care, denoted by t_F, from an interval $[\underline{t}, \overline{t}]$, where $\underline{t}$ and $\overline{t}$ are the lower and upper bounds, respectively, on the

Table 4.7 Panel size and follow-up appointment visit frequency

P	1400	1450	1500	1550	1600	1650	1700	1750
t_F	15.0	19.7	24.3	29.0	33.7	38.4	43.1	47.8

medically acceptable range of follow-up times. This gives each PCP a certain amount of wiggle room to affect the demand for their appointment slots. We assume that follow-up patients do not have acute episodes. This is a modeling convenience. In reality, a fraction of patients in the follow-up group may develop acute symptoms. So long as the rate at which follow-up patients develop acute symptoms is not affected by the choice of revisit interval (within the acceptable range mentioned above), our approach can be generalized to consider the possibility that patients in group P_F may develop acute symptoms.

With the above notation in hand, it follows immediately that r_F, the rate at which patients in follow-up care become inactive, equals $1/(k_F t_F)$. In equilibrium, we must have $r_A P_A = r_F P_F$, which leads to the result that a fraction $r_F/(r_A + r_F)$ of panel patients are inactive and the remainder are in follow-up care. Given P_A and P_F, we can also calculate the average daily demand for appointments and the requisite follow-up interval length for which the average demand equals the average capacity κ. In particular, this leads to the following capacity balance equation

$$t_F = \frac{P(1 + k_F)}{\kappa k_F} - \frac{1}{r_A k_F}. \tag{4.2}$$

Next, we illustrate how our model may be used in practice with the help of an example. We assume that every acute care visit gives rise to two follow-up visits on average and the following input parameters: 3.356 office visits per patient per year, which includes acute and follow-up visits[4] (Hsaio et al. 2010), and 260 working days per year (52 weeks, five days per week). This allows us to calculate $r_A = 0.0043$. Next, we find follow-up visit intervals for different panel sizes in increments of 50 for a PCP who works eight hours per day with 30-min appointment slots, i.e. $\kappa = 16$. Results are shown in Table 4.7.

Suppose follow-up visit intervals between 25 and 45 days are deemed acceptable. Then, the PCP can serve a panel between 1,500 and just under 1,750, so long as she adjusts the follow-up intervals accordingly. In the capacity balance equation (4.2) derived above, different PCPs can use different incidence rates, depending on the composition of their panels. The above calculations did not adjust for vacations (usually between 2 and 4 weeks per year), sick leaves (approximately 1 week per year), and planned time off for educational purposes (usually 1 week as well). If there is no provision to cover this loss in service capacity, available capacity should be reduced by 4–6 weeks, which in the case of

[4] This is the national average visit rate.

a PCP with 16 slots per day would amount to having either 14 or 15 appointment slots per day. In that case, the panel size calculations can be redone with an appropriate daily capacity.

The above method is a rudimentary approach for rough-cut capacity calculations. Panel size calculations that capture all of the important factors—e.g. different appointment lengths, demand from patients belonging to other PCPs' panels, and spoilage of slots, can be significantly more complicated. Next, we present a review of models found in the literature that deal with the problem of determining PCP panel sizes.

Similar to the approach we use above, Murray et al. (2007) provide a capacity balance equation that matches average demand (panel size × visits per patient per year) and available capacity (available provider slots per day × provider days per year). The average number of visits per patient per year may differ by panel due to different likelihood of clinic visits for different patient populations. For example, panels with different demographic characteristics such as age and gender may have different frequency of appointments. Therefore, panel sizes that are appropriate for two PCPs with the same clinic capacity may be different as their patients' medical needs may be different. Our model can also accommodate different incidence rates for different panels and it also considers PCPs' choice of time between follow-up visits.

Green et al. (2007) focus on the impact of panel size on the level of overflow frequency. The overflow frequency level is defined as the percentage of days when demand exceeds capacity. This study assumes that the number of patients who utilize PCP's capacity on any day has a binomial distribution. This model is then used to calculate the probability that demand exceeds capacity for each given panel size. The probability that an arbitrary patient utilizes PCP's capacity equals the average number of visits per day per patient in the PCP's panel. This formulation can be used to select a panel size based on a maximum acceptable overflow frequency.

Green and Savin (2008) take a queueing approach to evaluate the impact of panel size. The performance metrics include expected backlog, and the probability that a patient is able to obtain a same-day appointment. No-shows and cancelations are taken into account. For each fixed value of the probability that an arbitrary patient is able to receive same-day services, and upon assuming that all patients want to see a doctor on the day they call and as early as possible if same-day appointments are unavailable, the authors use simple queueing models to calculate panel sizes.

Robinson and Chen (2010) compare the cost of traditional and advance-access scheduling policies in terms of a weighted average of patients' waiting time and doctors' idle and overtime. They also include examples in which depending on problem parameters, switching from a traditional appointment system to an advanced-access system accommodates an increase of up to 30% in a physician's panel size while maintaining the same cost level.

All models, including the one we presented above, do not model patient preferences in terms of desired appointment dates and do not consider seasonal demand patterns. The models presented in Green et al. (2008, 2007) and Robinson and Chen (2010) are more suitable for Advanced (Open) access systems in which all patients are assumed to want same-day appointments. Our model considers the choice of follow-up inter-visit times, which affect panel size decisions, but this issue is not modeled in previous studies.

4.3.3 No-Shows

As seen from the analysis of data in Sect. 4.2, no-show rates can vary significantly across health care systems. High no-show and late cancelation rates can lead to a variety of unwanted outcomes—e.g. loss of revenue, longer patient wait times, poor quality of care, and variable provider workload patterns. The latter can increase the level of dissatisfaction among health care providers.

No-shows are the focus of papers in two bodies of literature—Health services research (HSR) and Operations research (OR). In the OR literature, papers assume that no-show rates are exogenous and focus on evaluating different booking strategies via mathematical models. Such strategies include overbooking by double or triple booking in certain slots, or reducing the length of each slot in an attempt to increase provider capacity utilization. Overbooking helps to reduce loss of capacity, but on days when the majority of scheduled patients show up, it could increase patients' in-clinic wait times and providers' overtime, leading to patient and provider dissatisfaction. We have anecdotal evidence that providers' willingness to accept overbooking is related to their remuneration and that providers are more willing to accept workload variability when their remuneration depends on the number of patient visits.

In the HSR literature, researchers first identify the reasons for no-shows and then propose strategies for eliminating them. The effect of such strategies is documented in empirical studies that compare no-show rates before and after the application of interventions. Common examples of causes of no-shows are forgetfulness, lack of knowledge about health consequences of missed appointments, appointments with unfamiliar providers, and language and transportation barriers. Clinics can respond by sending appointment reminders, educating patients, prioritizing patient-PCP matched appointments, making interpreters available, and either offering transportation assistance or linking patients with community services that offer such assistance. HSR literature contains a number of studies in which the use of strategies mentioned above has been shown to benefit clinics by reducing the incidence of no-shows. We provide a detailed review of both streams of literatures later in this section, after we present a model that can be used to choose an overbooking strategy in response to no-shows.

We have interacted with several clinics and health systems. In all cases, the number of patients that may be overbooked was strongly affected by the service providers' willingness to accept variable daily workload patterns, although there were significant differences in practices surrounding overbooking. Therefore, we present a model below to illustrate the problem faced by a service provider that has determined the maximum number of patients that may be overbooked and needs help in choosing the position of overbooked patients in his or her daily schedule. We also assume that service times are deterministic. Our model can be modified to consider the number of overbooks as a decision variable, and random service times. This, however, leads to a more complicated model (see Sect. 4.3.5 for an example)

The service provider in our model has κ regular advance-book appointment slots, indexed $i = 1, \ldots, \kappa$, and has decided to book up to $(b - \kappa)$ additional overbook appointments. The actual number of additional appointments that may be booked on a particular work day depends on how many patients call and agree to have appointments in overbook slots. That is, our model has two types of appointments: regular and overbook (O/B) appointments. All regular appointments are booked first. When κ appointments are already booked on a particular day and additional requests arise, patients are told that they can either book another day when a regular appointment may be available, or take one of the O/B appointment slots. If they agree to take an O/B slot, then they receive lower priority relative to regular patients. That is, an O/B patient can be served only when a regular-book patient does not show up and there is no previously scheduled O/B patient waiting for service.

We use c_w to denote the cost of patient waiting relative to physician overtime. In most practical situations, $c_w < 1$ would be the norm. Robinson and Chen (2010) demonstrate how c_w can be estimated from observations of the average queue length and physician utilization.

We also make several simplifying assumptions. These are: (i) all patients call in advance to book appointments, (ii) service times are constant, and (iii) patients and service providers are punctual. The same slot cannot be booked for more than one regular and one O/B patient. That is, double booking is allowed, but triple, quadruple or higher order booking is not allowed. These assumptions are based on direct observation of several clinics' operations.

Finally, we consider two variants of our model. In the first approach, patients pick one of the available O/B slots after the clinic reveals available O/B slots. In the second approach, the clinic decides in which slot to place each O/B request after learning that a patient wants to book an O/B slot. We present the two models in sequence. The appropriateness of which approach to use in a particular setting would depend on the strength of patients' preferences. For example, patients typically expect to be able to book in a slot of their liking in primary-care setting, but they are more likely to accept slots assigned by physician's offices in specialty and surgical clinics where provider capacity is more scarce.

Patients Choose O/B Slots: The clinic chooses x_i's before booking begins, where $i \in \{1, \ldots, b\}$. If $x_i = 1$, then a patient may double book an appointment in the ith slot. If $x_i = 0$, then double booking is not allowed in slot i. Even when $x_i = 1$, slot i may not be picked by an overbook request because patients may prefer other O/B slots that might be available, or insufficient O/B requests may arise with the result that some O/B slots are left unused. Note that patients are not required to book earlier available O/B slots first.

Let Z denote a $(1 \times b)$ vector of 0s and 1s, where a 0 in the ith position, with $i = 1, \ldots, \kappa$, indicates that the ith regular patient was a no-show and a 1 indicates that the patient showed up. Note that $Z_j = 0$ for every $j = \kappa + 1, \ldots, b$ because no regular patients are booked in these slots. Similarly, let Y denote a $(1 \times b)$ vector of 0s and 1s, where a 0 in the ith position indicates that a hypothetical patient that might have been double booked into that slot either chose not to book or was a no-show, and a 1 indicates that the hypothetical patient showed up. Given show probabilities, we can calculate the probability associated with each realization of vectors Z and Y. For some slot j, let N_j denote the random number of O/B patients waiting to be served after the commencement of either a service period or an idle period for the physician at the start of slot j. Then, we have

$$N_1(x) = x_1 Y_1 Z_1.$$

This means that at the first slot, an O/B patient will be found waiting only if both the regular and the O/B patient scheduled in that slot show up. Next, the count of waiting patients evolves as follows.

$$N_j(x) = [N_{j-1}(x) + x_j Y_j - (1 - Z_j)]^+ \quad \forall j = 2, \ldots, b.$$

We must also have

$$N_j(x) \geq 0 \quad \forall j = 1, \ldots, b.$$

Clearly, for each vector x, there are corresponding distributions for each N_j, knowing which we can calculate the clinic's overall cost. First, we can calculate total waiting time as follows:

$$W(x) = \sum_{i=1}^{b} N_i(x),$$

which comes from the fact that each patient waiting at time period i waits for one period until period $(i + 1)$. Similarly, the physician's work day ends at N_κ periods after κ because all those that are waiting at time κ are served one by one following κ. This gives rise to the following expected cost function:

$$\min_{\{x\}} \{E[C(x)] = c_w E[W(x)] + N_\kappa(x)\}, \tag{4.3}$$

subject to

$$\sum_{i=1}^{b} x_i \geq b - \kappa \tag{4.4}$$

$$x_i \in \{0, 1\} \quad \forall i = 1, \ldots, b. \tag{4.5}$$

For each x, the problem of evaluating $E[C(x)]$ is not difficult, but the problem of finding an optimal x is a combinatorial problem and its solution can take significant computational effort. We illustrate two approaches for finding $E[C(x)]$ for a given x. In the first approach, we assume that Y_j and Z_j are independent. In the second approach, this assumption is not required and we use a scenario-based formulation. For the first method, we exploit the fact that $N_j(x) \leq \min\{j, b-\kappa\}$, which comes from the fact that each appointment slot can have at most one extra (O/B) patient and there are at most $(b-\kappa)$ O/B patients. Then, for $1 \leq s \leq \min\{j-1, b-\kappa\}$, we have

$$P(N_j(x) = r \mid N_{j-1}(x) = s) = \begin{cases} 0 & \text{if } r \neq [s-1, s+1] \\ 1_{\{x_j=0\}}P(Z_j = 0) \\ +1_{\{x_j=1\}}P(Y_j = 0)P(Z_j = 0) & \text{if } r = s-1, \\ 1_{\{x_j=0\}}P(Z_j = 1) \\ +1_{\{x_j=1\}}P(Y_j = 0)P(Z_j = 1) \\ +1_{\{x_j=1\}}P(Y_j = 1)P(Z_j = 0) & \text{if } r = s, \\ 1_{\{x_j=1\}}P(Y_j = 1)P(Z_j = 1) & \text{if } r = s+1. \end{cases} \tag{4.6}$$

In the above expression and in the remainder of this chapter, $1_{\{\cdot\}}$ is a function that takes value one if the expression in the braces is true, and zero otherwise. Note that if $s = b - \kappa$, then x_j cannot equal 1 because no more than $(b-\kappa)$ overbooks are allowed. A similar expression can be written for the case in which $s = 0$. The key difference is that in that case $r = s - 1$ is not possible.

In the second approach, we assume that there are K equiprobable scenarios indexed by $k \in \{1, \ldots, K\}$. A scenario is a random draw from the underlying uncertainty in the arrival of O/B and scheduled patients and for each k, we have the corresponding vectors z^k and y^k. This allows us to write the clinic profile setup problem as follows.

$$x^* = \arg\min_x \sum_k c^k(x) \tag{4.7}$$

subject to

$$\sum_{i=1}^{b} x_i \geq b - \kappa \tag{4.8}$$

$$x_i \in \{0, 1\} \quad \forall i = 1, \ldots, b. \tag{4.9}$$

Furthermore,

$$c^k(x) = \min_{\{n_j^k\}} \left\{ c_W \sum_{i=1}^{b} n_i^k + n_\kappa^k \right\} \tag{4.10}$$

subject to

$$n_1^k = x_1 y_1^k z_1^k \tag{4.11}$$

$$n_j^k \geq n_{j-1}^k + x_j y_j^k - (1 - z_j^k) \quad \forall j = 2, \ldots, b \tag{4.12}$$

$$n_j^k \geq 0 \quad \forall j = 1, \ldots, b. \tag{4.13}$$

The second optimization problem is a linear program, but the first problem is an integer program with binary variables. For each scenario, the second problem calculates the number of O/B patients waiting at each potential service start epoch. The first problem finds the cost minimizing locations for O/B patients over all scenarios. When K is large, the solution to the above formulation approaches the exact formulation given earlier. The stochastic linear and integer programming literature includes a number of approaches for reducing the computational burden of solving these problems (see, e.g. Birge and Louveaux 1997). However, the problem remains computationally challenging for large K and b.

Clinic Assigns Patients to O/B slots: Consider now the situation in which the clinic chooses slots in which the first O/B request, the second O/B request, and so on will be booked. These slots are picked in advance. When the jth patient makes a request, (s)he is assigned to the pre-determined slot. We define $\{x_{ij}\}$ as clinic decision variables, where $x_{ij} = 1$ if the ith slot is assigned to the jth caller, provided that the jth caller makes a request. We also use notation $x_{i\cdot}$ to denote the sum of x_{ij} over all j and $x_{\cdot j}$ to denote the sum of x_{ij} over all i. In the interest of brevity, this formulation is presented only for the scenario-based approach.

The inner problem of finding the minimum cost associated with each scenario can be written as follows.

$$c^k(x) = \min_{\{n_j^k\}} \left\{ c_W \sum_{i=1}^{b} n_i^k + n_K^k \right\}, \tag{4.14}$$

subject to

$$n_1^k = (x_{1\cdot})(y_1^k)(z_1^k) \tag{4.15}$$

$$n_j^k \geq n_{j-1}^k + (x_{j\cdot})(y_j^k) - (1 - z_j^k) \quad \forall j = 2, \ldots, b \tag{4.16}$$

$$n_j^k \geq 0 \quad \forall j = 1, \ldots, b \tag{4.17}$$

That is, the inner problem remains unchanged with the difference that we use $x_{i\cdot}$ instead of x_i for each i. But the outer problem is now different, as shown below.

$$x^* = \text{argmin}_x \sum_k c^k(x), \tag{4.18}$$

subject to:

$$x_{i\cdot} \leq 1 \tag{4.19}$$

$$x_{\cdot j} \geq 1 \quad \forall j = 1, \ldots, b - \kappa \tag{4.20}$$

$$x_{ij} \in \{1, 0\} \quad \forall i = 1, \ldots, b. \tag{4.21}$$

The first constraint above ensures that no slot has more than two booked patients. The second constraint ensures that the program chooses locations for at least $(b - \kappa)$ O/B requests. The complexity of this problem is greater than the equivalent problem in which the patients chose which O/B slots to book because there are now b^2 binary variables, whereas in the earlier formulation, there were b binary variables. However, in many practical settings, commercially available optimization software may be used to obtain either optimal or near-optimal solutions to the above problem. Because such problems are solved relatively infrequently (e.g. either at the time of setting up a clinic profile or modifying it based on changed circumstances), it is not necessary to have very fast solution algorithms. We believe that the ability to obtain good solutions in several hours on moderately fast computer workstations would be reasonable, which should be possible with the help of advanced commercial software for solving linear and integer programs. We do not present an example in this section. Instead, we do so in Sect. 4.3.5, which combines overbooking with the choice of appointment lengths when addressing the clinic profile setup problem. In the remainder of this section, we summarize HSR and OR literatures dealing with no-shows

HSR literature: Some researchers propose quantitative methods for estimating each patient's no-show probability as a function of demographic characteristics, health status, or appointment-keeping history (Cashman et al. 2004; Goldman et al. 1982; Gruzd et al. 1986). However, there are also empirical studies that show that the prediction of attendance behavior using patients' demographic information or past appointment-keeping history is inaccurate (Dervin et al. 1978). Other factors such as transportation, personal schedule, patients' psychological anxiety about their appointments, and patients' perceptions regarding clinics' booking practices, e.g. double or triple booking, may also result in no-shows (Barron 1980; Lacy et al. 2004; Mitchell et al. 2007; Simth et al. 1994).

The HSR literature contains conflicting evidence about whether no-show rates increase in appointment lead time—see, for example, Bean and Talaga (1992), who review research on health care appointment breaking and find inconsistent evidence about whether days to appointment is a significant predictor of no-show behavior. In particular, some studies find that longer appointment lead times (delays) are correlated with higher patient no-shows (Gallucci et al. 2005; Lee et al. 2005; Whittle et al. 2008). In contrast, Dervin et al. (1978), Fosarelli et al. (1985), Irwin et al. (1981), Neinstein (1982), Starkenburg et al. (1988) find no statistically significant correlation between lead time and appointment-keeping behavior. The studies that find positive correlation between lead time and no-shows generally do not exclude same-day appointments from the analysis. No-show rates for same-day appointments are indeed low regardless of clinic environments (Simth and Yawn 1994), and need to be studied separately because those patients often consider their need to be urgent. Note that we do not include same-day appointments in our analysis of the correlation between lead times and no-show rates in Sect. 4.2.

We believe that the ambiguity in the health service research literature about the correlation between appointment lead time and no-shows may be, in part, due to the lack of rigorous multivariate statistical analysis. Most studies of appointment-keeping predictors do not address possible interactions and confounding among predictors (Melniknow et al. 1994). Patients' no-show behavior may be highly context-dependent (for example, forgetfulness, efficacy of reminder systems, change in health condition, or patients' other commitments), which would require statistical studies to include many more context-dependent variables. Neal et al. (2005) studied the reasons for missed appointments in primary-care setting with the help of a survey of patients and reported their findings as follows. Among the survey respondents, 49.4% of the patients said that they forgot about the appointments. In addition, 29.6% of the patients included a reason that the appointment was at an inconvenient time, and 15.8% included a reason that the appointment was not with the doctor of their choice. In addition, 25.0% of patients said that other commitment or competing priorities deterred them from showing up. For those patients who provided a reason why they forgot, 65.4% said that there was no reason or excuse, 26.9% said that they were distracted or preoccupied by other things, and only 7.7% of the patients said that it was because they waited too long.

Many HSR studies have shown that patient no-shows can be significantly reduced by patient education or appointment reminders (Campbell et al. 1994; Guse et al. 2003; Lee et al. 2003; Mitchell 2008; Roth et al. 2004). From a medical and clinic management point of view, it would be preferable to ensure attendance rather than using scheduling strategies to reduce the impact of broken appointments (Deyo et al. 1980). However, patient education or clinic intervention may not always succeed. In such cases, OR models may help mitigate the negative impact of no-shows on clinic operations. Next, we summarize OR models that account for patient no-shows.

OR Literature: Many operations research models have focused on how to mitigate the impact of no-shows. These papers do not consider patients' preferences for particular appointment days, time blocks, and service providers when modeling the appointment booking process. Note that the first formulation we presented in this section allowed patients to choose particular overbook slots at the time of making appointments. In what follows, we group studies based on commonality of assumptions pertaining to no-shows.

Several papers assume a common no-show probability distribution for all patients. For example, (LaGanga and Lawrence 2007) consider a general overbooking model that inflates the booking limit based on an average no-show rate, and evaluate the performance of overbooking by revenue, patient wait time, and physician overtime. They show that overbooking is beneficial especially when no-show rate is high. Kaandorp and Koole (2007) consider the clinic profile setup problem with fixed patient no-show probabilities while accounting for patient wait time, server idle time, and tardiness. They propose a local search algorithm that converges to an optimal schedule.

Kim and Giachetti (2006) consider a dynamic clinic profile setup problem when the clinic has stochastic no-show rates. The performance is evaluated by expected revenue and physician overtime, and the authors show that dynamically setting the clinic profile performs better than general overbooking when no-show rates are high or stochastic. Robinson and Chen (2010) compare the impact of no-shows on the performance of traditional appointment systems and the Advanced-Access systems by evaluating patient waiting time, doctor idle time and overtime. They identify the characteristics of the optimal overbooking policy, and show that Advanced-Access systems work better than traditional systems except when no-show rate is low.

There are models that assume patients' no-show rates increase with appointment lead time. For example, Green et al. (2008) use this assumption for capacity analysis of a single-server Advanced Access system through a queueing model. Liu et al. (2010) model a multiple-day appointment problem as a Markov decision process in which the clinics decide which appointment day to book the patient into upon receiving a request. Alternatively, the likelihood of no-shows could depend on a whole host of patient characteristics. There is a stream of literature that utilizes heterogeneous no-show probabilities for patients belonging to different classes to derive optimal schedules; see, for example, Muthuraman and Lawley (2008) and Zeng et al. (2010).

4.3.4 Urgent/Same-day Demand

Clinics often try to meet urgent or same-day demand by setting a target for the number of appointment slots that should be open at the start of a day to accommodate such requests. Models that can be used to address such problems have been discussed in Gupta and Wang (2008). In this section, we present a heuristic approach presented in Gupta and Wang (2008) as an example of relevant models. This approach ignores patients' preferences, for which Gupta and Wang (2008) discuss other approaches.

Consider a clinic that has m physicians, where physician i has κ_i total slots on an arbitrary workday, and $\kappa = \sum_{i=1}^{m} \kappa_i$ is the total clinic capacity. Non-urgent patients call-in advance, whereas urgent (same-day) patients call at the start of the workday. All urgent demand is met, even if that incurs overtime cost. We denote the cost of insufficient same-day capacity by c per-patient. The clinic's average contribution from each accepted regular appointment is r_1 when the patient visits his/her PCP and r_1' when the patient visits another physician. Corresponding parameters for same-day patients are r_2 and r_2'. A natural ordering of the revenue parameters is $r_1 \geq r_1'$ and $r_2 \geq r_2'$. In fact, a recent study has shown that patient-PCP mismatch reduces physicians' and clinic's revenues by approximately 15% per visit (O'Hare and Corlett 2004).

Let X_i denote the same-day demand for physician i. Then, the problem of reserving capacity for same-day access can be formulated as that of choosing booking limits $\mathbf{b}^*$, where $\mathbf{b}^* = \arg\max\{\Pi(\mathbf{b})\}$ is an optimal solution to the multi-dimensional newsvendor problem described below.

$$\Pi(\mathbf{b}) = E\left\{(r_2 + c)\sum_{i=1}^{m}(\kappa_i - b_i) - c\sum_{i=1}^{m}X_i - (r_2 - r_2')\sum_{i=1}^{m}(\kappa_i - b_i - X_i)^+ \right.$$
$$\left. - (r_2' + c)\left[\sum_{i=1}^{m}(\kappa_i - b_i - X_i)\right]^+\right\}.$$

$\Pi(\mathbf{b})$ is jointly concave in $\mathbf{b}$, which makes it straightforward to find $\mathbf{b}^*$.

Gerchak et al. (1996) study the operating room capacity reservation problem when both the number of elective surgery requests and the number of emergency surgeries are random. This study provides a stochastic dynamic programing model for the advance scheduling problem, while incorporating the tradeoffs among capacity utilization, overtime usage, and delays. The authors show that the optimal policy is often not a threshold policy, and that the optimal number of elective surgeries to schedule increases with the number of patients waiting for elective surgeries. The advance scheduling problem in Gerchak et al. is similar to the outpatient appointment scheduling in the sense that patients are divided into two groups (same-day (urgent) and advance-book (elective surgery patients.)

Dobson et al. (2011) propose a carve-out model that reserves a fraction of the daily capacity for urgent patients in primary-care setting. Under this model, urgent patients may be scheduled in routine (non-urgent) slots when all urgent slots are filled, but routine patients cannot access slots reserved for urgent patients. Urgent overflow requests are satisfied on the day of the appointment request, but non-urgent patients may be scheduled on later days. The authors model the evolution of the non-urgent appointment queue at the beginning of each day as a Markov chain, and minimize the cost of same-day demand overflow and non-urgent patients' delay. The authors consider two scenarios: when demand and capacity are balanced (base case), and when the system is overloaded. The performance of the carve-out models is compared to the Advanced-access system in which all patients are treated as urgent, and the zero-carve-out system in which no slots are reserved for urgent demand.

The authors' numerical experiments show that when the system is not overloaded, the optimal policy (among carve-out, Advanced Access, and zero-carve-out) depends both on the ratios of the cost of urgent overflow to the cost of non-urgent patient delay, and the arrival dynamics of the urgent and non-urgent patients. For overloaded systems, the trade-off between the benefit of serving a non-urgent patient and the cost of urgent overflow determines the optimal reservation level.

Papers that schedule patients of multiple priority groups for services such as MRI and CT scan are also relevant to the same-day capacity reservation problem. For example, Green et al. (2006) formulate the capacity management problem of a diagnostic medical system as a finite-horizon dynamic program and identify properties of the optimal policies. The model considers three patient classes:

advance-book outpatients whose appointments are scheduled in advance, inpatients whose needs are generated randomly during the day, and emergency patients whose demand needs to be served as soon as possible. The authors find that the performance of the proposed heuristics is most sensitive to the assumed cost of each unserved outpatient and inpatient.

Patrick et al. (2008) model the capacity allocation process as a stochastic dynamic program, and dynamically allocate remaining capacity to balance patient wait-time, revenue, and costs associated with capacity usage and denial of appointments. This model allows class-dependent penalty functions for patient waits. Demand is assumed to come from two sources: outpatients and inpatients, where inpatient demand is known at the beginning of each day and outpatient demand arrives throughout the day. The authors propose a linear value function approximation method to derive rules for booking different priority classes and use of overtime.

Papers discussed above do not model no-shows, cancelations and overbooking. In contrast, Chen and Robinson (2011) use stochastic linear programing to simultaneously set appointments for established patients and randomly-arriving same-day patients while taking into account patient no-shows, ancillary physician tasks, and additional indirect waiting costs for same-day patients.

Gupta and Wang (2008) and Wang and Gupta (2011) model patient preferences and the quality-of-care and revenue impact of matching patients with their PCPs when there are urgent (same-day) and nonurgent (advance-book) appointment requests. Note that these are the only papers that consider patient choice and urgent/nonurgent capacity allocation at the same time.

Overall, the quantitative literature adequately addresses key questions faced by clinic managers, but translational studies and software implementation are needed to achieve more widespread use of this methodology.

4.3.5 Appointment Lengths

The problem of choosing appointment lengths is also a well studied problem in the OR literature. A detailed review of papers dealing with this problem is available in Gupta and Denton (2008). There are two variants of this problem. In one approach, it is assumed that the number of appointments to be booked, sequence of bookings, and service time distributions of each appointment are known. Patients and service providers are assumed to arrive as scheduled and no-shows are not modeled.[5] The purpose of mathematical models belonging to this category is to determine the

[5] Note that no-shows can be modeled in this setup by assigning a non-zero probability (equal to no-show probability) to the event that the service time is zero (in case of a no-show) while ensuring that patients who do not show up do not incur a waiting cost.

appointment time of each patient in the sequence. Details of a formulation that uses this approach can be found in Denton et al. (2003). Several authors have refined (extended) this formulation in recent years; see, for example, Bagen and Querynne (2009) and Gul et al. (2011). We present a review of papers that have appeared after Gupta and Denton (2008) at a later point in this section. However, this model does not match well with how outpatient appointments are managed.

In the outpatient setting, it is more common to find situations in which clinics need to determine work profiles for each provider before any appointment requests arrive. This means clinics must determine the maximum number of appointments, denoted by n, that can be served by a particular provider in a work day and a base appointment length. Scheduled appointment durations are multiples of this base length, with the majority of appointment lengths equal to a single base length. For example, suppose the base length equals a unit of time. Then, for a physician with nominal capacity κ and no overbooking, possible appointment times are denoted by $1, \ldots, \kappa$. The problem facing the clinic is to determine which of these time slots to book for each arriving appointment request. Such problems are typically formulated as cost minimization problems and there is literature on these types of formulations. We present a model in this section to highlight the complexity of these problems.

We take a scenario-based approach where a scenario, denoted by k, specifies the number of appointment requests and a vector of service times. The number of requests that are accepted is capped at n, the maximum number that the physician is willing to serve on that work day. Note that when the set of possible start times is $\{1, \ldots, n\}$ and $n > \kappa$, then this represents a situation in which the physician is willing to accept $n - \kappa$ overbook appointments. The objective is to choose a vector of appointment start times that minimizes the sum of patient waiting times and service provider's tardiness relative to the length of workday κ. Patients and providers are assumed to be punctual, and providers are assumed not to have the ability to use idle time in a productive fashion. This means that physician idle time is undesirable and minimizing idle time is equivalent to minimizing tardiness with respect to the length of the work day. Consequently, it is not necessary to penalize physician idle time.

The scenario-based formulation is similar to the second model presented in Sect. 4.3.3. The clinic's decision variables are x_{ij}, where $x_{ij} = 1$ if the ith service start time is assigned to the jth caller, provided that the jth caller makes a request. The locations of start of services, i.e. x_{ij}s, are determined in advance. Similar to Sect. 4.3.3, we also use notation $x_{i\cdot}$ to denote the sum of x_{ij} over all j and $z^k = (z_1^k, \ldots, z_n^k)$ to denote realized service times of patients 1 through n. Note that if patient j upon booking an appointment does not show, then the corresponding z_j^k is zero. Similarly, if only $n^k \leq n$ patients book appointments in a particular scenario, then $z_j^k = 0$ for every $j > n^k$. If more than n requests arrive on a given day, then all requests in excess of n are asked to try another day.

Typically, clinic profiles are set well in advance and not changed in response to daily fluctuations in the number of appointment requests. For this reason, the model presented below does not explicitly consider multiple appointment days. Overflow to future days is modeled via a penalty for making patients wait. Finally, similar to Sect. 4.3.3, the relative value of physician overtime is treated as a unit of cost and the relative value of patient waiting is c_w, where $c_w < 1$ would be typical.

Throughout this section, we assume that when multiple patients are given the same appointment start time, the order of service among those patients is the same as the order of arrival of appointment requests. That is, for each i, the order of service is $x_{i,1}$ first, followed by $x_{i,2}$ and so on until $x_{i,n}$. We also define w_{i0}^k as the backlog of remaining work at the start of time slot i under scenario k. It is easy to see that

$$w_{1,0}^k = 0, \quad \text{and} \tag{4.22}$$

$$w_{i,0}^k = \left(w_{i-1,0}^k + \sum_{j=1}^{n} (x_{i-1,j})(z_j^k) - 1 \right)^+ \quad \text{for } i = 2, \ldots, \kappa. \tag{4.23}$$

The waiting time of the jth caller, if he or she is assigned to slot i, and he or she shows up, can be calculated recursively with the help of the following equations:

$$w_{i,1}^k = \begin{cases} w_{i,0}^k & \text{if } x_{i,1} > 0, \\ 0 & \text{otherwise} \end{cases} \tag{4.24}$$

$$w_{i,j}^k = \begin{cases} w_{i,0}^k + \sum_{u=1}^{j-1} (x_{i,u}) z_u^k & \text{if } x_{i,j} > 0, \\ 0 \end{cases} \tag{4.25}$$

Otherwise Eqs. 4.24 and 4.25 can be explained as follows. Every patient who is potentially assigned to slot i must wait at least an amount equal to the backlog of remaining work at the beginning of slot i. Furthermore, the first patient who calls for an appointment waits exactly equal to $w_{i,0}^k$ if she or he is assigned to slot i. For any other patient j, where $j \geq 2$, additional delay is possible. This delay equals the time it would take the service provider to serve all patients assigned to slot i who have higher priority and who show up.

The total waiting time in scenario k is $\sum_{i=1}^{\kappa} \sum_{j=1}^{n} w_{i,j}^k$. Similarly, the total amount by which the service provider is late with respect to the length of his or her work day is $\ell^k = \max_{\{j=1,\ldots,n\}} \{ (\sum_{i=1}^{\kappa} ((i + w_{i,j}^k + z_j^k)(x_{i,j})) - \kappa)^+ \}$. In this expression, $\sum_{i=1}^{\kappa} ((i + w_{i,j}^k + z_j^k)(x_{i,j}))$ is the time at which the patient who is the jth caller in sequence is served. This expression can be further simplified as shown in the formulation below, which contains the inner optimization problem for each set of $x_{i,j}$s.

$$c^k(x) = \min_{\{w_{i,j}^k, \ell^k\}} \left\{ c_w \sum_{i=1}^{\kappa} \sum_{j=1}^{n} w_{i,j}^k + \ell^k \right\}, \tag{4.26}$$

subject to

$$w_{1,0}^k = 0 \tag{4.27}$$

$$w_{i,0}^k \geq w_{i-1,0}^k + \sum_{j=1}^{n}(x_{i-1,j})(z_j^k) - 1 \quad \text{for } i \geq 2 \tag{4.28}$$

$$w_{i,1}^k \geq w_{i,0}^k - (1 - (x_{i,1})I_{\{z_1^k > 0\}})M \quad \text{for all } i \tag{4.29}$$

$$w_{i,j}^k \geq w_{i,0}^k + \sum_{u=1}^{j-1}(x_{i,u})z_u^k - (1 - (x_{i,j})I_{\{z_j^k > 0\}})M \quad \text{for all } i \text{ and } j \geq 2 \tag{4.30}$$

$$\ell^k \geq \sum_{i=1}^{\kappa}((i)(x_{i,j}) + w_{i,j}^k + z_j^k) - \kappa - (1 - x_{i,j})M \quad \text{for all } i,j \tag{4.31}$$

$$\ell^k \geq 0 \tag{4.32}$$

$$w_{i,j}^k \geq 0 \quad \forall i,j. \tag{4.33}$$

In the above formulation M is a large constant, which is used to ensure that the optimal choice of w_{ij}^k would be zero when either $x_{ij} = 0$ or $z_j^k = 0$.

The outer problem involves binary variables $x_{i,j}$s. It can be written as follows:

$$x^* = \arg\min_x \sum_k c^k(x), \tag{4.34}$$

subject to

$$x_{\cdot j} \geq 1 \quad \forall j = 1, \ldots, n \tag{4.35}$$

$$x_{ij} \in \{1, 0\} \quad \forall i,j. \tag{4.36}$$

The first constraint above ensures that the program chooses at least one location for each arriving request before the request arises. The complexity of this problem is high because it involves $(\kappa \cdot n)$ binary variables.

We solved several examples using our formulation above to shine light on the value of using this approach for setting a clinic's profile. The data used to generate these examples are as follows: $K = 500$ scenarios, $n = 3$, 4, 5 or 6 maximum appointments, $\kappa = 5$ available slots, show probability of 0.8 for each caller, appointment slot length = 1 unit of time, lognormal service time with mean = 1 unit of time and two levels of coefficient of variation $(C_s = 0.25, 0.75)$, and two levels of $c_w = 0.25$ and 0.75. Each scenario is specified by a vector of values z_j^k, $j = 1, \ldots, n$. The procedure described below generates all K scenarios for each value of n. First, we generate a random matrix of size $K \times n$, denoted Z_1, whose row index represents scenario and column index represent the caller index. Each element of Z_1 equals 1 with probability 0.8, and 0 with probability 0.2. Next, we generate another $K \times n$ matrix Z_2 whose kth row has the first n^k elements equal to 1 and the rest equal to 0. The parameter n^k is the minimum of n and a random sample from a Poisson distribution with parameter n. That is, the kth row represents a sequence of booking requests. Finally, a third matrix Z_3 is generated whose elements are random samples drawn from a lognormal distribution with mean 1 and the appropriate C_s (either 0.25 or 0.75). The value of z_j^k for each j and k is the product of (k, j)th elements of Z_1, Z_2 and Z_3. It is non-zero only if at least j callers try to book appointments and the jth caller shows up.

The above procedure is necessary because in our setting, the maximum number of appointments are chosen by the clinic, but the actual number of appointments on any given day depends on the demand. Put differently, suppose the clinic decides not to book more than 5 appointments. Then, on different days of operation, the actual number of appointment requests may be more or less than 5. If requests equal or exceed 5, then precisely 5 appointments are booked. If requests are less than 5, then all requests are booked. In either instance, appointments are booked into particular slots according to the solution obtained from our formulation.

Our focus in this chapter is not on developing methods for solving the problem in a computationally efficient manner. Therefore, we used commercial software (CPLEX 8.1) and solved instances of the problem involving a small number of appointments slots and patient arrivals. It took less than 1 minute to solve examples with $n = 3$ and $n = 4$, 5–9 min to solve examples with $n = 5$, and 28–51 min to solve examples with $n = 6$. We did not solve larger-sized problems because the computation time grows rapidly for $n > 6$. There are a variety of methods in stochastic programing literature that can be adapted to improve the computational difficulty of obtaining numerical solutions, which can be the focus of future research efforts.

The first set of results in Fig. 4.1 show the optimal appointment locations. In this figure, the caller index is denoted by upper-case letters. For each value of n, the optimal appointment slot reserved for each caller is shown. For example, when $C_s = c_w = 0.25$ (upper left panel), if the clinic allows at most 3 appointments, then the first caller is booked into slot 1, the second caller into slot 3 and the third caller into slot 2. In the same panel, we see that if the clinic were to allow up to 6 patients to book appointments, then the first caller is booked into slot 3, second caller into slot 2, third and fifth callers into slot 1, the fourth caller into slot 4, and the sixth caller into slot 5. That is, the first slot is double-booked, if needed. That happens only if 5 or more patients request appointments. In contrast, the upper right panel with $c_w = 0.75$ shows that the double booked slot is the fifth slot and caller number 5 and 6 are booked into that slot. The fact that the double-booked slot changes from being the first slot to the last slot as c_w changes from 0.25 to 0.75 is intuitively satisfying (see the $n = 6$ case in all four panels of Fig. 4.1). Double booking in an earlier slot decreases provider overtime (by increasing the probability of working this patient into a slot that becomes open on account of no-show), but at the expense of greater patient waiting. However, the sequence in which callers are assigned to available slots is not intuitive.

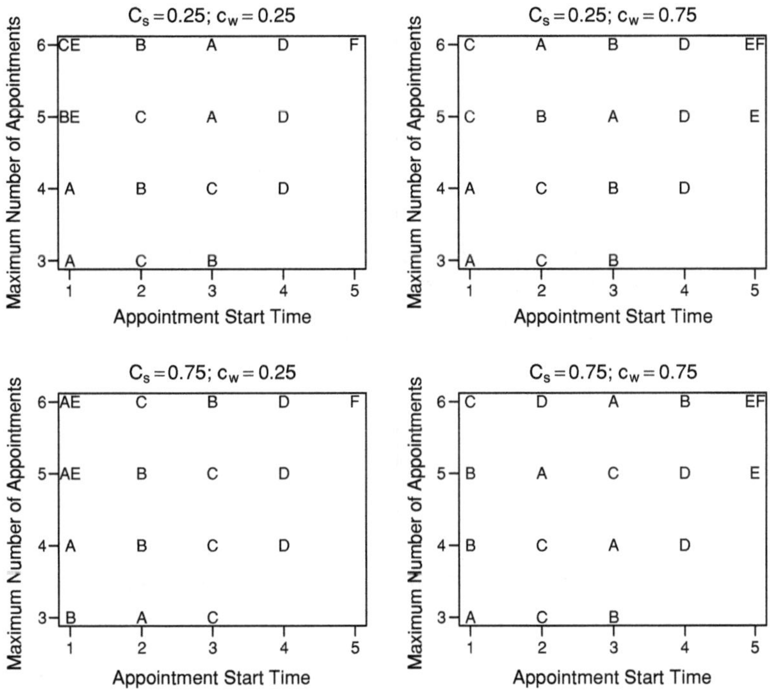

Fig. 4.1 Optimal clinic profile

We also summarize the average scheduled appointment length for a patient scheduled at each appointment start time in Fig. 4.2. Several previous studies have studied the magnitude of job allowances (time between two consecutive appointments) in situations where the number of patients seeking appointments and the sequence of appointments is assumed known, see, e.g. Denton et al. (2003). In the majority of such cases, the job allowances are found to have a dome shape. That is, job allowances are smaller both for appointments that occur at the beginning and at the end of the schedule. In contrast, Fig. 4.2 shows that job allowances can follow different patterns depending on the maximum number of appointments, and the values of C_s and c_w. These results are also not straightforward to explain on an intuitive basis.

Next, we summarize papers that have appeared in the OR literature on the topic of setting appointment lengths. As mentioned earlier in this section, these papers do not directly address the problem that arises in the context of outpatient clinics because they assume that at least one of the following are known: the number of appointments to be booked and/or the sequence of bookings. Begen and Queyranne (2009) consider the problem of determining an optimal schedule that minimizes the total expected overage and underage costs for a single operating room for a given sequence of jobs with discrete random durations. An underage cost occurs when a job finishes before the next job's start time and an overage cost occurs when a job

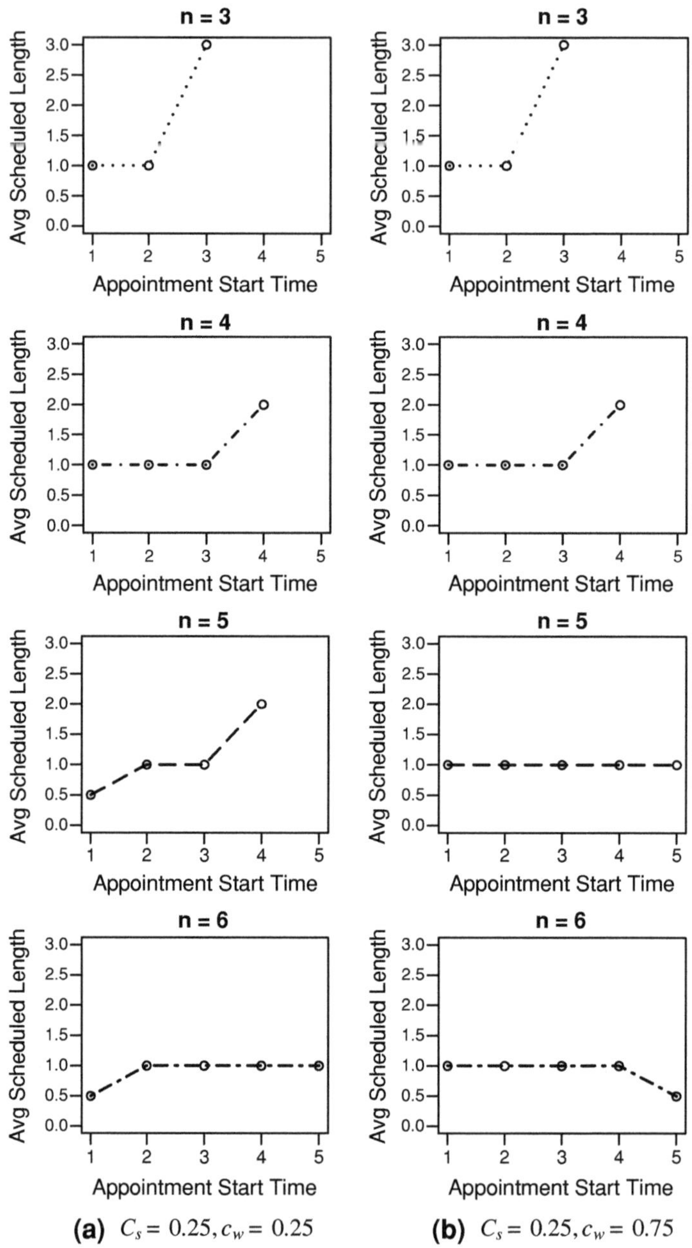

Fig. 4.2 Average scheduled appointment lengths

finishes after the next jobs' start time. The authors show that the objective function is L-convex under some conditions on the cost parameters and that there is an optimal integer appointment schedule that minimize the expected total cost.

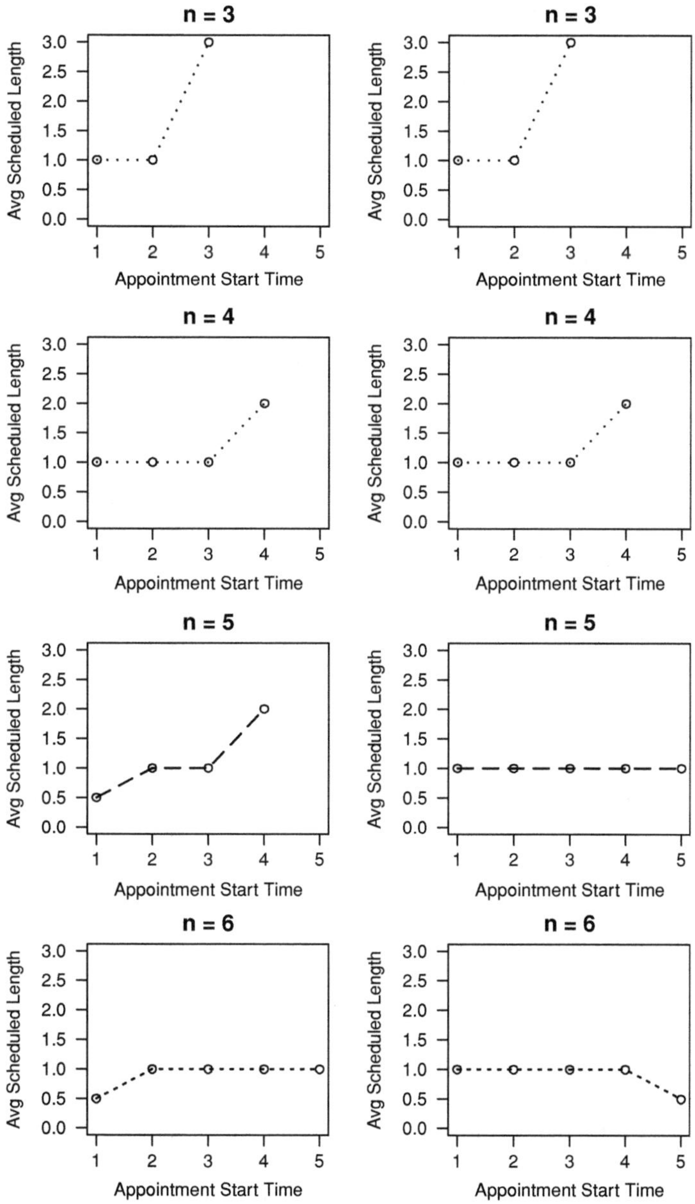

(c) $C_s = 0.75$, $c_w = 0.25$ **(d)** $C_s = 0.75$, $c_w = 0.75$

Fig. 4.2 continued

Begen et al. (2011) extend this problem to an environment in which the service time distributions are not known and only a set of independent sample duration data is available. They show that the total expected overage and underage cost is convex under a sufficient condition on cost parameters, and drive bounds on the number of samples required to obtain near-optimal solutions with a high probability.

Kong et al. (2010) model the appointment scheduling problem as a robust min-max problem in which they assume the mean and covariance estimates of the service durations are known, and use the worst case distribution to obtain the schedule. The authors show that in a congested system with two types of patients, there is an optimal schedule such that the probability of waiting for each patient is identical for most appointments, except the first and last few slots. The optimal schedule has the following features: schedule patients with more variable service times first, allocate near zero appointment lengths to the first few patients, then schedule a break before switching to the class of patients with lower service time variability.

Gul et al. (2011) use discrete event simulation to evaluate heuristics for sequencing and setting scheduled surgery lengths to minimize patient waiting times and physician overtime. The sequencing rules studied include increasing or decreasing mean procedure times, increasing variance of procedure times, and increasing coefficient of variation of procedure times. Similarly, scheduled surgery time for the $(i + t)$th patient is set equal to $A_{i+1} = A_i + h_i$, where $A_1 = 0$ and h_i is a selected percentile of procedure i duration (also known as *job hedging*). The authors show that simple heuristics, such as those they consider, can outperform the current practice, and that job hedging can reduce patient wait times.

4.3.6 Patient Preferences

Patients who attempt to book a non-urgent appointment do not necessarily want the first available appointment slot with any available physician. Instead, they typically wish to book an appointment with a doctor of choice at a convenient time of day that fits their schedules (Jennings et al. 2005; Olowokure et al. 2006). Patients' preferences may also depend on urgency of their medical needs and the schedule of appointments they hold with other clinics/providers because patients generally want to minimize number of trips to the clinic/health system. Patients with urgent needs often want quick access to any physician and a familiar physician is preferred (Cheraghi-Sohi et al. 2008). Clinics can improve patients' satisfaction by paying attention to their preferences. In addition, evidence shows that clinics benefit by accommodating patients' preferences because matching patients with their preferred doctors not only improves quality and continuity of care (Doescher et al. 2004), but also allows physicians to provide more value-added services to their patients (O'Hare et al. 2004). In addition, matching patients with their PCPs and offering them a convenient appointment time can reduce no-shows and thereby improve operational efficiency (Barron 1980; Carlson 2002; Simth and Yawn 1994).

Clinics may wish to account for patients' preferences at the clinic profile setup stage. However, the number of a physician's appointments available in each block of time (e.g. an hour) is limited and physicians also have preferences concerning their work hours. Therefore, there is a relatively small degree of flexibility in adjusting clinic profile setup to match patients' preferences. In contrast, clinics have a great deal of flexibility to dynamically match patients' preferences with available appointment slots at the booking stage; see for example Wang and Gupta (2011). Therefore, we focus on the appointment booking stage for incorporating patients' preferences in a dynamic fashion.

Individual patient preferences may be difficult to estimate from data because a high proportion of patients do not visit clinics frequently. In addition, booking preferences may differ by patient and change over time for the same patient. Wang and Gupta (2011) show that it is reasonable to aggregate preference information by physician panel, and use panel-level information to guide appointment booking decisions. In their model, each patient is asked to provide physician and time combinations that are acceptable to him or her, and the clinic decides whether to offer an appointment slot within the patient's acceptable set while accounting for anticipated future requests. Patients are not asked to rank order their acceptable combinations, because the clinic is interested in matching as many patient requests as possible with the available capacity. If the clinic asks its patients to rank order acceptable appointment slots, it would not be reasonable to book a patient with his or her lower ranked choice when a higher ranked choice is available. Moreover, if the clinic honors patients' ranking of different appointment slots, then this approach will lead to a first-come-first-served appointment system with reduced ability to place more patients in their acceptable combinations. By only obtaining patients' acceptable combinations, the clinic may book some patients in appointment slots that are less frequently requested and thus increase its chance of booking later arriving patients into their acceptable slots.

In the remainder of this section, we present a summary of the approach presented in Wang and Gupta (2011). In that paper, the appointment booking problem is modeled as a Markov Decision Process. A single-day appointment booking problem is considered and decision epochs are chosen such that there is at most one booking attempt at each decision epoch. Time is counted backwards. The system state is denoted by $s = (s_{i,j})$, an $m \times b$ matrix where the (i, j)th entry is the number of slots booked in time block j for physician i, $i = 1, \ldots, m$ and $j = 1, \ldots, b$.

Let $u_t(s)$ be the maximum expected revenue from time t onwards at the clinic level, $t = 1, \ldots, \tau$, and τ is the earliest time period that the clinic accepts a booking request for the appointment day. Then the clinic-level expected revenue function can be written as

$$u_t(s) = \sum_{\ell=1}^{m} \lambda_t^{\ell} u_t^{\ell}(s) + \left(1 - \sum_{\ell=1}^{m} \lambda_t^{\ell}\right) u_{t-1}(s), \tag{4.37}$$

where

$$u_t^{\ell}(s) = \sum_{\text{all(I,J)}} p_{I,J}^{\ell} \max_{(i,j)\in(I,J)} \left\{ r_{1,\ell}^{i} + u_{t-1}(s + e_{i,j}), u_{t-1}(s) - \pi_t \right\} \tag{4.38}$$

is the expected revenue from time t onward at the panel level, λ_t^ℓ is the probability that a panel ℓ patient arrives in period t, I is the set of acceptable physicians, J is the set of acceptable times, and $p_{I,J}^\ell$ is the probability that an arbitrary panel ℓ patient chooses $\{I,J\}$ as his or her set of acceptable physician and time combinations. The cost parameter $r_{1,\ell}^i$ is the average revenue from an advance-book panel i patient who visits physician ℓ, and π_t is the penalty cost of delaying an arriving patient's appointment request in period t.

Upon assuming that same-day appointment requests arrive at the beginning of the day and that the clinic optimally matches them with available capacity, the expected revenue calculated in period 0 (i.e. the appointment day) is

$$u_0(s) = E\left\{ r_2 \sum_{i=1}^{m} \min\{X_i, (\bar{\kappa}_i - \bar{s}_i)\} r_2' \min\left\{ \sum_{i=1}^{m} (\bar{\kappa}_i - \bar{s}_i - X_i)^+, \sum_{i=1}^{m} (X_i - \bar{\kappa}_i + \bar{s}_i)^+ \right\} \right.$$
$$\left. - c\left(\sum_{i=1}^{m} X_i - \sum_{i=1}^{m} (\bar{\kappa}_i - \bar{s}_i) \right)^+ \right\}, \qquad (4.39)$$

where X_i is the same-day requests from panel i patients, and $\bar{\kappa}_i$ and $\bar{s}_i$ are the total capacity and total number of appointments booked for physician i, respectively. The cost parameters r_2 and r_2' denote the average revenue for a patient-PCP matched and mismatched visits, respectively. When the clinic is unable to accommodate a same-day appointment request with its available capacity, a cost c is incurred, which can be interpreted as either overtime cost or the cost of using more expensive resources (such as after-hour clinics) to serve the urgent need. In Eq. 4.39, the first term is the expected revenue from same-day patient-PCP matched appointments, the second term is the expected revenue from patient-PCP mismatched visits, and the third term is the expected cost due to excess same-day demand.

Wang and Gupta (2011) partially characterize an optimal booking policy for the above formulation. They also propose several heuristics, which rely on the partial characterization of an optimal policy. The paper presents many numerical examples which show that it is beneficial to account for patient preferences, especially when demand and supply are imbalanced. The overall approach is easy to implement and could be incorporated into existing appointment systems and their web-based interfaces.

4.4 Future Directions and Challenges

In this paper, we discussed six key problems that are important for AS design. From a clinic's perspective, these problems arise simultaneously and not in isolation as models typically assume. For example, clinic capacity and panel sizing decisions need to consider no-shows, urgent requests, service time variability and patient preferences. However, if models were to try to consider all of these features simultaneously, they would quickly become intractable. It is important therefore to identify implementable rules that result in near-optimal capacity choices with respect to a variety of performance metrics. The efficacy of such rules can be tested via models, e.g. by checking if these rules are optimal under certain cases, and via numerical comparisons or simulation models. We believe that such studies can also lead to greater acceptance of modeling approaches among practitioners.

The management of no-shows has attracted significant attention from the OR community. Many ideas developed in these studies can be implemented to improve capacity management in presence of no-shows. However, widespread use of OR models is still not common, which may be in part due the lack of software tools to help clinic managers make overbooking decisions. Similarly, the problem of setting appointment lengths has attracted much attention. However, the version of this problem that is commonly studied in the literature is more suitable for setting scheduled durations of surgeries, rather than outpatient appointments. Outpatient clinics can benefit from model-based approaches for determining appointment lengths and the position of overbooks in service providers' schedules.

Health systems struggle with what metrics to use to drive capacity and AS design decisions. For example, some use the time to the third available appointment slot at the start of a randomly chosen day as a measure of ease of access. Others measure the percent of patients whose appointments are scheduled within 14 days of their identified desired date. Clearly, when such metrics are put in place, providers respond by changing their practice styles to produce good results on the chosen metrics. This affects the tradeoff between efficiency (capacity utilization) and responsiveness. More research is needed to identify intuitively appealing and easy-to-compute metrics that clinic managers can use to improve efficiency and responsiveness in presence of strategic response by providers [see Gupta et al. (2006) for an example of such metrics for clinics that implement Advanced Access].

Many health systems use the Internet to communicate with patients and the use of such means of communication is likely to increase in the future. Health systems have begun offering phone and e-consults with service providers for seasonal ailments, and certain types of routine follow-up appointments and prescription refills. If more patients use these means of communicating with their service providers, it may be necessary to adapt AS design to allow time in service providers' schedules for such activities.

Acknowledgments The authors are grateful to Dr. Brian Hertz, Internal Medicine, Hines VA Medical Center and Associate Professor of Internal Medicine, Loyola University, Chicago, for his comments and suggestions for improving an earlier version of this chapter.

References

Barron W (1980) Failed appointments. Who misses them, why they are missed, and what can be done. Prim Care 7(4):563–574

Bean AG, Talaga G (1992) Appointment breaking: causes and solutions. J Health Care Mark 12(4):14–25

Begen MA, Queyranne M (2009) Appointment scheduling with discrete random durations. In: Proceedings of the twentieth annual ACM-SIAM symposium on discrete algorithms, Society for Industrial and Applied Mathematics, Philadelphia, SODA '09, pp 845–854

Begen MA, Levi R, Queyranne M (2011) A sampling-based approach to appointment scheduling. http://www.ivey.uwo.ca/faculty/MBegen/ (working paper)

Birge JR, Louveaux F (1997) Introduction to stochastic programming. Springer Series in Operations Research and Financial Engineering, New York

Buzacott JA, Shanthikumar JG (1993) Stochastic models of manufacturing systems. Prentice Hall, Englewood Cliffs

Campbell JR, Szilagyi PG, Rodewald LE, Doane C, Roghmann KJ (1994) Patient-specific reminder letters and pediatric well-child-care show rates. Clin Pediatr 33(5):268–272

Carlson B (2002) Same-day appointments promise increased productivity. Manag Care 11(12):43–44

Cashman SB, Savageau JA, Lemay CA, Ferguson W (2004) Patient health status and appointment keeping in an urban community health center. J Health Care Poor Underserved 15(3):474–488

Cayirli T, Veral E (2003) Outpatient scheduling in health care: A review of literature. Prod Oper Manag 12(4):519–549

Chen RR, Robinson LW (2011) Sequencing and scheduling appointments with potential call-in patients (Working Paper). http://ssrn.com/abstract=1871125

Cheraghi-Sohi S, Hole A, Mead N, McDonald R, Whalley D, Bower P, Roland M (2008) What patients want from primary care consultations: a discrete choice experiment to identify patients' priorities. Ann Fam Med 6(2):107–115

Clague JE, Reed PG, Barlow J, Rada R, Clarke M, Edwards RH (1997) Improving outpatient clinic efficiency using computer simulation. Int J Health Care Qual Assur Inc Leadersh Health Serv 10(4-5):197–201

Denton B, Gupta D (2003) A sequential bounding approach for optimal appointment scheduling. IIE Trans 35(11):1003–1016

Dervin JV, Stone DL, Beck CH (1978) The no-show patient in the model family practice unit. J Fam Pract 7(6):1177–1180

Deyo RA, Inui TS (1980) Dropouts and broken appointments: a literature review and agenda for future research. Med Care 18(11):1146–1157

Dobson G, Hasija S, Pinker EJ (2011) Reserving capacity for urgent patients in primary care. Prod Oper Manag 20:456–473

Doescher MP, Saver BG, Fiscella K, Franks P (2004) Preventive care: does continuity count. J Gen Intern Med 19(6):632–637

Elkhuizen SG, Das SF, Bakker PJM, Hontelez JAM (2007) Using computer simulation to reduce access time for outpatient departments. Qual Saf Health Care 16(5):382–386

Fosarelli P, DeAngelis C, Kaszuba A (1985) Compliance with follow-up appointments generated in a pediatric emergency room. Am J Prev Med 1(3):23–29

Foster EM, Hosking MR, Ziya S (2010) A spoonful of math helps the medicine go down:an illustration of how health care can benefit frommathematical modeling and analysis. BMC Med Res Methodol 10:60–70

Gallucci G, Swartz W, Hackerman F (2005) Brief reparts: impact of the wait for an initial appointment on the rate of kept appointments at a mental health center. Psychiatr Serv 56:344–346

Gerchak Y, Gupta D, Henig M (1996) Reservation planning for elective surgery under uncertain demand for emergency surgery. Manag Sci 42(3):321–334

Goldman L, Freidin R, Cook EF, Eigner J, Grich P (1982) A multivariate approach to the prediction of no-show behavior in a primary care center. Arch Intern Med 142(3):563–567

Green LV, Savin S (2008) Reducing delays for medical appointments: a queueing approach. Oper Res 56(6):1526–1538

Green LV, Savin S, Wang B (2006) Managing patient service in a diagnostic medical facility. Oper Res 54(1):11–25

Green LV, Savin S, Murray M (2007) Providing timely access to care: what is the right patient panel size. Jt Comm J Qual Patient Saf 33(4):211–218

Gruzd DC, Shear CL, Rodney WM (1986) Determinants of no-show appointment behavior: the utility of multivariate analysis. Fam Med (18):4

Gul S, Denton B, Fowler J, Huschka T (2011) Bi-criteria scheduling of surgical services for an outpatient procedure center. Prod Oper Manag doi:10.1111/j.1937-5956.2011.01232.x. http://dx.doi.org/10.1111/j.1937-5956.2011.01232.x

Gupta D, Denton B (2008) Appointment scheduling in health care: challenges and opportunities. IIE Trans 40:800–819

Gupta D, Wang L (2008) Revenue management for a primary care clinic in the presence of patient choice. Oper Res 56(3):576–592

Gupta D, Potthoff S, Blowers D, Corlett J (2006) Performance metrics for advanced access. J Health care Manag 51(4):246–259

Guse CE, Richardson L, Carle M, Schmidt K (2003) The effect of exit-interview patient education on no-show rates at a family practice residency clinic. J Am Board Fam Pract 16:399–404

Ho CJ, Lau HS (1992) Minimizing total cost in scheduling outpatient appointments. Manag Sci 38(12):1750–764

Hsiao CJ, Cherry DK, Beatty PC, Rechtsteiner EA (2010) National ambulatory medical survey report: 2007 summary. National health statistics reports, Number 27 Available on the web at http://www.cdc.gov/nchs/data/nhsr/nhsr027.pdf, Cited March 7, 2011

Irwin CE Jr, Millstein SG, Shafer MAB (1981) Appointment-keeping behavior in adolescents. J Pediatr 99(5):799–802

Jennings BM, Loan LA, Heiner SL, Hemman EA, Swanson KM (2005) Soldiers' experiences with military health care. Mil Med 170(12):999–1004

Johnson SE, Newton WP (2002) Resource-based relative value units: a primer for academic family physicians. Fam Med 34(3):172–176

Kaandorp GC, Koole G (2007) Optimal outpatient appointment scheduling. Health Care Manag Sci 10:217–229

Kaplan EH, Johri M (2000) Treatment on demand: an operational model. Health Care Manag Sci 3(3):171–83

Kim S, Giachetti R (2006) A stochastic mathematical appointment overbooking model for health care providers to improve profits. IEEE Trans Syst, Man Cybern—Part A: Syst 36(6):1211–19

Kong Q, Lee CY, C-P T, Zheng Z (2010) Scheduling arrivals to a stochastic service delivery system using copositive cones (Working paper)

Lacy NL, Paulman A, Reuter MD, Lovejoy B (2004) Why we don't come: patient perceptions on no-shows. Ann Fam Med 2:541–545

LaGanga LR, Lawrence SR (2007) Clinic overbooking to improve patient access and increase provider productivity. Decis Sci 38(2):251–276

Lee CS, McCormick PA (2003) Telephone reminders to reduce non-attendance rate for endoscopy. J R Soc Med 96(11):547–548

Lee V, Earnest A, Chen M, Krishnan B (2005) Predictors of failed attendances in a multi-specialty outpatient centre using electronic databases. BMC Health Serv Res 5(1):51

Liu N, Ziya S, Kulkarni VG (2010) Dynamic scheduling of outpatient appointments under patient no-shows and cancellations. Manuf Serv Oper Manag 12(2):347–364

Mandel D, Zimlichman E, Wartenfeld R, Vinker S, Mimouni FB, Kreiss Y (2003) Primary care clinic size and patient satisfaction in a military setting. Am J Med Qual 18(6):251–255 November/December

Melnikow J, Kiefe C (1994) Patient compliance and medical research. J Gen Intern Med 9(2):96–105

Mitchell AJ, Selmes T (2007) Why don't patients attend their appointments? Maintaining engagement with psychiatric services. Adv Psychiatr Treat 13:423–434

Mitchell V (2008) Same-day booking. Can Fam Phys 54(3):379–383

Murray M, Davies M, Boushon B (2007) Panel size: how many patients can one doctor manage?. Fam Pract Manag 14(4):44–51

Muthuraman K, Lawley M (2008) A stochastic overbooking model for outpatient clinical scheduling with no-shows. IIE Trans 40:820–837

Neal R, Hussain-Gambles M, Allgar V, Lawlor D, Dempsey O (2005) Reasons for and consequences of missed appointments in general practice in the UK: questionnaire survey and prospective review of medical records. BMC Fam Pract 6(1):47 doi:10.1186/1471-2296-6-47

Neinstein LS (1982) Lowering broken appointment rates at a teenage health center. J Adolesc Health Care 3(2):110–113

O'Hare CD, Corlett J (2004) The outcomes of open-access scheduling. Fam Pract Manag 11(1):35–38

Olowokure B, Caswell M, Duggal H (2006) What women want: convenient appointment times for cervical screening tests. Eur J Cancer Care 15:489–492

Patrick J, Puterman ML, Queyranne M (2008) Dynamic multipriority patient scheduling for a diagnostic resource. Oper Res 56(6):1507–1525

Plantinga LC, Fink NE, Finkelstein FO, Powe NR, Jaar BG (2009) Association of peritoneal dialysis clinic size with clinical outcomes. Perit Dial Int 29(3):285–291

Puterman ML (1994) Markov decision processes: discrete stochastic dynamic programming. Wiley, New York

Robinson LW, Chen RR (2003) Scheduling doctors' appointments: optimal and empirically-based heuristic policies. IIE Trans 35(3):295–307

Robinson LW, Chen RR (2010) A comparison of traditional and open-access policies for appointment scheduling. Manuf Serv Oper Manag 12:330–346

Robinson LW, Chen RR (2010) Estimating the implied value of the customer's waiting time. Manuf Serv Oper Manag 13:53–57

Roth JP, Kula TJ, Jr, Glaros A, Kula K (2004) Effect of a computer-generated telephone reminder system on appointment attendance. Seminars in orthodontics 10(3):190–193, doi:10.1053/j.sodo.2004.05.001, technology in the Orthodontic Office

Schoenmeyr T, Dunn PF, Gamarnik D, Levi R, Berger DL, Daily BJ, Levine WC, Sandberg WS (2009) A model for understanding the impacts of demand and capacity on waiting time to enter a congested recovery room. Anesthesiology 110(6):1293–304

Smith CM, Yawn BP (1994) Factors associated with appointment keeping in a family practice residency clinic. J Fam Pract 38(1):25–29

Starkenburg RJ, Rosner F, Crowley K (1988) Missed appointments among patients new to a general medical clinic. N Y State J Med 88(9):437–435

Wang WY, Gupta D (2011) Adaptive appointment systems with patient preferences. Manuf Serv Oper Manag 13(3):53–57

Weiss EN (1990) Models for determining estimated start times and case orderings in hospital operating rooms. IIE Trans 22(2):143–150

Whittle J, Schectman G, Lu N, Baar B, Mayo-Smith MF (2008) Relationship of scheduling interval to missed and cancelled clinic appointments. J Ambul Care Manag 31(4):290–302

Zeng B, Turkcan A, Lin J, Lawley M (2010) Clinic scheduling models with overbooking for patients with heterogeneous no-show probabilities. Ann Oper Res 178(1):121–144

Chapter 5
Operating Theatre Planning and Scheduling

Erwin W. Hans and Peter T. Vanberkel

Abstract In this chapter we present a number of approaches to operating theatre planning and scheduling. We organize these approaches hierarchically, which serves to illustrate the breadth of problems confronted by researchers. At each hierarchical planning level we describe common problems, solution approaches and results from studies at partner hospitals.

5.1 Introduction

Within the Operations Research/Operations Management (OR/OM) health care literature, operating theatre (OT) planning and scheduling is one of the most popular topics. This is not surprising, as many patients in a hospital undergo surgical intervention in their care pathway. For a hospital, the OT accounts for more than 40% of its revenues and a similar large part of its costs (HFMA 2005). An efficient OT department thus significantly contributes to an efficient health care delivery system as a whole.

An extensive overview and taxonomy of the OT planning and scheduling literature is given by Cardoen et al. (2010a). They conclude that the majority of the research is directed at planning and scheduling of elective patients at an operational level of control, and take a deterministic approach. Furthermore, they

E. W. Hans (✉) · P. T. Vanberkel
Department of Operational Methods for Production & Logistics, Center for Health Care Operations Improvement & Research, University of Twente, Enschede, The Netherlands
e-mail: e.w.hans@utwente.nl

P. T. Vanberkel
e-mail: p.t.vanberkel@utwente.nl

R. Hall (ed.), *Handbook of Healthcare System Scheduling*,
International Series in Operations Research & Management Science 168,
DOI: 10.1007/978-1-4614-1734-7_5, © Springer Science+Business Media, LLC 2012

observe that only half of the literature contributions consider up- or down-stream hospital resources, and few papers report about implementation in practice. This appears to be a common problem in OR/OM health care literature (Brailsford et al. 2009). An up-to-date online bibliography of the OT management literature is maintained by Dexter (2011), and a structured literature review of OR in the management of operating theatres is given by Guerriero and Guido (2011).

In this chapter we address OT planning problems on three hierarchical managerial levels: strategic, tactical and offline operational planning, as introduced in Sect. 5.2.

The remainder of this chapter addresses recent work in each of these three levels of control. Section 5.2 outlines the planning and control functions on the aforementioned hierarchical levels in an OT department. Section 5.3 addresses the strategic problem of determining the target utilization of an OT department. Section 5.4 addresses the strategic problem of determining the number of surgical teams required during the night to deal with emergency cases. Section 5.5 addresses the strategic decision whether to use emergency operating theatres. Section 5.6 addresses the tactical problem of determining a master surgery schedule (a day-to-day allocation of operating theatres to surgical specialties) that levels the workload in subsequent departments (wards). Section 5.7 addresses the offline operational problem of scheduling elective surgeries with stochastic durations, and sequencing them in order to reduce access time of emergency surgeries. We will use a wide array of OR techniques, including discrete-event and Monte Carlo simulation, statistical modeling and meta-heuristics.

5.2 A Hierarchy of Resource Planning and Control in Operating Theatres

Competitive manufacturing companies make planning and control decisions in a hierarchical manner (Zijm 2000). For example, the long-term decision of what products to manufacture is at the top of the hierarchy and the real-time decision of whether to discard a specific part due to its quality is at the bottom of the hierarchy. In general the reliance of one decision on another defines the hierarchy. Many planning and control frameworks classify decisions into the three hierarchical levels—strategic, tactical and operational—as suggested by Anthony (1965). Similar hierarchical planning and control frameworks have been proposed for health care (see Hans et al. 2011). Hans et al. refine the classical hierarchy by splitting the operational level into an offline and online operational level, where the former is the *in advance* short-term decision making, and the latter the monitoring and control of the process in *real-time*. In the remainder of this section we outline the main OT planning and control functions on these four hierarchical levels.

5.2.1 Strategic Planning and Control

To reach organizational goals, the strategic level addresses the dimensioning of core OT resources, such as the number of OTs, the amount of personnel, instruments (e.g. X-ray machines), etc. It also involves case mix planning, i.e. the selection of surgery types, and the determination of the desired patient type volumes (Vissers et al. 2001). Agreements are made with surgical services/specialties concerning their annual patient volumes and assigned OT time. The dimensioning of subsequent departments' resources (e.g. ward beds) is also done (Vanberkel and Blake 2007). Strategic planning is typically based on historical data and/or forecasts. The planning horizon is typically long-term, e.g. a year or more.

5.2.2 Tactical Planning and Control

The tactical level addresses resource usage over a medium term, typically with a planning horizon of several weeks (Blake and Donald 2002; Wachtel and Dexter 2008). The actual aggregate patient demand (e.g. waiting lists, appointment requests for surgery) is used as input. In this stage, the weekly OT time is divided over specialties or surgeons, and patient types are assigned to days. For the division of OT time, two approaches exist (Denton et al. 2010). When a closed block planning approach is used, each specialty will receive a number of OT blocks (usually OT-days). In an (uncommon) open block planning approach, OT time is assigned following the arrival of requests for OT time by surgeons.

On the tactical level, the surgery sequence is usually not of concern. Instead, on this level it is verified whether the planned elective surgeries cause resource conflicts for the OT, for subsequent departments (ICU, wards), or for required instruments with limited availability (e.g. X-ray machines). The design of a Master Surgical Schedule is a tactical planning problem.

5.2.3 Operational Planning and Control (Offline)

The offline operational level addresses scheduling of specific patients to resources (and as a consequence, the sequencing of activities) and typically involves a planning horizon of a week. It encompasses the rostering of OT-personnel, and reserving resources for add-on surgeries (Dexter et al. 1999). In addition, it addresses the sequencing of surgeries (Denton et al. 2007), to prevent critical resource conflicts, e.g. regarding X-ray machines, instrument sets, surgeons, etc. When there are no dedicated emergency OTs, the sequencing of the elective surgeries can also aid in spreading the planned starting times of elective surgeries (which are "break-in moments" for emergency surgeries) in order to reduce the emergency surgery waiting time (Wullink et al. 2007).

5.2.4 Operational Planning and Control (Online)

The online operational level addresses the monitoring and control of the day-to-day activities in the OT. Obviously at this level of control, all uncertainty materializes and has to be dealt with. If necessary, surgeries are rescheduled, or even canceled (Dexter et al. 2004; McIntosh et al. 2006). This is usually done by a day coordinator in the OT department. Emergency surgeries, which have to be dealt with as soon as possible, are scheduled, and emergency OT teams may have to be assembled and dispatched to the first available OT. If there are emergency OTs, these emergency surgeries are dispatched to these OTs. If there are no such OTs, they are scheduled within the elective surgical schedule.

In summary, strategic planning typically addresses capacity dimensioning decisions, considering a long planning horizon of multiple years. Tactical planning addresses the aggregate capacity allocation to patient types, on an intermediate horizon of weeks or months. Offline operational planning addresses the in-advance detailed capacity allocation to elective patients, with a short planning horizon of days and up to a few weeks. Online operational planning addresses the monitoring and control of the process during execution, and encompasses for example reacting to unforeseen events.

5.3 Strategic: The Problem with Using Target OT Utilization Levels

Utilization of operating theatres is high on the agenda of hospital managers and researchers and is often used as a measure of efficiency, both introspectively as well as in benchmarking against other OT departments. As a result, much effort is spent trying to maximize OT utilization, sometimes without understanding the factors affecting it. Using straightforward statistical analysis we show how the target OT utilization of a hospital depends on the patient mix and the hospital's willingness to accept overtime. This work is described in detail in Houdenhoven et al. (2007). Similarly, the erroneousness of target *ward* occupancies is studied by Harper and Shahani (2002) and discussed by Green in Hall (2006).

5.3.1 General Model

There are various ways to compute the utilization rate. We define the OT utilization as the expected total surgery duration (including changeover/cleaning time) divided by the amount of time allotted (see Fig. 5.1):

$$\text{Expected OT utilization} = \frac{\text{expected total surgery duration}}{\text{alloted time}} \tag{5.1}$$

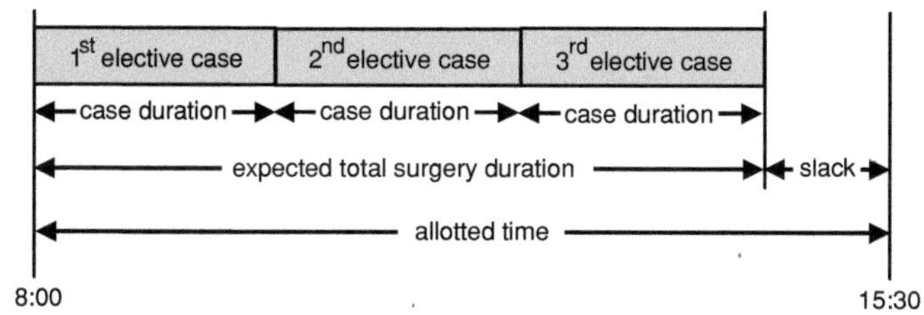

Fig. 5.1 Timeline for surgical cases

Our approach can be easily extended to deal with more extensive definitions of OT utilization.Note that the case duration includes the time required to clean and prepare the room for the next patient (i.e. the turnover time). The amount of allotted time is computed as follows:

$$\text{Alloted time} = \text{expected total surgery duration} + \text{slack time} \tag{5.2}$$

where the slack time (reserved capacity to account for variability) is determined in such a way that a certain frequency of overtime is achieved. This is a managerial choice: slack time reduces cancelations and/or costly overtime, but also reduces OT utilization. The frequency of overtime depends on the distribution of the total surgery duration and can be computed according to:

$$\text{Frequency of overtime} = P(\text{total surgery duration} > \text{allotted time}) \tag{5.3}$$

Now more formally, let μ_s and σ_s denote the average and standard deviation of elective surgical case durations of type s, and let n_s denote the number of cases completed in one block. A type s may correspond with the surgeries of, for example, a surgical specialty or a specific surgeon. Likewise, n_s^e, μ_s^e and σ_s^e denote the same for emergency cases. All these parameters are based on historical data. It follows that the total expected duration of all elective cases in one OT block is $n_s \times \mu_s$ and the standard deviation of the total duration of these n_s cases equals $\sqrt{n_s \times \sigma_s^2}$ (assuming durations are mutually independent). Accordingly:

$$\text{Expected total surgery duration} = n_s \times \mu_s + n_s^e \times \mu_s^e \tag{5.4}$$

$$\text{Total surgery duration std. deviation} = \sqrt{n_s \times \sigma_s^2 + n_s^e \times \left(\sigma_s^e\right)^2} \tag{5.5}$$

The accepted risk (or frequency) of overtime is denoted by r_s. Now we can complete Eq. 5.2. The amount of allotted time required to achieve an overtime frequency of r_s can be computed as follows:

$$\text{Alloted time} = n_s \times \mu_s + n_s^e \times \mu_s^e + \alpha(r_s)\sqrt{n_s \times \sigma_s^2 + n_s^e \times \left(\sigma_s^e\right)^2} \tag{5.6}$$

where $\alpha(r_s)$ is a function yielding probability r_s. The outcome of this function depends on the distribution of the surgery duration. Using $\alpha(r_s)$ in this way allows the approach to be independent of the surgery duration distribution, i.e. function $\alpha(r_s)$ can be changed to reflect various distributions. Using Eqs. 5.4 and 5.6 we can complete formula (5.1) for the expected OT utilization as a function of the frequency of overtime as follows:

$$\text{Expected OT utilization} = \frac{n_s \times \mu_s + n_s^e \times \mu_s^e}{n_s \times \mu_s + n_s^e \times \mu_s^e + \alpha(r_s)\sqrt{n_s \times \sigma_s^2 + n_s^e \times \left(\sigma_s^e\right)^2}} \tag{5.7}$$

5.3.2 General Results

We use formula (5.7) for the expected OT utilization to illustrate the relationship between OT utilization, patient mix and overtime frequency. In a theoretical scenario where there is no surgery duration variability (i.e. $\sigma_s = \sigma_s^e = 0$), the expected OT utilization is obviously 100%.

As a case study we consider Erasmus Medical Center in Rotterdam, the Netherlands. OT management in this hospital accepts a 30% risk of overtime. For simplicity, they assume that the total surgery duration follows a normal distribution $\sim N\left(n_s \times \mu_s + n_s^e \times \mu_s^e, \sqrt{n_s \times \sigma_s^2 + n_s^e \times \left(\sigma_s^e\right)^2}\right)$. Using straightforward statistical analysis we can show that $\alpha(r_s) = 0.5$ when the acceptable frequency of overtime is 30%. This is shown as follows. Let X be the total surgery duration, then:

$$\begin{aligned}
30\% &= P\left(X > n_s \times \mu_s + n_s^e \times \mu_s^e + \alpha(r_s)\sqrt{n_s \times \sigma_s^2 + n_s^e \times \left(\sigma_s^e\right)^2}\right) \\
&\Leftrightarrow P\left(X \le n_s \times \mu_s + n_s^e \times \mu_s^e + \alpha(r_s)\sqrt{n_s \times \sigma_s^2 + n_s^e \times \left(\sigma_s^e\right)^2}\right) = 0.7 \\
&\Leftrightarrow P\left(\frac{X - n_s \times \mu_s - n_s^e \times \mu_s^e}{\sqrt{n_s \times \sigma_s^2 + n_s^e \times \left(\sigma_s^e\right)^2}} \le \alpha(r_s)\right) = 0.7 \\
&\Leftrightarrow P(Z \le \alpha(r_s)) = 0.7
\end{aligned}$$

where $Z \sim N(0, 1)$. It follows that $\alpha(r_s) = 0.5$.

We use 2 years of historical data from the aforementioned hospital. We consider three different surgical specialties (i.e. three different patient mixes) and for each we show the trade-off between expected OT utilization and overtime frequency. This is illustrated in Fig. 5.2.

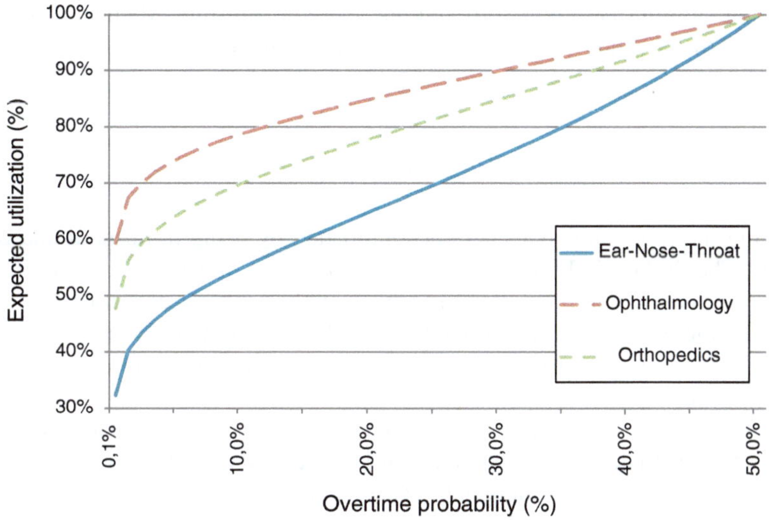

Fig. 5.2 Trade-off between overtime probability and expected utilization

The calculated expected OT utilization can also be regarded as a target utilization, or benchmark. Figure 5.2 shows that a single OT utilization target will result in different overtime frequencies for each specialty. For example, a target utilization of 80% will result in an overtime frequency of approximately 12% for ophthalmology but an overtime frequency of approximately 35% for ENT. In general, a low risk of overtime and a complex patient mix will result in a low utilization rate. If the accepted risk of overtime is higher and the patient mix less complex, then a higher utilization can be achieved. Given that overtime is expensive (and perhaps limited by collective bargaining agreements), this example illustrates the inadequacy of a single target OT utilization as a performance metric. It also illustrates the importance of taking case mix characteristics into account when comparing utilization figures between different OT departments.

5.4 Strategic: On-Call or In-House Nurses for Overnight Coverage for Emergency Cases?

Treating emergency patients is a common activity for most hospitals. Likewise, the OT must be available to provide emergency operations 24 h/day. The night shift (e.g. from 11:00 p.m. to 7:30 a.m.) is typically the most expensive shift to staff due to collective labor agreements and the inconvenient hours. Determining minimum cost staffing levels that provide adequate coverage to meet emergency demand is a strategic problem. In this section we describe a case study to determine appropriate night shift staffing levels at Erasmus Medical Center. The outcomes of the study were successfully implemented.

5.4.1 General Problem Formulation

Covering the night shift is usually accomplished by using in-hospital and on-call nurses. The in-hospital nurses are stationed in the hospital while waiting for emergency cases. The on-call nurses wait at their homes for emergency cases (typically there is a requirement that they can be present in the hospital within a set time of being requested to do so) and are typically cheaper than in-hospital teams. In general, a single nurse can support exactly one case at a time but can complete any number of cases in series until the end of the shift. The decision required in this problem is to determine how many in-hospital and on-call nurses are necessary to meet the demand for emergency cases. Timeliness is of the essence here, as these emergency cases may be very urgent.

When the first emergency case presents for surgery during a night shift, in-house nurses respond. Depending on the hospital policy and the total number of in-house nurses, an on-call nurse may be called in. In other words, some hospitals may wait until 1, 2, ... or all in-house nurses are busy before calling in a nurse from home, while other hospitals may wait until all in-house nurses are busy and an emergency case is present. For each subsequent emergency case, this process is repeated. Note that nurses are available to complete multiple surgeries per night and are available again after completing a surgery. Finally surgeries cannot be preempted. In this subsection we assume the hospital's policy for calling an on-call nurse is fixed, although determining this policy is, in and of itself, an interesting research question.

There are generally two types of emergency cases: those that need to be started immediately and those that can be delayed before being started. The former we refer to as emergent cases and the latter as urgent cases. The acceptable delay, or safety interval, for starting an urgent case varies: "for example a facility may consider it imperative for a patient with a ruptured abdominal aortic aneurysm to be operated on within 30 min of arrival, while a patient with an amputated finger should be operated on within 90 min of arrival, and a patient with a perforated gastric ulcer should be operated on within 3 h of arrival" (Oostrum et al. 2008a).

By incorporating the acceptable delays for urgent cases it is possible to postpone urgent case demand to a later cheaper shift, and/or postpone the case until busy in-house nurses are free. To examine these possibilities in detail, Oostrum et al. (2008a) use a discrete-event simulation and a case study at Erasmus Medical Center Rotterdam (Erasmus MC). To illustrate the benefits of postponing surgeries, the authors compare results with surgery postponements with the approach of Dexter and O'Neill (2001) where surgery postponements are not used. In the following subsection we provide an overview of the results.

5.4.2 General Results

Current practice at Erasmus MC had a team composition of nine in-house nurses and two on-call nurses. Using the approach of Dexter and O'Neill, a team of eight in-house nurses and two on-call nurses was determined to be appropriate. A number of other team compositions were considered, ranging from a total of 11 nurses to a total of six. Each team composition represented a what-if scenario in the simulation model. The simulation model was used to determine the number of surgery cases starting later than required.

To compute the cost of each team composition, observe that—since the number of working hours does not depend on the team composition—we only need to look at the cost of idle staff. Under Dutch law, the costs for nurses who wait during the night shift are 107.5% of the regular hourly daytime wage for in-house nurses, and 106% for nurses on-call. We thus compute the cost of waiting nurses in each team composition as follows:

$$\begin{aligned}\text{Cost of waiting} - (&\text{number of in-housenurses} \times 1.075 \\ &+ \text{number of on-call nurses} \times 1.06) \times \text{hourly wage}\end{aligned}$$

Figure 5.3 displays the cost of waiting and percentage of surgeries starting late for the considered team compositions, where we assumed for simplicity that a regular hour's wage is 1. It shows that current practice of nine in-house and two on-call nurses performs the best. However, the waiting cost can be decreased by approximately 18.5% by switching to a team composition of five in-house and four on-call nurses, at the expense of a 2% increase of late starts.

For policy making, managers can use results like these to see the relative performance cost associated with each staff assignment. The decision autonomy remains with the policy makers and they are left to determine if cheaper staffing levels justify a decrease in performance.

For more extensive results, we refer to Oostrum et al. (2008a), where the authors present the distribution of cases starting later than required, surgical specialty specific results, results for multiple nurse types and an extensive sensitivity analyses. The sensitivity analyses showed that the approach can be generalized for use in other centers.

Oostrum et al. (2008a) report that heavy involvement of clinical staff in this project was essential for the following reasons. Staff assessed the safety intervals for urgent patients to ensure changes did not negatively affect patient's safety. They validated the discrete-event simulation model, and suggested various scenarios for sensitivity analyses. The visualizations provided by the computer simulation aided to convince them of the final conclusions. As a result, despite the negative impact on their salary, the staff accepted the adjustment of the team composition to five in-house and four on-call nurses. For Erasmus MC this intervention resulted in an annual cost saving of 275,000 euro.

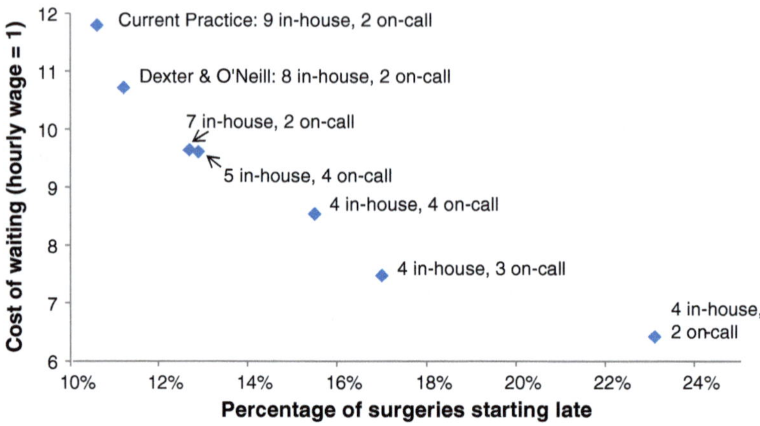

Fig. 5.3 Cost of waiting and late surgery starts for various team compositions

5.5 Strategic: Emergency Operating Theatres or Not?

During regular working hours, most hospitals either perform emergency operations in dedicated emergency OTs, or in regular elective patient OTs. For the second option a certain amount of slack is scheduled in order to fit in emergency cases without causing excessive cancelations of elective cases. The choice to use Policy 1 (reserving capacity in dedicated emergency OTs) or Policy 2 (reserving capacity in multiple regular emergency OTs) is the strategic decision addressed in this section. The difference between these two policies is illustrated graphically in Fig. 5.4.

The flow of patients is summarized as follows: "Emergency patients arriving at a hospital that has adopted the first policy, will be operated immediately if the dedicated OT is empty and will have to queue otherwise, whereas patients arriving at a hospital that has adopted the second policy can be operated once one of the ongoing elective cases has ended. Other planned cases will then be postponed to allow the emergency operation" (Wullink et al. 2007).

Policy 1 has the advantage that the first emergency case of the day can begin without delay, but all following cases may be subject to delay. Furthermore this policy means only the emergency OTs need to be equipped for emergency cases. Finally, as a result of emergency surgeries, elective surgeries will experience no delay (Bhattacharyya et al. 2006; Ferrand et al. 2010) and elective OTs will experience no overtime (Wixted et al. 2008).

Policy 2 cannot guarantee any emergency case will begin without delay, but since emergency cases can be completed in more OTs, an opening (i.e. a case finishing) for the subsequent cases may happen sooner than in Policy 1. The benefits from this policy essentially result from flexibility. To ensure this flexibility (and the corresponding benefits) multiple (or all) of the OTs must be equipped to deal with emergency cases.

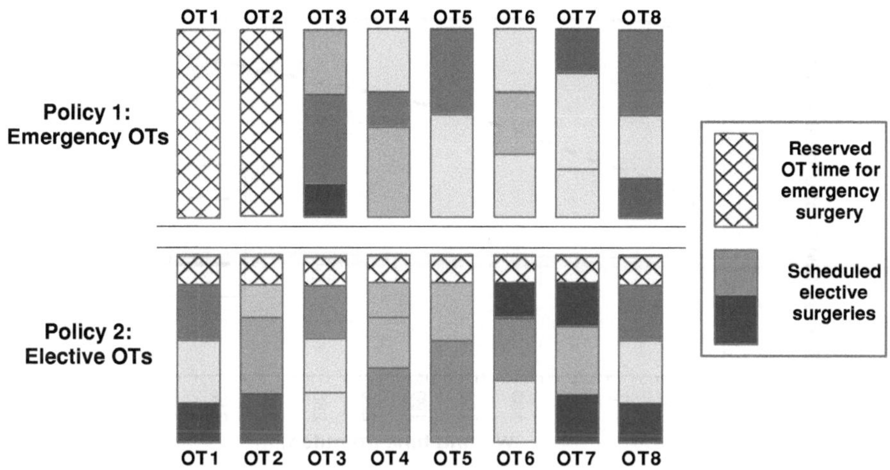

Fig. 5.4 Cost of waiting and late surgery starts for various team compositions

5.5.1 General Problem Description

The decision that is required is to determine how to reserve OT capacity for emergency cases, i.e. according to Policy 1 or Policy 2. There are advantages and disadvantages of both policies introduced above. Due to the stochastic nature of emergency cases (arrivals and surgery durations) choosing the best policy is not immediately obvious. To compare the policies we suggest evaluating the following metrics:

- *emergency surgery waiting time*: the total delay, or the delay past what is allowed to receive emergency surgery.
- *elective surgery waiting time*: the difference between the planned and actual starting time of an elective surgery.
- *OT overtime*: the time used for surgical procedures after the regular block time has ended.
- *OT utilization*: the ratio between the total used operating time for elective procedures and the available regular time.

  The following instance parameters are taken into account: elective surgery volume and duration characteristics, emergency surgery arrival and duration characteristics.

5.5.2 General Results

We summarize a case study (presented in detail in Wullink et al. 2007) where discrete-event simulation was used to prospectively evaluate both policies. The

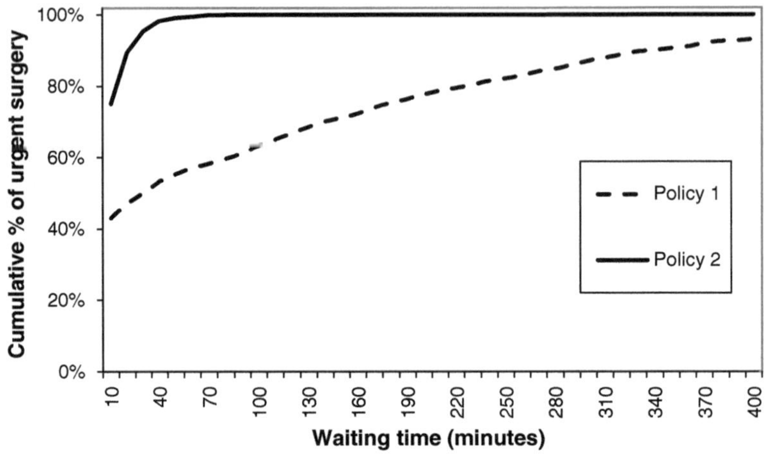

Fig. 5.5 Cumulative percentage of emergency patients in Policy 1 and 2 (simulation results)

Table 5.1 Summary of simulation results for Policy 1 and 2

	Policy 1	Policy 2
Total overtime per day	10.6	8.4
Mean number of OTs with overtime per day	3.6	3.8
Mean emergency patient's waiting time	74 (±4.4)	8 (±0.5)
OT utilization (%)	74	77

case study was used to support decision making at Erasmus MC. When applying Policy 2, the hospital decided that all of their 12 OTs would be equipped to handle emergency cases. In Policy 1, with emergency capacity allocated to 1 dedicated emergency OT, the remaining free OT time is allocated exclusively to elective OTs. In Policy 2, with emergency time allocated to each elective OT, the reserved OT time is distributed evenly over all elective OTs. Figure 5.5 and Table 5.1 summarize the results from the discrete-event simulation.

From Table 5.1 it is clear that Policy 2 outperforms Policy 1 on all given outcomes.

Under Policy 1, all emergency patients were operated on within 7 h with a mean waiting time of 74 (±4.4) min. Under Policy 2, all emergency patients were operated upon within 80 min with a mean waiting time of 8 (± 0.5) min. OT utilization for Policy 1 was 74 and 77% for Policy 2. Policy 1 resulted in 10.6 h of overtime on average per day and Policy 2 resulted in 8.4. Policy 2, with emergency capacity allocated to all elective OTs, thus substantially outperforms Policy 1, on all outcomes measured.

Table 5.2 summarizes the results of additional simulation experiments in which we vary the number of emergency OTs (0, 1, 2 or 3) as well as the number of

Table 5.2 Simulation results: (1) average and (2) maximum emergency surgery waiting time (min), (3) percentage of emergency surgeries that has to wait, (4) average elective surgery waiting time (min)

	Number of emergency OTs			
Elective OTs used for emergency	0	1	2	3
0	–	21.9	2.4	0.5
		3,026	949	292
		4.4%	2.4%	1.1%
		12.6	12.6	12.6
5	1.3	0.6	0.3	0.1
	204.9	152.7	113.1	83.3
	4.5%	2.9%	1.5%	0.7%
	32.3	21.2	14.2	11.4
10	0.5	0.3	0.1	0.1
	94.2	76.3	63.8	50.2
	4.2%	2.6%	1.3%	0.6%
	22.2	16.0	12.1	10.3
15	0.3	0.2	0.1	0.0
	60.3	52.3	43.3	36.0
	4.0%	2.5%	1.2%	0.5%
	18.6	14.9	11.6	10.0

elective OTs used for emergency surgeries (0, 5, 10 or 15). We use the case mix of the previous experiment, but resize the problem to 15 elective OTs (instead of 12). Furthermore, approximately 10% of the surgeries are emergency surgeries. The results show that Policy 2 [dealing with emergencies in (some) elective OTs] results in improved emergency waiting performances, at the expense of increased waiting time of the elective surgeries. A mixed policy combines the advantages of both policies—the table can be used as a guideline to make a trade-off.

5.6 Tactical: Designing a Master Surgical Schedule to Level Ward Usage

Managers are inclined to solve problems at the moment they occur (i.e. on the operational level). In Hans et al. (2011) we refer to this phenomenon as the "real-time hype" of managers. For health care managers, while inundated with operational problems, the universal panacea for all productivity-related problems is "more capacity". It is thereby often overlooked to tactically allocate and reorganize the available resources, which may turn out to be even more effective, and will certainly be cheaper. However, due to its longer (intermediate) planning horizon, tactical planning is less tangible and inherently more abstract than operational planning. In the majority of our health care process optimization research projects we find that the tactical planning level is typically not formalized and overlooked. Tactical planning decisions are rather a result of historical development ("This year's tactical plan is last year's tactical plan"), than a result of periodic planning. We also find they have often evolved to hard constraints for operational planning ("We don't do orthopedic patients on Wednesday afternoons. Why? Well, we just don't!").

This is also typical for the tactical planning of OTs, the block planning or Master Surgical Scheduling (MSS) problem, which concerns the weekly allocation of OT-days to surgical specialties (or surgeons). To a surgeon: "operating theatre 6 on Monday is *her/his* OT". Re-allocating OT-days may however lead to a more stable workload in subsequent departments (wards, ICU), and even reduce the required capacity of these departments. In this section we present a model to analyze and improve the impact of the MSS on the resource usage in subsequent departments.

5.6.1 General Problem Description

Tactical OT planning typically involves the assignment of OT capacity to aggregate patient groups (i.e. patient cohorts) for a fixed planning horizon. This assignment should reflect the strategic goals of the hospital. For example, consider a planning horizon of one month and a hospital with a strategic goal to complete 1,000 orthopedic surgeries over the next six months, then the orthopedic surgical specialty should be assigned enough OT capacity to complete 1000/6 $\approx$ 167 surgeries per month.

The tactical plan is used to organize capacity over an intermediate planning horizon such that long-term goals are met and to create a structure from which operational level planning can be based. In the OT this is usually accomplished with a MSS. The MSS defines which surgical specialties operate on which days during the planning horizon. Such a schedule allows the surgical specialties to plan their other functions, such as outpatient clinics, education, etc. The schedule also allows the OT department to make its own planning decisions, such as how many pieces of equipment are needed each day, what are the staffing levels, when can OT maintenance happen, etc.?

When a MSS is being developed, not all of the details about the planning horizon are known, i.e. which patients will show up, which doctors will be available, etc. What is known is that a certain volume of patients with a certain case mix is expected. Hence the assignment of patient cohorts (not individual patients) to OT time is the primary factor considered when designing a MSS.

A MSS represents a repetitive pattern over a certain number of days (say Q). For each day $q \in \{1, 2, \ldots, Q\}$ in the MSS each of the I available OTs has to be assigned to one of the available surgical specialties. More precisely, the MSS is described by the assignment of a surgical specialty j to each OT block b_{iq}, where

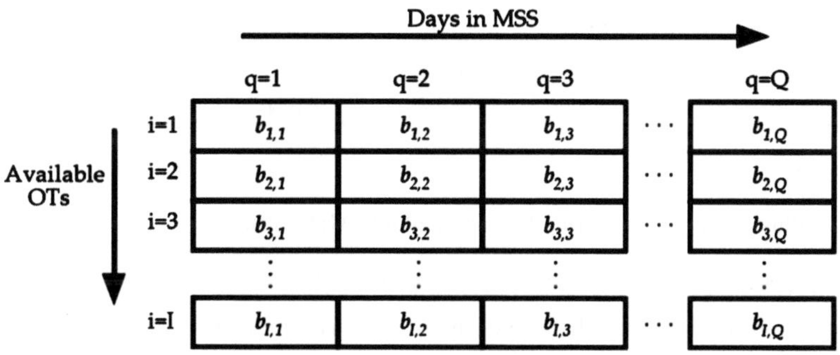

Fig. 5.6 Example empty Master Surgery Schedule (MSS)

$i \in \{1, 2, \ldots, I\}$ and. Using this notation, an empty MSS (i.e. before specialties have been assigned OT blocks) is shown in Fig. 5.6, where each cell represents an OT block. It is common that multiple blocks are assigned to a single specialty on the same day.

The MSS is defined for period Q and executed repeatedly. Let M be the maximum length of stay (LOS) of any patient. Figure 5.7 displays how the multiple MSS cycles repeat and how patients overlap.

In this section we describe a model by Vanberkel et al. (2011a). The objective of the model is to make a cyclical assignment of OT time to patient cohorts for an intermediate term planning horizon, such that strategic "production levels" and performance goals are achieved. We allow for a stochastic LOS and, for a given MSS, compute a number of workload metrics associated with recovering surgical inpatients. This approach does not find the optimal MSS but rather evaluates MSS proposals. Adopting this approach to be used in conjunction with a search heuristic to find the best MSS proposal is of course a natural and very plausible extension.

The aim is to determine the number of patients in recovery as a function of the MSS. We do this by modeling the recovering patient cohorts with binomial distributions. We then add these discrete distributions (with convolutions) to determine the number of patients recovering. Once we know the number of patients recovering, we predict a number of workload metrics including admissions, ongoing inpatient care, discharges and specialized inpatient care.

Consider a single patient who is recovering from surgery and each day has the option of staying or being discharged. From historical data we can compute the probability of being discharged and conversely the probability of staying for each day of the patient's LOS. Now consider a cohort of patients with similar discharge probabilities. From probability theory it is known that when multiple experiments have two (and only two) outcomes, then the probability for the number of experiments resulting in each outcome can be computed with a binomial distribution (assuming experiments are independent and identically distributed). Thus on any day and for each patient cohort, we can compute the number of discharges and consequently we know the number of patients who will remain until

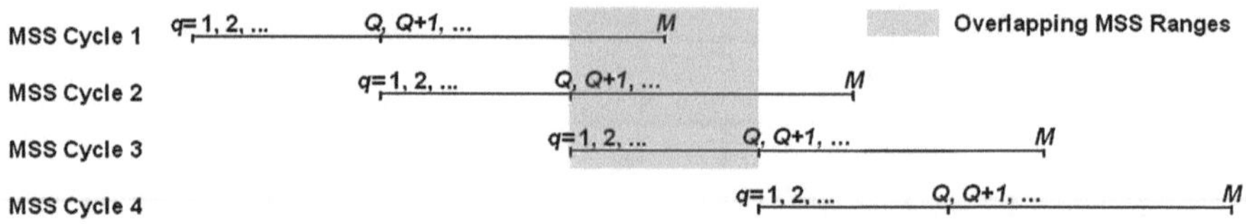

Fig. 5.7 Illustration of the overlap between multiple MSS cycles

tomorrow. For a given MSS and using historic records, we can compute the number of admission to the ward (i.e. the number of completed inpatient surgeries each day) for each patient cohort. Thus for each patient cohort we have a distribution for the admission rate and using a binomial distribution we have a distribution for the discharge rate and we can easily compute the ward occupancy distribution. Finally, using discrete convolutions we can compute the overall ward occupancy. The formal model description follows.

Assume that each surgical specialty represents a single patient cohort. Let the MSS be defined such that b_{iq} is an OT block where $i \in \{1, 2, \ldots, I\}$ indexes the OTs and $q \in \{1, 2, \ldots, Q\}$ the days in a cycle. Let each surgical specialty j be characterized by two parameters c^j and d_n^j, where c^j is a discrete distribution for the number of surgeries carried out in one OT block and d_n^j the probability that a patient, who is still in the ward on day n, is to be discharged that day ($n = 0, 1, \ldots, L^j$, where L^j denotes the maximum LOS for specialty j).

Using c^j and d_n^j as model inputs, for a given MSS the probability distribution for the number of recovering patients on each day q can be computed. The required number of beds is computed with the following three steps. *Step 1* computes the distribution of recovering patients from a single OT block of a specialty j; i.e. we essentially pre-calculate the distribution of recovering patients expected from an OT block of a specialty. In *Step 2*, we consider a given MSS and use the result from *Step 1* to compute the distribution of recovering patients given a single cycle of the MSS. Finally in *Step 3* we incorporate recurring MSSs and compute the probability distribution of recovering patients on each day q.

Step 1. For each specialty j we use the binomial distribution to compute the number of beds required from the day of surgery $n = 1$ until $n = L^j$. Since we know the probability distribution for the number of patients having surgery (c_j), which equates to the number of beds needed on day $n = 0$, we can use the binomial distribution to iteratively compute the probability of needing beds on all days $n > 0$. Formally, the distribution for the number of recovering patients on day n is recursively computed by:

$$h_n^j(x) = \begin{cases} c^j(x) & \text{when } n = 0 \\ \sum_{k=x}^{c^j} \binom{k}{x} (d_{n-1}^j)^{k-x} (1 - d_{n-1}^j)^x h_{n-1}^j(k) & \text{otherwise} \end{cases}.$$

Step 2. We calculate for each OT block b_{iq} the impact this OT block has on the number of recovering patients in the hospital on days q, $q + 1$, ... If j denotes the specialty assigned to OT block b_{iq}, then let $\bar{h}_m^{i,q}$ be the distribution for the number of recovering patients of OT block b_{iq} on day $m = 1, 2, \ldots, Q, Q + 1, \ldots$ It follows that:

$$\bar{h}_m^{i,q} = \begin{cases} h_{m-q}^j & \text{if} \quad q \leq m < L^j + q \\ \mathbf{0} & \text{otherwise} \end{cases}$$

where 0 means $\bar{h}_m^{i,q}(0) = 1$. Let H_m be a discrete distribution for the total number of recovering patients on day m resulting from a single MSS cycle. Since recovering patients do not interfere with each other we can simply iteratively add the distributions of all the OT blocks corresponding to the day m to get H_m. Adding two independent discrete distributions is done by discrete convolutions which we indicated by " $*$ ". For example, let A and B be two independent discrete distributions. Then $C = A * B$, which is computed by:

$$C(x) = \sum_{k=0}^{\tau} A(k)B(x - k)$$

where τ is equal to the largest x value with a positive probability that can result from $A * B$ (e.g. if the maximum value of A is 3 and the maximum value of B is 4, then when convoluted the maximum value of the resulting distribution is 7, therefore in this example $\tau = 7$). Using this notation, H_m is computed by:

$$H_m(x) = \bar{h}_m^{1,1} * \bar{h}_m^{1,2} * \cdots * \bar{h}_m^{1,Q} * \bar{h}_m^{2,1} * \cdots * \bar{h}_m^{I,Q}$$

Step 3. We now consider a series of MSSs to compute the steady-state probability distribution of recovering patients. The cyclic structure of the MSS implies that patients receiving surgery during one cycle may overlap with patients from the next cycle. In the case of a small Q patients from many different cycles may overlap.

In Step 2 we have computed H_m for a single MSS in isolation. Let M be the last day where there is still a positive probability that a recovering patient is present in H_m. To calculate the overall distribution of recovering patients when the MSS is repeatedly executed we must take into account $\lceil M/Q \rceil$ consecutive MSSs. Let H_q^{SS} denote the probability distribution of recovering patients on day q of the MSS cycle, resulting from the consecutive MSSs. Since the MSS does not change from cycle to cycle, H_q^{SS} is the same for all MSS cycles. Such a result, where the probabilities of various states remain constant over time, is referred to as a steady-state result. Using discrete convolutions, H_q^{SS} is computed by:

$$H_q^{SS}(x) = H_q * H_{q+Q} * H_{q+2Q} * \cdots * H_{q+\lceil M/Q \rceil Q}$$

From this result a number of workload metrics can be derived. To determine the demand for ward beds from the variable H_q^{SS} consider the following example. Let the staffing policy of the hospital be such that they staff for the 90th percentile of demand and let D_q denote the ninetieth percentile of demand on day q. It follows that D_q is also the number of staffed beds needed on day q, and is computed from H_q^{SS} as follows:

$$D_q = \max\left\{x | H_q^{SS}(x) \leq 0.9\right\}$$

In practice, patients tend to be segregated into different wards depending on the type of surgery they received. To incorporate this segregation into the model and to consequently have recovering patient distributions for each ward, a minor modification needs to be made to the model. Let W_k be the set of specialties j whose patients are admitted to ward k. Then in Step 2 we only have to consider those OT blocks assigned to a specialty in W_k and continue with the calculations.

Ward occupancy alone does not fully account for the workload associated with care for recovering patients. During patient admissions and discharges the nursing workload can increase. From the model the probability distribution for daily admissions and discharges can be computed. To compute the admission rate, set $d_1^j = 1$ for all j and repeat the steps above. The resulting H_q^{SS} will denote the admissions on day q.

The discharge rate is the rate at which patients leave the ward and can be computed by adding an additional calculation in Step 1. Let D_n^j be a discrete distribution for the number of discharges from specialty j on day n which is computed as follows:

$$\mathbb{P}\left(D_n^j = x\right) = \sum_{k=x}^{C^j} \binom{k}{x} \left(d_n^j\right)^x \left(1 - d_n^j\right)^{k-x} \mathbb{P}\left(h_n^j = k\right)$$

Finally, after computing D_n^j, one can set $h_n^j = D_n^j$ and continue with Step 2. By doing so, the resulting H_q^{SS} will denote the distribution for daily discharges for each day q of the MSS.

The inherent assumption of the described method is that all patients with a patient cohort have equal probability of being discharged and that it is independent of other patients, i.e. it is assumed that patients are identically distributed and independent. The independence assumption implies that the amount of time one patient is in the hospital does not influence the amount of time another patient is in the hospital. This seems like a natural assumption in most cases and appropriate so long as surgeries are rarely canceled due to a bed shortage (cancelations due to bed shortages create a dependency). The identically distributed requirement means that we must compute the number of beds needed tomorrow (and the number of case completed in one OT block), for all identically distributed cohorts of patients separately. In other words, the parameters of the binomial distribution must reflect all of the patients in a given cohort.

5.6.2 General Results

The model was applied at the Netherlands Cancer Institute—Antoni van Leeuwenhoek Hospital (NKI-AVL)—to support the design of a new MSS. Selected results from Vanberkel et al. (2011b) are summarized in this subsection.

Management at NKI-AVL strives to staff enough beds such that for 90% of the week days there is sufficient coverage. This implies that on 10% of the days they will be required to call in additional staff. Using the model a number of MSS proposals were evaluated and eventually staff chooses an MSS that the model predicted would lead to a balanced ward occupancy.

An unbalanced ward occupancy makes staff scheduling, and ward operations, difficult. Early in the week, beds would be underutilized whereas later in the week, beds would become highly utilized and the risk of a shortage would increase. Such peaks and valleys represent variation in the system which possibly could be eliminated with a different MSS. This variation leads to significant problems, particularly as the wards approach peak capacity. For example, when inpatient wards reach their peak capacity and a patient admission is pending, staff often scrambles to try and make a bed available. If one cannot be made available, additional staff is called in (or in rare cases when additional staff cannot be found, the elective surgery is canceled), which causes extra work for OR planners, wasted time for surgeons and extra anxiety for patients. When a bed was made available, it often means a patient was transferred from one ward to another (often to a ward capable of caring for the patient but not the designated one) or discharged. Either way, extra work is required by ward staff and there is a disruption in patient care. Although completely eliminating such problems is likely not possible without an exorbitant amount of resources, sound planning ahead of time may help to minimize occurrences.

After implementing the new MSS, the ward occupancy was observed over a 33-week period. From these observations, probability distributions of beds used for each day of the MSS cycle were derived. Using Chi-square goodness-of-fit tests, these observed distributions were compared to those projected by the model. Six of the seven projected distributions (one for each day of the MSS cycle) were found to be a good fit for the observed data at a level $\alpha = 0.05$, while for the seventh day, this was true at a level $\alpha = 0.2$. Figure 5.8 compares the projected ward occupancy with the observed ward occupancy during the 33-week period.

5.6.3 Discussion

The main benefit of using the model was to be able to quantify the concerns of ward staff, thereby providing a platform from which they could begin to negotiate a solution. Staff was quick to embrace the model output, particularly after seeing several modifications to the original MSS, at which point they were able to roughly predict model output for a given modification.

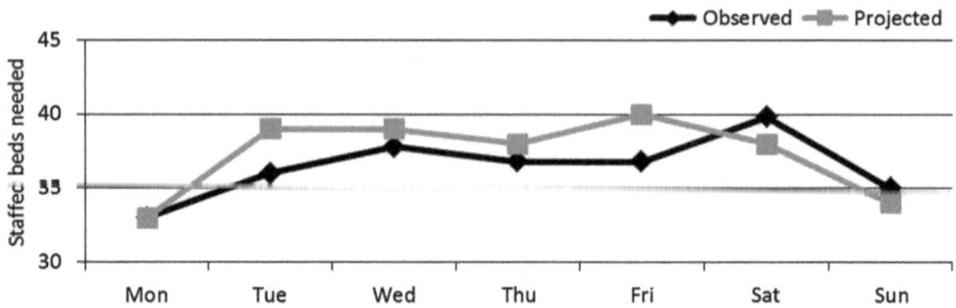

Fig. 5.8 Comparison of the projected and observed (90th percentile) ward occupancies

In this project we treated the equipment and physician schedule restrictions as unchangeable. It is possible that further improvements in the ward occupancy could have been achieved if these restrictions were relaxed. In this way the model can be used to illustrate the benefits of buying an extra piece of equipment or of changing physicians' schedules. An additional restriction, which if relaxed may have allowed further improvements, is the assignment of wards to surgical specialties. In other words, in addition to changing when a specialty operates, it may prove advantageous to change which ward the patients are admitted to after surgery. Finally, we chose the best MSS from those created through swapping OR block and surgical specialty assignments. It is possible that a search heuristic may have found a better MSS, although it would have required the many surgical department restrictions to be modeled and the more complex model may not have garnered the same level of staff understanding and support.

Oostrum et al. (2008b) propose another approach, where the MSS is planned in more detail: here it comprises a cyclical schedule of frequently occurring elective surgery *types*. The resulting combinatorial optimization problem is to determine a MSS that balances OT utilization and ward occupancy. By scheduling surgery types, the surgeon/surgical specialty can assign a patient's name at a later time, without affecting the performance of the MSS. The model considers stochastic OT capacity constraints and empirical LOS distributions. As the resulting problem is NP-hard, heuristics are provided. For a review on the suitability and managerial implication of this particular MSS approach see Oostrum et al. (2010).

5.7 Operational: Elective Surgery Scheduling and Sequencing

Operational planning and scheduling of operating theatres is arguably one of the most popular topics in the health care OR literature. The literature reviews of Cardoen et al. (2010a) and Guerriero and Guido (2011) outline many contributions regarding the elective surgery scheduling and sequencing literature. Cardoen et al. (2010b) also propose a classification scheme for OT planning and scheduling problems, which contains four descriptive fields $\langle\alpha|\beta|\gamma|\delta\rangle$. Here, α holds the patient characteristics, β the delineation of the decision, γ the extent to which uncertainty is incorporated and δ the performance measures.

In previous work (Hans et al. 2008) we demonstrated that by combining advanced optimization techniques with extensive historical statistical records on surgery durations, the OT department utilization can be improved significantly. We demonstrated that, if slack time is reserved in OTs according to the method described in Sect. 5.3.1 (particularly Eq. 5.6, the portfolio effect can be exploited in a local search meta-heuristic as follows. By swapping surgeries between OTs (1 swap or 2 swap), the total slack time of both involved OTs is affected. By clustering surgeries with similar duration variability characteristics, the total slack time is reduced due to the portfolio effect. This principle can be used in a local search heuristic to minimize the total slack time, and thus free OT time. A result of the portfolio optimization is that the fragmentation of the free OT time is minimized. In fact, OTs in resulting solutions are either filled to a great extent with surgery and slack time, or are empty. As a result, OTs can be closed, or time is freed to perform more surgeries.

In this section we discuss the optimization of the elective surgery schedule, in order to minimize emergency surgery waiting time. This problem follows from Policy 2 outlined in Sect. 5.5 (i.e. emergency surgeries are dealt with in elective OTs).

5.7.1 General Problem Description

Emergency surgery waiting time increases a patient's risk of postoperative complications and morbidity. When dealing with emergency patients according to Policy 2 (Sect. 5.5), waiting time will occur when all elective OTs are busy. Typically, at the beginning of the regular working day, all OTs will be busy with long procedures, as surgeries are often scheduled according to the longest processing time rule. As a result, emergency surgeries that arrive just after the start of the elective program may have to wait a long time, as surgeries cannot be preempted. This pleads for scheduling a short surgery at the beginning of the day, to obtain a so called "Break-in-Moment" (BIM), at an early time for emergency surgeries. Extending on this idea, we may sequence the elective surgeries within their assigned OTs in such a way, that their expected completion times, which are BIMs for emergency surgery, are spread as evenly as possible. We do not re-assign surgeries to other OTs, but instead only re-sequence elective surgeries within their assigned OT. This is illustrated in Fig. 5.9: the BIMs are clearly spread more evenly after re-sequencing the surgeries.

The problem of sequencing elective surgeries in such a way that the BIMs are spread as evenly as possible (or, alternatively, the break-in-intervals/BIIs are minimized) is in fact a new type of scheduling problem. This innovative idea was a result of a MSc thesis project at Erasmus MC (Lans et al. 2006), where it was proven that the problem is NP-hard by reduction from three-partition.

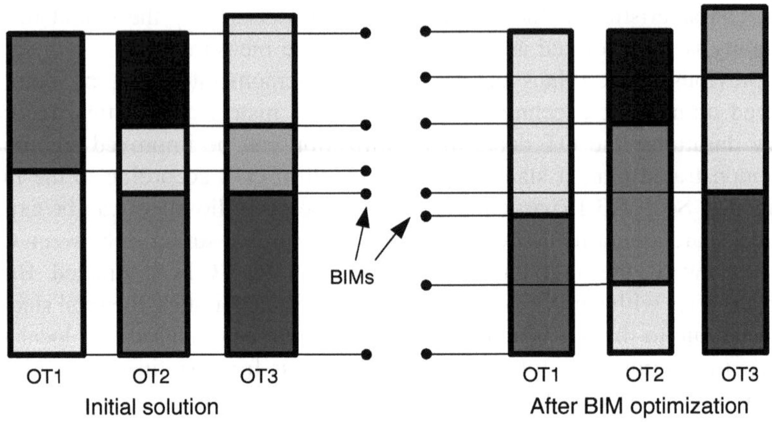

Fig. 5.9 Example BIM optimization

We assume, as illustrated in Fig. 5.9, that surgeries are executed directly after another, i.e. there is no planned slack between surgeries. The planning horizon is within a day, and starts on the first moment when all OTs are scheduled to have elective surgeries. If all OTs start at the same time, then this time marks the start of the planning horizon. It ends on the first moment when there is an OT without a scheduled surgery, since after this moment there are infinitely many BIMs. The objective is to lexicographically minimize the largest break-in-intervals (BIIs). In other words, we minimize the largest BII, then the second largest (without affecting the largest), etc. The reason that we do not only minimize the largest BII is that the expected duration of the shortest surgery is a lower bound to the longest BII. This can be seen as follows: assuming all OTs start at the same time, placing the shortest surgery at the beginning of its OT gives a BII that cannot be shortened.

In forthcoming work we will propose various exact and heuristic approaches for the BIM/BII optimization problem. Here we give the results of a Simulated Annealing (SA) local search heuristic, which iteratively swaps surgeries within their sequence. The SA method uses the following parameters: start temperature 0.2, final temperature 0.0001, Markov chain length 150, decrease factor 0.8. We fix the shortest surgery at the beginning of its OT.

5.7.2 General Results

We generate instances with the case mix of Sect. 5.5 (academic hospital Erasmus MC), scaled to fill 4, 8 or 12 OTs. Surgeries are scheduled "First Fit" (Hans et al. 2008). First Fit assigns surgeries from the top of the list to the first available OT plus an amount of slack (Sect. 5.3.1, Eq. 5.6) to achieve a 30% probability of overtime caused by surgery duration variability, until no surgery can be found

Table 5.3 Average frequency of break-in-interval size (initial solution→SA solution; 260 instances per parameter setting)

No. of OTs	Reduced flexibility	>90 min	>75 min	>60 min	>45 min	>30 min	>15 min
4	No	1.01→0.29	1.51→0.67	2.01→1.50	2.72→2.84	4.09→5.52	5.51→7.11
		−71.3%	−55.6%	−25.4%	4.4%	35%	29%
4	Yes	1.01→0.30	1.51→0.74	2.00→1.59	2.72→2.85	4.10→5.47	5.55→7.01
		−70.3%	−51%	−20.5%	4.8%	33.4%	26.3%
8	No	0.48→0.00	0.82→0.01	1.21→0.09	1.97→0.46	3.84→3.75	6.89→10.22
		−100%	−98.8%	−92.6%	−76.6%	−2.3%	48.3%
8	Yes	0.47→0.00	0.82→0.02	1.23→0.11	1.94→0.56	3.82→3.91	6.88→10.02
		−100%	−97.6%	−91.1%	−71.1%	2.4%	45.6%
12	No	0.33→0.00	0.69→0.00	0.95→0.02	1.47→0.11	3.14→1.35	6.97→10.49
		−100%	−100%	−97.9%	−92.5%	−57%	50.5%
12	Yes	0.36→0.00	0.70→0.00	0.95→0.02	1.46→0.13	3.15→1.58	6.92→10.26
		−100%	−100%	−97.9%	−91.1%	−49.8%	48.3%

anymore that fits in the remaining OT capacity. Each instance has two variants: with *full* flexibility (all surgery sequences are allowed), and with *reduced* flexibility (randomly, $\frac{1}{12}$th of the first surgeries are fixed on this position in their OT, and $\frac{1}{12}$th of the last surgeries are fixed on this position in their OT). For example, surgeries on children are typically done first, and surgeries after which extensive OT cleaning is required are typically done last.

Table 5.3 presents the results for the SA algorithm. It compares the solutions found by SA to the initial First Fit solution (which does not aim to optimize BIM/BIIs). Particularly, it shows the frequency of the BIIs of size >15, >30, …, >90 min. Each number is an average over 260 instances (52 weeks of 5 working days). SA solves each instance in less than 2 s. Clearly, the large intervals are eliminated to a great extent, the more so when there are more OTs (and thus more BIMs).

The question now is what impact these optimized BIMs/BIIs have on emergency surgery waiting time, particularly given the fact that elective surgery durations are stochastic, and the BIMs are *expected* surgery completion times. Table 5.4 presents the results of a Monte Carlo simulation of 260 instances with 12 OTs and *reduced* sequencing flexibility. The elective surgeries are assumed to have a lognormal distribution. The emergency surgeries arrive according to a Poisson process (on average 5.1 arrivals/day), and are served on a FCFS basis. Elective surgeries are not preempted.

We observe that the BIM/BII optimization by SA, despite the reduced flexibility, has a significant impact on emergency surgery waiting. For example, the relative number of first emergency patients who wait at most 10 min increases by 69% from 28.8 to 48.6%. The improvement decreases with every next arriving emergency patient of the day. This may be expected, as these emergency patients increasingly distort the original schedule.

Table 5.4 Waiting time for the first, second and third arriving emergency patients (12 OTs, run length 780 days, maximum relative error 10%, minimum confidence level 90%)

Waiting time (min)	First emergency surgery		Second emergency surgery		Third emergency surgery	
	Initial solution (%)	SA solution (%)	Initial solution (%)	SA solution (%)	Initial solution (%)	SA solution (%)
<10	28.8	48.6	34.9	44.9	40.4	46.2
<20	53.0	75.8	56.9	73.6	63.0	69.8
<30	70.5	90.9	71.8	87.2	76.3	86.7

5.7.3 Discussion

BIM/BII optimization has a big impact on emergency surgery waiting. More research is required into exact solution approaches, and perhaps applications of BII/BIM optimization in other sectors. For health care, it is easy to implement: it only requires re-sequencing of elective surgeries. As a first step, managers are advised to plan the shortest surgery at the beginning of the regular working day.

5.8 Future Directions

The OT department offers challenging planning and control problems on all hierarchical levels of control. While operational planning and control has received a lot of attention from the OR/OM in health care research community, tactical planning is less exposed, and research has had less of an impact in practice due to its inherent complexity. In our experience, decision support software tools mostly focus on the operational planning level, whereas tools for the tactical planning level are scarce and are too simplified or limited in scope to deal with tactical decision making. Future research therefore has to focus on the tactical level, to a greater extent. This raises opportunities to expand the scope beyond the OT department. From our survey of health care models that encompass multiple departments we concluded that researchers often model hospitals in a way that reflects the limited/departmental view of health care managers (Vanberkel et al. 2010). The research scope should particularly include the polyclinics, where new patients are taken in, and the wards, which are typically managed to follow the OT department but whose workloads may be leveled significantly by tactically optimizing the OT's master surgery schedule. Ultimately, we should aim to optimize the entire patient care pathway.

Acknowledgments The hospitals Erasmus MC and Netherlands Cancer Institute, and all co-authors involved in the various research projects described here: Boucherie RJ, Harten WH van,

Houdenhoven M van, Hulshof PJH, Hurink JL, Kazemier G, Lans M van der, Lent WAM van, Oostrum JM van, Wullink G.

References

Anthony RN (1965) Planning and control systems: a framework for analysis. Harvard Business School Division of Research, Boston

Bhattacharyya T, Vrahas MS, Morrison SM, Kim E, Wiklund RA, Smith RM, Rubash HE (2006) The Value of the dedicated orthopaedic trauma operating room. J Trauma 60:1336–1341

Blake JT, Donald J (2002) Using integer programming to allocate operating room time at Mount Sinai Hospital. Interfaces 32(2):63–73

Brailsford SC, Harper PR, Patel B, Pitt M (2009) An analysis of the academic literature on simulation and modelling in health care. J Simul 3:130–140

Cardoen B, Demeulemeester E, Beliën J (2010a) Operating room planning and scheduling: a literature review. Eur J Oper Res 201:921–932

Cardoen B, Demeulemeester E, Beliën J (2010b) Operating room planning and scheduling problems: a classification scheme. Int J Health Manag Inf 1(1):71–83

Denton BT, Viapiano J, Vogl A (2007) Stochastic optimization of surgery sequencing and start time scheduling decisions. Health Care Manag Sci 10(1):13–24

Denton BT, Miller A, Balasubramanian H, Huschka T (2010) Optimal allocation of surgery blocks to operating rooms under uncertainty. Oper Res 58(4):802–816

Dexter F (2011) Website: http://www.franklindexter.com/bibliography_TOC.htm

Dexter F, O'Neill L (2001) Weekend operating room on-call staffing requirements. AORN J 74:666–671

Dexter F, Macario A, Traub RD (1999) Which algorithm for scheduling add-on elective cases maximizes operating room utilization? Anesthesiology 91:1491–1500

Dexter F, Epstein RH, Traub RD, Xiao Y (2004) Making management decisions on the day of surgery based on operating room efficiency and patient waiting times. Anesthesiology 101:1444–1453

Ferrand Y, Magazine M, Rao U (2010) Comparing two operating-room-allocation policies for elective and emergency surgeries. In: Johansson B, Jain S, Montoya-Torres J, Hugan J, Yücesan E (eds) Proceedings of the 2010 winter simulation conference

Guerriero F, Guido R (2011) Operational research in the management of the operating theatre: a survey. Health Care Manag Sci 14:89–114

Hall R (2006) Patient flow: reducing delay in health care delivery. Springer, New York

Hans EW, Wullink G, Houdenhoven M, van Kazemier G (2008) Robust surgery loading. Eur J Oper Res 185:1038–1050

Hans EW, van Houdenhoven M, Hulshof PJH (2011) A framework for health care planning and control. Memorandum 1938, Department of Applied Mathematics, University of Twente, Enschede

Harper PR, Shahani AK (2002) Modelling for the planning and management of bed capacities in hospitals. J Oper Res Soc 53(1):11–18

HFMA (2005) Achieving operating room efficiency through process integration. Technical report. Health Care Financial Management Association

McIntosh C, Dexter F, Epstein RH (2006) The impact of service specific staffing, case scheduling, turnovers, and first-case starts on anesthesia group and operating room productivity: a tutorial using data from an Australian hospital. Anesth Analg 103:1499–1516

van der Lans M, Hans EW, Hurink JL, Wullink G (2006) Anticipating urgent surgery in operating room departments. BETA working paper WP-158, ISSN: 1386–9213, University of Twente

van Houdenhoven M, Hans EW, Klein J, Wullink G, Kazemier G (2007) A norm utilisation for scarce hospital resources: evidence from operating rooms in a Dutch university hospital. J Med Syst 31(4):231–236 van Oostrum JM, van Houdenhoven M, Vrielink MMJ, Klein J, Hans EW, Klimek M, Wullink G, Steyerberg EW, Kazemier G (2008a) A simulation model for determining the optimal size of emergency teams on call in the operating room at night. Anesth Analg 107:1655–1662

van Oostrum JM, van Houdenhoven M, Hurink JL, Hans EW, Wullink G, Kazemier G (2008b) A master surgical scheduling approach for cyclic scheduling in operating room departments. OR Spectr 30(2):355–374

van Oostrum JM, Bredenhoff E, Hans EW (2010) Suitability and managerial implications of a master surgical scheduling approach. Ann Oper Res 178(1):91–104

Vanberkel PT, Blake JT (2007) A comprehensive simulation for wait time reduction and capacity planning applied in general surgery. In: Anderson JG, van Merode GG (eds) Special issue on Simulation in Health Care. Health Care Manag Sci 10(4):373–385

Vanberkel PT, Boucherie RJ, Hans EW, Hurink JL, Litvak N (2010) A survey of health care models that encompass multiple departments. Int J Health Manag Inform 1(1):37–69

Vanberkel PT, Boucherie RJ, Hans EW, Hurink JL, van Lent WAM, van Harten WH (2011a) An exact approach for relating recovering surgical patient workload to the master surgical schedule. J Oper Res Soc (forthcoming)

Vanberkel PT, Boucherie RJ, Hans EW, Hurink JL, van Lent WAM, van Harten WH (2011b) Accounting for Inpatient Wards when developing master surgical schedules. Anesth Analg (forthcoming)

Vissers JMH, Bertrand JWM, De Vries G (2001) A framework for production control in health care organizations. Prod Plan Control 12:591–604

Wachtel RE, Dexter F (2008) Tactical increases in operating room block time for capacity planning should not be based on utilization. Anesth Analg 106(1):215–222

Wixted JJ, Reed M, Eskander MS, Millar B, Anderson RC, Bagchi K, Kaur S, Franklin P, Leclair W (2008) The effect of an orthopedic trauma room on after-hours surgery at a level one trauma center. J Orthop Trauma 22(4):234–236

Wullink G, Houdenhoven M, van Hans EW, Oostrum JM, van der Lans M, Kazemier G (2007) Closing emergency operating rooms improves efficiency. J Med Syst 31(6):543–546

Zijm WHM (2000) Towards intelligent manufacturing planning and control systems. OR Spectr 22(3):313–345

Chapter 6
Appointment Planning and Scheduling in Outpatient Procedure Centers

Bjorn Berg and Brian T. Denton

Abstract This chapter provides a summary of the planning and scheduling decisions for outpatient procedure centers. A summary and background of outpatient procedure centers and their operations is provided along with the challenges faced by managers. Planning and scheduling decisions are discussed and categorized as either long-or short-term decisions. Examples and results are drawn from the literature along with important factors that influence planning and scheduling decisions. A summary of open challenges for the operations research community is presented.

6.1 Introduction

Outpatient procedure centers (OPCs), also known as ambulatory surgery centers (ASCs), are a growing trend for providing specialty health care procedures (surgical or non-surgical) in the U.S. From 1996 to 2006, the rate of visits to OPCs in the U.S. increased by 300% while the rate of similar visits to surgery centers in a hospital setting remained constant (Cullen et al. 2009). The increase in OPC visit frequency is in part due to the patient benefits for surgery in an OPC including lower costs, appointment systems that are often more amenable to patient

---

B. Berg (✉) · B. T. Denton
Edward P. Fitts Department of Industrial and Systems Engineering,
North Carolina State University, Raleigh, NC 27695, USA
e-mail: bpberg@ncsu.edu

B. T. Denton
e-mail: bdenton@ncsu.edu

R. Hall (ed.), *Handbook of Healthcare System Scheduling*,
International Series in Operations Research & Management Science 168,
DOI: 10.1007/978-1-4614-1734-7_6,

preferences, the ability to recover at home, lower complication rates, lower infection rates, and shorter procedure durations.

Many procedures previously required resources only available in hospital settings; however, advances in medical care and technology have made it possible to provide these services through minimal (or non) invasive procedures that can be provided at low risk in outpatient settings. Such procedures often use methods such as laparoscopy, endoscopy, or laser surgery. The improvement and simplification of the care process that results from these advances translates into lower costs and the expectation to see more patients in these environments. As a result OPCs are often associated with higher profit, for certain types of procedures, and high daily patient throughput.

The differences in the OPC and hospital settings create challenges for OPCs. Patient appointment scheduling, staff scheduling, allocation of equipment and resources, and decisions about how to interface with the rest of the health care system each have their own nuances in an OPC setting. OPCs operate for a fixed period (e.g. 8 A.M.–5 P.M.) typically Monday to Friday. Since most of the procedures done in OPCs are elective in nature, OPC managers are presented with more opportunity than hospital-based practices to decide and influence how to allocate their patient demand. Improving advanced planning and daily appointment scheduling systems can play an influential role in an OPC's efficiency and utilization. However, in order to optimally plan and design patient schedules there are many factors to consider including staff and resource levels, pre and post procedure processes, and patient characteristics such as case mix, no-shows, and short notice add-on patients.

From an operations management perspective there are many criteria used to evaluate the performance of OPCs. Patient waiting time, staff and resource utilization, patient throughput, and overtime costs are all important criteria related to the cost and quality of care provided. However, making decisions based on these criteria can be complicated because some criteria, such as patient waiting and resource utilization, are competing. In other words, changes that positively affect one often negatively affect the other. Furthermore, there are many stakeholders, such as patients, nurses, providers (surgeons, physician specialists), and administrators, with varying prospectives about the importance of each criterion.

In this chapter we provide an overview of patient planning and scheduling in OPCs. We also discuss issues that influence these types of decisions including procedure and recovery duration uncertainty, availability of staff and physical resources, common bottlenecks, demand uncertainty, and patient behavior. We give special attention to the unique challenges for OPC managers and how they relate to patient planning and scheduling.

The remainder of this chapter is organized as follows. In the following section we provide a general background on OPC operations. In Sect. 6.3 we describe some of the challenges faced in making long-term planning and short-term scheduling decisions. We discuss several specific types of decisions and provide two examples based on a real outpatient procedure center. In Sect. 6.4 we discuss the factors that affect OPC planning and scheduling decisions. Where relevant, we provide a review of the literature on methods that have been used to address these factors. Finally, we conclude by discussing some future research opportunities.

6.2 Background

OPCs are also known by various terminologies including ambulatory surgery centers, ambulatory procedure centers, outpatient surgery centers, and same day surgery centers. While the terms surgery and procedure are used interchangeably in these references, the health care services provided in these settings are generally classified as requiring more specialized care than can be provided in an office visit, but less intensive than the care provided in a hospital setting.

Procedures most commonly provided in OPCs include endoscopies of both the large and small intestines for colorectal cancer screening, lens extraction and insertion for cataract care, and administration of pain management agents into the spinal canal (Cullen et al. 2009). Other common procedures include certain orthopedic procedures, urological procedures, tonsillectomies, gallbladder removal, and various cosmetic surgeries. The wide spectrum of services now offered at OPCs means that many patients are candidates. However, requirements are generally more strict concerning the health state of the patient due to the lack of supporting care for emergencies that are otherwise available in a hospital.

Some OPCs specialize in a specific type of procedure, such as endoscopy suites where the facility is equipped and staffed to provide various endoscopic procedures such as colonoscopies or esophagogastroduodenoscopies (EGDs), while other OPCs are shared by providers from a variety of specialties. Other health care service settings that are not commonly classified as OPCs but have many similarities in how care is provided include catheterization labs, chemotherapy infusion centers, and various diagnostic settings such as those for CT scans. While OPCs are not directly part of a hospital, many are affiliated with a local hospital. As a result it is often necessary to coordinate planning and scheduling decisions for staff with other commitments. For example, some providers may work certain days at an OPC and other days at the affiliated hospital.

OPCs have multiple stages of care, each involving many individual activities. The stages for a patient can be aggregated into intake, procedure, and recovery. The resources most commonly associated with each stage of a typical OPC are listed in Table 6.1. In the intake stage the patient first checks in to the OPC. Next, they are called back to change into a procedure gown, physiological information is recorded, and the patient's proper preparation (e.g. fasting) is ensured. The patient may also consult with the provider (e.g. surgeon, endoscopist, or other type of proceduralist depending on the type of OPC) or nurse at this stage of the process. The procedure begins once a procedure room is available, the patient is ready, and the necessary staff and physical resources are available. Certain procedures may require support staff such as nurses or technicians who are responsible for specialty equipment such as diagnostic imaging devices. OPCs affiliated with academic

Table 6.1 The resources at each stage of a typical outpatient procedure center

	Intake	Procedure	Recovery
Resources	• Check-in Staff	• Providers • Nurses • Procedure Rooms • Anesthesiologists	• Nurses
	• Nurses	• Support Staff	• Recovery Beds
	• Intake Beds	• Procedure Specific Equipment (e.g. endoscope, arthroscope, laproscope)	

teaching hospitals may have medical fellows assisting in the procedure. Following the procedure, the patient proceeds to recovery where they recover from any anesthetic and await a follow-up consultation with the provider prior to being discharged.

The provider and staff may continue with the next procedure where the previous patient recovers depending on resource availability and other activities. The start time of the next procedure is dependent on many factors. First, the procedure room must be *turned over* following each procedure. During turn over material resources are restocked, equipment is sterilized, and the room is prepared for the next procedure. In between procedures the provider's activities may include consulting with other patients, dictating notes from previous procedures, or other administrative activities.

Figure 6.1 illustrates the typical activities a patient may go through on the day of their procedure. Many of these activities are brief in duration, but they often require multiple resources (e.g. nurse, provider, recovery bed, procedure room). High resource dependency combined with uncertainty in activity durations, and the high volume of patients each day, make coordinating the entire process challenging. Uncertainty arises from a number of sources including uncertainty in procedure and recovery durations, no-shows, short notice add-on patients, patient punctuality, staff availability, and patients requiring additional resources such as an interpreter. Challenges also arise due to the need to coordinate all of the activities for many patients (often 30 or more) within a fixed period of time (e.g. 8 A.M –5 P.M). If the completion of procedures runs beyond the planned closing time then overtime costs result.

There are many opportunities for bottlenecks in the patient flow process. Common bottlenecks include procedure rooms, recovery beds, providers and their teams, anesthesiologists, and equipment that needs to be sterilized between each procedure. Because the OPC operates on a daily basis it is not likely to reach a steady state. It is also not uncommon for bottlenecks to shift throughout the day. For example, intake is often a bottleneck at the beginning of the day as patients start to arrive; later in the day recovery may become a bottleneck as recovery beds fill up. The occurrence of bottlenecks can be influenced by many factors including

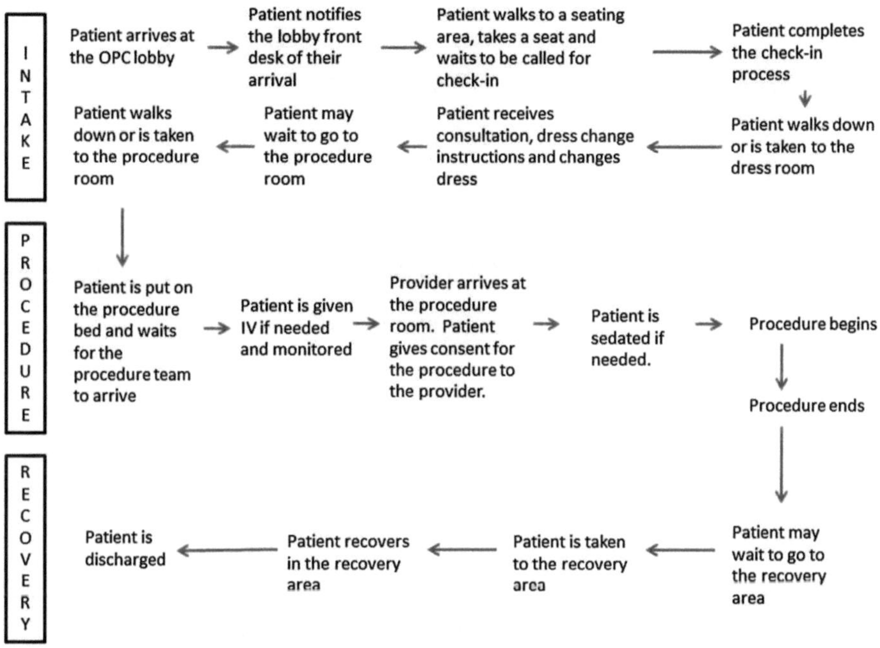

Fig. 6.1 Patient activities during intake, procedure, and recovery stages of the process in a typical OPC

provider availability during the day, patient punctuality, procedure room turn over time, and variation in procedure mix during the day resulting from the sequencing of procedures.

Figure 6.2 depicts the patient flow process in a particular OPC studied by Gul et al. (2011). In this example, the intake and recovery area resources referred to as pre/post rooms are pooled, i.e., the same rooms are used for intake and recovery. Pooling the intake and recovery stage resources can increase flexibility in how limited space is used, reduce variation in the number of patients in intake and recovery, and reduce the risk of intake or recovery becoming a bottleneck in the system. It may also reduce the number of nurses needed overall, or else reduce the need for nurses to move from intake to recovery during the day as the number of patients in each area changes. However, equipping areas to be used for both intake and recovery may result in higher design costs since the entire area needs to be capable of serving multiple purposes. An alternative is to separate intake and recovery resulting in a linear (rather than reentrant) flow of patients through the OPC.

Some OPCs choose to staff and equip procedure rooms for complete flexibility for all types of procedures. This creates flexibility in the assignment of patients and providers to rooms. As a result, a first-come first-serve queue discipline could be used in the procedure stage to reduce the risk of procedure rooms becoming a

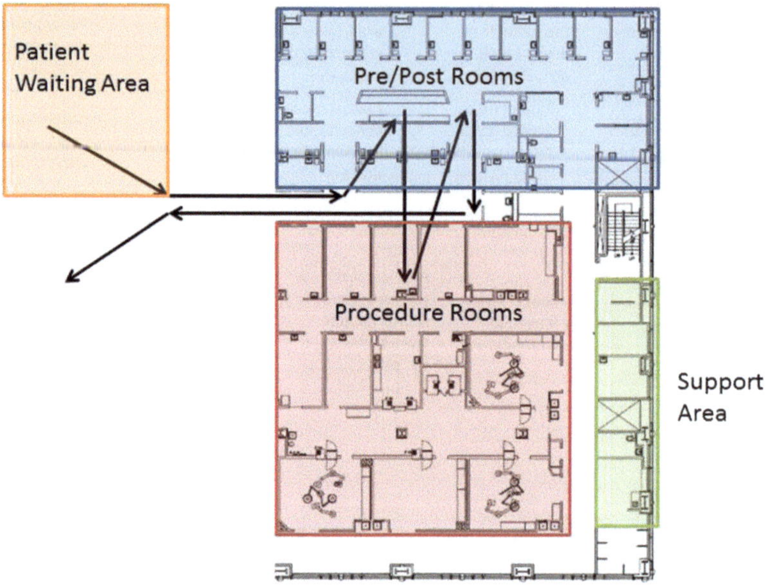

Fig. 6.2 An example of a common layout for an OPC and the patient flow process

bottleneck. OPCs that provide a wider variety of procedures, however, may choose to allocate specific procedures to specific rooms thereby saving equipment costs and allowing staff to specialize in a service. For example, certain procedures such as endoscopies may frequently use imaging equipment during the procedure, but outfitting each procedure room with imaging equipment may not be desirable due to the associated high capital costs. Further flexibility may be attained by not assigning patients to specific providers prior to their procedure. This could reduce patient waiting and increase utilization of OPC resources; however, the preferences of the patients for certain providers, and the benefits of continuity of care from clinic to OPC must be considered. Each of these opportunities for flexibility and resource pooling is specific to a particular OPC. The related decisions must carefully weigh the costs and benefits associated with increased flexibility.

Uncertainty has a significant impact on planning and scheduling decisions for OPCs. Some sources of uncertainty can be reduced with some cost and effort, while others are largely unavoidable. For example, OPC managers may be able to mitigate no-shows by calling patients in advance. On the other hand, the uncertainty in procedure and recovery duration is often difficult or impossible to reduce. This is because it is difficult to predict the complexity of a patient's procedure or their physiological reaction to a sedation agent following the procedure. However, by incorporating these sources of uncertainty in the planning and scheduling process, through the use of appropriate methods, such as simulation, queueing, and stochastic optimization, the extent to which the efficiency of the OPC is affected can be reduced.

6.3 Planning and Scheduling

The need to coordinate resources across multiple stages (intake, procedure, recovery) makes patient scheduling and planning a challenge to OPC managers. OPCs share many similarities with the scheduling of outpatient clinics and surgical practices. However, there are several differences. First, the complexity of the patient flow process is much higher than that of a typical outpatient clinic because the overall process involves multiple steps and many types of resources. Second, OPCs do not have the same planning and scheduling complexities as hospital-based practices, such as the need to manage inpatients and trauma cases that arise during the day. Therefore, there are typically more opportunities to improve efficiency through better planning and scheduling decisions.

Previous articles provide reviews of appointment scheduling in several settings including outpatient clinics (Cayirli and Veral 2003) and hospital surgical practices (Gupta 2007; Guerriero and Guido 2011). There are also reviews in areas such as operating room planning (Cardoen et al. 2010) and surgical process scheduling (Blake and Carter 1997) that are not specific to OPCs. In this chapter we focus specifically on patient planning and scheduling for OPCs. In the remainder of this section we discuss the most significant issues related to longer term planning and short-term scheduling decisions.

6.3.1 Long-Term Planning

OPC managers face many decisions in planning and scheduling appointments, both short and long term. Long-term planning and scheduling decisions include the following:

- How far in advance should the appointment system be open to ensure adequate access for patients and flexibility in staff schedules (e.g., weeks or months)?
- How many patients should be scheduled in a day and what is the best mix of different types of patients and procedures?
- Should any appointment slots be left open for procedures that are likely to be scheduled on short notice?
- Should additional patients be scheduled to compensate for no-shows?
- What is the required nurse staffing?
- How many procedure rooms are needed, and how should procedure rooms be assigned to providers?

In this section we discuss each of these decisions and we provide specific examples of how they arise in the OPC setting. We also review some of the relevant literature related to these types of decisions.

The *booking horizon* determines how far into the future an OPC will schedule patient appointments. Selecting the length of the booking horizon is an important planning decision that requires coordination among staff schedules. If an OPC is going to make appointments available for a future date, administrative managers need to ensure that the necessary resources will be available on that date. Using a longer booking horizon allows schedulers and patients greater flexibility in choosing an appointment. However, a longer booking horizon also requires an OPC to design and commit to a staffing schedule far in advance. Furthermore, changes in staff availability over time may cause disruptions to schedules, requiring cancellations and rescheduling which can be a source of patient dissatisfaction.

Short booking horizons have been shown to be successful in some outpatient clinic settings. In order to mitigate the effects of no-shows and cancellations in an outpatient clinic, heuristic policies for dynamically scheduling requested appointments to specific days have been shown to work well by Liu et al. (2010). In their study, the authors assume that the no-show and cancellation rates increase with appointment delay. That is, patients have a higher propensity to not attend their appointment when the difference in their request date and appointment date are large. The authors use a Markov decision process to dynamically assign patients an appointment date when they call to request an appointment. This decision is based on the current number of appointments scheduled on each day in the booking horizon. They show that their proposed heuristics, including a two-day booking horizon, perform particularly well in the context of high patient demand. However, booking horizons in OPCs will typically be longer since many procedures require adequate advanced notice in order for patients to prepare for the procedure.

The number of patients to plan for each day affects the distribution of workload over time, and therefore staffing and other resource planning decisions. Further, when multiple types of procedures are scheduled, determining the right mix of procedures can influence planning decisions. Scheduling too many patients can result in high patient waiting time, overtime costs, and in some cases cancellations. The problem of dynamically allocating appointments to patients over time has been considered in the context of diagnostic resources by Patrick et al. (2008). The authors consider the problem of planning in the presence of patient wait time targets that require patients to be scheduled within a predefined time window. The authors use approximate dynamic programming methods and show that by carefully using overtime the patient wait list can be successfully managed.

The number and mix of procedures that can be scheduled depends on the availability of providers performing certain procedures. Further, OPC managers must decide whether patients should be scheduled to see specific providers, or whether there is flexibility in which provider performs each patient's procedure. While allowing provider flexibility decreases the bottleneck effect at the procedure stage, certain patients or procedures may require the skill or consultation of a specific provider. Furthermore, patients often have a preference for a certain provider.

OPC managers must also decide on the booking policy to be used. Two common alternatives are *block booking* and *open booking*. In block booking, a provider or group of providers is reserved specific procedure rooms on a recurring basis for certain days and times on a weekly or monthly schedule. Patients are then scheduled into blocks by their provider who is free to allocate patients provided the total procedure time can be completed in the allocated block. On the other hand, open booking consists of allocating patient appointment requests on a first-come first-serve basis for a given day of service. The OPC constructs a schedule of patient/provider room assignments, in some cases allocating multiple procedure rooms for a single provider, shortly before the day of service (e.g. 24 hours in advance). Thus, in open booking systems the OPC is treated more as a pooled resource.

Allocating certain types of procedures to specific rooms is common, and provides a means of balancing workload and resource requirements that may be necessary when there are a wide variety of procedures. Procedure information including type, provider, and type of anesthesiology have been used to classify and allocate procedures to rooms in an OPC by Dexter and Traub (2002). The authors used heuristics such as the earliest available start time, or the latest available start time, to allocate a procedure to a specific room at the time of scheduling. They compared the heuristics using a discrete event simulation model where multiple surgical groups shared procedure rooms. Similarly, some studies have compared online (decisions are made when appointment is requested) and offline (decisions are made after all appointment requests have been made) algorithms for allocating procedures to procedure rooms (Dexter et al. 1999). In order to maximize procedure room efficiency, Dexter et al. (1999) concluded that it was optimal to allocate additional procedures in descending order of expected duration to rooms with the least amount of available time that was still sufficient to accommodate the additional procedure.

In some OPCs there is a need to ensure that there is sufficient space in the schedule for high priority procedures that need to be scheduled on short notice. This is another example of competing criteria in OPC planning. For example, filling a schedule with appointments scheduled in advance will help maximize capacity utilization; however, any procedures that need to be scheduled on short notice will likely be disruptive to the OPC operations and cause high patient waiting and overtime. Erdogan and Denton (2011) study this problem in the context of a single server and provide evidence that allocating time at the end of the day is optimal provided that patients do not have a high indirect waiting cost, i.e., the urgency is such that they can afford to wait until the end of the day to complete their procedure.

The number of cases scheduled on a daily basis directly influences revenue. The problem of deciding how many elective surgery cases to schedule on a particular day has been considered by Gerchak et al. (1996). The authors consider the decision of whether or not to accept an additional elective case while faced with the uncertainty of how much space to leave for potential urgent add-on cases that arise stochastically in the future. Scheduling up to and no more than a predefined number of elective cases each day is common in practice. This is referred to as a *control limit* or *cut-off* policy. Formulating the problem as a stochastic dynamic program with the competing criteria of revenue, overtime, and wait time, the authors show that the optimal number of elective cases to schedule on a day is related to the number of elective surgery cases on the wait list, as opposed to being of a control limit type. That is, the optimal numbers of elective cases to schedule does not follow a strict control limit, but will dynamically change based on the number that are waiting to be scheduled.

Many OPCs face high no-show rates and need to schedule additional patients to compensate for lost revenue. This is commonly referred to as *overbooking*. Dynamically allocating patient appointment requests to appointment slots for a single day with patient no-shows has been considered using overbooking by Muthuraman and Lawley (2008). The authors assume that appointment slots are equally spaced, visit durations are exponentially distributed, and no-show rates vary based on patient attributes. Revenue, patient waiting, and overtime are used as criteria in their objective in the context of an outpatient clinic. In addition to sequential scheduling decisions, overbooking along with careful planning of appointment schedules has also been demonstrated to help mitigate the burden of no-shows in OPCs (Berg et al. 2011).

The capacity of an OPC to see patients depends on staff availibility and physical resources (procedure rooms, recovery beds). The nursing staff required for OPCs is often an important consideration for planning decisions since nurses are necessary at each stage of the process. OPC nursing staff may be dedicated to specific responsibilities and stages, or they may be more flexible and *float* to where they are needed in the OPC. While the latter case provides more flexibility and can mitigate bottlenecks, this requires that the nursing staff be highly skilled with experience in multiple settings.

Example: Optimal Allocation of Procedure Rooms

In this section we provide a specific example of a long range planning decision based on an analysis of an endoscopy suite reported by Berg et al. (2010). The example involves determining how many procedure rooms to assign to endoscopists, and how the decision affects competing performance criteria.

The endoscopy suite considered in this example is part of a large academic medical center and follows the general process structure in Fig. 6.1. Appointments can be made up to 12 weeks in advance and schedules typically fill up within the last 48 hours. Patients arrive at the endoscopy suite according to a predetermined set of assigned appointment times. Intake is staffed by six nurses, the number of procedure rooms and endoscopists available on a given day can both range between four and eight, and the recovery stage includes three rooms with eight beds in each room.

As illustrated in Fig. 6.3, opening two procedure rooms for each provider will allow providers to move to their next procedure while the previous procedure room is being turned over. Thus, the allocation of an additional procedure room can reduce provider waiting time and increase patient throughput per provider. However, the costs of staffing and equipping two procedure rooms for each provider is high relative to the total number of patients that can be seen in the endoscopy suite.

Figure 6.4 compares the utilization rates for procedure rooms and endoscopists as well as patient throughput to the number of endoscopists operating in an

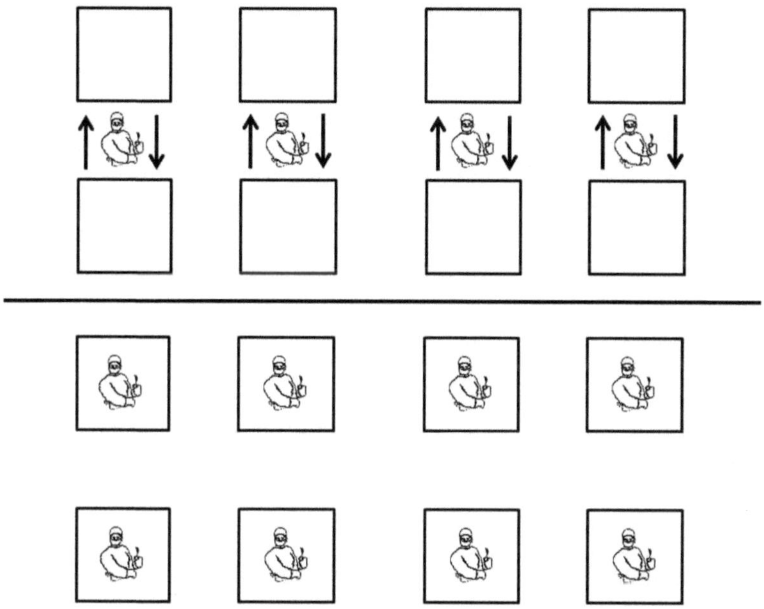

Fig. 6.3 Two scenarios for allocating providers to procedure rooms

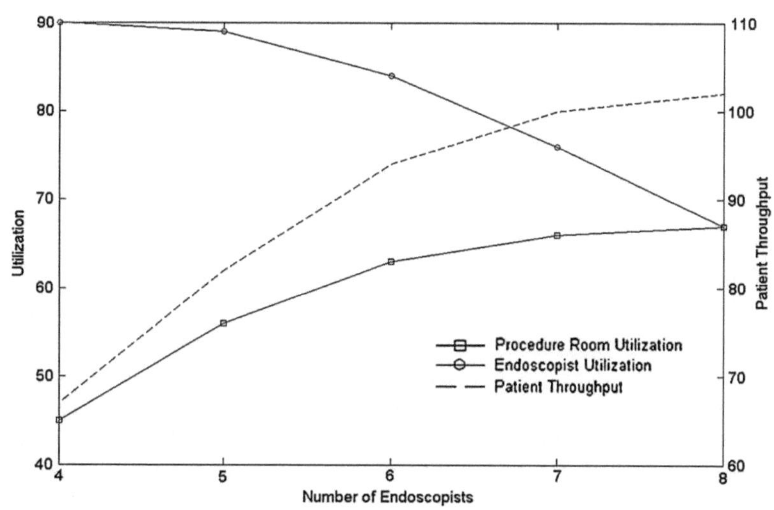

Fig. 6.4 Expected endoscopist and procedure room utilization and patient throughput as a function of the number of endoscopists in the endoscopy suite

endoscopy suite with eight procedure rooms. As the number of endoscopists operating within the eight procedure rooms increases from four to eight, endoscopist utilization decreases, but total procedure room utilization and patient throughput both increase. These results illustrate the type of tradeoff in performance criteria that OPC managers face in making long-term planning decisions.

In addition, daily processes can also affect long-term planning decisions. For example, the decision of allocating procedure rooms to providers is influenced by the time required to turn over a room. If room turn over time is short relative to procedure time, fewer procedure rooms may be necessary. However, with longer turn over times more procedure rooms may be desirable to avoid bottleneck effects at the procedure stage.

6.3.2 Short-Term Scheduling

The remainder of this section focuses on short-term scheduling challenges in OPCs. Research related to short-term scheduling decisions has received more focus than that of long-term planning and scheduling for OPCs. Challenges for short-term planning in OPCs include the following:

- How should procedures be sequenced throughout the day?
- When should patients be scheduled to arrive at the OPC?
- When is it necessary to cancel procedures?

The resources involved in the procedure stage of the process are often the most expensive and constraining to the OPC. Therefore the procedure is frequently the bottleneck in the system, and as a result much of the existing literature has focused on scheduling procedures. In this section we discuss examples of each of the above decisions in the context of OPCs. We also present a standard single server model that has been used for scheduling of OPCs. Finally, we provide a specific example of appointment scheduling in the context of an endoscopy suite.

Although the procedures in OPCs are done in high volumes and may be considered to be routine, there is often a large amount of uncertainty in the time required for the procedure. The high uncertainty is a result of many factors that influence the procedure duration including procedure type, individual provider, type of anesthetic, and patient physiological characteristics (Dexter et al. 2008). Figure 6.5 illustrates the uncertainty in procedure durations for colonoscopies performed in a particular outpatient endoscopy suite. It illustrates two features that are common for any type of procedure. First, there is a finite time (5 minutes in this example) for which the probability of being below is very low. Second, there is a long tail indicating a low (but non-zero) probability the procedure will take a very long time. Long tails such as this are a result of unpredictable complications associated with procedures. For example, a patient who receives a routine colonoscopy may have multiple polyps discovered requiring biopsies that significantly lengthen the procedure time. While a variety of distributions have been found useful for modeling purposes (Cayirli and Veral 2003), the log-normal distribution is often found to be an appropriate fit (Strum et al. 2000; Zhou and Dexter 1998).

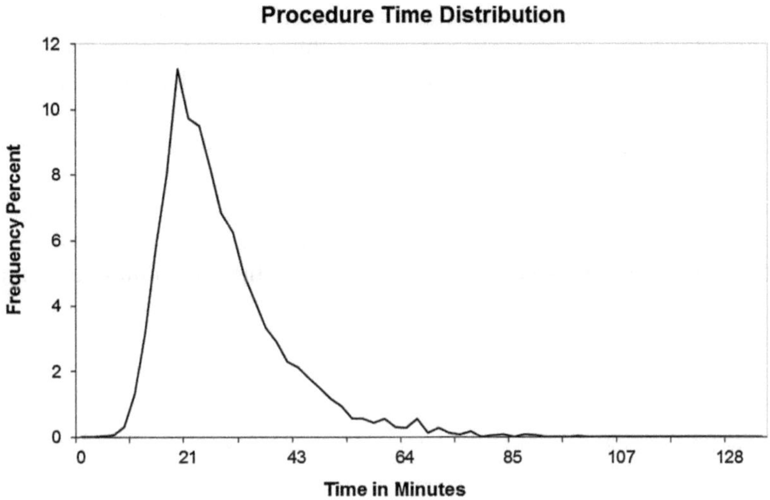

Fig. 6.5 The procedure duration distribution for colonoscopies can have a long tail due to many factors

As an example of a short-term daily scheduling problem, we discuss the single server appointment scheduling problem. The single server problem is a useful example because OPCs can often be disaggregated into multiple single server problems in which each procedure room corresponds to a server. Berg et al. (2011) show that this can be a reasonable approximation when the procedure room is the bottleneck in the overall process. The appointment times for each patient $i = 1,\ldots,n$, denoted by vector **a**, must be decided upon in advance. Suppose that the objective is to minimize the weighted sum of costs, c_i^w and c^o, associated with expected patient waiting time and overtime, respectively. The patient waiting times and overtime, $w_i(\mathbf{d},\mathbf{a})$ and $o(\mathbf{d},\mathbf{a})$, are functions of a vector of random variables, **d**, the durations for each patient's procedure, and a vector of appointment times, **a**. The objective can be formulated as follows:

$$\min_{\mathbf{a}}\{\sum_{i=1}^{n} c_i^w E[w_i(\mathbf{d},\mathbf{a})] + c^o E[o(\mathbf{d},\mathbf{a})] | \mathbf{a} \in A\}, \tag{6.1}$$

and the waiting and overtime can be written as

$$w_1 = 0, \quad w_i = \max\{0, w_{i-1} + d_{i-1} - a_i + a_{i-1}\},$$
$$\text{and} \quad o = \max\{0, a_n + w_n + d_n - p\}$$

where p is the planned length of the OPC day and A represents the feasible region of appointment schedules that adhere to a specific OPC's constraints. Constraints may include requirements to schedule procedures for a certain provider during the hours they are working at the OPC (as opposed to associated hospital or clinical practice) or constraints on allowable or preferred sequences of procedures during the day.

The single server example illustrates the tradeoff that administrative managers must consider between multiple criteria, in this case patient waiting time and overtime. The focus of short-term scheduling problems such as this is typically on *direct* waiting time, i.e. the time the patient spends waiting beyond their appointment time on the day of service. This is in contrast to *indirect* waiting time which measures the total time from an appointment request to the day of service (indirect waiting is a common criterion for long-term planning problems).

The stochastic nature of procedure times and other activities in OPCs makes finding optimal schedules very challenging. In practice, schedules are commonly based on the mean procedure time. Thus, the appointment times for patient arrivals are defined as follows:

$$a_i = a_{i-1} + \mu_{i-1}, \quad \forall i \tag{6.2}$$

where the first patient arrives at the beginning of the day ($a_1 = 0$) and μ_i represents the procedure duration mean for patient i.

Because the above scheduling rule is easy to implement it is commonly used in practice. However, it typically leads to very high expected patient waiting times. This is a result of procedures having duration distributions with long tails and waiting time accumulating for each patient throughout the day. For example, if the service time distribution is symmetric then there is a probability of 0.5 that a procedure will run longer than the allotted time, and each time this occurs the waiting time accumulates.

Many heuristics for determining appointment schedule times for outpatient clinics have been proposed and examined (Bailey 1952; Ho and Lau 1992; Robinson and Chen 2003). Specific to OPCs, setting interarrival times through *hedging* may be useful to reduce patient waiting time at the risk of increase overtime (Gul et al. 2011). Hedging refers to using a percentile (e.g., 50th, 65th) of a procedure's duration distribution to set appointment times. Elaborating on the heuristic in (2), job hedging can be represented by

$$a_i = a_{i-1} + \mu_{i-1} + \gamma, \quad \forall i \tag{6.3}$$

where γ represents the additional time added to act as a buffer to reduce the likelihood of a patient waiting.

Denton et al. (2007) demonstrated that the sequencing decisions have a high impact on the performance of an appointment schedule, especially when overtime and patient waiting time costs are relatively evenly matched. Further, the authors demonstrated that the simple heuristic of sequencing procedures by decreasing procedure duration variance can provide significant improvements. Sequencing patients with greater variability in their procedure duration or propensity to not attend their appointment later in the day can lead to lower expected costs (Berg et al. 2011). However, combining procedure sequencing and start time scheduling leads to a challenging stochastic combinatorial optimization problem. As a result, many studies have considered heuristics. In the context of scheduling multiple procedure types by procedure duration, the shortest processing time (SPT) heuristic has been shown to work well in OPCs over other heuristics such as

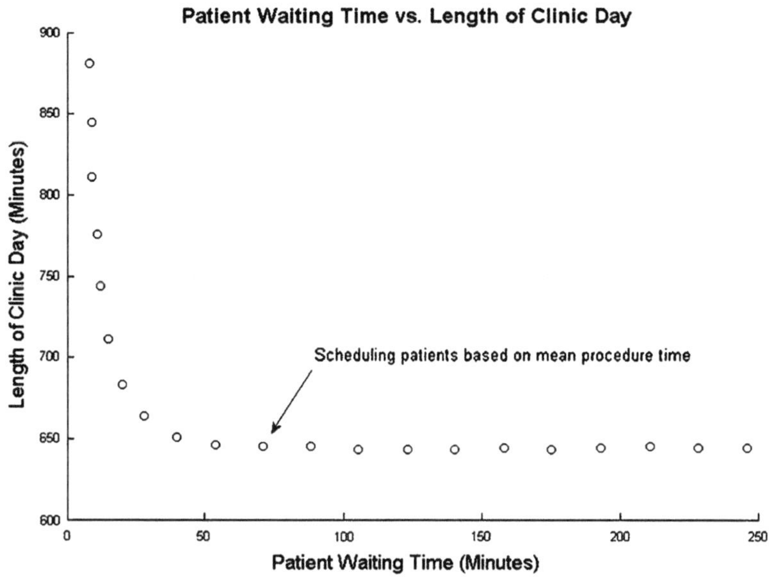

Fig. 6.6 Expected length of day (time to complete all cases) versus expected patient waiting time (averaged over all patients) with respect to the interarrival time for the patient arrival schedule

sequencing according to longest processing time, procedure variation, and a procedure's coefficient of variation (Gul et al. 2011).

Example: Appointment Scheduling in an OPC

In OPC settings, it has been demonstrated that using hedging can often reduce expected patient waiting time significantly with minimal effect on the expected length of day (time to complete all procedures). As an example drawn from Berg et al. (2010), Fig. 6.6 illustrates this in the context of the endoscopy suite described in Sect. 6.3.1.1.

In this example, each endoscopist has their own set of patients that are scheduled according to the heuristics defined in (2) and (3). That is, there is a patient arrival *stream* for each individual endoscopist in the suite. The appointment schedule generated by using the procedure duration means for interarrival times is identified in Fig. 6.6. This corresponds to the heuristic defined in (2). The hedging parameter in (3), γ, is varied to generate the rest of the appointment schedules in Fig. 6.6.

The appointment schedules in Fig. 6.6 illustrate the tradeoff in the competing criteria that is made in designing appointment schedules. The results in this example show that using interarrival times for patients greater than the procedure duration mean can reduce patient waiting time while not incurring a significantly longer length of the clinic day. In Fig. 6.6, the length of the clinic day is correlated with overtime and is the same as overtime when $p = 0$ for example, as defined in (1).

6.4 Factors Influencing Scheduling

In this section we identify some of the most important factors that detract from efficient performance of OPCs, and must be considered in planning and scheduling. These include uncertainty in intake and recovery durations, variation in patient demand and provider availability, material resources, and patient characteristics and behavior.

6.4.1 Intake and Recovery

Just as procedure durations vary significantly by procedure types and patient characteristics, so do the durations for intake and recovery (Huschka et al. 2007). When resources are limited in intake (e.g. nurses) or in recovery (e.g. recovery beds) these stages in the process can affect planning and scheduling. Figure 6.7 illustrates the variation associated with intake and recovery at an endoscopy suite. Variation in intake time is due to the varying levels of preparation required for different procedures. For example, less invasive procedures may have the patient enter the procedure room directly upon arrival, while others may involve additional intake activities such as administration of anesthetic. Recovery times can vary as well, since certain procedures may require different sedation methods which can influence the time it takes for a patient to recover following a procedure. Thus, the uncertainty in the duration of intake and recovery coupled with the limited capacity in each stage may deserve careful consideration as appointment schedules are designed.

The uncertainty in recovery duration can have very different effects on an OPC than the intake stage due to the nature of recovery being at the end of the process. High recovery utilization rates can result in the entire system backing up. This is particularly true if there is no recovery alternative for patients finishing their procedure other than recovering in the procedure room, thus blocking subsequent procedures from beginning.

Due to the similarities in OPC recovery areas and the post anesthesia care unit (PACU) in hospitals, drawing on surgery scheduling insights from hospital-based practices can be informative to recovery planning for OPCs. Queueing models are often used in these environments, but the assumption of a steady state may be restrictive in the setting of an OPC. Schoenmeyr et al. (2009) justify their model assumptions based on historical data and show that the arrival process into the PACU following surgery can be modeled as a Poisson process. They use their model and simulation to conclude that significant decreases in PACU congestion

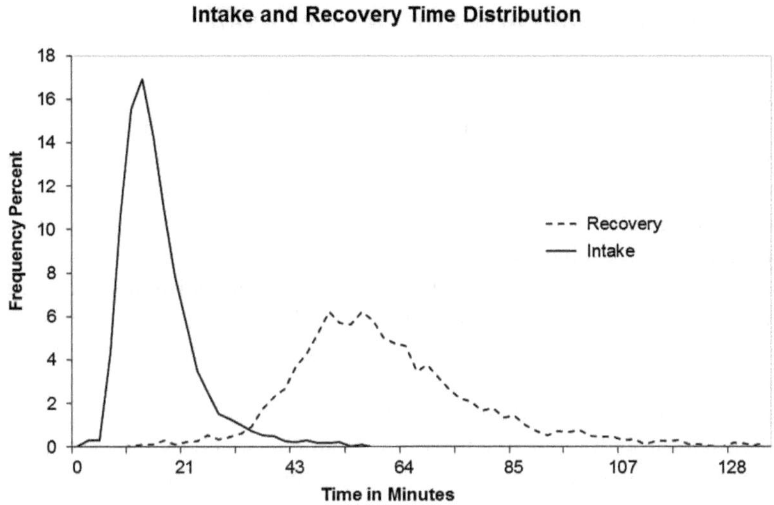

Fig. 6.7 The distributions for intake and recovery durations can have high variances contributing to potential bottlenecks in these stages

could be gained by proportionally small changes in capacity. However, this relationship is sensitive to the number of procedures planned.

Controlling the sequence in which procedures are performed across multiple procedure rooms can help balance the arrival rate into the PACU. Although many providers prefer to have longer procedures earlier in the day, discrete event simulation has been used to show that this sequencing rule may perform poorly as the variation of the longer procedures can disrupt the schedule later in the day by Marcon Dexter (2006). Furthermore, the PACU tends to be empty for much of the beginning of the day, and then has a peak of workload following completion of the first procedures of the day. The authors conclude that sequencing heuristics that balance the longer procedures at the beginning and end of the day tend to smooth the flow of patients into the PACU.

In the scheduling literature, when jobs remain on a machine following processing, and there is no buffer capacity, it is referred to as *blocking*. Blocking and *no-wait* scheduling problems have been discussed in several manufacturing contexts (Hall and Sriskandarajah 1996). A similar situation occurs in OPCs; when the recovery room is full, patients may start their recovery in a procedure room. However, this blocks the use of the procedure room and can cause delays. Augusto et al. (2010) explicitly modeled the possibility of patients recovering in an operating room (OR) as a mixed integer program. The authors recommend a decision rule for when to use the OR for recovery, based on case load and the ratio of ORs to recovery beds. Although this problem was formulated in the context of a hospital practice, the relationship between the ORs and PACU is analogous to OPCs with procedure rooms and shared recovery areas.

6.4.2 Patient Demand and Provider Availability

Variation in supply and demand can create scheduling challenges and inefficiencies for an OPC. The problem of supply and demand being mismatched is very common in many industries and is prevalent in OPCs. Patient demand variation can be high from week to week as well as from day to day. Even more, month to month variation may be high as demand for procedures may be high when patients have time off (e.g. summer for students) or when patients will be less active (e.g. winter for orthopedic patients). Further, supply factors contributing to the supply and demand mismatch include provider availability and upstream referring sources. The first, provider availability, may result from variation in provider schedules for a variety of reasons, such as vacation, administrative or research obligations, or attending a conference for their specialty. The second, referrals, depends on an OPC's affiliation with other practices. For example, specialty clinic consultations result in newly generated referrals for procedures at the OPC. Thus, the OPC's position downstream in the overall health service supply chain exposes them to variation associated with other upstream practices. Figure 6.8 illustrates the weekly variation for procedures in an endoscopy suite affiliated with a large academic medical center.

The challenge of leveling patient demand across available capacity in order to gain operational efficiencies needs to be considered when attempting to accommodate patient appointment preferences. The loss of efficiency resulting from demand variation can include being under (or over) staffed, resources being under utilized, and patients having poor access to services as well as long wait times at the OPC. Schedules for nurses, other personnel, and physical resources are often fixed day to day and week to week. Thus, supply is not easily varied to match demand.

6.4.3 Material Resources

Materials management contributes to the operating costs of an OPC. This includes the purchasing, ordering, inventory, and opportunity costs for any medical and surgical supplies that an OPC uses. Examples include medical equipment, lab equipment, surgical instruments, and medical apparel.

Sterilization of procedure equipment can be a timely as well as resource intensive process. For example, the sterilization of endoscopes in an endoscopy suite requires trained personnel, disinfection and sterilization equipment, and can take a up to a few hours to process. Further, since procedure equipment such as endoscopes are expensive, purchasing additional equipment is not always feasible. Single-use equipment for certain types of procedures has the advantage of avoiding the costs of sterilization and maintenance, but has been found to be very costly in the long run (Schaer et al. 1995). The tradeoff between the capital costs

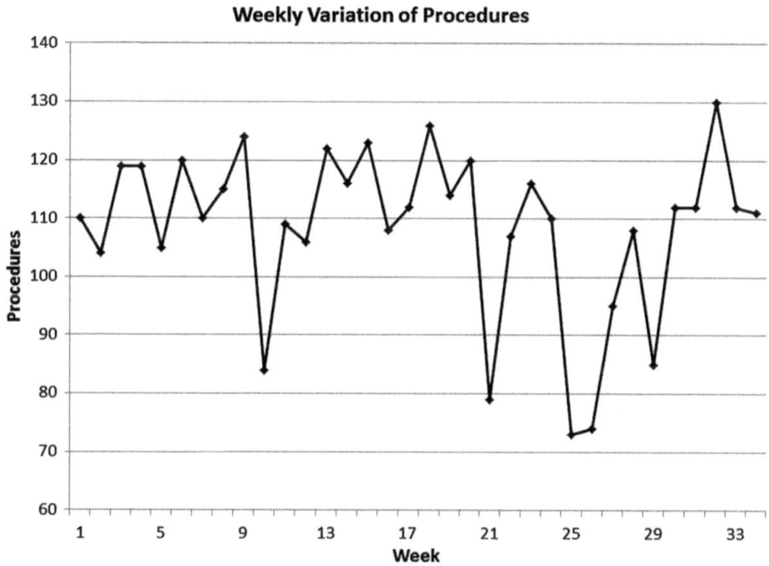

Fig. 6.8 The number of procedures done each week in an endoscopy suite vary week to week. Data are presented from July to February

of equipment and the effects of limited resources on an OPCs efficiency needs to be considered in both the long-term planning and short-term scheduling contexts.

The tradeoff between the use of mobile and fixed diagnostic resources is another example of material resource planning. Many procedures require the use of diagnostic resources, but equipping every procedure room with such resources can be expensive. While mobile equipment affords flexibility in the location and use of the equipment, the mobile equipment may be cumbersome and/or difficult to set up and use. Therefore, there is a natural tradeoff between the cost of investing in mobile diagnostic resources and the flexibility such resources offer to the scheduling process.

The design of surgical equipment kits for OPCs requires careful consideration. Different types of procedures require different supplies. Preparing universal kits that contain the supplies and equipment necessary for all procedure types can be costly as it requires high inventory levels; however, preparing kits for individual procedures can be time intensive and susceptible to errors in packing kits. As a result there are challenging decisions about how best to tradeoff cost and the benefits of flexibility.

Efforts to use appointment scheduling information to manage the inventory of physical material resources has also been considered. Generally, OPCs use economic order quantity (EOQ) models to manage inventory levels. However, using just in time (JIT) models that are based on when procedures are scheduled in an OPC has been proposed by Epstein and Dexter (2000). The authors use simulation and conclude that while there may be possible savings in a JIT system used in conjunction with the appointment scheduling system, it is unlikely that the savings would be substantial when compared to the cost of implementing such a system. Thus, traditional EOQ models with higher inventory levels are likely best for OPCs.

6.4.4 Patient Characteristics and Behavior

The patient population served by an OPC is likely to be diverse in their characteristics as well as how they interact with the health care system. Relevant patient characteristics include age, gender, and physiological background, which are often correlated with procedure times, and therefore can be useful for appointment scheduling. For example, obese patients tend to be at higher risk of complications, and have longer procedure and recovery times. By patient behavior, we primarily refer to patients' (non) attendance and punctuality, as well as their preference for certain appointment times. Designing appointment schedules that compensate for patient behavior is a challenge faced by OPC managers.

An OPC's ability to serve a patient case mix relies on its ability to adapt to a variety of patient characteristics, preferences, and behavior. Cayirli et al. (2006) demonstrated that the performance of an appointment schedule is very sensitive to patient characteristics and behavior such as walk-ins (add-ons or patients that need to be scheduled the same day), no-shows, and punctuality. Although the authors' analysis was specific to a clinical office setting (primary care), the role of patient characteristics and behavior in scheduling decisions is informative to OPCs.

No-shows occur when patients do not attend their scheduled appointment and do not cancel beforehand. No-shows have been reported in OPC settings and present a challenge to managers of many types of health care practices (Adams et al. 2004; Sola-vera et al. 2008). The reasons for patients failing to adhere to their scheduled appointments include illness, stress about the procedure, improved symptoms, forgetting about the appointment, improper preparation for the procedure, or balking when informed about the cost of the procedure. In many ambulatory settings, *advanced access* has become a popular method for dealing with the uncertainty in patient demand (Murray and Berwick 2003). Advanced access refers to scheduling appointments for the same day that they are requested and "doing today's work today." This scheduling policy requires providers being able to match demand with supply and not having any backlog of appointment requests. By offering appointments to patients on the same day that they call, providers reduce the problem of patients failing to attend their previously scheduled appointment as well as patients having long delays for an appointment. However, due to the preparation necessary for many OPC procedures, advanced access is not a feasible policy for appointment scheduling in OPCs.

In contrast to patients failing to attend their scheduled appointments, many OPCs (especially those affiliated with a hospital) will also receive high priority add-on cases that need to be fit into the current day's schedule. For example, endoscopy suites are sometimes asked to see a patient with indications of colorectal cancer on short notice. Heuristics were evaluated via simulation to determine how to allocate add-on cases to specific procedure rooms in order to maximize utilization (Dexter et al. 1999). Dynamically scheduling appointment times while considering no-show rates and uncertainty in future demand has also been examined as a stochastic programming formulation (Erdogan and Denton 2011). A dome shaped schedule is observed for routine patients (non-add-ons) where patients earlier and later in the day are scheduled closer together and patients in the middle of the day are given more time between arrivals.

Patients receiving surgery in OPCs may have a preference for the day and time of their appointments. In a survey of cataract surgery patients, the authors found that the patients value appointment flexibility very highly and strongly preferred morning appointments (Dexter et al. 2009). Due to the high cost of OPC resources and the challenges in balancing supply and demand, patient preferences are often not as high a priority for managers when compared to other environments such as primary care. Incorporating the consideration of patient preferences into OPC planning and scheduling decisions is an important direction for future research.

6.5 Operations Research Challenges

As demand for services in OPCs continues to rise, the need to provide services in a cost-effective manor makes planning and scheduling in OPCs an important challenge for OR researchers and practitioners. Considerable effort has been put into scheduling inpatient surgeries and ambulatory clinics where queueing and mathematical programming methods are applicable to single stage and single server environments. However, a number of unique challenges remain in planning and scheduling for the OPC setting.

The multi-stage (intake, procedure, recovery) and multi-server nature of OPCs make optimization models that accurately represent the system a challenge to formulate. The single server model presented in Sect. 6.3.2 illustrated the challenges in designing an appointment schedule with competing criteria for a single stage and single provider. However, the design of an OPC appointment schedule may need to include multiple servers in the model since there are many shared resources between each server such as nurses, equipment, and procedure rooms. Further, there is uncertainty in the intake and recovery stages that will impact the design of an appointment schedule. Finally, all of the activities required for a patient's procedure need to occur within a limited time frame. The complex interactions between many resources across multiple patient care stages requires significant coordination and conveys the challenges in formulating models for OPCs

Due to the complexity of OPCs, mathematical programming models may not always be possible, or even desirable. The complexity of OPCs, resulting from multiple stages and the coordination of many resources, makes discrete event simulation a natural methodology. While descriptive simulation models that accurately represent an OPC are helpful in diagnosing bottlenecks and evaluating hypothetical scenarios, simulation optimization methods could be used to make optimal or near optimal planning and scheduling decisions. This remains on open challenge for future research.

In addition to developing new models, there is also a need for implementable recommendations that can be gleaned from this body of research. The process of making such recommendations includes demonstrating the value of a model's solution (with data from real OPCs) and abstracting easy to implement rules or insights. Advanced OR models can serve as a means to evaluate the effectiveness of easier to implement scheduling rules.

6.6 Conclusions

This chapter has summarized typical OPC operations, described the similarities, differences, and interactions between OPCs and other health care service settings, and has explained some of the unique challenges in the planning and scheduling decisions that OPC managers face. The decisions were categorized as either long-term planning decisions or short-term scheduling decisions and were presented with models and results drawn from examples in the literature. Factors that influence OPC planning and scheduling decisions were summarized along with methods used to address these challenges.

There has been a lot of research and focus on appointment scheduling in the context of ambulatory clinics and hospital-based surgery practices. While some of these methods are relevant to planning and scheduling in OPCs, the unique nature of OPCs presents challenges that have yet to receive the same attention. With demand for surgery in the outpatient setting continuing to rise, designing appointment systems specific to OPCs that accommodate timely access to services while utilizing resource efficiently will continue to increase in importance.

The complexity of OPCs will lead to opportunities for the development of new models and methodological advances, particularly in the areas of stochastic optimization methods such as stochastic programming, stochastic dynamic programming, and simulation optimization.

Acknowledgments This project was funded in part by the National Science Foundation under grant CMMI-0844511.

References

Adams L, Pawlik J, Forbes G (2004) Nonattendance at outpatient endoscopy. Endoscopy 36(5):402–404

Augusto V, Xie X, Perdomo V (2010) Operating theatre scheduling with patient recovery in both operating rooms and recovery beds. Comput Ind Eng 58(2):231–238

Bailey N (1952) A study of queues and appointment systems in hospital out-patient departments, with special reference to waiting-times. J R Stat Soc Ser B (Methodol) 14(2):185–199

Berg B, Denton B, Nelson H, Balasubramanian H, Rahman A, Bailey A, Lindor K (2010) A discrete event simulation model to evaluate operational performance of a colonoscopy suite. Med Decis Mak 30(3):380–387

Berg B, Denton B, Erdogan S, Rohleder T, Huschka T (2011) Optimal booking strategies for outpatient procedure centers. North Carolina State University working paper

Blake J, Carter M (1997) Surgical process scheduling: a structured review. J Soc Health Syst 5(3):17–30

Cardoen B, Demeulemeester E, Beliën J (2010) Operating room planning and scheduling: A literature review. Eur J Oper Res 201(3):921–932

Cayirli T, Veral E (2003) Outpatient scheduling in health care: A review of literature. Prod Oper Manag 12(4):519–549

Cayirli T, Veral E, Rosen H (2006) Designing appointment scheduling systems for ambulatory care services. Health Care Manag Sci 9(1):47–58

Cullen K, Hall M, Golosinskiy A (2009) Ambulatory surgery in the united states, 2006. Natl Health Stat R (11)

Denton B, Viapiano J, Vogl A (2007) Optimization of surgery sequencing and scheduling decisions under uncertainty. Health Care Manag Sci 10(1):13–24

Dexter F, Traub R (2002) How to schedule elective surgical cases into specific operating rooms to maximize the efficiency of use of operating room time. Anesth Analg 94(4):933–942

Dexter F, Macario A, Traub R (1999) Which algorithm for scheduling add-on elective cases maximizes operating room utilization?: Use of bin packing algorithms and fuzzy constraints in operating room management. Anesthesiology 91(5):1491–1500

Dexter F, Dexter E, Masursky D, Nussmeier N (2008) Systematic review of general thoracic surgery articles to identify predictors of operating room case durations. Anesth Analg 106(4):1232–1241

Dexter F, Birchansky L, Bernstein J, Wachtel R (2009) Case scheduling preferences of one surgeon's cataract surgery patients. Anesth Analg 108(2):579–582

Epstein R, Dexter F (2000) Economic analysis of linking operating room scheduling and hospital material management information systems for just-in-time inventory control. Anesth Analg 91(2):337–343

Erdogan S, Denton B (2011) Dynamic appointment scheduling with uncertain demand. INFORMS J Comput (in press)

Gerchak Y, Gupta D, Henig M (1996) Reservation planning for elective surgery under uncertain demand for emergency surgery. Manag Sci 42(3):321–334

Guerriero F, Guido R (2011) Operational research in the management of the operating theatre: a survey. Health Care Manag Sci 14(1):89–114

Gul S, Denton B, Fowler J, Huschka T (2011) Bi-criteria scheduling of surgical services for an outpatient procedure center. Prod Oper Manag 20(3):406–417

Gupta D (2007) Surgical suites' operations management. Prod Oper Manag 16(6):689–700

Hall N, Sriskandarajah C (1996) A survey of machine scheduling problems with blocking and no-wait in process. Oper Res 44(3):510–525

Ho C, Lau H (1992) Minimizing total cost in scheduling outpatient appointments. Manag Sci 38(12):1750–1764

Huschka T, Denton B, Gul S, Fowler J (2007) Bi-criteria evaluation of an outpatient procedure center via simulation. In: Proceedings of the 39th conference on Winter simulation: 40 years! The best is yet to come, IEEE Press, pp 1510–1518

Liu N, Ziya S, Kulkarni V (2010) Dynamic scheduling of outpatient appointments under patient no-shows and cancellations. Manuf Serv Oper Manag 12(2):347–364

Marcon E, Dexter F (2006) Impact of surgical sequencing on post anesthesia care unit staffing. Health Care Manag Sci 9(1):87–98

Murray M, Berwick D (2003) Advanced access. J Am Med Assoc 289(8):1035–1040

Muthuraman K, Lawley M (2008) A stochastic overbooking model for outpatient clinical scheduling with no-shows. IIE Trans 40(9):820–837

Patrick J, Puterman M, Queyranne M (2008) Dynamic multi-priority patient scheduling for a diagnostic resource. Oper Res 56(6):1507–1525

Robinson L, Chen R (2003) Scheduling doctors' appointments: optimal and empirically-based heuristic policies. IIE Trans 35(3):295–307

Schaer G, Koechli O, Haller U (1995) Single-use versus reusable laparoscopic surgical instruments: a comparative cost analysis. Am J Obstet Gynecol 173(6):1812–1815

Schoenmeyr T, Dunn P, Gamarnik D, Levi R, Berger D, Daily B, Levine W, Sandberg W (2009) A model for understanding the impacts of demand and capacity on waiting time to enter a congested recovery room. Anesthesiology 110(6):1293–1304

Sola-vera J, Sáez J, Laveda R, Girona E, Fegarcía sepulcre M, Cuesta A, Vázquez N, Uceda F, Pérez E, Sillero C (2008) Factors associated with non-attendance at outpatient endoscopy. Scand J Gastroenterol 43(2):202–206

Strum D, May J, Vargas L (2000) Modeling the uncertainty of surgical procedure times: Comparison of log-normal and normal models. Anesthesiology 92(4):1160–1167

Zhou J, Dexter F (1998) Method to assist in the scheduling of add-on surgical cases-upper prediction bounds for surgical case durations based on the log-normal distribution. Anesthesiology 89(5):1228–1232

Chapter 7
Human and Artificial Scheduling System for Operating Rooms

P. S. Stepaniak, R. A. C. van der Velden, J. van de Klundert and A. P. M. Wagelmans

Abstract Operating theatres experience dynamic situations that result from unanticipated developments in scheduled cases, arrival of emergency cases and the scheduling decisions made during the day by the operating room coordinator (ORC). The task of the ORC is to ensure that operating rooms (ORs) finish on time and that all scheduled cases as well as the emergency cases are completed. At the end of each day, however, ORs may finish too early or too late because cases have experienced delays or been canceled. Delays or cancelations add to the patient's inherent anxiety associated with surgery and engenders anger and frustration. They have been shown to be an important determinant of patient dissatisfaction across the continuum of preoperative-operative-postoperative care. Recent research (Stepaniak et al. (2009) Anesth Analg 108:1249–1256) addresses how the risk attitude of an ORC affects the quality of the scheduling decision making. In this chapter you will learn about the interaction between the personality of both a human and an artificial OR scheduler, learn about the effects on the decision the OR scheduler makes and the quality of the resulting OR schedule. Therefore, we formalize risk attitudes in heuristics developed to solve the real-time scheduling problems ORCs face during the day.

P. S. Stepaniak (✉) · R. A. C. van der Velden · J. van de Klundert
Institute of Health Policy and Management, Erasmus University Rotterdam, Rotterdam, The Netherlands
e-mail: pieter.stepaniak@gmail.com

R. A. C. van der Velden
e-mail: Ronald.van.der.velden@gmail.com

J. van de Klundert
e-mail: vandeklundert@bmg.eur.nl

A. P. M. Wagelmans
Econometric Institute, Erasmus School of Economics, Erasmus University Rotterdam, Rotterdam, The Netherlands
e-mail: wagelmans@ese.eur.nl

R. Hall (ed.), *Handbook of Healthcare System Scheduling*,
International Series in Operations Research & Management Science 168,
DOI: 10.1007/978-1-4614-1734-7_7,

7.1 Introduction

Operating rooms (ORs) are relatively scarce resources. Poor scheduling and misuse of ORs can provide opportunities for conflict and competition. Hospital management determines the available operating room (OR) capacity and assigns capacity to the different medical specialties. Increases in the efficiency of use of the ORs results in more production and therefore more revenue for the hospital. However, increasing this efficiency is sometimes easier said than done. Picture the following not uncommon situation. Due to poor case scheduling, OR staff is forced to stand around idly, and expensive nursing, anesthesia and support staff are wasted on some days. On other days, the OR staff works beyond regular working hours to finish the workload on that day. There are situations where surgeons/anesthesiologists arrive too early or too late in the OR and teams are not always ready at the scheduled time. Sometimes the capacity in the OR is insufficient for patients who arrive in the emergency department, which causes scheduled patients to be denied surgery that day, or for staff to work late. Such situations frequently result in nurses, doctors, management and patients becoming extremely frustrated. When looking at an OR in an era in which both cost-containment and quality of health care are considered of prime importance, hospitals simply have to utilize ORs effectively and efficiently. An important tool to achieve this goal is well-designed scheduling systems.

This handbook offers guidance on how to improve health care by improving the delivery of services through application of state-of-the-art scheduling systems. For instance, capacity planning, scheduling patients, staff and nurses are addressed. Every chapter has in common that whatever scheduling system has to be implemented on a day-to-day, hour-to-hour or second-to-second basis, a decision is made by a human being: a scheduler. In this chapter you will learn about the relations between the personality of an OR scheduler, the decision the OR scheduler makes and the quality of the resulting OR schedule. The methods, materials and results in this chapter are based on published scientific publications (Stepaniak et al. 2009; Stepaniak 2010).

7.2 Problems and Formulations

7.2.1 *Surgical Case Scheduling*

In this chapter, we will consider 'surgical case scheduling' as the process of assigning a given set of cases for a certain day to ORs and defining start times for these cases, in order to maximize OR efficiency (or to minimize OR inefficiency). We can view this as a two-stage process.

The first stage of this process consists of a pre-assignment of one or more days in advance. In this stage, there is much scheduling flexibility since both patients and personnel are not yet informed on their detailed planning. However, after the schedule has been created, it is communicated to all people involved.

The second stage then takes place during the day of operation. Unexpected events (cases may take far more time than scheduled; cases can be cancelled due to no-show or the patient not being ready for surgery) may force the schedule to be revised. Another possibility is the arrival of an emergency case that needs to be added to the schedule as quick as possible. Both types of events can influence the start times of other cases. Also, it might be necessary to exchange cases between ORs. In the end, these changes will also influence the time at which the last case in each room is finished. When cases are still waiting after the regular operating hours, they may be assigned to the service room where an extra stand-by team is available to perform these last cases.

In order to optimize the schedules, decisions made in the first stage should already take into account the events that may occur in the second stage, although exact information about these events is not available. The same is true for decisions made in the second stage: when reacting to a case taking more time than expected, one also has to consider the possibility of an emergency case arriving later that day.

We will define this scheduling process and the measure of inefficiency in a more formal way in Sect. 7.3.

7.2.2 Planning Framework

The flow of activities in the OR through surgical case planning, directing and controlling, and then back to planning again can be formalized by a planning and control cycle. Because there are some differences between industry and service-oriented industries (Vissers and Beech 2005; Morton 2009; Royston 1998; Delesie 1998) a production control framework for hospitals has been developed, which is illustrated in Fig. 7.1 Production control framework. Characteristic for this framework is that patients, processes and chains are the basis for organizing care and it deals with balancing effective, efficiency and timely care. The framework is based on an analysis of the design requirements for hospital production control systems (de Vries et al. 1999; Vissers et al. 2001) and builds on the production control design concepts developed (Bertrand et al. 1990). It is then applied in the context of the OR.

In this chapter the decisions made on the first four levels of the model are given. The focus of this chapter is on the fifth level of the production control framework as applied to the OR. This level concerns the actual scheduling of patients, given planning rules and service requirements for the coming days or weeks. In addition, we look at the process of rescheduling cases in reaction to unforeseen events like delays and arrival of emergency cases. We consider processes used in facilitating day-to-day activities that need to be performed to deliver timely, effective and efficient care for the patient.

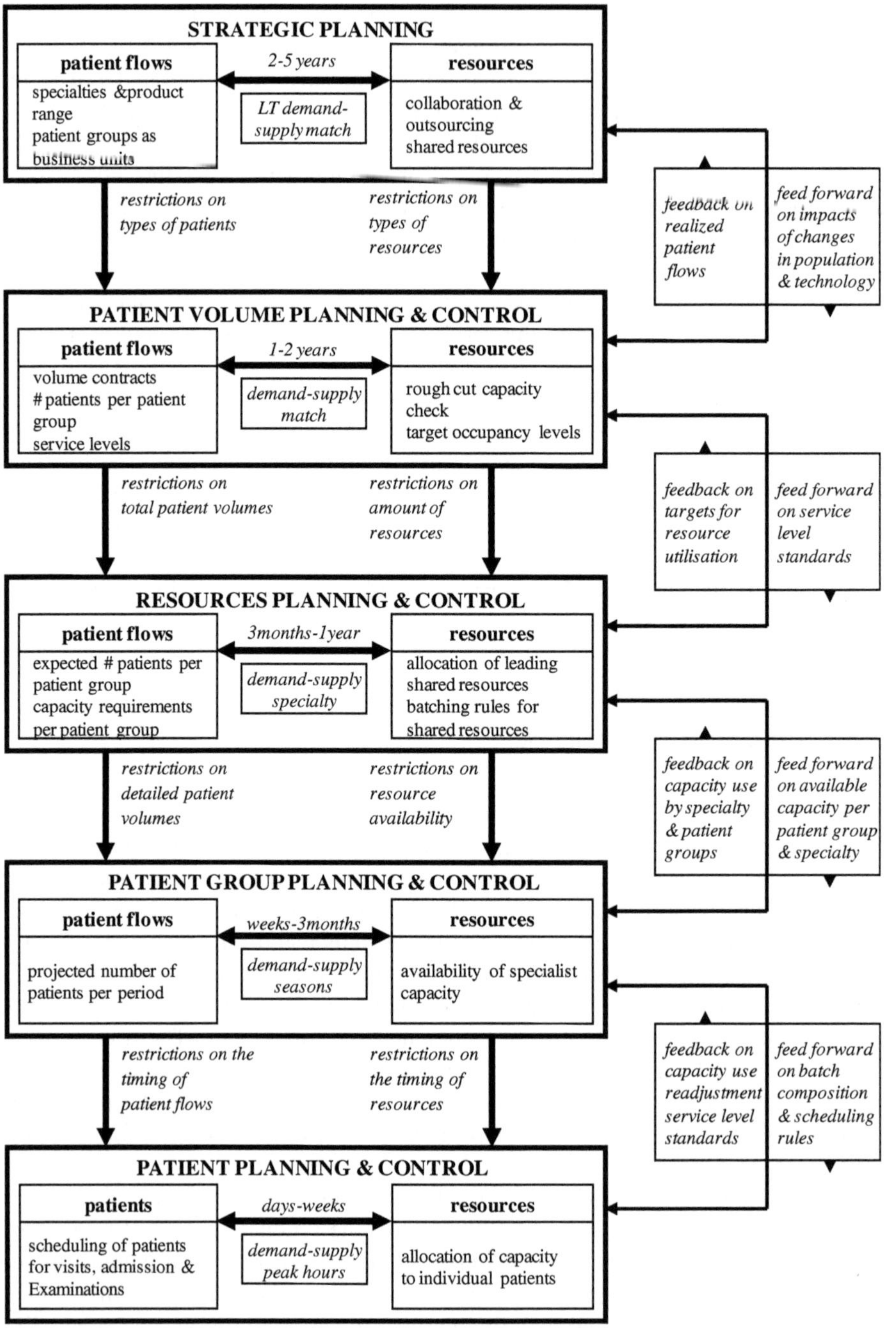

Fig. 7.1 Production control framework

7.2.3 Relevance

Surgical delay has been shown to be an important determinant of patient satisfaction across the continuum of preoperative-operative-postoperative care (Tarazi et al. 1998). Delays in scheduled surgical cases affect patient satisfaction even more than the intraoperative anesthesia experience (Brown et al. 1997).

Delays in surgery resulting from cancellations, bumping of cases and poor scheduling can have a significant impact on the quality of care for scheduled cases as well (Reason 2005). Delays only add to the patient's inherent anxiety associated with surgery and engender anger and frustration. The OR, by its very nature, is an extremely stressful, uncertain, dynamic and demanding environment where staff members need to manage multiple highly technical tasks, often simultaneously (Reason 2005; Silen-Lipponen et al. 2005). Other factors also impact the system within the OR. Examples are individual, group and organizational performance issues such as team and time management, interpersonal skills, leadership, workload distribution, dynamic decision making, human machine interface, problem detection, capture of errors (slips, mistakes, fixation bias), loss of situational awareness, high mental and physical workload, fatigue, environmental stress, production pressure and personal life stress (Weinger et al. 1990). Moreover, the dynamics of the OR are complex because they form a point of intersection among multiple groups with their own agendas and requirements.

OR staff carry out their sometimes long working days under time pressure. The Joint Commission on the Accreditation of Healthcare Organizations has identified time pressures to start or complete the procedure as one of four contributing factors to increased wrong site surgery (ACOG Committee Opinion 2006). Similar to other professions, the undue pressures of time that result from falling behind create stress that can lead to cutting corners or inadvertent error. Relative to other hospital settings, errors in the OR can be catastrophic (i.e., wrong site surgery, retained foreign body, unchecked blood transfusions). In some cases these errors can result in high-profile consequences for the patient, surgeon or hospital (Makary et al. 2006). In other words, poor scheduling and the subsequent induced variations in processes harm outcomes.

Based on the time required to construct schedules as well as the quality of resulting schedules (Beaulieu et al. 2000; Carter and Lapierre 2001) evidence indicates that case scheduling in practice often is performed poorly (Litvak and Long 2000; McManus et al. 2003). Additionally, methods that improve the reliable estimate of surgical cases naturally lead to improved timeliness, efficiency, and effectiveness of OR processes (Dexter 2000; Dexter et al. 2001, 2003; Lapierre et al. 1999; Wickizer 1991).

Reasoning along these lines, Edwards Deming concluded that the real enemy of quality is variation in processes. A main objective in operations management is therefore to identify sources of variation (Tannat 2002). Although variation exists in every process and always will, controlling the identified variation helps managers and clinicians to improve efficiency by aligning the health service delivery processes towards the desired results (McLaughlin and Kaluzny 2006). Indeed, an OR scheduling process that reduces the census variability of the OR can improve the flow of surgical patients to downstream inpatient units, resulting in a more even and predictable patient care burden (Litvak et al. 2005). Furthermore, accurate preoperative scheduling of surgical episodes is critical to the effort to minimize variability in the length of the surgical day and to maintain on-time starts for cases to follow (Litvak et al. 2005).

7.2.4 Formal Problem Definition

We will now turn to a more formal definition of the surgical case scheduling problem. In our definition, the input of the problem consists of:

- A set of n ORs $\{1\ldots n\}$. A subset of these rooms is available for emergency cases. One room is designated as the service room. All cases starting after time T need to be performed in this room.
- A set of case types. For each case type, we have an estimate of the stochastic distribution of the case durations. In this chapter, we assume that these durations follow a log-normal distribution with two parameters. A subset of these case types are emergency case types. The arrivals of each emergency case type follow a stochastic process.
- A set of cases C that can be divided into the set of elective cases and a set of emergency cases. Notice that the emergency cases are not part of the problem's initial input. These cases are implicitly defined by the arrival processes of the emergency case types. They become known only at the time of arrival. The duration $d(c)$ of each case $c \in C$ is only known when the case finishes.
- Regular working hours during which all ORs are opened. We assume they open at time 0 and close at time T. Any cases that have started before T are guaranteed to finish, even if this means that the room has to stay open after T.

In the first stage, each case is assigned an OR and a start time. In the second stage, these assignments can be changed when necessary. Eventually these actions lead to the actual start and end time of the individual cases as well as the closing times C_i of each room i The inefficiency measure discussed earlier can then be defined as $Eff = \sum_i (T - C_i)^+ + \beta \cdot \sum_i (C_i - T)^+$ where $(x)^+ = \max(x, 0)$ and β is the relative cost of overtime.

The objective function can be modified in several ways if we include additional scenarios. First, elective cases can be canceled if not enough regular time is available. We define the set $C^c \subseteq C$ of canceled cases and incur a penalty for each canceled case, which is proportional to the length of the case: $\alpha \cdot \sum_{c \in C^c} d(c)$. Also, for emergency cases we introduce the requirement that they are started within a certain time limit. For each case that violates this requirement, we incur a fixed penalty δ. Let the violating cases be collected in set C^v; then the total penalty value becomes $\delta \cdot |C^v|$.

Having specified the input and the objective function, we now turn to the constraints of the problem, thus defining the solution space available to the Operating Room Coordinator (ORC). First, we assume that the assignment of scheduled cases is given, as is the linear order of the cases per OR. Thus the order of the cases cannot be modified, except for the insertion of emergency cases. Emergency cases can only be scheduled in dedicated ORs, which typically have slack time to accommodate emergency cases. Cases that have already started cannot be interrupted (preempted) for emergency cases. Further, emergency cases cannot be canceled. When a case for an OR is canceled, it is the last scheduled case in the linear order of cases assigned to that room. As an alternative to being cancelled, the last scheduled case can be moved to the service OR to be scheduled after time T. Cancelation and referral decisions cannot be undone. The schedulers do not have information about future arrivals of emergencies or durations of cases other than the information described in the problem input.

7.3 Prior Research

The scheduling of patients in the OR has been studied extensively over the past 40 years. In a review of surgical suite scheduling procedures, Magerlein and Martin (1978) discuss methods for planning patients in advance of their surgical dates, as well as techniques for assigning patients to ORs at specific times of a day. Dexter et al. (1999a, b) used online and offline bin-packing techniques to plan elective cases and evaluated their performances using simulation. A goal-programming model to allocate surgeries to ORs is explored by Ozkarahan (2000). Marcon et al. (2003) present a tool to assist in the planning negotiation between the different actors of the surgical suite. Linear programming models have also been proposed for the planning and scheduling of ORs' activities (Guinet and Chaabane 2003; Jebali et al. 2005). Fei et al. (2004) proposed a column generation approach to plan elective surgeries in identical ORs. Lamiri et al. (2008) present an optimization model and algorithms for elective surgery planning in ORs with uncertain demand for emergency surgery. Their problem consists of determining a plan that specifies the set of elective cases that would be performed in each period over a planning horizon (1 or 2 weeks). The surgery plan should minimize costs related to the over-utilization of ORs and costs related to performing elective surgeries.

The problem addressed in this chapter is related to scheduling problems in which the objective is a weighted function of the makespan and penalties for rejected cases. Such scheduling problems with rejection have been studied for various single objective functions, finding a single optimal solution for case scheduling.

Charnetski (1984) uses simulation to study the problem of assigning time blocks to surgeons on a first-come, first-served basis when the goal is to balance the waiting cost of the surgeon and the idle cost of the facilities and operation room personnel. The proposed heuristic recognizes that different types of procedures have different service time distributions and sets case allowances based on the mean and standard deviation of the individual procedure times. Dexter et al. (1999c) uses computer-based hypothetical OR suites to test different OR scheduling strategies aimed at maximizing OR utilization. OR utilization depends greatly on (and increases) as the average length of time patients wait for surgery increases.

In Van der Velden (2010), methods are developed that take into account multiple objectives. Also, classification trees are used to partition a set of input cases into different subsets and determine optimal heuristics for each subset.

7.4 Applications

We have observed that the personalities of ORCs differ among hospitals in relation to the ORCs willingness to take on more risk in their daily planning, with respect to the risk of cases running late but filling more gaps. This was our motivation for analyzing the effect of risk aversity of an ORC on OR efficiency.

7.4.1 About the Operating Room Coordinator

The person responsible for the surgical schedule is the ORC. The ORC observes the daily variation in this schedule and takes the necessary actions such that scheduled and non-scheduled cases are performed without ending too late in too many ORs at the end of the day. ORCs are the people who maintain a safe and orderly flow of patients in the OR. The position of the ORCs is one that requires highly specialized skills. Moreover, the job can be notoriously stressful, depending on many variables (equipment, specialist, arrival of emergency/acute cases, delay in schedules, human factors, communication, etc.). In addition, they are generally assertive but calm under pressure, and they are able to follow and apply rules and yet be flexible when necessary. The ORC starts with a given schedule and deals with the turn of events as it materializes while performing scheduled cases and emergency cases as they newly arrive. Their jobs involve frequent communication with the various stakeholders such as anesthetists, surgeons and other OR staff. The ORC may cancel scheduled cases, or defer them to the service OR. Their responsibilities include rearranging case and staff assignments, as some OR cases take more or less time than originally planned, and unplanned acute patients require surgery. All other cases have to be performed, potentially yielding overtime work. The task of the ORC is therefore to balance the costs of working overtime with the effects that cancellations have on patient satisfaction and patient health.

There are observed differences among the personalities of the ORCs with regard to their willingness to accept more risk concerning their daily planning. The hypothesis is tested that the relationship between the personality of an ORC, and especially the risk an ORC is willing to take of cases running late, influences OR efficiency. In this section, we discuss an empirical test performed on the ORCs. In Sect. 7.6, we turn to a simulation model developed to test a large range of risk attitudes on an extensive data set. We will use data from the Sint Franciscus Gasthuis (SFG), Rotterdam, The Netherlands.

7.4.2 Human Risk Attitudes

A decision maker is said to be risk-averse if he prefers less risk to more risk, all else being equal. In the OR, a risk-averse decision maker wants all the ORs to be finished before the end of the working day without any chance of running late. The opposite of risk aversion is risk-seeking. A risk-seeking decision maker will prefer more risk to less risk, and accepts the possibility of running late, all else being equal.

There are numerous contributions to the conceptualization of subjective orientation toward risk (Sitkin and Pablo 1992; Weber et al. 1998; Trimpop et al. 1999). Some studies analyze the interaction between personality feature variables, which are not risk attitudes. These variables have been linked to decision-making on risky courses of action (Zuckerman 1990), impulsiveness (Eysenck and Esenck 1977) and decision-making style (Franken 1988). Zuckerman (1994, 2002) developed the Zuckerman–Kuhlman Personality Questionnaire (ZKPQ) to assess personality along five-dimensions. The results of the ZKPQ have been replicated across several studies. These results have shown for example that risk-taking is related to scores on the ZKPQ impulsive sensation seeking scale (Zuckerman 1990). Zuckerman (1990, 2002), Zuckerman and Kuhlman (2000) defines sensation seeking as a need for new and complex experiences and a willingness to take risk for one's own account. He has found that high sensation seekers tend to anticipate lower risk than low sensation seekers do, even for new activities. This finding indicates that a high sensation seeker is more likely to look for opportunities that provide the chance to take a risk, and that the will to take risks seems less threatening to this specific type of individual.

To assess personality versus risk-taking relationship of an ORC, the ZKPQ test and subsequent scores can be applied. We have performed this calculation for the ORCs at the SFG. ZKPQ scores on impulsive sensation seeking can be grouped as follows: the scores of very low and low were considered to be risk-averse, the average scores were considered risk-neutral and the high and very high scores were considered to be non risk-averse. In 2006, prior to the start of the study, the ORCs in the SFG were informed about this study, whereas in 2007 they were not. The ZKPQs for every ORC are given in Table 7.1.

7.4.3 Analyzing Differences Between Risk Attitude Groups

In order to analyze which risk attitude creates maximum OR efficiency, the ORCs expectations with regard to how the OR program would materialize is registered every working day. This expectation, or prognosis, is proposed by the ORC and he

Table 7.1 ZKPQ score per ORC

ORC	ZKPQ score (%)
#1	81
#2	92
#3	25
#4	32

informs the anesthetist on duty of this. When making the prognosis, the following aspects are estimated and noted by the ORC:

- Which OR(s) need(s) time after business hours;
- Which OR(s) are on schedule;
- The amount of available OR capacity for emergency surgery during the period from 2 PM until 4 PM. This capacity is designated for patients already on the waiting list and for emergency patients outside or inside the hospital who may possibly need emergency/acute surgery.

If at 4 PM, all the above-mentioned aspects have been accurately estimated, we say that the ORCs prognosis has materialized. In all other cases, the prognosis has not materialized. Further we measured:

- Whether the prognosis of the ORC made at 2 PM coincides with the actual situation at 4 PM (% of all prognoses made);
- Accurate prognosis made at 2 PM that specific ORs would need extra time after regular working hours (% of all prognoses made);
- The average end time of all ORs;
- The average end time of all ORs still running after 4 PM;
- The average number of ORs in progress after 4 PM;
- The number of unnecessary rejections of planned elective patients.

Operating room inefficiency is defined as the sum of under-utilized OR time and over-utilized OR time multiplied by the relative cost of overtime (Dexter et al. 2004). This definition takes into account the negative effects of not using the expensive operating theatres and having to work outside regular working hours.

The significance of the difference in the average end of program time between risk-averse and risk-seeking ORCs is tested using a factorial ANOVA ($p = 0.05$). After filling in the ZKPQ test and measuring the outcomes during a five month period, the results are as in Table 7.2, which shows the quantitative results of the two groups in 2009–2010.

We observe that the non risk-averse ORC makes a better prognosis concerning the development of the OR program. The average end times of the OR are almost 30 min later compared to the risk-averse ORs. The number of rejected patients is lower when a non risk-averse ORC makes decisions. Further, between the ORCs there is no difference in the average end times of ORs after 4:00 PM.

We studied the sample variance among OR-day combinations. For the study period we used Levene's test of homogeneity of variances. With $p = 0.865$ (2008)

Table 7.2 Main results per type ORC per study period

Working days	Non risk-averse		Risk-averse	
	2009 119	2010 121	2009 120	2010 122
The prognosis of the ORC made at 2 PM matches the actual outcome at 4 PM (% of all prognoses made)	84	81	48	58
Accurate prognosis made at 2 PM that specific ORs will require extra time after regular working hours (% of all prognoses made)	84	79	31	41
Average end time all ORs	3.51 PM (±9 min)	3.42 PM (±11 min)	3.18 PM (±11 min)	3.21 PM (±14 min)
The average end time of all ORs still running after 4 PM	4:20 PM (±18 min)	4:18 PM (±14 min)	4:16 PM (±17 min)	4:19 PM (±17 min)
The average number of ORs in progress after 4 PM (%)	13.8 (±2.5)	11.3 (±2.5)	8.8 (±1.3)	11.3 (±3.8)
The number of unnecessary rejections of planned elective patients	7	9	19	22

and $p = 0.213$ (2009), we can conclude that in both study periods we have equal variances. We performed the one-way ANOVA to compare means of case duration of the four ORCs. With a p value of 0.583 we accept the hypotheses of equal means for the case duration for the four ORCs.

Based on the results we calculated the mean inefficiency per OR per day by considering each OR-day to be independent of all others. The relative cost of overtime in our study is 1.50. The cost per hour of over-utilized OR time includes: indirect costs, intangible costs, and retention and recruitment costs incurred on a long-term basis from staff working late. The mean inefficiency per OR per day for the risk-averse ORC is 0.86 (SD 0.24). For the non risk-averse ORC, the mean inefficiency per OR per day is 0.42 (SD 0.18). This means that the non risk-averse ORC causes a lower OR inefficiency.

7.4.4 Modeling Risk Aversity in Scheduling Algorithms

The research described in the previous section confirms our presumption that risk aversity leads to inefficiency. However, since the number of ORCs in a hospital is limited, it is hard to obtain enough data for a more extensive test. We have therefore developed a simulation model that allows us to measure the impact of risk attitude on the number of canceled tasks, overtime and inefficiency.

Simulation Model

We simulate separate, independent working days using discrete event simulation: the system is modeled by means of a chronologically ordered discrete set of events. As these events are processed one at a time, the state of the system changes and new events may be generated. The simulation starts at 8:00 a.m. and ends when all regular ORs have completed their final case. Because we compare the simulation results with real life day-per-day data from the SFG, we have chosen not to consider interdependencies between working days, e.g., by rescheduling canceled cases the next day.

In each room, we start the first case at 8:00 a.m. When a case starts, the corresponding 'finish event' is generated using the historic duration of the case (so that we can compare our outcomes with historic data). Of course the rescheduling heuristics do not use this generated duration, but work with the parameters of the distribution of the duration of cases of that type. After a case has finished, 9 min is scheduled for cleaning time. After cleaning, the next case assigned to the room starts as soon as possible (if there is one). Cases cannot start more than 60 min earlier than scheduled.

During the simulation, an artificial ORC makes decisions that may change the schedule. For reasons of computation times, we have limited the frequency by which rescheduling is considered. A first rescheduling occurrence is at 8 a.m. when the newly arrived cases are considered, possibly leading to modifications of the original schedule. During the day we consider rescheduling whenever a case finishes with an ending time that differs 15 min or more from the scheduled ending time. Rescheduling is also considered when a new emergency case arrives, and at 16.00, the scheduled closing time of the ORs. Finally, rescheduling is considered at least every 60 min.

Rescheduling must take the following rules into account:

- The sequence of elective cases within an OR is fixed and cannot be changed during the day.
- When an emergency/acute case arrives, it is placed in the series 'non-scheduled'. There is no room assigned to this specific case.
- If before 4 p.m. there is OR capacity available in a room then the next scheduled elective case or urgent/acute case is started.
- Scheduled cases can be moved from the originally assigned room to the service OR or can be canceled.
- Cases that are not yet assigned to any room can be assigned to a room or to the service (so that they are performed after 4 p.m.).

- Canceled cases or cases moved to the service OR cannot be scheduled again in the day schedule (before 4 p.m.).
- Cases cannot be paused or stopped once they have started

Parameterizing Risk Attitude

To evaluate a feasible decision in our heuristic approach at time t, we sample a fixed number of scenarios, each of which completely specifies all arrivals of emergency cases after t, and the durations of all cases to be completed after t according to the scheduling decisions made. We define the cost of a scenario by the cost of the optimal solution for the offline problem as specified by a scenario. Since we want to evaluate a feasible solution at time instant t, we in fact consider the conditional cost of a scenario, i.e., the cost of an optimal solution for the scenario, under the condition that the decision under consideration is indeed taken at time t.

We subsequently define risk attitude on the basis of the scenarios that are taken into account when evaluating decisions. Risk averse ORCs are modeled by considering only a subset of scenarios with high conditional cost for the decision under consideration, whereas risk seeking ORCs are modeled by considering only a subset of scenarios that have low conditional cost for the decision under consideration. In the end, both types of ORCs choose the decision that they evaluate as best.

To formalize this idea, consider the outcomes of a decision for a set of M scenarios. To evaluate the decision, a family of functions is used. Each of these functions sorts the costs under the different scenarios and then takes the average of a subset of these sorted costs. Family members differ in the subset that is used and different subsets represent different risk attitudes. The subsets depend on parameters $\varphi \in [0,1], \omega \in (0,1)$ as follows. Let x be the vector of sorted outcomes with x_i an element of this vector. We assume x_1 is the smallest cost (best case) and x_M is the largest cost (worst case). For given φ and ω we define a function $f_{\varphi,\omega}(x)$ on the vector x of sorted outcomes as follows:

$$f_{\varphi,\omega}(x) = \frac{1}{\omega M} \sum_{i=1+\lfloor \varphi(1-\omega)M \rfloor}^{\lceil \omega M + \varphi(1-\omega)M \rceil} x_i,$$

which is the average of the outcomes with indices between the boundaries $1 + \varphi(1-\omega)M$ and $\omega M + \varphi(1-\omega)M$, which is an interval containing ωM outcomes.

We have three special cases:

- For $\varphi = 0$ we have $f_{0,\omega}(x) = \frac{1}{\omega M} \sum_{i=1}^{\lceil \omega M \rceil} x_i$, which corresponds to the average of the first ωM elements in vector x.
- For $\varphi = 1$ we have $f_{1,\omega}(x) = \frac{1}{\omega M} \sum_{i=1+\lfloor (1-\omega)M \rfloor}^{M} x_i$, which corresponds to the average of the last ωM elements in vector x.

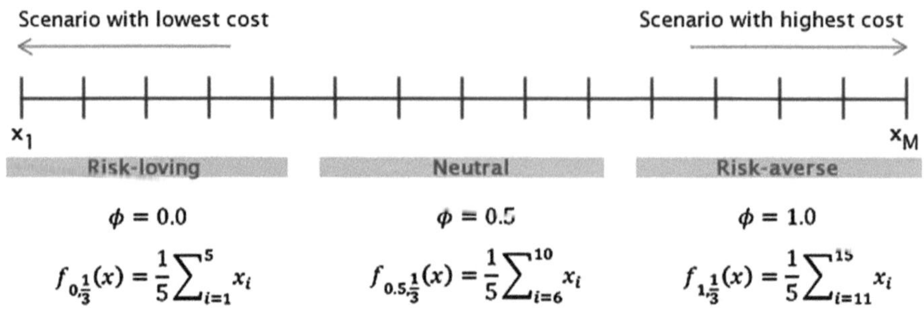

Fig. 7.2 Averaging outcomes

- For $\varphi = 0.5$ we have $f_{0.5,\omega}(x) = \frac{1}{\omega M}\sum_{i=1+\lfloor 0.5(1-\omega)M\rfloor}^{\lceil \omega M+0.5(1-\omega)M\rceil} x_i = \frac{1}{\omega N}\sum_{i=1+\lfloor 0.5M-\omega M\rfloor}^{\lceil 0.5M+0.5\omega M\rceil} x_i$, which corresponds to the average of the middle ωM elements of vector x.

We can view these cases in a more practical, human way:

- A person with $\varphi = 0$ would be a risk seeker, who only takes the best possible outcomes into account and does not care about any scenario that would result in a worse outcome.
- A person with $\varphi = 1$ would be a risk-averse person, whose decisions are guided by worst things that may possibly happen.
- A person with $\varphi = 0.5$ bases his or her decision on the more usual outcomes, ignoring the real extreme cases (good or bad) cases.

This is illustrated in Figure 7.2, where we assume $\omega = 0.3$ and $M = 15$. Note that the three person types all take the average of $\omega M = 5$ observations.[1] However, the non risk-averse ORC averages the five best outcomes while the risk-averse person averages the five worst outcomes. The average person takes some observations in between while ignoring the extreme outcomes on both sides.

The rescheduling heuristic uses Monte Carlo optimization. A Monte Carlo experiment is a class of computational algorithms that relies on repeated random sampling to compute their results. In our study we use it as follows. It starts by generating a set of scenarios. A scenario consists of a random realization for the duration of each of the remaining cases including a set of randomly generated emergency cases still to arrive. For each scenario all assignments of future arrivals to ORs are enumerated. These assignments decisions are complemented by optimal decisions regarding cancelation of elective cases and rescheduling of elective cases in the service OR. Optimality is regarded here with respect to a aforementioned cost function, which serves as the objective function. The cost of a scenario

[1] In the preceding text, we have assumed that all values are integral. In our implementation, we first calculate ωM and round this down; also, the limits for the summation are rounded down

is set to equal the minimum costs (over all assignments for the emergency cases generated in the scenario) of the created optimal schedule per assignment. The rationale behind using the cost of minimum cost schedules for optimal assignments is that this coincides with the scheduling objectives taken into account during the day.

Data and Parameter Settings

The simulation is based on a 3-month period in the year 2009. The total number of surgical cases in this period amounts to 3,027, of which 301 are emergency cases and 39 are acute cases. The number of ORs is ten. For every surgical case we know the scheduled and actual case duration; scheduled and actual start and end time; whether the case is elective, urgent or acute; and the scheduled and actual OR where the case is performed. Holidays and weekends are excluded from the data. Based on the data, all relevant events on the days of surgery and the adjustments can be simulated and the outcomes can be compared to the historical outcomes.

For each surgery we have estimated the parameters of the lognormal distribution that can be used to estimate the case duration. All electives cases were known at 8 a.m., the beginning of the working day. For emergency arrivals, we do not exactly know the time at which they arrived. We will assume the following about their arrival:

- Around 50% of the emergency cases arrive between the end of the previous day and 8:00 a.m. (SFG, 2010). These emergency cases are considered at the start of the day. The remaining emergency cases arrive at a random time between 8 a.m. and 4 p.m.
- The simulation uses historical urgent and acute cases.
- The subset of ORs to which emergency cases can be assigned may vary per day.

To generate random urgent and acute case arrivals between 8:00 and 16:00 for the scenarios, we have collected data about the arrivals of emergency cases in 2008. We assume that the time of day arrivals occur according to a non-homogeneous Poisson process with a piecewise constant arrival rate. The arrival rates are estimated using the mean number of arrivals per 30 min time interval. For each random arrival, we sample a random emergency case from the historical data set. The state of the system at a certain time of the day consists of the status of the planning: the starting and ending times of all cases that have been completed, the starting times and expected duration of the cases that are being performed at that moment, the ordered lists of cases scheduled for future execution in each of the rooms, the list of cases that will be performed in the service OR and finally the list of cases that have been canceled and the cases that have not yet been assigned to any room.

Because SFG aims to avoid cancelation of cases at all costs, we set the corresponding parameter at infinity very large positive value (i.e., $\alpha = 1{,}000{,}000$). In order to find suitable values for the weights β and γ, we have presented actual

ORCs with several dilemmas in which there is a choice between an amount of overtime and another amount of service:

- If there are at 3:30 p.m. two cases to perform, of which one has a scheduled duration of 45 min and the other a scheduled duration of 60 min, which one (or both) of these cases are moved to the service OR?
- Would you rather start a very important case with a scheduled duration of 140 min in the scheduled OR at 2:50 p.m. or at 4 p.m. in the service OR? And would you start the same case at 2:20 p.m. in the scheduled OR or at 4 p.m. in the service OR?
- Would you prefer to perform a case with a scheduled duration of 90 min in the service OR, or would you rather schedule this very same case in a OR with only 60 min of capacity left? And, what would you do if only 45 min of capacity is left?

We suppose that the one who is answering a question balances two types of costs: cost of overtime and costs of moving the operation to the service OR. Let us look at the first question in the third bullet. Suppose that the ORC decides to schedule the case in an OR with only 60 min of capacity left. The ORC prefers 30 (90−60) min expected overtime above 90 min service time. To state it differently, the costs assigned to 30 min of overtime are lower than the costs of 90 min operating in the service OR. Then 30 min x cost overtime <90 min x cost of service time. Then the cost ratio of overtime to service time is <3. We can conclude that the ORC prefers overtime more than three times over service time. Based on the choices made by the ORCs, we set $\beta = 2$ and $\gamma = 1$ (i.e., 1 min of overtime is twice as costly as 1 min of work in the service room). In our experiments, we have considered 30 scenarios while evaluating each possible decision. The choice of 30 scenarios is based on the fact that in real life a rational choice takes into account the cognitive limitations of both knowledge and cognitive capacity of the human being (Simon 1991).

7.4.5 Simulation Results

It is interesting to find out the effects of different risk attitudes when we assume that human capacity will have a hard time analyzing a large number of scenarios. Therefore, in our comparison of simulation results with the historic outcomes, we will use a simulation with 50 scenarios. We now present the results (*based on 50 scenarios*) in comparison with the historical data in Table 7.3.

The last column gives the historical results. The three preceding columns give the results for various choices of the risk aversion parameter φ. The first column are the result for $\varphi = 0$, the most risk seeking variant. The next columns use $\varphi = 0.5$, and $\varphi = 1$, the most risk-averse variant. The simulation results show that the process of cancelation works realistically. At the same time, it reveals that the

Table 7.3 Comparison between results simulator and historical data

	Non risk- averse policy	Mean policy	Risk-averse policy	Historical results
Rejected cases	24	27	30	25
Overtime (min)	5,238	4,060	4,745	2,291
Service time (min)	9,121	10,964	11,269	12,871
Value objective function	24,019,597	27,019,084	30,020,759	25,017,453

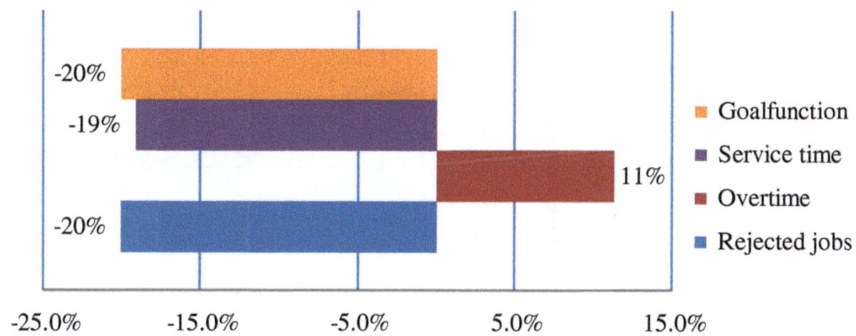

Fig. 7.3 Effect of non risk-averse policy as compared to risk-averse policy (based on 50 scenarios)

preferences regarding overtime versus referral to a service OR may work differently in practice than stated by the ORCs in the presented dilemmas.

The modeling of risk aversion is especially interesting as it models the effect of variations of risk attitude between ORCs. Figure 7.3 compares the results of a risk-minded heuristic ($\varphi = 0$) with a risk-averse heuristic ($\varphi = 1$). The risk-minded heuristics result in less service time, less cancellations and a better objective function value. It does, however, generate more overtime.

Because the SFG specifically wants to avoid cancelation of cases at all costs, α was set at a relatively large value (1,000,000). As there are many hospitals there may be different approaches towards cancelation of cases. To make a more general analyses we therefore set α (arbitrally) tot 100. Figures 7.4, 7.5 and 7.6 show the results of this more general analysis of how each of the three objective function components varies in value with φ. We see the same trend concerning the effect and direction of different risk attitudes on the three components of the goal function as in Table 7.3, but with different values.

We clearly see that risk aversion leads to an increase in the number of cancellations, increase in service time and decrease in overtime. A risk-averse person focuses on the worst scenarios (which may include a larger number of emergency case arrivals or longer expected case durations). Since service time is limited, the presumption of an increased workload will lead to more cancellations.

Fig. 7.4 Risk aversion versus rejected patients

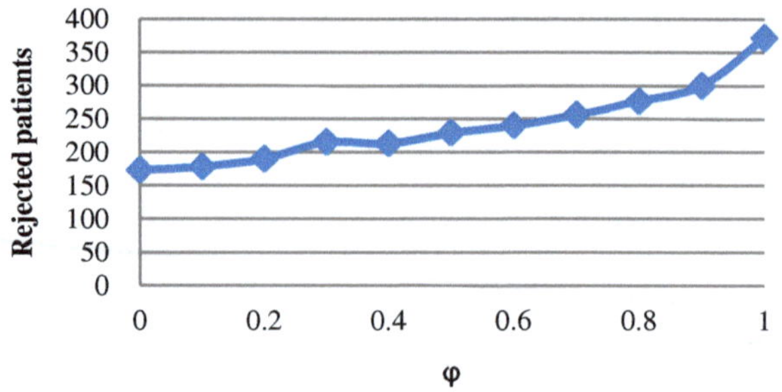

Fig. 7.5 Risk aversion and overtime

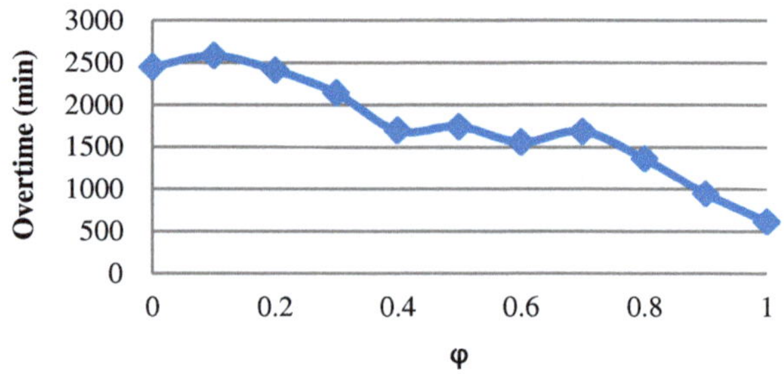

Fig. 7.6 Risk aversion and service time

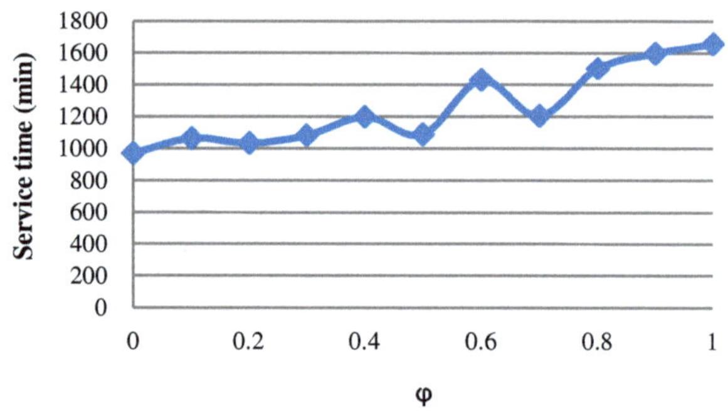

7.5 Further Research

We modeled the daily dynamics faced by the OR and especially how risk aversion influences the quality of the scheduling decisions. Our results are consistent with the findings in the literature: a high sensation seeker is likely to look for opportunities that provide the chance to take a risk, and this risk will seem less threatening to this kind of individual. The results confirm earlier findings that a non risk-averse ORC creates lower costs and fewer rejected patients compared to a risk-averse ORC as well as a higher utilization during working days. When recruiting an ORC, it may be helpful to consider risk-aversion one of the selection criteria.

Though there is much evidence to support the link between personality and risk-taking, the literature shows that the exact nature is still unclear. It could be interested to find what happens in the mind of a risk-taker that is significantly different from what occurs in the mind of a non risk-taker. Further, in our research we choose one axis of interest: sensation seeking. But there are other axes, such as neuroticism-anxiety, aggression-hostility, activity, and sociability that can be important, necessary, or completely determinative for an ORC's success in planning the schedule. This has to be analyzed in future studies with a larger population of ORCs. We suggest repeating the study in other hospitals and further improvement of the heuristics in the process. More generally, improvement of the heuristics is an interesting direction for further research. The results of these research will contribute to improved timeliness, efficiency, and effectiveness of OR processes.

References

ACOG Committee Opinion (2006) Patient safety in the surgical environment. Obstet Gynecol 107:429–433

Beaulieu H, Ferland JA, Gendron B, Michelon P (2000) A mathematical programming approach for scheduling physicians in the emergency room. Health Care Manag Sci 3:19–200

Bertrand JWM, Wortmann JC, Wijngaard J (1990) Production control: a structural and design oriented approach. Elsevier, Amsterdam

Cao Z, Zhang Y (2007) Scheduling with rejection and non-identical job arrivals. J Syst Sci Complex 20:529–535

Cao Z, Yang XA (2009) PTAS for parallel batch scheduling with rejection and dynamic job arrivals. Theor Comput Sci 410:27–29

Cao Z, Wang Z, Zhang Y, Liu S (2006) On several scheduling problems with rejection or discretely compressible processing times. Lecture notes in computer science, Springer, Beijing, pp 90–98

Carter MW, Lapierre SD (2001) Scheduling emergency room physicians. Health Care Manag Sci 4:347–360

Charnetski JR (1984) Scheduling operating room surgical procedures with early and late completion penalty costs. J Oper Manag 5:91–102

de Vries G, Bertrand JWM, Vissers JMH (1999) Design requirements for healthcare production control systems. Prod Control Plan 10:559–569

Delesie L (1998) Bridging the gap between clinicians and health managers. Eur J Oper Res 8:28–35

Dexter F, Macario A (2004) When to allocate operating room time to increase operating room efficiency. Anesth Analg 98:758–762

Dexter F, Traub RD (2000) Sequencing cases in the operating room: predicting whether one surgical case will last longer than another. Anesth Analg 90:975–979

Dexter F, Macario A, Traub RD (1999a) Which algorithm for scheduling add-on elective cases to maximizes operating room utilization? Use of bin packing algoritms and fuzzy constraints in operating room management. Anesthesiology 91:1491–1500

Dexter F, Macario A, Traub RD, Hopwood M, Lubarsky DA (1999b) An operating room scheduling strategy to maximize the use of operating room block time: computer simulation of patient scheduling and survey of patients preferences for surgical waiting time. Anesth Analg 89(1):7–20

Dexter F, Macario A, Traub RD, Hopwood M, Lubarsky DA (1999c) An operating room scheduling strategy to maximize the use of operating room block time: computer simulation of patient scheduling and survey of patients' preferences for surgical waiting time. Anesth Analg 89:7–20

Dexter F, Epstein RH, Marsh HM (2001) A statistical analysis of weekday operating room anesthesia group staffing costs at nine independently managed surgical suites. Anesth Analg 92:1493–1498

Dexter F, Traub RD, Macario A (2003) How to release allocated operating room time to increase efficiency: predicting which surgical service will have the most underutilized operating room time. Anesth Analg 96:507–512

Engels DW, Karger DR, Kolliopoulos SG, Sengupta S, Uma RN, Wein J (2003) Techniques for scheduling with rejection. J Algorithms 49:175–191

Epstein L, Noga J, Woeginger GJ (2002) On-line scheduling of unit time cases with rejection: minimizing the total completion time. Oper Res Lett 30:415–420

Eysenck SBG, Esenck HJ (1977) The place of impulsiveness in a dimensional system of personality description. Br J Soc Clin Psychol 16:57–68

Fei H, Chu C, Artiba A, Meskens N (2004) Planification des salles opératoires : résolution par la génération de colonnes et la programmation dynamique, 2ème Conférence Francophone en Gestion et Ingénierie des Systèmes Hospitaliers, GISEH, Mons, Belgique, 9–11 Sept

Fleischer R, Wahl M (2000) Online scheduling revisited. J Sched 3:343–353

Franken RE (1988) Sensation seeking, decision making styles and preference for individual responsibility. Pers Individ Differ 9:136–146

Jebali A, Hadjalouane AB, Ladet P (2005). Operating rooms scheduling, International Journal of Production Economics, Corrected Proof, Accessed 29 June 2005 (in press)

Karger DR, Phillips SJ, Torng E (1996) A better algorithm for an ancient scheduling problem. J Algorithms 20:400–430

Lamiri M, Xie X, Dolgui A, Grimaud F (2008) A stochastic model for operating rooms planning with elective and emergency surgery demands. Eur J Oper Res 185:1026–1037

Lapierre SD, Batson C, McCaskey S (1999) Improving on-time performance in health care organisations: a case study. Health Care Manag Sci 2:27–34

Litvak E, Long MC (2000) Cost and quality under managed care: irreconcilable differences? Am J Manag Care 6:305–312

Litvak E, Buerhues PI, Davidoff F, Long M et al (2005) Managing unnecessary variability in patient demand to reduce nursing stress and improve patient safety. J Qual Patients Saf 31:330–338

Magerlein JM, Martin JB (1978) Surgical demand scheduling: a review. Health Serv Res 13(4):418–433

Makary MA, Sexton BJ, Freischlag JA, Millman EA et al (2006) Patient safety in surgery. Ann Surg 243:628–635

Marcon E, Kharraja S, Simmonet G (2003) The operating theatre scheduling: an approach centered on the follow-up of the risk of no realization of the planning. Int J Prod Econ 85(1):83–90

McLaughlin CP, Kaluzny AD (2006) Continuous quality improvement in health care. 3rd edn. Center for Health Services Research, University of North Carolina at Chapel Hill, Chapel Hill

McManus ML, Long MC, Cooper A et al (2003) Variability in surgical caseload and access to intensive care services. Anesthesiology 98:1491–1496

Megow N, Uetz M, Vredeveld T (2006) Models and algorithms for stochastic online scheduling. Math Oper Res 31:513–525

Möhring RH, Radermacher FJ, Weiss G (1984) Stochastic scheduling problems: general strategies. Zeitschrift für Operations Research 28:193–260

Möhring RH, Schulz AS, Uetz M (1999) Approximation in stochastic scheduling: the power of LP-based priority policies. J ACM 46:924–942

Morton A (2009) Analysis: What's the difference between a hospital and a bottling factory. Br Med J 339:2727

Ozkarahan I (2000) Allocation of surgeries to operating rooms by goal programming. J Med Syst 24(6):339–378

Reason J (2005) Safety in the operating theatre part 2: human error and organizational failure. Qual Saf Health Care 14:56–60

Royston G (1998) Shifting the balance of care into the 21st century. Eur J Oper Res 105:267–276

Rudin JF (2001) Improved bounds for the on-line scheduling problem. Ph.D. thesis, The University of Texas at Dallas

Sgall J (1998) On-line scheduling: a survey. Online algorithms: the state of the art. Comput Sci 1442:196–231

Simon H (1991) Bounded rationality and organizational learning. Organ Sci 2:125–134

Sitkin SB, Pablo AL (1992) Reconceptualizing the determinants of risk behaviour. Acad Manag Rev 17:9–38

Stachota P, Normandin P (2003) Reasons registered nurses leave or change employment status. J Nurs Adm 33(2):111–118

Stepaniak PS (2010) Modeling and management of variation in the operating theatre. Ph.D. thesis, Erasmus University Rotterdam

Stepaniak PS, Mannaerts GHH, de Quelerij M, de Vries G (2009) The effect of the operating room coordinators risk appreciation on operating room efficiency. Anesth Analg 108:1249–1256

Stepaniak PS, Heij C, Mannaerts GHH, de Quelerij M, de Vries G (2010) Modeling procedure and surgical times for current procedural terminology-anesthesia-surgeon combinations and evaluation in terms of case-duration prediction and operating room efficiency: a multicenter study. Anesth Analg 106:1232–1245

Tannat G (2002) Design for six sigma: launching new products and services without failure. Gower Publishing Limited, New York

Thomson TP, Brown H (2002) Turnover of licensed nurses in skilled nursing facilities. Nurs Econ 20(2):66–69

Trimpop RM, Kerr JH, Kirkcaldy BD (1999) Comparing personality constructs of risk-taking behaviour. Pers Individ Differ 26:237–254

van der Velden R (2010) Multi-objective analysis of online and offline surgical scheduling heuristics. Master thesis, Erasmus University

Vissers J, Beech R (2005) Health operations management. Patient flow logistics in health care. In: Vissers J, Beech R (eds) Routledge, London

Vissers JMH, Bertrand JWM, De Vries G (2001) A framework for production control in health care organisations. Prod Control Plan 12:591–604

Weber EU, Hsee CK, Sokolowska J (1998) What folkore tells about risk and risk taking? Cross-cultural comparisons of America, German and Chinese proverbs. Organ Behav Hum Decis Process 75:170–186

Wickizer TM (1991) Effect of hospital utilization review on medical expenditures in selected diagnostic areas: an exploratory study. Am J Public Health 81:482–484

Zuckerman M (1990) The psychophysiology of sensation seeking. J Pers 59:313–345

Zuckerman M (1994) An alternative five-factor model for personality. In: Halverson CF, Kohnstamm GA, Martin RP (eds) The developing structure of temperament and personality from infacy to adulthood. Lawrence Erlbaum, Hillsdale, pp 53–68

Zuckerman M (2002) Zuckerman–Kuhlman personality questionnaire (ZKPQ): an alternative five factorial. In: DeRaad B (ed) Big five assessment. Hogerefe and Huber Publishers, Seattle

Zuckerman M, Kuhlman M (2000) Personality and risk taking: common biosocial factors. J Pers 68:999–1029

Chapter 8
Bed Assignment and Bed Management

Randolph Hall

Abstract Beds are a critical resource for serving patients in hospitals, but also provide a place where patients queue for needed care. Bed requirements result from medical needs along with the hospital's effectiveness at reducing average length of stay and hospitalization rates. Hospitals can reduce the need for beds by reducing the unproductive portion of the patient's stay (e.g., waiting for a test) and by reducing the portion of time when beds are unoccupied. Hospitals must also synchronize discharges with admissions to minimize time of day and day of week variations in bed occupancy levels. Finally, beds must be managed as part of the overall hospital system so that shortages do not cause delays or cancellations in the emergency department or surgery.

8.1 Introduction

Hospital size is measured in many ways, but most often by the number of in-patient beds. When the Los Angeles County decided to replace its old general hospital (LA County/University of Southern California, or LAC/USC) in 1997, county supervisors approved a hospital with 600 licensed in-patient beds, far less than the old hospital, which was staffed for nearly 750 in-patient beds and licensed for almost 1,400. The decision to reduce the number of in-patient beds remains controversial to this day.

R. Hall (✉)
Epstein Department of Industrial and Systems Engineering,
University of Southern California, Los Angeles, CA 90089-0193, USA
e-mail: rwhall@usc.edu

R. Hall (ed.), *Handbook of Healthcare System Scheduling*,
International Series in Operations Research & Management Science 168,
DOI: 10.1007/978-1-4614-1734-7_8,

In reality, the number of in-patient beds is only one determinant of a hospital's ability to serve patients. Since the 1930s, when the original LAC/USC hospital was constructed, the practice of medicine has changed for the better. The demographics of hospital patients have also changed, and so has the landscape of competing hospitals in the region. It is accepted today that long patient stays are neither good for the health of patients nor a good expenditure of money. By reducing patient stays, more patients can be served with the same number of beds.

LAC/USC has also evolved in the types of cases it sees. Today, the vast majority of its admissions enter through the emergency department (ED) rather than as scheduled procedures. Although the number of in-patient beds was reduced, the county significantly expanded its ED, providing more than 100 ED beds in the new hospital.

In the 1930s, it was common to build hospitals with open bed wards with many patients residing in the same room. Patients in new hospitals are now given private rooms, offering more flexibility to use beds for different types of patients and to serve them better. Reduced length of stay, changes in cases, and changes in room design are indicative of the fact that counting beds alone does not tell the whole story as to a hospital's abilities to serve its patients.

The need for hospital beds results from rates of hospitalization (i.e., the rate at which people are admitted and discharged from hospitals), efficiency and the average length of stay (LOS) for patients. The latter has declined significantly in recent decades. In the US, the average length of stay was nearly 8 days in 1960 (OECD 2009, 2011) declining to 6.4 days in 1990 and 4.8 days in 2007 (NCHS 2010), a trend that holds for most age groups and health conditions. In the Netherlands, the decline has been even more dramatic, from more than 20 days in 1960 to less than 6 in 2009. LOS averages 4–7 days in most OECD countries, with only Japan falling far outside this range with an average above 18 days (OECD 2011). Efficient hospitals can achieve average lengths of stay well below 4 days.

Among OECD Countries in 2007, the number of acute hospital beds/capita ranged from 1.0/1,000 people in Mexico to 8.2/1,000 people in Japan, with an average of 3.85 (slightly more than France and slightly less than Greece; OECD 2011). The average bed occupancy among OECD countries is 75%, and ranges from 60% in Mexico to 89% in Canada.

According to the American Hospital Association (2010), the US is served by nearly 5,800 hospitals and nearly 950,000 staffed beds (about one bed for every 320 people), each hospital averaging 160 beds. These hospitals range in size from just a few beds in rural communities to more than 1,000 in major urban health centers. Nearly 90% of the nation's hospitals are classified as community hospitals, of which 60% operate as part of a system and another 30% are affiliated with other hospitals through networks.

Both hospitalizations and length of stay depend on the health of the population, which is also related to age. The average LOS for those over 85 within the U.S. was 5.6 days in 2007 (still shorter than the average LOS for all people in 1990). "In 2007, those aged 65 years and over accounted for just 13% of the US population, but 37% of the hospital discharges, and 43 percent of the days of care."

(Hall et al 2009). Those over 65 are admitted to hospitals at nearly three times the rate of the average person.

Emergency departments in the US saw 124 million people in 2008 (41 visits/100 persons), resulting in nearly 17 million hospitalizations (5.6/100 persons). According to the 2007 hospital discharge survey (2009), total hospitalizations averaged 11.44/100 persons/year. Thus, half of all admissions come via the emergency department. Between 1980 and 2000, hospitalization rates declined by 25% overall and have remained steady since. In other OECD countries, hospitalization rates range from about 6/100 persons/year (Mexico) to 26 (Austria).

While some number of beds is necessary to serve health needs, health systems have found ways to improve health while also reducing the number of beds. This can be accomplished by reducing the need for hospitalization and reducing the length of stay.

The remainder of this chapter is divided into three sections. First, in Sect. 8.2, we describe the factors that affect the need for in-patient hospital beds in a community as well as bed management terminology. Next, in Sect. 8.3, we review the literature on bed management. Finally, in Sect. 8.4, we provide the directions for future research.

8.2 Defining the Need for Beds

Beds are needed to accommodate patients during their hospital stays, for recuperation, observation, tending to wounds and administration of a range of therapies. By providing more beds, hospitals expand their capacity to provide this range of services to more patients and, consequently, expand their capacity to perform more scheduled operations and procedures and accommodate more unscheduled emergency cases. The demand for beds is a function of the following factors:

Health and age of the population: Community health programs aim to reduce the need for hospitalization through prevention programs; therapies delivered through out-patient clinics can also restore patient health and circumvent the need for hospitalization. However, as people age, increased rates of hospitalization are inevitable, and therefore the age distribution of communities has a large effect on the need for hospital beds. The complexity of cases is measured with the *case mix index* (CMI), which can be correlated to average hospital length of stay. In the US, the CMI is an average among diagnostic-related groups (DRGs) for Medicare patients, which is also a measure of cost reimbursement.

Technology: A factor in the reduction of hospitalization rates in recent decades has been introduction of minimally invasive surgical procedures (e.g., laser guided cataract surgery and laparoscopic surgery) that can be performed in an out-patient setting, eliminating the need for in-patient beds or reducing the length of stay. Alternatives to general anesthesia also reduce the need for hospitalization.

Efficiency and quality in serving patients: Much of the time spent by patients in hospital beds is not medically necessary. While the bed is a point where patients are served, it is also a point where patients wait—for a diagnostic test, surgery, discharge. The length of stay for patients is often symptomatic of the hospital's efficiency in delivering care to its patients. Hospitals need to reduce the *unproductive* portion of the patient's length of stay. Hospitals also need to ensure that patients receive appropriate care and are not discharged prematurely, necessitating a hospital readmission.

Efficiency in managing beds: The cost of building and equipping the space for an average hospital bed exceeds $1 million in much of the US, and the average cost per day for a hospital stay runs in thousands of dollars. For such a high-valued resource, it is essential for hospitals to minimize the downtime between the discharge of one patient and intake of the next. Improved coordination, so that the departure of a patient is both predicted in advance and instantly communicated to housekeeping and intake, can make it possible for a new patient to be quickly assigned to a room. Hospitals need to reduce the portion of time that beds *are unoccupied.*

The focus of this chapter is on reducing unproductive bed time and unoccupied bed time, so that more patients can be served, patients spend less time in hospitals, and resources can be used more efficiently.

Hospitals should also strive to reduce the need for hospitalization by improving patient health in out-patient settings, including the introduction of technology that reduces the need for hospitalization.

As an illustration, Ham et al. (2003) compared length of stay at Kaiser Permanente (KP) of California to other Medicare patients in California, other Medicare patients in the US and the UK National Health System, finding that KP achieved substantially less bed use through reduced hospitalization and shorter stays. They conclude that: "The NHS can learn from Kaiser's integrated approach, the focus on chronic diseases and their effective management, the emphasis placed on self care, the role of intermediate care, and the leadership provided by doctors in developing and supporting the model of care."

8.2.1 Classification of Bed Types

Bed management would be much simpler if all beds were the same, one substituting for the next. It would also be simpler if hospitals had flexibility to add and subtract beds as needed, or were not limited by regulation on the number of patients they can admit. The United States' Agency for Health Care Research and Quality AHRQ (2011a) has defined in-patient bed capacity of hospitals as follows:

"*Licensed beds*: The maximum number of beds for which a hospital holds a license to operate. Many hospitals do not operate all of the beds for which they are licensed.

Physically available beds: Beds that are licensed, physically set up, and available for use. These are beds regularly maintained in the hospital for the use of patients, which furnish accommodations with supporting services (such as food, laundry, and housekeeping). These beds may or may not be staffed but are physically available.

Staffed beds: Beds that are licensed and physically available for which staff is on hand to attend to the patient who occupies the bed. Staffed beds include those that are occupied and those that are vacant.

Unstaffed beds: Beds that are licensed and physically available and have no current staff on hand to attend to a patient who would occupy the bed.

Occupied beds: Beds that are licensed, physically available, staffed and occupied by a patient.

Vacant/available beds: Beds that are vacant and to which patients can be transported immediately. These must include supporting space, equipment, medical material, ancillary and support services, and staff to operate under normal circumstances. These beds are licensed, physically available and have staff on hand to attend to the patient who occupies the bed."

Thus, at any point of time, the number of beds available for patients can be no more than the number of licensed beds, the number of available beds and the number of staffed beds. Further, nurse staffing can be constrained by regulation. In the US, hospitals certified to participate in Medicare are required to "have adequate numbers of licensed registered nurses, licensed practical (vocational) nurses, and other personnel to provide nursing care to all patients as needed".[1] The American Nursing Association (ANA 2011) has advocated for hospitals to create:

1. Nurse Staffing Plans—Direct care nurses contribute to development of hospital-wide plans, by unit and shift, that set nurse staffing levels based on patient acuity and needs at any given time, available support staff and other factors.
2. Nurse-to-Patient Ratios—A specific, legally mandated minimum ratio, varying based on the type of unit.
3. Disclosure of Staffing Levels—Hospitals must publicly report nurse staffing levels so staffing plans can be reviewed by hospital staff, patients, the public or a regulatory body.

Individual states have legislated standards for nurse-to-patient ratios. California was the first to enact such a law in 1999, followed by implementation of department specific standards throughout the state in 2004 (Spetz et al. 2000; Terasawa et al. 2010). Through the imposition of such ratios, the number of available beds is sometimes reduced due to insufficient nurse staffing.

Beyond limits on the number of beds in aggregate, hospitals are also constrained by the number of beds of any given type. While some bed types may substitute for others, availability of the right types of beds can limit a hospital's ability to admit particular patients. AHRQ (2011a) classifies beds as follows:

---

[1] Chapter IV: Centers for Medicare & Medicaid Services, Department of Health and Human Services, Subchapter g: standards and certification. 42 CFR 482.23(b).

"*Adult Intensive Care* (*ICU*): Can support critically ill/injured patients, including ventilator support.

Medical/Surgical: Also thought of as "Ward" beds.

Burn or Burn ICU: Either approved by the American Burn Association or self-designated. (These beds should not be included in other ICU bed counts.)

Pediatric ICU (*PICU*): The same as adult ICU, but for patients 17 years and younger.

Pediatrics: Ward medical/surgical beds for patients 17 and younger.

Psychiatric: Ward beds on a closed/locked psychiatric unit or ward beds where a patient will be attended by a sitter.

Negative pressure/isolation: Beds provided with negative airflow, providing respiratory isolation. Note: This value may represent available beds included in the counts of other types.

Operating rooms: An operating room that is equipped and staffed and could be made available for patient care in a short period."

Other bed classifications include:

Post Anesthesia Care Unit (*PACU*) beds, found within surgical departments.

"*Step-down*" beds, or beds that transition between an ICU bed and a general hospital bed.

Telemetry beds, which provide continuous electronic monitoring, particularly for heart rate and rhythm and breathing, either at bedside or from a nursing station.

Finally, beds may reside within wards, units or departments that are classified by medical specialty, grouping patients having similar conditions, both to provide specialized care and to offer efficiency. Examples include burns, maternity, psychiatric, pediatric, neurology and detoxification. Hospitals themselves are classified according to the type of care offered, which may include specialized tertiary or quaternary care (for instance, transplant procedures), trauma care or, at the other end of the spectrum, rehabilitation.

Bed scheduling is naturally complicated by the provision of more specialized bed types, as well as their elevated importance. In the period from 1984 to 2000, critical care beds increased in numbers in the US, while in-patient beds of all types declined (Halpern et al. 2004). Hospitals increasingly focus on more complex cases, which demands specializations.

8.2.2 Measuring the Performance of Bed Management

Within the nomenclature of queueing systems, beds act as servers and patients act as customers. Arrivals occur when patients are ready to be placed in a bed, which may occur after being seen in an emergency department, when ready to leave a PACU or simply upon admission to a hospital. The queue represents the set of patients waiting to be placed in a bed. Departures occur when the patient is discharged and transported out of his or her room. In a general sense, hospitals seek to:

Maximize throughput per bed: the number of patients discharged per bed per unit time.
Minimize waiting time for beds: the length of time from when a patient is ready to be placed in a bed until the patient is in the bed.
Maximize occupancy: the proportion of time that a bed is occupied by a patient.
As a byproduct, hospitals also seek to minimize the number of patients that cannot be accommodated due to blocking or delays, who either forego treatment or go elsewhere for treatment.

Maximizing Throughput

Throughput is maximized when the *bed cycle* is minimized, representing the time from when one patient is discharged and leaves the room until the next patient is discharged and leaves the room.[2] Many hospitals follow a cycle comprising the following steps:

1. *Notification time*: from when patient leaves until the bed management system is notified that the patient has left.
2. *Housekeeping response time*: from notification until housekeeping arrives at the room to prepare the bed for the next patient.
3. *Cleaning time*: for preparation of the bed for the next patient.
4. *Notification time*: from completion of cleaning until bed management is notified that the bed is ready for the next patient.
5. *Assignment time*: from notification until a specific patient is assigned to the bed.
6. *Transportation time*: from assignment until the patient is placed in the room.
7. *Intake time*: the process by which the patient is admitted into a bed, including the transfer of all information to nursing staff for the care of the patient.
8. *Use time*: when patient occupies a bed until the attending physician orders discharge.
9. *Discharge time*: a period when the steps of discharge (e.g., providing instructions to patients, delivering medications, arranging for transportation) are completed.
10. *Wait for transportation*: from when the discharge process is complete until the patient is transported out of the room.

The patient is not physically present in the bed for steps 1–6, and would not be present for all of steps 7–10 if he or she has been temporarily transported elsewhere for a procedure or test (in which case the bed is held for the patient's return). The bed throughput, T, equals the inverse of the mean bed cycle time, C.

---

[2] A departure can also occur due to the death of a patient.

When the steps are performed sequentially, T is the inverse of the sum of the individual cycle components:

$$T = 1/C = 1/\sum_{i=1}^{10} t_i$$

where:
t_i = the average length of step i

Bed throughput is increased by shortening or eliminating individual steps. For instance, systems can be created to more quickly dispatch housekeeping or transportation teams, or to speed up the discharge process. Bed throughput can also be increased by shortening the patient's stay (steps 7–10), which depends on:

Medical opinion: of the attending physician, deciding when a patient is ready for discharge.
Standards of care: defining how long a patient should normally remain in the hospital for a particular condition.
Medical advancements: creating new technologies and modalities of care that make it medically unnecessary for a patient to spend as long in the hospital.
Co-Morbidities: defining the overall patient health and the ability of the patient to rapidly recover.
Placement: whether the patient has a place available to further recuperate upon discharge, which can be affected by homelessness, whether family members are available for support or whether space is available in a rehabilitation hospital.

Bed throughput could also be increased by creating systems that permit steps to be performed simultaneously. For instance, a patient might be assigned and transported as soon as the bed is vacated, assuming that housekeeping can quickly ready the room during the intervening time. A high throughput also depends on having a queue of patients ready to be assigned to each type of bed, thus keeping the assignment time from growing due to the absence of patients.

The capacity per bed, *c,* differs from bed throughput, and represents the maximum rate at which a bed can accommodate patients. It differs from bed throughput in Step 5, the assignment time. When there is no patient ready for assignment to a bed, Step 5 is elongated, reducing throughput but not capacity. It is also possible for other steps to be elongated due to a shortage of resources—no transportation staff, housekeeping staff, etc. We define capacity (for sequential steps) as:

$$c = 1/C' = 1/\sum_{i=1}^{10} t'_i$$

where C' is the average cycle time when no step is elongated due to a shortage of resources or patients, defined by the times t'_i, each representing the average length of an un-delayed cycle step. Hospitals strive to attain throughputs that approach the capacity of their beds by making the individual steps as short as possible.

The average Bed Length of Stay (BLOS) represents the average time that a patient is physically assigned to an in-patient bed (from intake to departure), thus equaling:

$$\text{BLOS} = \sum_{i=7}^{10} t_i$$

BLOS typically (but not always) comprises the majority of the bed's cycle time and, therefore, it is important to minimize BLOS in order to maximize throughput and capacity. If a patient spends time in multiple beds, the average total length of stay, LOS, is the sum of the $\underline{\text{BLOS}}$ times for all beds in which he or she resided, plus any time transporting the patient between beds.

The average turnover time, TT, is the unoccupied portion of the bed cycle, or more specifically:

$$\text{TT} = \sum_{i=1}^{6} t_i$$

Minimizing turnover time acts to increase the bed occupancy, and is accomplished either through improved efficiency or ensuring that the number of beds is well matched to demand (thus minimizing delays in the assignment step due to the absence of waiting patients).

Minimizing Waiting Time and Total Stay

The waiting time depends on the rate at which patients present for care, the number of beds available of each type and the capacity per bed. Hospitals can control waiting time by controlling throughput and capacity and by controlling arrivals. They can also directly reduce average waiting time, *W*, by minimizing assignment and transportation time, placing the patient in the bed as immediately as possible after the bed is ready to be occupied.

The average total stay, TS, is the sum of the average waiting time and the average total length of stay:

$$\text{TS} = W + \text{LOS},$$

where,

LOS = the average total length of stay (accounting for all beds occupied by each patient from intake to discharge).

For the patient's benefit and for efficiency, it is desirable to minimize total stay, but it is particularly desirable to minimize waiting time because this is when patients do not reside in a bed that matches their medical need.

Arrivals occur due to both scheduled and unscheduled (principally emergency) cases and both are controllable to a degree. Scheduled cases are typically planned well in advance, and can be set according to projected bed availability (accounting for nursing schedules, for instance) and seasonal trends. Unscheduled cases are affected by the management of the emergency department. While an emergency department is either morally or legally required (for instance, the US' Emergency Medical Treatment and Labor Act, EMTALA) to see all presenting emergency patients, regardless of ability to pay, an ED does influence the arrival of emergency cases via ambulance. Hospitals sometimes move to "*divert*" status due to back-ups in emergency, in which case patients may (but not always) be routed to alternate hospitals. Doctors also influence waits in the following ways:

Admission decision: a doctor decides whether a patient is admitted to an in-patient bed for medical reasons, but this is a judgment call, sometimes influenced by bed availability and patient and family preference (and their persuasiveness). In some hospitals the patient may receive priority for surgery as a consequence of being admitted, even though he or she has been stabilized and could have been discharged to await surgery.

Assignment decision: the doctor also decides the type of bed to which the patient is assigned. The hospital has the greatest flexibility in managing waits when the patient is assigned to a general medical/surgical bed. For instance, telemetry beds are in limited supply, but even so doctors will assign patients to telemetry as a precaution, when not medically indicated (Chen and Hollander 2007).

In some situations, the bed manager must also decide whether to upgrade a patient to a type of bed that is equipped beyond need, should that be the only bed available. Doing so may reduce waiting in the short-run, but cause subsequent delay for patients who truly need that type of specialized bed.

When all beds of a needed type are occupied, then the following may occur:

- Patients will become "*boarders*" in the emergency department, meaning they have been seen and admitted, but are resting in a temporary location, perhaps in an examination room, in a temporary holding room or even on a gurney in a hallway. Boarders inhibit the ability of the emergency department to see additional patients, and exacerbate queues in waiting rooms (Gallager and Lunn 1990; Howell et al. 2008; Proudlove et al. 2003).
- It may be impossible to move a patient from one bed type to another, for instance from ICU to a general medical/surgical bed.
- Surgical cases may be postponed because there is no place for the patient to recover once surgery is completed.

Thus, failure to accommodate patients in beds can block progress in other parts of the hospital. In busy emergency departments, it is not unusual for patients to wait a day or more to be assigned to an in-patient bed.

Maximizing Occupancy

The occupancy for a particular bed, o, is the proportion of time that a bed is occupied by a patient, and represents the ratio of the average bed length of stay, BLOS, to the average cycle time, C:

$$o = \mathrm{BLOS}/C.$$

For economic reasons, hospitals strive for high total occupancy (o) levels, representing:

$$o = \sum_{j=1}^{N} o_j/N$$

where,

o_j = occupancy for bed j
N = number of licensed beds

A high occupancy results naturally from minimizing turnover time, in part through efficiency and in part by ensuring that patients arrive at a sufficient rate to fill beds to capacity. As mentioned earlier, the average bed occupancy in OECD countries is 75%. Lower occupancy levels create severe financial stress, as hospitals cannot recover their fixed capital and operating costs. Many hospitals operate with occupancies above 90%, which creates another type of stress in managing resources and waits for beds. While it is not impossible to operate at this level, it is very difficult to accommodate time varying demands as well of the assignment of each patient type to exactly the right bed type.

Hospitals do not always have the capability to measure occupancy with precision because they do not have the systems to constantly monitor which beds are occupied and which are not. Instead, they may take a "*census*" (e.g., a count) of patients at a particular time of day (e.g., midnight), every day. Dividing the census by the number of beds provides the occupancy. Such a measure does not reflect variations in bed occupancy throughout the day (see Sect. 8.2.3), and can overestimate what occupancy might be if averaged over time.

Occupancy measures are also flawed in that they do not easily discriminate between *productive occupancy* and *unproductive occupancy*. We define the former as the time when a bed is occupied by a patient who medically needs to be there, whereas the latter is time when a bed is occupied by a patient waiting for something to happen (e.g., waiting for surgery or a test). Thus, traditional occupancy measures conflate "service time" with "waiting time" (from queueing nomenclature), because one cannot be distinguished from the other. It is, thus, a mistake for a hospital to add beds simply because it has a high occupancy, because the problem may be a long LOS due to waits for tests or other factors.

Another possible flaw is that the hospital simply does not know whether a bed is occupied or not at the time of the census, which may be due to false or delayed records. Few hospitals have the ability to automatically record or detect when a patient first arrives and last leaves a bed, and therefore they rely on potentially inaccurate manual recordings. Nurses may fail to record a patient's discharge immediately, either due to distractions or because the nurse does not want it to be known that a bed has become available.

As discussed in Chap. 2, Little's formula prescribes the relationship between the long-term average waiting time, queue size and arrival rate for queueing systems. It can also be used to characterize occupancy as a function of average length of stay and throughput:

$$oN = \lambda(\text{BLOS})$$

where λ is defined as the rate at which patients are admitted to the N beds of a given type.[3] Admission rate will in the long-run always equal the throughput, which measures the discharge rate. oN, the occupancy multiplied by the number of beds, represents the census averaged over time, which equals the product of the throughput and the average length of stay. If a hospital admits 30,000 patients per year with an average four-day length of stay, then:

$$oN = 30,000 \text{ patients/year (4 bed days/patient) (1 year/365 days)} = 329 \text{ beds}$$

If the hospital has 350 beds, then occupancy is 0.94 (94%) and if the hospital has 400 beds then occupancy is 0.82 (82%). Thus, occupancy might increase as a result of any of these actions: (1) decreasing number of beds, (2) increasing admissions or (3) increasing average length of stay (not all of which are desirable). Occupancy might also be increased by reducing the turnover time (steps 1–6 of the bed cycle).

Examples of Hospital Data

Table 8.1, Figs. 8.1 and 8.2 provide examples of data used to track in-patient workload for nursing and bed management staff. Specific transactions, such as admissions and discharges, generate work for the staff, which must be balanced against staffing and bed availability. Changes in the time of day patterns in admissions and discharges can change the balance in workload from shift to shift as well as affect occupancy levels by time of day. Patterns of admissions and discharges also vary from month to month. In Sect. 8.3, we will explore specific implications of time variability for bed management.

[3] Little's formula is accurate when bed-to-bed transport times are excluded from the LOS calculation.

Table 8.1 Monthly transactions by shift

	Day shift	Evening shift	Night shift
IP admits	88	202	75
PRE admits	82	142	5
IP discharges	77	79	22
Transfers	253	322	115
Cancels	42	60	16
Edits of patient record	300	384	236
Totals for month	842	1,189	469

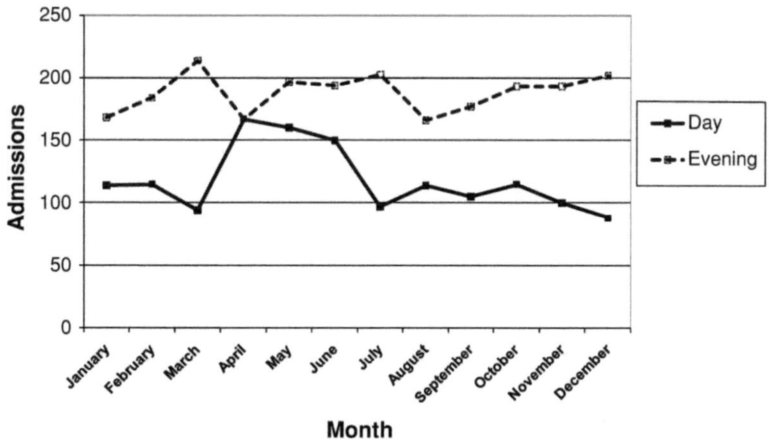

Fig. 8.1 Transactions by shift and month of year

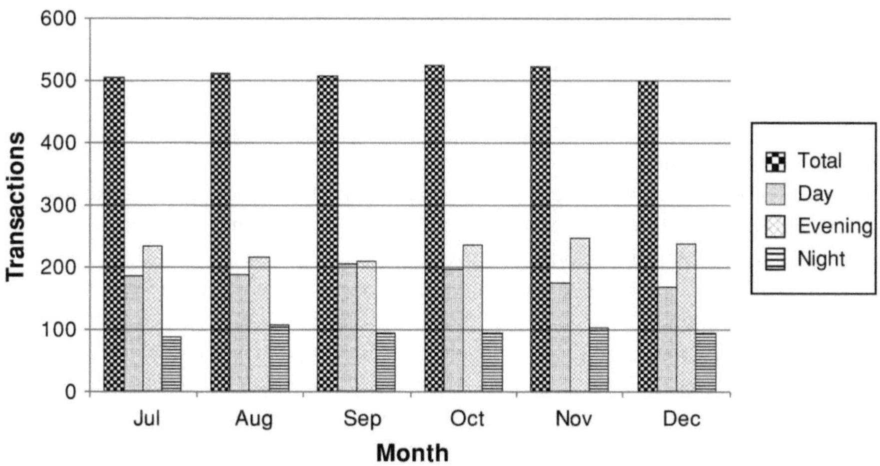

Fig. 8.2 Total transactions by shift and month of year

8.2.3 Accounting for Time Variability

Little's equation is accurate when occupancy is averaged across all times of day and LOS is calculated in equally fine increments of time. When the bed census is taken only at one time of day, but LOS is measured in finer increments, a mismatch occurs, and Little's formula will provide an inconsistent result. Suppose, for instance, that all patients are placed in a bed at 8:00 p.m. one day and leave two days later at 8:00 a.m., with a length of stay of 36 h. Suppose too that census is taken every day at midnight, and that patients are admitted at the rate of 100/day. Then, by Little's formula:

$$oN = 100 \text{ patients/day } (36 \text{ h/patient}) (1 \text{ day/24 days}) = 150 \text{ beds}$$

If the hospital were to have 200 beds, then Little's formula would predict an occupancy of 75%, which is true when averaged over 24 h of day. However, census would vary from 200 occupied beds between 8:00 p.m. and 8:00 a.m. (100 patients from each of two days) and just 100 occupied beds between 8:00 a.m. and 8:00 p.m. (just the 100 patients who arrived the prior day). If one were to always take census at midnight, then occupancy would be 100%, whereas, if census were always taken at noon, then occupancy would be 50%.

The midnight census gives results consistent with Little's formula if patients are assigned to rooms by the night, and LOS is measured in integer days. This would mean operating like a hotel, booking rooms a night at a time. So, for the example, because every person is assigned two nights, LOS becomes 2 days, not 36 h, and Little's formula produces an ***oN*** value of 200 beds. While this approach produces consistency, it does not accurately portray time variations in occupancy, because patients may be admitted (and sometimes discharged) at all hours.

Although the example is simple, it illustrates how bed occupancy does vary by time, and is related to:

Admission of emergency cases: which occur with greater frequency in evening hours, due to the prevalence of violence and accidents, and due to the presentation of patients outside of their normal work and school hours. Admissions often occur at the highest rates on weekend evenings when alcohol- and drug-related injuries are particularly common.

Completion of scheduled surgeries: which typically do not occur on weekends, and are concentrated in the afternoons. Patients emerge from surgery around the time when emergency patient arrivals are growing.

Patient discharge and departures: which often occur toward the middle of the day, and sometimes later.

Putting these factors together, peak occupancy typically occurs in the early morning hours, up until the time patients begin to be discharged. Occupancy also varies by day of week, often lowest on Mondays prior to the completion of the first surgeries of the week (though the pattern could be different at hospitals with large emergency volumes).

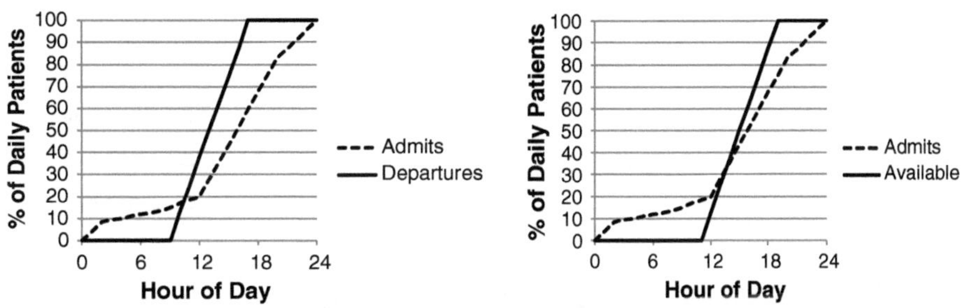

Fig. 8.3 Time varying patterns for admits, departures and available beds

To achieve a high overall occupancy, hospitals need to manage bed utilization at all times of day and all days of week through control of discharge and surgery schedules (Allder et al. 2010 summarizes key issues).

Example of Variations by Time of Day

As an illustration of time variation, we consider here an example where patients are admitted from scheduled elective surgery and from emergency in equal numbers. Elective surgery admits are spread between noon and 8:00 p.m. and emergency admits are spread throughout the day, peaking between 8:00 p.m. and 2:00 a.m., with a lull between 2:00 a.m. and 8:00 a.m. The dashed lines in Fig. 8.3 represent cumulative admits in total by time of day, shown as a percentage of the daily total.

Departures occur at a steady rate during the daytime, beginning at 9:00 a.m. and ending at 5:00 p.m., as shown on the left, but become available 2 h later, as shown on the right (also plotted as cumulative percentages of the daily total). Some observations:

- To circumvent "boarding", a number of beds equaling 20% of the daily intake must be held in reserve at midnight to accommodate additional admits in the early morning hours. Thus, it would be impossible to achieve 100% occupancy at a midnight census while circumventing boarding.
- On the other hand, if 20% of the daily intake is held in reserve, there would be a substantial surplus of beds later in the afternoon (about 40% of daily intake would be vacant around 6:00 p.m.).
- The two-hour lag between a patient departure and a bed becoming available increases the hospital's bed requirement by an amount approximating 5% of the daily intake. This time delay translates into either more boarding or more beds.
- Likewise, patterning the discharge process to match the intake, so that the two follow the same time-of-day pattern, would reduce the need for beds and reduce boarding.

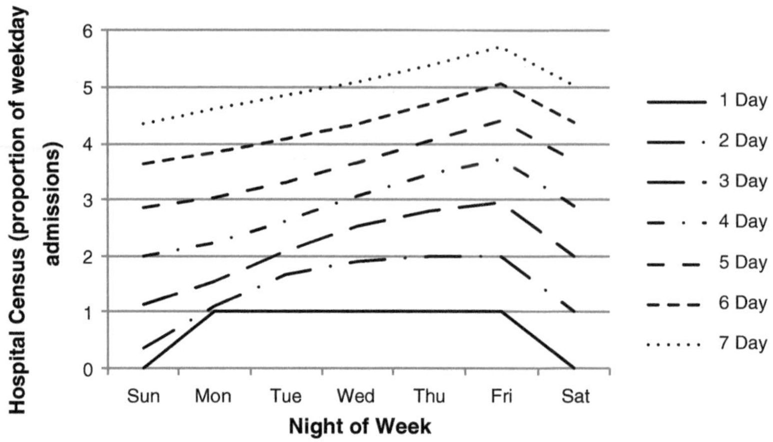

Fig. 8.4 Hospital census as function of day of week and average length of stay

The important conclusion is that time-of-day patterns matter in achieving strong performance in the measures of occupancy and waiting time.

Example of Variations by Day of Week

It is common for hospitals to only schedule surgeries on weekdays, leaving weekends only for emergency cases. This leads to fluctuations in census by night of week, peaking on Friday evening, and dropping to a minimum on Sunday evening. For illustration, we consider a hospital where length of stay is represented by a shifted Poisson distribution, and where intake only occurs on weekdays. The distribution is shifted by one day, and thus there is zero probability of a stay less than one day. The mean for the length of stay varies from one day to seven days in the example.

Hospital census is plotted in Fig. 8.4, shown as a proportion of weekday admissions. The daily mean census is always (5/7) of the mean length of stay (because admits occur on five out of the week's seven days). Further, the daily variations in census are smoothed out as the mean length of stay increases. When the mean is just one day, census drops by 100% on Saturday and Sunday evenings. For a seven day length of stay, census rises 30% from Sunday night to Friday night. The tactical implications are as follows:

- By not scheduling surgeries on weekends, one can expect significant variations in census by day of week.
- If the hospital is successful in reducing average length of stay, daily variations will be exacerbated.

- Hospitals need to consider approaches for scheduling surgeries that offset these effects, perhaps by scheduling cases with longer stays at the end of the week and scheduling more cases early in the week (Bekker and Koeleman 2011).

8.2.4 Bottlenecks

As will be discussed in the following chapter on queueing networks, the bottleneck represents the step in a queueing network with limiting capacity. It tends to be the last place where large queues accumulate. In a serial system (all customers follow the same sequential path), the bottleneck is the step with the minimum capacity. If capacities are reasonably balanced, however, there may be no obvious bottleneck, and queues might accumulate at different places at different times.

Other than beds, possible limiting steps in a hospital include the emergency department, surgery and radiology, all of which are important for smooth patient flow (Hall 2005). Any of these can significantly impede throughput when capacity is insufficient. For beds themselves, the limiting factor might be a type of bed, such as ICU, if the number of beds of that type is not well balanced with the distribution of patient needs across bed types. The bed capacity is further limited by other supporting hospital departments, including:

Pharmacy: ability to rapidly fill prescriptions, particularly at time of discharge.
Transportation: availability of people and equipment to move patients from place to place.
Nursing: whether beds are closed due to unavailability of nurses, and the time required to process patients at intake and discharge.
Records: if reliant on paper records, the time needed to move charts from place to place within hospitals.
Laboratory: to complete needed tests during the hospital stay.

When beds are the bottleneck, queues may "spill back" to prior stages, for instance through back-ups in the emergency department or delays for scheduled surgeries.

8.3 Literature

The literature on bed management is extensive in many disciplines, including operations research, statistics, public health and medicine. For instance, as early as 1954, Bailey had developed queueing models to analyze hospital capacities (Bailey 1954, 1956).

A common feature of the literature is a focus on modeling and managing beds as a critical hospital resource, recognizing beds as either a hospital gateway or bottleneck, and evaluating implications of bed management on a diverse set of performance goals, including health outcomes. Literature reviews can be found in Anderson et al. (2001) Baillie et al. (1997) and Kusters (1983).

While our focus is on the literature emerging from the operations research field, it is important to recognize the contributions of work targeting process changes, in particular that of the Institute for Health Care Improvement. For instance, Resar et al. (2011) cite four key elements: predicting capacity, predicting demand, developing a plan, and evaluating a plan. Testing the concept, a real-time demand management system at University of Pittsburgh Medical Center (UPMC) at Shadyside reduced patient waits and boarding, and also reduced the number of patients who left the emergency department without being seen.

There is also an extensive literature (not covered here) on statistical modeling of patient length of stay, as well as evaluation of the performance of medical doctors in predicting length of stay for their own patients. Beyond the general surveys in Baillie et al. (1997); Kusters (1983) and Marshall et al. (2005) discuss more recent developments. The key questions in the literature entail selecting appropriate probability distributions, incorporating knowledge of the patient's condition and therapy to make these distributions more precise, and updating distributions over time after the patient has been in the hospital. A challenge is to accurately model the tails of these distributions, given that some patients spend far longer in the hospital than others.

The remainder of this section examines the literature on bed management from three perspectives: (1) capacity and occupancy, (2) admissions and (3) discharge. Each represents an aspect of control. In queueing theory terms, these amount to selecting the number of servers, controlling arrivals and controlling departures.

8.3.1 Capacity and Occupancy Management

Capacity management determines the number of beds and allocates them across specialties. Modeling efforts have focused on representing intake and discharge as stochastic processes and understanding tradeoffs between the costs of adding beds versus the benefits of reducing waits for beds. Green (2005) reviews methods for managing hospital capacity, as reference. One approach is to model hospital beds as a queueing system (Gorunescu et al. 2002a, 2002b; Green and Nguyen 2001), modeling intake and discharge processes and their effects on patient waits and lost demand (because of blocking at full occupancy).

Lapierre et al. (1999) utilize a time series model of patient census for allocation across specialties, accounting for variations by the hour across the week. Cochran and Bharti (2006a, b) utilize a combination of queueing and simulation models to analyze interdependencies between hospital units, considering dynamic reallocation of bed types, as well as blocking effects and targeted utilization levels.

Harrison et al. (2005) created detailed stochastic models for bed occupancy, accounting time varying rates that reflect day of week and seasons of the year.

Discharge probabilities, for instance, depend on the day of week and current length of stay. The model is used to examine effects of size, mix of patients by length of stay and effectiveness of smoothing admission rates of patients.

Another approach is to utilize multi-objective programming, accounting for the multiple aims for bed management. Li et al. (2009) utilized goal programming as a decision aid accounting for customer service and profits, which was demonstrated at a public hospital in China. Other mathematical programming approaches include network flow models (accounting for relationships between departments, such as Elif et al. 2006) and non-linear programming (reflecting relationships between capacity and service parameters; Kokangul 2007).

Hospitals inherently experience considerable randomness and variability that is hard to capture in analytical models. For this reason, simulation has been the tool of choice in many studies examining hospital capacities and allocation of hospital capacities over time. Examples include Bagust et al. (1999), El-Darzi et al. (1998), Harper and Shahani (2002), Kao and Tung (1981), Kim et al. (1999), Kokangul (2007) and Ridge et al. (1998). Such approaches provide a more detailed representation of system dynamics (often suitablefor setting capacities), but are not amenable to complex scheduling decisions.

8.3.2 Hospital Admissions

Patients are admitted to hospitals based on the medical judgment of doctors, but also based on the ability of the hospital to accommodate patients. Milsum et al. (1973) outline the decision-making framework surrounding admissions, distinguishing the American model of physicians who are granted hospital privileges to attend to patients, versus the alternative of hospital specialists who separately screen patients for admission. They present flow models for admissions that link medical decisions to the allocation of specific beds to accommodate patients.

Patient admissions can be divided into scheduled cases versus unscheduled (typically through emergency). Scheduled can be further categorized into patients that are drawn from waiting lists, scheduled via appointments, or scheduled via add-on appointments. A common goal is to control scheduled admissions based on predicted future occupancies along with predicted future requirements to accommodate unscheduled emergency cases. Another goal is to keep the hospital occupancy at a high (or sometimes consistent) level, while maintaining a good service level for emergency cases (e.g., minimizing waits for admission to beds or minimizing the number of boarders). It is also important to minimize cancellations of scheduled surgeries, in the event that resources are insufficient at the time of surgery (Utley et al. 2003).

Kolesar (1970), for instance, modeled transitions in hospital occupancy levels with Markovian state transition probabilities, and then formulated linear programs to optimize admissions, for instance maximizing average long-run occupancy while satisfying an overflow constraint. While effective at demonstrating basic tradeoffs, this approach did not account for time variations in rates, which are inherent to bed management systems.

Another approach has been to assign patients to admission dates based on patient preferences (e.g., desired time windows or desired dates for surgeries), for instance using linear programming as a resource allocation tool (Dantzig 1969) or heuristically assigning patients to date according to localized performance objectives combining cost and patient convenience (Connors 1970).

Control models have also been used, for which the approach is to reject patients once the occupancy exceeds set thresholds (e.g., Shonick and Jackson 1973). Similarly, it is possible to optimize quotas based on anticipated workload, or to admit patients based on projected day-of-week load profiles by specialty (Adan and Vissers 2002; Bekker and Koeleman 2011; Gallivan and Utley 2005), perhaps leveling loads by scheduling surgeries with different recovery times on different days of the week. Beyond availability of beds, demands on nursing staff may be a consideration in a hospital ward's ability to accept new patients, as considered by Offsend (1972).

It should be kept in mind that surgery is the biggest single source of scheduled hospital cases, and therefore effective bed scheduling requires coordination with surgical scheduling. Because surgeries must be scheduled around availability of operating rooms, surgeons and support teams, bed availability is not always the controlling factor for surgery schedules, though recent research has investigated their interrelationship (Vanberkel et al. 2010). The underlying randomness in length of stay and number of emergency cases leaves considerable uncertainty in bed availability, making it difficult, as a matter of practice, to reserve beds for specific patients (Gallivan et al. 2002; Gerchak et al. 1996).

8.3.3 Hospital Discharge

The literature on discharge planning has focused on continuity of care as patients transition out of the hospital, including issues such as correct medication, access to needed out-patient services, and communication with patients (e.g., Kripalani et al. 2007, 2011; Forster et al. 2003). For instance, Moore et al (2003) concluded: "the prevalence of medical errors related to the discontinuity of care from the inpatient to the outpatient setting is high and may be associated with an increased risk of rehospitalization." It is therefore important to effectively execute discharges to circumvent future demands on hospital capacity. Other research has examined the effectiveness of social interventions (e.g., provision of out-patient services or help in transportation) that enable patients to be discharged early (e.g., Evans and Hendricks 1993).

More specifically related to scheduling, some hospitals, such as at the Mayo Clinic Agency for Health Care Research and Quality, AHRQ (2011b), Manning et al. (2007), have instituted appointment systems that assign specific times for patients to leave hospitals. This approach facilitates the coordination of patient services at time of discharge, provides support for patients and family members so they can prepare to leave the hospital, and can help synchronize discharges with expected hospital admissions (thus providing more consistent occupancy levels throughout the day). Manning et al. found that 60% of patients were given a posted discharge appointment time at Mayo and of these 60% were discharged within 30 min of the planned appointment time.

Further information about discharge appointments can be found through the Institute for Health Care Improvement's Transforming Care at the Bedside Initiative Institute for Health Care Improvement, (IHI 2004). Beyond setting appointments, IHI recommends that discharge rounds be made in advance of the discharge day, to create checklists of all steps needed for discharge, and provide assurance that the steps are followed.

8.4 Future Directions

Beds are a critical resource for hospitals, constrained by physical size and design, staffing and licensing. As a result, beds are often the bottleneck that controls the flow of patients through the hospitals, limiting the ability of surgery to schedule patients and limiting the flow of emergency patients into in-patient beds. To serve the needs of more patients, hospitals need to pursue three tactics: (1) reducing the need for hospitalization, (2) reducing the length of stay and turnover time and (3) ensuring that sufficient beds are available to meet true needs.

An extensive literature exists for predicting and modeling length of stay, occupancy, admission rates and discharge rates, as well as a literature on controlling admission of patients to hospitals. Discharge planning and length of stay have also been studied from a medical perspective and literature exists on process improvement to reduce length of stay.

At present, much less is known about the relationship between process improvements and models for occupancy and admission. While it is convenient to treat a hospital bed as a server, like a normal queueing system, the reality is that the bed stay is a mixture of service time and queue time (waiting for needed hospital services). Process improvements attempt to reduce wasted time and thus reduce hospital stays. However, the details of queueing and service steps, which occur during patient stays, are not well represented in the modeling literature.

Likewise, the literature on discharge planning is mostly focused on health outcomes along with process improvements, with little written on optimizing discharge schedules. Synchronization of discharges with admissions can reduce bed requirements (or alternately reduce boarding of patients or cancellation), but so far systems for discharge planning have not achieved this level of sophistication.

Returning to the story of LAC/USC Hospital, at the time when its replacement was being planned, the average length of stay was about seven days, well above the national average. LAC/USC was able to reduce that value by about a day, offering the equivalent of 150 beds in new capacity, similar to the number of beds that would be lost in moving to the new hospital. At LAC/USC and elsewhere, one must continually question whether the number of beds is needed to serve the population, or whether the size is needed to accommodate queues of patients waiting for hospital services. Hospitals should be sized according to the need to serve patients, and not to accommodate queues of patients waiting for care.

To implement these ideas, it will be important in the future for hospitals to improve their technology for tracking patient activities from point of admission to discharge, and possibly beyond. The gaps mentioned in our capabilities result from the absence of information about what truly happens to the patient, moment by moment, during his or her hospital stay. More precise and complete data sets will open the door for better scheduling, reduced length of stay and higher quality for patients.

Acknowledgment My appreciation goes to David Belson for his contributions to understanding of bed management based on his extensive experience working with California hospitals.

References

Adan IJBF, Vissers JMH (2002) Patient mix optimisation in hospital admission planning: a case study. Int J Oper Prod Manag 22:445–461

Agency for Health Care Research and Quality, AHRQ (2011a) Agency releases standardized bed definitions. http://www.ahrq.gov/research/havbed/definitions.htm. Accessed 7/9/2011

Agency on Health Care Research and Quality, AHRQ (2011b). Posting expected discharge date facilitates communication, leads to on-time patient departures and high levels of satisfaction. http://www.innovations.ahrq.gov/content.aspx?id=2177. Accessed 18 July 2011

Allder S, Silvester K, Walley P (2010) Managing capacity and demand across the patient journey. Clin Med 10:13–15

American Hospital Association (2010) Fast facts on US hospitals. Chicago, Illinois

American Nursing Association, ANA (2011) Safe nurse staffing laws in state legislatures. http://www.safestaffingsaveslives.org/WhatisANADoing/StateLegislation.aspx. Accessed 7/9/2011

Anderson J, Bernath V, Davies J, Greene L, Ludolf S (2001) Literature review on integrated bed and patient management. Centre for Clinical Effectiveness. Monash Institute of Public Health, Victoria

Bagust A, Place M, Posnett JW (1999) Dynamics of bed use in accommodating emergency admissions: stochastic simulation model. Br Med J 319:155–159

Bailey NTJ (1954) Queueing for medical care. Appl Stat 3:137–145

Bailey NTJ (1956) Statistics in hospital planning and design. J R Stat Soc B Appl Stat 5:146–157

Baillie H, Wright W, McLeod A, Craig N, Leyland A, Drummond N, Boddy A (1997) Bed occupancy and bed management. Report of CSO Project K/OPR/2/2/D248, Public Health Research Unit, University of Glasgow

Bekker, R and Koeleman, PM (2011) Scheduling admissions and reducing variability in bed demand. Health Care Manag Sci 14:237–249

Chen EH, Hollander JE (2007) When do patients need admission to a telemetry bed? J Emerg Med 33:53–60

Cochran JK, Bharti A (2006a) Stochastic bed balancing of an obstetrics hospital. Health Care Manag Sci 9:31–45

Cochran JK, Bharti A (2006b) A multi-stage stochastic methodology for whole hospital bed planning under peak loading. Int J Industrial Sys Eng 1:8–36

Connors MM (1970) A stochastic elective admissions scheduling algorithm. Health Serv Res 5:308–319

Dantzig GB (1969) A hospital admission problem. Stanford University Operations Research Technical Report, Stanford

El-Darzi E, Vasilakis C, Chaussalet T, Millard PH (1998) A simulation modelling approach to evaluating length of stay, occupancy, emptiness and bed blocking in a hospital geriatric department. Health Care Manag Sci 1:143–149

Elif A, Cote MJ, Lin C (2006) A network flow approach to optimizing hospital bed capacity decisions. Health Care Manag Sci 9:391–404

Evans RL, Hendricks RD (1993) Evaluating hospital discharge planning: a randomized clinical trial. Med Care 31:358–370

Forster AJ et al (2003) The incidence and severity of adverse events affecting patients after discharge from the hospital. Ann Intern Med 138:161–167

Gallager EJ, Lunn SG (1990) The etiology of medical gridlock: causes of emergency department overcrowding in New York City. J Emerg Med 8:785–790

Gallivan S, Utley M (2005) Modelling admissions booking of elective in-patients into a treatment centre. IMA J Manag Math 16:305–315

Gallivan S, Utley M, Treasure T, Valencia O (2002) Booked inpatient admissions and hospital capacity: mathematical modeling study. Br Med J 324:280–282

Gerchak Y, Gupta D, Henig M (1996) Reservation planning for elective surgery under uncertain demand for emergency surgery. Manage Sci 42:321–334

Gorunescu F, McClean SI, Millard PH (2002a) A queueing model for bed-occupancy management and planning of hospitals. J Oper Res Soc 53:19–24

Gorunescu F, McClean SI, Millard PH (2002b) Using a queueing model to help plan bed allocation in a department of geriatric medicine. Health Care Manag Sci 5:307–312

Green L (2005) Capacity planning and management in hospitals. In: Brandeau ML, Sainfort F, Pierskalla WP (eds) Operations research and health care, handbook of methods and applications. Springer, New York

Green LV, Nguyen V (2001) Strategies for cutting hospital beds: the impact on patient service. Health Serv Res 36:421–442

Hall RW (2005) Patient flow: reducing delay through improved health care delivery. Springer, New York

Hall MJ, DeFrances CJ, Williams SN, Golosinskiy A, Schwartzman A (2009) National hospital discharge survey: 2007 summary. National Health Statistics Reports, No 29, 26 Oct

Halpern NA, Pastores SM, Greenstein RJ (2004) Critical care medicine in the US 1985–2000: an analysis of bed numbers, use, and costs. Crit Care Med 32:1254–1259

Ham C, York N, Sutch S, Shaw R (2003) Hospital bed utilization in the NHS, Kaiser Permanente, and the US Medicare programme: analysis of routine data. Br Med J 327:1257–1260

Harper PR, Shahani AK (2002) Modelling for the planning and management of bed capacities in hospitals. J Oper Res Soc 53:11–18

Harrison GW, Shafer A, MacKay M (2005) Modeling variability in hospital bed occupancy. Health Care Manag Sci 8:325–344

Howell E, Bessman E, Kravet S, Kolodner K, Marshall R, Wright S (2008) Active bed management by hospitalists and emergency department throughput. Ann Intern Med 149: 804–810

Institute for Health Care Improvement, IHI (2004) Transforming care at the bedside. Cambridge, Massachusetts

Kao EPC, Tung GG (1981) Bed allocation in a public health care delivery system. Manage Sci 27:507–520

Kim S-C, Horowitz I, Young KK, Buckley TA (1999) Analysis of capacity management of the intensive care unit in a hospital. Eur J Oper Res 115:36–46

Kokangul A (2007) A combination of deterministic and stochastic approaches to optimize bed capacity in a hospital unit. Comput Methods Programs Biomed 90:56–65

Kolesar P (1970) A Markovian model for hospital admission scheduling. Manage Sci 16:B384–B396

Kripalani S, Jackson AT, Schnipper JL, Coleman EA (2007) Promoting effective transitions of care at hospital discharge: a review of key issues for hospitalists. J Hosp Med 2:314–323

Kripalani S et al (2011) Deficits in communication and information transfer between hospital-based and primary care physicians, implications for patient safety and continuity of care. J Am Med Assoc 297:831–841

Kusters RJ (1983) Patient scheduling: a review. Report EUT/BDK/3, Department of Industrial Engineering and Management Science, Eindhoven University of Technology

Lapierre SD, Goldsman D, Cochran R, DuBow J (1999) Bed allocation techniques based on census data. Socio-Econ Plan Sci 33:25–38

Li X, Beullens P, Jones D, Tamiz M (2009) Optimal bed allocation in hospitals. In: Barichard ME, Xavier G, Vincent T (eds) Multiobjective programming and goal programming. New York, Springer

Manning DM et al (2007) In-room display of day and time patient is anticipated to leave hospital: a discharge appointment. J Hosp Med 2:13–16

Marshall A, Vasilakis C, El-Darzi E (2005) Length of stay-based patient flow models: recent developments and future directions. Health Care Manag Sci 8:213–220

Milsum JH, Turban E, Vertinsky I (1973) Hospital admission systems: their evaluation and management. Manage Sci 19:646–666

Moore C, Wisnivesky J, Williams S, McGinn T (2003) Medical errors related to discontinuity of care from an inpatient to an outpatient setting. J Gen Intern Med 18:646–651

National Center for Health Statistics NCHS (2010) Health, US, 2010 with special feature on death and dying. Center for Disease Control and Prevention, Atlanta

OECD (2009) Health at a glance: OECD indicators. OECD Publishing, Paris

OECD (2011) OECD health data 2011. OECD Publishing, Paris

Offsend FL (1972) A hospital admission system based on nursing workload. Manage Sci 19: 132–138

Proudlove NC, Gordon K, Boaden R (2003) Can good bed management solve the overcrowding in accident and emergency departments? Emerg Med J 20:149–155

Resar R, Nolan K, Kaczynski D, Jensen K (2011) Using real-time demand capacity management to improve hospitalwide patient flow. Jt Comm J Qual Patient Saf 37:217–227

Ridge JC, Jones SK, Nielsen MS, Shahani AK (1998) Capacity planning for intensive care units. Eur J Oper Res 105:346–355

Shonick W, Jackson JR (1973) An improved stochastic model for occupancy-related random variables in general-acute hospitals. Oper Res 21:952–965

Spetz J, Seago JA, Coffman J, Rosenoff E, O'Neil E (2000) Minimum nurse staffing ratios. California acute care hospitals. Center for the Health Professions, University of California, San Francisco

Terasawa E, Harrington SE, Sathyanarayan A (2010) The effect of California's minimum nurse staffing law on emergency department closure. ASHE conference paper

Utley M, Gallivan S, Treasure T, Valencia O (2003) Analytical methods for calculating the capacity required to operate an effective booked admissions policy for elective inpatient services. Health Care Manag Sci 6:97–104

Vanberkel PT, Boucherie RJ, Hans EW, Hurink JL, van Lent WAM, van Harten WH (2010) An exact approach for relating recovering surgical patient workload to the master surgical schedule. J Oper Res Soc 62:1851–1860

Chapter 9
Queuing Networks in Healthcare Systems

Maartje E. Zonderland and Richard J. Boucherie

Abstract Over the last decades, the concept of patient flow has received an increased amount of attention. Healthcare professionals have become aware that in order to analyze the performance of a single healthcare facility, its relationship with other healthcare facilities should also be taken into account. A natural choice for analysis of networks of healthcare facilities is queuing theory. With a queuing network a fast and flexible analysis is provided that discovers bottlenecks and allows for the evaluation of alternative set-ups of the network. In this chapter we describe how queuing theory, and networks of queues in particular, can be invoked to model, study, analyze, and solve healthcare problems. We describe important theoretical queuing results, give a review of the literature on the topic, discuss in detail two examples of how a healthcare problem is analyzed using a queuing network, and suggest directions for future research.

9.1 Introduction

With an aging population, the rising cost of new medical technologies, and a society wanting higher quality care, the demand for healthcare is increasing annually. In European countries, such as the Netherlands, healthcare expenditures

M. E. Zonderland (✉) · R. J. Boucherie
Stochastic Operations Research & Center for Healthcare Operations Improvement and Research, University of Twente, Postbox 217, 7500 AE, Enschede, The Netherlands
e-mail: m.e.zonderland@utwente.nl

R. J. Boucherie
e-mail: r.j.boucherie@utwente.nl

M. E. Zonderland
Division I, Leiden University Medical Center, Postbox 9600, 2300 RC, Leiden, The Netherlands

R. Hall (ed.), *Handbook of Healthcare System Scheduling*,
International Series in Operations Research & Management Science 168,
DOI: 10.1007/978-1-4614-1734-7_9, © Springer Science+Business Media, LLC 2012

consume around 10% of the GDP. In the United States this percentage is even bigger at 16% (Organisation for Economic Co-operation and Development 2011) (2008 data). Since the supply of healthcare is finite, policy makers have to ration care and make choices on how to distribute physical, human, and monetary resources. Such choices also have to be made at the hospital level (e.g., which patient groups will be treated in this hospital), and on a departmental level (e.g., who gets which available bed).

An immediate consequence of rationing resources is the evolution of queues. This brings us immediately to queuing theory, which is the mathematical theory that studies queues. The methods available in this field can support healthcare professionals in their decision making. Already in 1952, Bailey recognized that queuing theory would be of value to make a trade-off between patient waiting time and healthcare provider idle time: short waiting time means a low provider utilization rate, while low provider idle time results in long waiting times (Bailey 1952). With queuing theory a balance between these two performance measures can be found. Another example is calculating the required number of beds on a nursing ward that ensures the patient rejection rate stays below a certain threshold (Bruin et al. 2010). Finally, consider an example from the operating room (OR), where a queuing model can be used to find the optimal amount of OR time to allocate to semi-urgent patients. A surplus of allocated OR time results in an empty OR (a waste of resources), while a shortage will result in elective patients who need to be canceled to accommodate the semi-urgent patients. The challenge is to find a balance (Zonderland et al. 2010). The book chapter by Linda Green (2008) provides an overview of queuing theory applications in healthcare.

9.1.1 Some General Queuing Concepts

A queue can generally be characterized by its arrival and service processes, the number of servers, and the service discipline (Fig. 9.1). The arrival process is specified by a probability distribution that has an arrival rate associated with it, which is usually the mean number of patients who arrives during a time unit (e.g., minutes, hours, or days). A common choice for the probabilistic arrival process is the Poisson process, in which the inter-arrival times of patients are independent and exponentially distributed.

The service process specifies the service requirements of patients, again using a probability distribution with associated service rate. A common choice is the exponential distribution, which is convenient for obtaining analytical tractable results. The number of servers in a healthcare setting may represent the number of doctors at an outpatient clinic, the number of MRI scanners at a diagnostic department, and so on. The service discipline specifies how incoming patients are served. The most common discipline is First Come First Serve (FCFS), where patients are served in order of arrival. Other examples are briefly addressed in Sect. 2.2.5. Some patients may have priority over other patients (see Sect. 2.2.6).

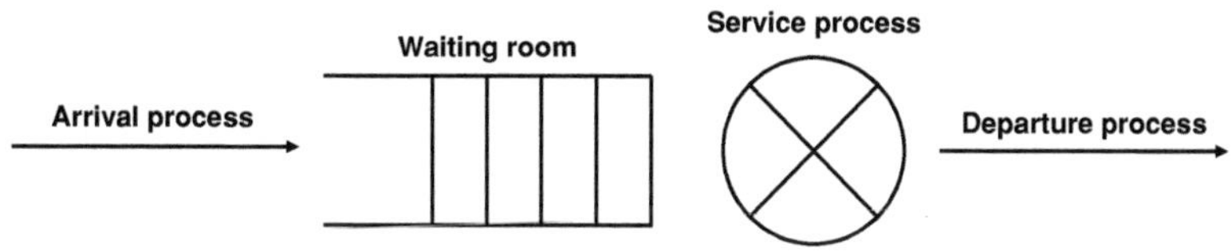

Fig. 9.1 A simple queue

This can be such that the service of a lower priority patient is interrupted when a higher priority patient arrives (preemptive priority), or the service of the lower priority patient is finished first (non-preemptive priority).

Typical measures for the performance of the system include the mean sojourn time, $\mathbb{E}[W]$, the mean time that a patient spends in the queue and in service. The sojourn time is a random variable as it is determined by the stochastic arrival and service processes. The mean waiting time, $\mathbb{E}[W^q]$, gives the mean time a patient spends in the queue waiting for service. How $\mathbb{E}[W]$ and $\mathbb{E}[W^q]$ are calculated depends, among other things, on the choice for the arrival and service processes, and is given for several basic queues in Sect. 2.2.

Kendall's Notation

All queues in this chapter are described using the so-called Kendall notation: $A/B/s$, where A denotes the arrival process, B denotes the service process, and s is the number of servers. There are several extensions to this notation, see for example (Winston 1994). Clearly, there are many distinctive cases of queues:

$M/M/1$: The single-server queue with Poisson arrivals and exponential service times. The M stands for the *M*arkovian or *M*emoryless property. $M/D/1$: The single-server queue with Poisson arrivals and *D*eterministic service times. $M/G/1$: The single-server queue with Poisson arrivals and *G*eneral (i.e., not specified) service time distribution.

Other arrival processes may also apply: consider for example the $D/M/1$, $G/M/1$ and $G/G/1$ queue. All of the forms above also exist in the case of multiple servers ($s > 1$).

The load of the queue is defined as the mean utilization rate per server, which is the amount of work that arrives on average per time unit, divided by the amount of work the queue can handle on average per time unit. Suppose our server is a single doctor in an outpatient clinic, then the load specifies the fraction of time the doctor is working. The load, ρ, equals the amount of work brought to the system per time unit, i.e. the patient arrival rate, λ, multiplied by the mean service time per patient, $\mathbb{E}[S]$:

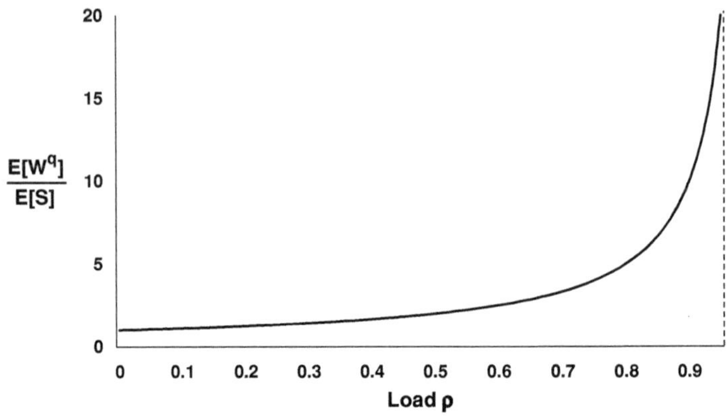

Fig. 9.2 The relationship between load ρ and mean waiting time $\mathbb{E}[W^q]$ for the $M/M/1$ queue with Poisson arrivals and exponential service times

$$\rho = \lambda \mathbb{E}[S]. \tag{9.1}$$

The load is the fraction of time the server, working at unit rate, must work to handle the arriving amount of work. It is required that $\rho < 1$ (in other words, the server should work less than 100% of the time). If $\rho > 1$, then on average more work arrives at the queue than can be handled, which inevitably leads to a continuously growing number of patients in the queue waiting for service, i.e., an unstable system. Only when the arrival and service processes are deterministic (i.e., the inter-arrival and service times have zero variance), the load may equal 1. The mean waiting time, $\mathbb{E}[W^q]$, increases with load ρ. As an illustration, consider a single-server queue with Poisson arrivals and general service times (the so-called $M/G/1$ queue), with mean $\mathbb{E}[S]$ and squared coefficient of variation (scv) c_S^2, which is calculated by dividing the variance by the squared mean. For this queue, the relationship between ρ and $\mathbb{E}[W^q]$ is characterized by the Pollaczek–Khinchine formula (Cohen 1982):

$$\mathbb{E}[W^q] = \mathbb{E}[S]\, \frac{\rho}{1-\rho}\, \frac{1+c_S^2}{2}, \tag{9.2}$$

In Fig. 9.2 the relation is shown graphically for $c_S^2 = 1$. We see that the mean waiting time increases with the load. When the load is low, a small increase therein has a minimal effect on the mean waiting time. However, when the load is high, a small increase has a tremendous effect on the mean waiting time. As an illustration, increasing the load from 50 to 55% increases the waiting time by 10%, but increasing the load from 90 to 95% increases the waiting time by 100%! This explains why a minor change (for example a small increase in the number of patients) can result in a major increase in waiting times as sometimes seen in outpatient clinics. Formulas such as (2) allow for an exact and fast quantification

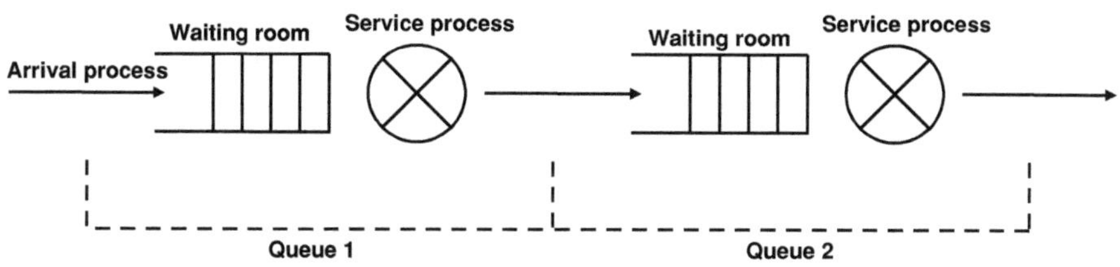

Fig. 9.3 The $M/M/1$ tandem queue

of the relationships between (influencable) parameters and system outcomes. Queuing theory is a very valuable tool to identify bottlenecks and to calculate the effect of removing them.

We conclude this subsection with a basic queuing network: the $M/M/1$ tandem queue. In this network we have two queues with exponential service, which are placed in series. Patients arrive at the first queue according to a Poisson process with rate λ. When the service at the first queue is completed, the patient is routed immediately to the second queue. Upon service completion at this queue, the patient leaves the system. At both queues the service discipline is FCFS, and there is an infinite waiting room (see Fig. 9.3). It can be shown that the mean sojourn time in the entire system, $\mathbb{E}[W]$, is just the sum of the mean sojourn times in the individual queues, $\mathbb{E}[W_j]$ for queue j:

$$\mathbb{E}[W] = \mathbb{E}[W_1] + \mathbb{E}[W_2], \tag{9.3}$$

since the departure process from each queue has the same characteristics as its input process. This remarkable result can be generalized to larger networks of queues, as is shown in Sect. 2.3.2.

9.1.2 Queuing Networks in Healthcare

When patients share and use multiple resources, a queuing network usually arises. Consider, for example, a patient that visits the Orthopedic outpatient clinic and then needs to have an X-ray at Radiology; or the surgical patient who is operated in the OR, then cared for at the intensive care unit (ICU) and subsequently cared for in a nursing ward. The formulation and analysis of these queuing network models is usually not straightforward. This likely explains why (discrete-event) simulation (Law and Kelton 1991) is a commonly used approach to analyze healthcare problems. Simulation models are robust in terms of the setting they can represent, however they are very time consuming to develop and require a vast amount of data (-analysis). Also, the resulting model is, with a few exceptions, not generic and thus not suitable to represent other problems or organizations other than the one it was build for.

In this chapter we describe how queuing theory, and networks of queues in particular, can be invoked to study, analyze, and solve healthcare problems. In Sect. 9.2 we provide an introduction to the theory of queues and queuing networks. In Sect. 9.3 we give a review of the literature on the topic, and discuss in detail two examples of how healthcare problems are analyzed using queuing networks. In the last section we suggest directions for further research. Given the numerous modeling opportunities of queuing networks, many difficult healthcare problems can, and hopefully will, be solved in the future. The literature references on applications of queuing theory in healthcare are included in the categorized ORchestra bibliography (Research Institute CHOIR 2011), provided by research institute CHOIR from the University of Twente, Enschede, the Netherlands.

9.2 Basic Queuing Networks

In this section we discuss several basic queuing networks. We start by introducing the Poisson process, which is a basic element in many queuing systems. We then proceed to the building blocks for the networks: the individual queues. We conclude by describing various queuing networks.

9.2.1 The Poisson Process

As mentioned in Sect. 1.1, the Poisson process is commonly used to model the arrival of customers to a queue, and in general to model independent arrivals from a large population. As an example, consider patient arrivals at a hospital emergency department (ED). They originate from a large population (the demographic area surrounding the hospital) and usually arrive independently. The probability that an arbitrary person has an urgent medical problem is very small. Then it can be shown that the arrival process tends to a Poisson process (Bruin et al. 2010).

The Poisson process is common in real world processes and has many interesting and for analysis very useful properties. For example, the number of ticks a Geiger counter records is a Poisson process. This example also indicates that merging or splitting Poisson processes independently results in Poisson processes, as this corresponds to joining two lumps of radioactive material or breaking one lump into parts. Or, for the population example, ED arrivals from a population subgroup (men, women, children, ...) are also Poisson.

For a Poisson process, the time between two successive arrivals is exponentially distributed (Wolff 1989). A very important property of the exponential distribution is that it is memoryless: the probability that the inter-arrival time exceeds $u + t$ time units, given that it already has exceeded u time units, equals the probability that the inter-arrival time exceeds t time units. Mathematically, a random variable X that has an exponential distribution satisfies:

$$\mathbb{P}(X > u + t | X > u) = \mathbb{P}(X > t), \quad \forall u, t \geq 0. \tag{9.4}$$

We may also rephrase this property as: what happens in the future is independent of what happened in the past. Because of this Markovian or memoryless property, the complexity of analyzing systems with this property significantly reduces, as we show in the subsequent subsections.

9.2.2 Basic Queues

We introduce the most commonly used queues: single and multi-server queues with Poisson arrivals and exponential or general service times. Unless mentioned otherwise, we consider the FCFS service discipline and queues with infinite capacity for waiting patients.

9.2.2.1 The $M/M/1$ Queue

In an $M/M/1$ queue, patients arrive according to a Poisson process with rate λ and exponentially distributed service requirement with mean service time $\mathbb{E}[S]$. The service rate per unit time is $\mu = \frac{1}{\mathbb{E}[S]}$, the number of patients that would be completed per time unit when the system would continuously be serving patients. As denoted in Sect. 1.1, the load of the queue is $\rho = \lambda\mathbb{E}[S]$, where it is required that $\rho < 1$, that is, the amount of work brought into the queue should be less than the rate of the server. The number of patients present in the queue at time *t*, i.e., those waiting in line and in service, is obtained from Markov chain analysis.

Let *N*(*t*) record the number of patients in the system at time *t*. Then $N = (N(t), t \geq 0)$ is a Markov chain with state space $\mathbb{N}_0 = \{0, 1, 2, \ldots\}$, arrival rate λ, which is the rate at which a transition occurs from a state with *n* patients to a state with $n + 1$ patients, and departure rate μ from state *n* to state $n - 1$.

We are interested in the probability P_n that at an arbitrary point in time in statistical equilibrium the system contains *n* patients[1]:

$$P_n = \lim_{t \to \infty} \mathbb{P}(N(t) = n). \tag{9.5}$$

The probability P_n also reflects the fraction of time that the system contains *n* patients. The total probability may be seen as an amount of fluid of total volume 1 that is distributed over the states of the Markov chain and flows from state to

[1] We consider the system in statistical equilibrium only, as is customary in queuing theory. For the $M/M/1$ queue, relaxation or convergence to equilibrium usually occurs fast. See Green et al. (2001) for a discussion on the validity of equilibrium analysis.

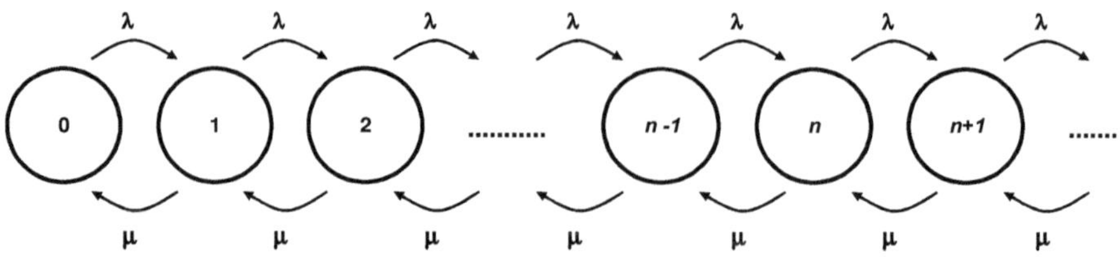

Fig. 9.4 Transition rates in the $M/M/1$ queue

state according to the transition rates (for the $M/M/1$ queue the arrival and departure rates). The system is in statistical equilibrium when these flows out of state n balance the flows into state n for each state n, $n = 0, 1, 2, \ldots$ (see Fig. 9.4) . Mathematically, this is expressed as:

$$\begin{aligned} \lambda P_0 &= \mu P_1, \\ (\lambda + \mu)P_1 &= \lambda P_0 + \mu P_2, \\ (\lambda + \mu)P_2 &= \lambda P_1 + \mu P_3, \\ &\vdots \end{aligned} \tag{9.6}$$

and in general:

$$\begin{aligned} \lambda P_0 &= \mu P_1, \\ (\lambda + \mu)P_n &= \lambda P_{n-1} + \mu P_{n+1} \quad \text{for} \quad n > 0. \end{aligned} \tag{9.7}$$

Since P_n is a probability, the summation of all probabilities P_n, $n = 0, 1, \ldots$, should equal unity:

$$\sum_{n=0}^{\infty} P_n = 1. \tag{9.8}$$

Using Eq. 9.7 and this additional property, we derive the queue length distribution P_n :

$$\begin{aligned} P_0 &= 1 - \rho, \\ P_n &= (1 - \rho)\rho^n \quad \text{for} \quad n > 0. \end{aligned} \tag{9.9}$$

Note that P_0, also called the normalization constant, denotes the probability that there are zero patients present, but also the fraction of time the queue is empty. Further, ρ is the probability there are one or more patients present, and the fraction of time the queue is busy.

The PASTA Property

In a queuing system with Poisson arrivals, the probability that an arriving patient finds n patients in the queue is equal to the fraction of time the queue contains n patients. This property is referred to as Poisson arrivals see time averages (PASTA) (Wolff 1989).

Usually, queuing systems with non-Poisson arrival processes do not conform to this property. For example, consider the $D/D/1$ queue with deterministic inter-arrival and service times. Time is equally distributed in slots of length one, and the service time is half a slot. Suppose that at the start of each time slot a patient arrives (so the inter-arrival time is one slot). Then the queue is empty upon arrival for all patients, while half of the time the queue contains one patient.

The mean number of patients in the queue, $\mathbb{E}[L]$, including those in service, is given by:

$$\mathbb{E}[L] = \sum_{n=0}^{\infty} nP_n = \frac{\rho}{1-\rho}. \tag{9.10}$$

Since ρ is the mean utilization rate of the server, the mean number of patients waiting, $\mathbb{E}[L^q]$, equals:

$$\mathbb{E}[L^q] = \frac{\rho}{1-\rho} - \rho = \frac{\rho^2}{1-\rho}. \tag{9.11}$$

Using a basic result in queuing theory, known as Little's law, the relationship between the mean number of patients in the queue, $\mathbb{E}[L]$, and the mean sojourn time, $\mathbb{E}[W]$, can be explicitly quantified as follows (Little 1961):

$$\mathbb{E}[L] = \lambda\mathbb{E}[W]. \tag{9.12}$$

This also holds for the relationship between the mean number of patients waiting for service, $\mathbb{E}[L^q]$, and the mean waiting time in the queue, $\mathbb{E}[W^q]$:

$$\mathbb{E}[L^q] = \lambda\mathbb{E}[W^q]. \tag{9.13}$$

Note that the equilibrium distribution and performance measures are characterized by the single parameter ρ and can be calculated in a straightforward manner. As we will see in the subsequent subsections, this is more involved for more complicated queuing systems.

Little's Law
The simple relationship $\mathbb{E}[L] = \lambda\mathbb{E}[W]$, presented in 1961 by Little (1961), is known as Little's law. It relates the mean number of patients in the queue, $\mathbb{E}[L]$, the average arrival rate, λ, and the mean time the patient spends in the queue, $\mathbb{E}[W]$.

A common intuitive reasoning for obtaining Little's law is the following. Suppose patients pay 1 Euro for each time unit they spend in the queue. On average, the queue receives $\mathbb{E}[L]$ Euro per time unit, since there are on average $\mathbb{E}[L]$ patients present in the queue. Alternatively, if each patient would pay upon entering the queue for its entire time spent in the queue, a patient would on average have to pay $\mathbb{E}[W]$ to finance the entire stay. Since each time unit on average λ patients enter the queue, the amount received by the queue per time unit then equals $\lambda\mathbb{E}[W]$. Both methods of payment must result in the same benefit for the queue, thus $\mathbb{E}[L] = \lambda\mathbb{E}[W]$. The formal proof actually follows the lines of this reasoning. It is remarkable that Little's law requires only mild assumptions on the system in equilibrium, and is valid irrespective of the number of servers, distribution of the arrival and service processes, queuing and service order. Thus Little's law applies to many types of queues.

9.2.2.2 The $M/M/s$ Queue

The $M/M/s$ queue is the multi-server variant of the $M/M/1$ queue. Patients arrive with rate λ, each patient is served by one server and a patient waits in queue when all servers are occupied. There are s servers so that the maximum service rate of the queue is $s\mu$, where μ is the service rate of the individual servers. If the number of patients in the queue, n, is less than the number of servers, s, the service rate equals $n\mu$ (see the transition rate diagram in Fig. 9.5) . Again it is required that the amount of work that arrives per time unit (ρ) is less than the maximum service rate, i.e., $\rho = \lambda\mathbb{E}[S] < s$. The equilibrium distribution is obtained from:

$$\begin{aligned} \lambda P_0 &= \mu P_1, && \\ (\lambda + n\mu)P_n &= \lambda P_{n-1} + (n+1)\mu P_{n+1} && \text{for} \quad n < s, \\ (\lambda + s\mu)P_n &= \lambda P_{n-1} + s\mu P_{n+1} && \text{for} \quad n \geq s. \end{aligned} \tag{9.14}$$

Thus

$$P_n = \frac{\rho^n}{m(n)} P_0, \tag{9.15}$$

where

$$m(n) = \begin{cases} n! & \text{for} \quad 0 \leq n < s, \\ s^{n-s} s! & \text{for} \quad n \geq s. \end{cases} \tag{9.16}$$

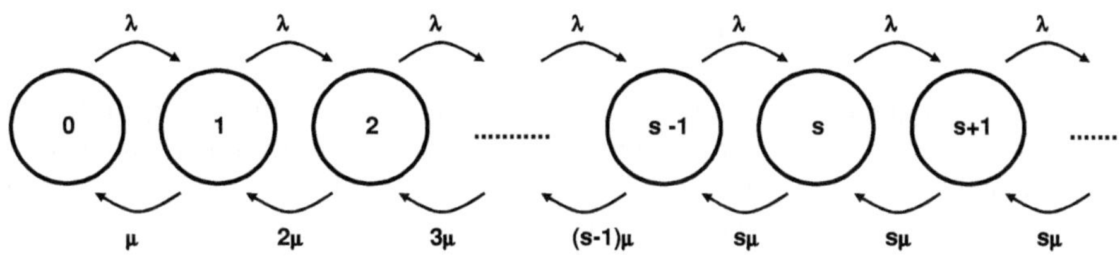

Fig. 9.5 Transition rates in the $M/M/s$ queue

Invoking the normalization condition (9.8), we obtain:

$$P_0 = \left(\sum_{n=0}^{s-1} \frac{\rho^n}{n!} + \frac{\rho^s}{s!} \frac{s}{s-\rho} \right)^{-1}. \tag{9.17}$$

For $s = 1$, Eqs. 9.15–9.17 reduce to the queue length distribution for the $M/M/1$ queue (9.9). The probability P_s deserves special attention; this is the fraction of time all servers are occupied, and because of the PASTA property, also the fraction of arriving patients that find all servers occupied. Thus the probability that a patient will be served immediately upon arrival is $1 - \sum_{n=s}^{\infty} P_n = \sum_{n=0}^{s-1} P_n$, and the probability that a patient has to wait is $\sum_{n=s}^{\infty} P_n$. The latter probability can be calculated using the Erlang-C formula (Gross et al. 2008):

$$P_{s^+} = \mathbb{P}(n \geq s) = \frac{\rho^s}{s!} \frac{s}{s-\rho} P_0. \tag{9.18}$$

There are several Erlang-C calculators available online to compute P_{s^+}, see e.g. (Free University 2010 and Westbay Online Traffic Calculators 2010). The mean number of patients waiting for service is:

$$\mathbb{E}[L^q] = \sum_{n=s+1}^{\infty} (n-s) P_n = \frac{\rho}{s-\rho} P_{s^+}. \tag{9.19}$$

By applying Little's law we find the mean waiting time:

$$\mathbb{E}[W^q] = \frac{\mathbb{E}[L^q]}{\lambda}. \tag{9.20}$$

The mean sojourn time is then obtained by adding the mean service time to the mean waiting time:

$$\mathbb{E}[W] = \mathbb{E}[S] + \mathbb{E}[W^q]. \tag{9.21}$$

The mean number of patients in the queue can be calculated by adding the mean number of patients in service, ρ, to the mean number of patients waiting (Gross et al. 2008):

$$\mathbb{E}[L] = \rho + \mathbb{E}[L^q]. \tag{9.22}$$

9.2.2.3 The $M/M/s/s$ Queue

The $M/M/s/s$ queue, or Erlang loss queue, is different from the $M/M/s$ queue in that it has no waiting capacity. Thus when all servers are occupied, patients are blocked and lost (i.e., they leave and do not come back). This type of queue is very useful when modeling healthcare systems with limited capacity, where patients are routed to another facility when all capacity is in use. Examples are nursing wards and the ICU. Figure 9.6 gives the transition rates for this queue.

We obtain:

$$\begin{aligned} \lambda P_0 &= \mu P_1 \\ (\lambda + n\mu)P_n &= \lambda P_{n-1} + (n+1)\mu P_{n+1} \\ \lambda P_{s-1} &= s\mu P_s, \end{aligned} \tag{9.23}$$

with solution:

$$P_n = \frac{\rho^n/n!}{\sum_{i=0}^{s} \rho^i/i!} \quad \text{for} \quad 0 \leq n \leq s, \tag{9.24}$$

where $\rho = \lambda \mathbb{E}[S]$. Surprisingly, (9.24) also holds for general service times (the $M/G/s/s$ queue) and is thus insensitive to the service time distribution (Gross et al. 2008). The probability that all servers are occupied, is often called the blocking probability, and is given by:

$$P_s = \frac{\rho^s/s!}{\sum_{i=0}^{s} \rho^i/i!}. \tag{9.25}$$

Formula (9.25) is often referred to as the Erlang loss formula, or Erlang-B (Gross et al. 2008). For large s, the direct calculation of P_s by using (9.25) often introduces numerical problems. The following stable recursion exists where these problems are avoided (Zeng 2003).

Recursion for Erlang-B

Step 1.
Set $X_0 = 1$.
Step 2.
For $j = 1, \ldots, s$ compute

$$X_j = 1 + \frac{jX_{j-1}}{\rho}. \tag{9.26}$$

Step 3.
The blocking probability P_s is given by

$$P_s = \frac{1}{X_s}. \tag{9.27}$$

□

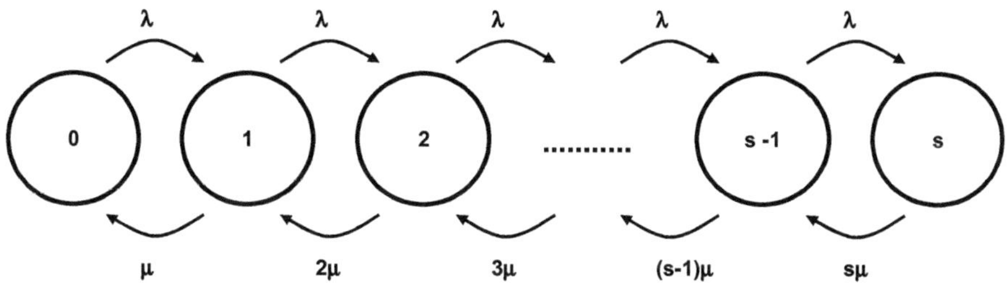

Fig. 9.6 Transition rates in the $M/M/s/s$ queue

Another option is to use one of the Erlang-B calculators available online, see e.g. Patient Flow Improvement Center Amsterdam (2010)and Westbay Online Traffic Calculators (2010). The performance measures are given by:

$$\mathbb{E}[L] = \rho(1 - P_s), \quad \mathbb{E}[W] = \mathbb{E}[S]. \tag{9.28}$$

As we have seen in this subsection, the computation of the blocking probabilities can be quite involved. The infinite server, or $M/M/\infty$ queue, is often used to approximate the $M/M/s/s$ queue for a large number of servers. In this queue, upon arrival each patient obtains his own server. The queue length has a Poisson distribution with parameter ρ, where $\rho = \lambda\mathbb{E}[S]$, and is thus given by

$$\begin{aligned} P_n^\infty &= \frac{\rho^n}{n!} P_0, \quad \text{where} \\ P_0^\infty &= e^{-\rho}. \end{aligned} \tag{9.29}$$

The blocking probability for the system with s servers is approximated by Tijms (2003):

$$P_s \approx \sum_{n \geq s}^{\infty} P_n^\infty. \tag{9.30}$$

9.2.2.4 Queues with General Arrival and/or Service Processes

For the $M/M/s$ queue a single parameter suffices to calculate the queue length distribution and related performance measures. However, assuming exponentiality of the distributions involved in a queuing process is not always a valid choice. When the coefficient of variation is not close to 1 (the value for the exponential distribution) other probability distributions should be used to obtain reliable outcomes, since the variance of the inter-arrival and service times has strong influence on the performance measures.

Results for non-exponential systems are scarce and are often characterized via the scv, c^2. In general, when the scv increases, the variability in the related queuing system also increases. In this subsection we will focus on results for mean waiting times. Additional results are given in the books (Gross et al. 2008; Tijms 2003; Wolff 1989). The software package QtsPlus that accompanies (Gross et al. 2008) supports the calculation of many relevant performance measures, is freely available online (QtsPlus Software 2010) and implemented in MS Excel, but also has an open source variant.

For the $M/G/1$ queue the Laplace—Stieltjes transform for the waiting time distribution is known. From this result, we obtain the Pollaczek–Khinchine formula (Cohen 1982) that characterizes the waiting time in the single-server queue with Poisson arrivals and general service times:

$$\mathbb{E}[W^q] = \mathbb{E}[S]\,\frac{\rho}{1-\rho}\,\frac{1+c_S^2}{2}, \tag{9.31}$$

where c_S^2 denotes the scv of the service time. The mean sojourn time for the $G/M/1$ queue is:

$$\mathbb{E}[W] = \frac{\mathbb{E}[S]}{1-\sigma}, \tag{9.32}$$

where σ is the unique root in the range $0<\sigma<1$ of the following equation:

$$\sigma = \bar{A}(\mu - \mu\sigma), \tag{9.33}$$

with $\bar{A}$ the Laplace–Stieltjes transform of the inter-arrival time and $\mu = \frac{1}{\mathbb{E}[S]}$ (Wolff 1989). For the $G/G/1$ queue the following approximation solution is often used (Tijms 2003):

$$\mathbb{E}[W^q] \approx \mathbb{E}[S]\frac{\rho}{1-\rho}\frac{c_A^2+c_S^2}{2}, \tag{9.34}$$

where c_A^2 denotes the scv of the arrival process. This result includes the $G/M/1$ queue and is exact for the $M/G/1$ queue.

It is hard to determine the exact effect of using the exponential distribution to represent a non-exponential process. As a rule of thumb, we suggest that as long as the actual variance is below that of the exponential distribution, then the exponential distribution provides a conservative estimate. In other words, the calculated expectations of the queue length and waiting times will over-estimate the actual values. Such a conservative estimate is for instance useful when a strategic decision that does not involve a lot of detail needs to be made.

For the mean waiting time in the $G/G/s$ queue the following approximation is very useful (Gross et al. 2008):

$$\mathbb{E}[W^q] \approx \mathbb{E}[W^q_{(M/M/s)}]\frac{c_A^2+c_S^2}{2}, \tag{9.35}$$

where $\mathbb{E}[W^q_{(M/M/s)}]$ denotes the mean waiting time in the $M/M/s$ queue with identical λ and μ. In (Gross et al. 2008) lower and upper bounds on $\mathbb{E}[W^q]$ are also provided. Using the results for $\mathbb{E}[W^q]$, Little's law can be applied to determine the mean number of patients in the queues mentioned in this subsection.

9.2.2.5 Service Disciplines

So far, we only discussed the FCFS service discipline. Other options are processor sharing (PS) and Last Come First Serve (LCFS). We will elaborate on queuing networks with these kind of queues in Sect. 2.4.2.

In the PS service discipline, all arriving patients are immediately served, thus there is no queuing. A single server is shared equally among patients, where each patient class may have its own service requirement. For the $M/M/1 - \text{PS}$ queue the queue length distribution, P_n, is identical to that of the $M/M/1 - \text{FCFS}$ queue (9.9). Intuitively, this can be explained as follows. The server works at rate μ, and when there are n patients in the queue, an individual patient is served with rate $\frac{\mu}{n}$. However, since n patients are served simultaneously, the overall completion rate is still μ ($\frac{\mu}{n} \cdot n = \mu$). Since the patient arrival rate equals λ, the flow in and out of the queue is identical to that of the $M/M/1 - \text{FCFS}$ queue.

The $M/M/1 - \text{LCFS}$ queue with preemptive resume can be seen as a stack, for instance of patient files, where a single server (the doctor) works on the top item of the stack. Whenever a new item is added, the server immediately starts working on this item. However, when the server returns to the previous item, it resumes service (i.e., the queue is work conserving). The queue length distribution is again given by (9.9), where the same argument holds as for the $M/M/1 - \text{PS}$ queue.

9.2.2.6 Miscellaneous Queuing Results

In this subsection we briefly mention a couple of other queuing results. Some of the results that can be obtained for $G/G/1$ queues are exact, but do not transfer to queuing networks. In particular, the equilibrium distribution at arrival instants in the $G/M/1$ queue is:

$$P_n = (1 - \sigma)\sigma^n, \tag{9.36}$$

where σ is defined as in (9.33).

The equilibrium distribution of the $M/M/1$ queue and the $G/M/1$ queue at arrival epochs have a geometric form. At arbitrary epochs, the equilibrium distribution for the $M/G/1$ and $G/M/1$ queues is not available in an amenable form. These distributions, however, can be obtained using the theory of matrix geometric queues. To this end, we introduce the class of so-called phase-type distributions (Latouche and Taylor 2002). A distribution is of phase-type if it can be represented as a continuous time Markov chain on the phases such that the chain remains in a phase during an exponential time and jumps from phase to phase according to transition probabilities, see Latouche and Taylor (2002) for details. It is interesting to observe that each probability distribution that attains positive values, only, can be approximated arbitrarily closely by a phase-type distribution. Using phase-type distribution for respectively the service time and inter-arrival time distribution, the equilibrium distributions for the $M/\mathrm{Ph}_r/1$ and $\mathrm{Ph}_s/M/1$ queues are available in closed form. For these queues, the state description requires the number of patients *n and* the phase of the service or inter-arrival times r resp. s. The equilibrium distribution is obtained in closed form:

$$P_n = P_0 R^n, \quad n = 0, 1, 2, \ldots, \tag{9.37}$$

where P_0 and P_n are r resp. s vectors over the phases of the service or inter-arrival times and R is an $r \times r$ or $s \times s$ matrix over these phases. The result generalizes to the $\mathrm{Ph}_r/\mathrm{Ph}_s/1$ queue where P_0 and P_n become rs vectors recording the joint phases of inter-arrival and service times. Although the form (9.37) is geometric, obtaining the matrix R is quite involved and goes beyond the scope of this chapter, see Latouche and Ramaswami (1999) for details. We specifically mention this queue since phase-type distributions are common in healthcare. For example the length of stay in geriatric care has been modeled using phase-type distributions (Fackrell 2009).

Instead of joining the queue, patients may be impatient and leave the queue before service. When this happens upon arrival, it is called balking. When patients leave after waiting some time, it is referred to as reneging. In the $M/M/s/s$ queue it is assumed that patients who are blocked are lost to the system. When blocked and/or impatient patients return to the queue after some time, we have a retrial queue (Gross et al. 2008).

In this subsection we have considered only queues with a single class of patients. When more than one patient class arrives at the queue, and classes have priority over one another, we have a priority queue (Wolff 1989). In the case of preemptive priority, the service of the low priority patient is interrupted immediately when a higher prioritized patient arrives. Afterward, the service of the low priority patient is resumed (work conserving) or may have to start allover again (work is lost). In the case of non-preemptive priority, a patient that is already in service is completed first.

Vacation queues are a generalization of the $M/G/1$ queue, where the server may take a vacation (i.e., becomes idle for a certain amount of time), also when there are patients in the queue (Wolff 1989). A generalization of the vacation queue is the polling model, where a single server visits multiple queues (Takagi 2000). In this chapter we restrict our focus to networks of queues with continuous availability.

9.2.3 Networks of Exponential Queues

Now that we have defined the building blocks, we can proceed to queuing networks. We start with networks of exponential queues with either a single or multiple servers.

9.2.3.1 Tandem Networks

Consider a tandem network of J queues that are placed in series. All queues have infinite waiting room, a single server, and the service requirement at queue j, $j = 1,\ldots,J$, has an exponential distribution with mean service time $\mathbb{E}[S_j]$. Patients arrive at queue 1 according to a Poisson process with rate λ. Upon service completion at queue j the patient routes to queue $j+1$, $j = 1,\ldots,J-1$, and finally departs from queue J.

From Burke's theorem (Burke 1956) it follows that the departure process of a queue with Poisson arrivals and exponential service times is again a Poisson process with the same rate as the arrival process, and that departures from queue 1 before time t_0 are independent of the queue length of queue 1 at time t_0. This fundamental result indicates that the queue length at time t_0 in queue 1 and queue 2 are statistically independent. Hence, for the tandem queue of Fig. 9.3

$$P(n_1,n_2) = \mathbb{P}(N_1 = n_1, N_2 = n_2) = (1-\rho_1)\rho_1^{n_1}(1-\rho_2)\rho_2^{n_2}, \quad n_1,n_2 \geq 0, \quad (9.38)$$

where $\rho_1 = \lambda\mathbb{E}[S_1]$, $\rho_2 = \lambda\mathbb{E}[S_2]$, and N_j is the random queue length at queue j in equilibrium. Continuing this argument, for a tandem network of J queues, we obtain the so-called product-form solution (Tijms 2003):

$$P(n_1,\ldots,n_J) = \prod_{j=1}^{J}(1-\rho_j)\rho_j^{n_j}, \quad (9.39)$$

where $\rho_j = \lambda\mathbb{E}[S_j]$. This elegant result leads us to open Jackson networks with general patient routing.

9.2.3.2 Open Jackson Networks

We now consider a network consisting of J single-server queues. The external arrival process at queue j, $j = 1,\ldots,J$, is Poisson distributed with rate γ_j, $\gamma_j \geq 0\ \forall j$. Each queue j has an exponentially distributed service requirement with mean service time $\mathbb{E}[S_j]$. Patients are routed from queue i to queue j with state independent routing probability r_{ij}, $0 \leq r_{ij} \leq 1$, i.e., a fraction r_{ij} of patients served at queue i routes to queue j. The parameter r_{i0} denotes the fraction of patients leaving the network at queue i. The total arrival rate λ_j at queue j is given by:

$$\lambda_j = \gamma_j + \sum_{i=1}^{J}\lambda_i r_{ij}, \quad j = 1,\ldots,J, \quad (9.40)$$

and is composed of the arrivals to queue j from outside and inside the network. A queuing network with these characteristics is called an open Jackson network, named after James R. Jackson who first studied its properties in 1957 (Jackson 1957). In Fig. 9.7 an example of an open Jackson network is given.

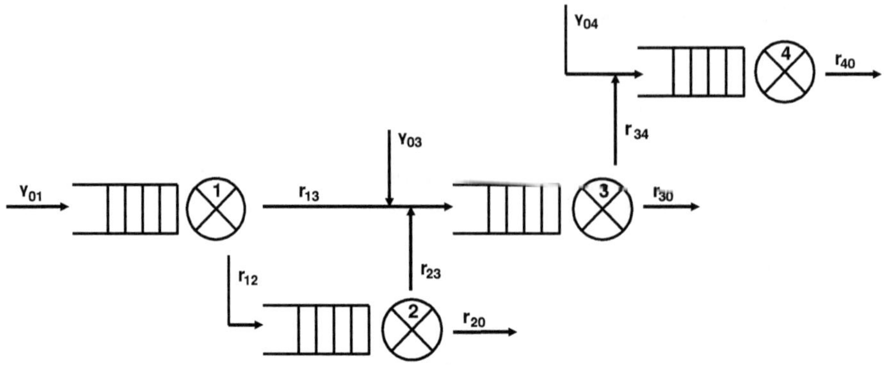

Fig. 9.7 An example of an Open Jackson Network with four queues and patient routing from queues 1→2, 1→3, 2→3, and 3→4. External arrivals occur at queue 1, 3, and 4; departures occur at queue 2, 3, and 4

According to Jackson's theorem (Jackson 1957), the product-form solution for this type of network is given by:

$$P(n_1, \ldots, n_J) = \prod_{j=1}^{J} (1 - \rho_j)\rho_j^{n_j}, \quad n_j \geq 0, \quad j = 1, \ldots, J, \tag{9.41}$$

where $\rho_j = \lambda_j \mathbb{E}[S_j]$.

The Power of Jackson's Theorem

From Jackson's theorem it follows that per queue only a single parameter, ρ_j, is required for the calculation of $P(n_1, \ldots, n_J)$. Consequently, only J parameters are required to analyze the entire network! This result is surprising since usually many parameters are required to characterize a probability distribution.

Since the queues in the network act as if they are independent $M/M/1$ queues, the performance measures are easy to compute:

$$\mathbb{E}[L_j] = \frac{\rho_j}{1 - \rho_j}, \quad \mathbb{E}[W_j] = \frac{\mathbb{E}[L_j]}{\lambda_j}. \tag{9.42}$$

The mean sojourn time for an arbitrary patient can be calculated using Little's law:

$$\mathbb{E}[W] = \frac{\sum_{j=1}^{J} \mathbb{E}[L_j]}{\sum_{j=1}^{J} \gamma_j}. \tag{9.43}$$

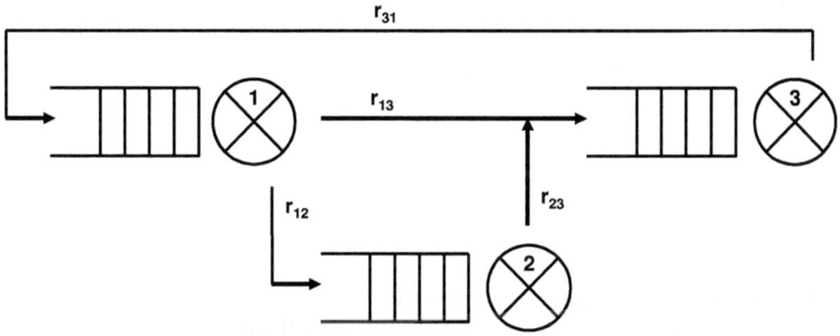

Fig. 9.8 An example of a closed Jackson network with three queues and patient routing from queues 1→2, 1→3, 2→3, and 3→1

Note that this is not equal to $\sum_{j=1}^{J} \mathbb{E}[W_j]$, since patients may not visit all queues in the network or visit some queues several times. Jackson's result can be extended to the multi-server case. We obtain:

$$P(n_1, \ldots, n_J) = \prod_{j=1}^{J} \frac{\rho_j^{n_j}}{m(n_j)} P_{0j}, \tag{9.44}$$

where $\rho_j = \lambda_j \mathbb{E}[S_j]$,

$$m(n_j) = \begin{cases} n_j! & \text{for } 0 \leq n_j < s_j, \\ s_j^{n_j - s_j} s_j! & \text{for } n_j \geq s_j, \end{cases} \tag{9.45}$$

and $s_j \geq 1$ for $j = 1, \ldots, J$. The normalization constant P_{0j} is given by

$$P_{0j} = \left(\sum_{n_j=0}^{s_j-1} \frac{\rho_j^{n_j}}{n_j!} + \frac{\rho_j^{s_j}}{s_j!} \frac{s_j}{s_j - \rho_j} \right)^{-1}. \tag{9.46}$$

9.2.3.3 Closed Jackson Networks

A Jackson network where the external arrival rates $\gamma_j = 0\ \forall j$ and the departure probabilities $r_{i0} = 0\ \forall i$, is a called a Gordon–Newell or closed Jackson network, since patients do not enter or leave (see Fig. 9.8) .

The finite number N of patients that is present in the network is continuously routed among J queues according to the state independent routing probabilities r_{ij}. For the single-server case we obtain a product-form solution (Gordon and Newell 1967):

$$P(n_1, \ldots, n_J) = B(N)^{-1} \prod_{j=1}^{J} \rho_j^{n_j}, \tag{9.47}$$

where $\sum_{j=1}^{J} n_j = N$. In this formula *B*(*N*) is called the normalization constant. In the open network variant, the expression $\prod_{j=1}^{J}(1-\rho_j)$ is actually the normalization constant and easy to compute. In the closed network variant, *B*(*N*) is given by:

$$B(N) = \sum_{\sum_{j=1}^{J} n_j = N} \prod_{j=1}^{J} \rho_j^{n_j}. \tag{9.48}$$

Calculating *B*(*N*) can be quite cumbersome, even for small *N*. Buzen's algorithm (1973) is very helpful in this case and works as follows.

Buzen's Algorithm

Step 1.
Define

$$G_j(k), \quad \text{where} \quad j = 0, \ldots, J \quad \text{and} \quad k = 0, \ldots, N, \tag{9.49}$$

with initial values

$$G_1(k) = \rho_1^k, \quad G_j(0) = 1. \tag{9.50}$$

Step 2.
Recursively compute

$$G_j(k) = G_{j-1}(k) + \rho_j G_j(k-1). \tag{9.51}$$

Step 3.
The normalization constant is given by:

$$B(N) = G_J(N). \tag{9.52}$$

□

Buzen's algorithm can also be used to compute other performance measures of interest. The marginal probability that n_j patients are present at queue *j* is given by:

$$P(n_j) = B(N)^{-1} \rho_j^{n_j} \left[G_J(N-n_j) - \rho_j G_J(N-n_j-1)\right]. \tag{9.53}$$

The mean number of patients present at queue *j* is given by:

$$\mathbb{E}[L_j] = \sum_{n_j=1}^{N} \rho_j^{n_j} B(N)^{-1} G_J(N-n_j). \tag{9.54}$$

The Closed Jackson Network can also be extended to the multi-server case. The product-form solution is then given by:

$$P(n_1,\ldots,n_J) = B(N)^{-1}\prod_{j=1}^{J}\frac{\rho_j^{n_j}}{m(n_j)}, \tag{9.55}$$

where $\sum_{j=1}^{J} n_j = N$, $sm(n_j)$ is given by (9.45), and

$$B(N) = \sum_{\sum_{j=1}^{J} n_j = N}\prod_{j=1}^{J}\frac{\rho_j^{n_j}}{m(n_j)}. \tag{9.56}$$

For the multi-server case *B*(*N*) can also be calculated using Buzen's algorithm.

In a closed single-server Jackson network the mean waiting time and mean number of patients at queue *j* can be calculated without evaluating *B*(*N*) (Gross et al. 2008). This algorithmic approach is called mean value analysis (MVA). We present the basic algorithm, but MVA has been extended to many other queuing systems, see Adan and van der Wal (2011).

MVA Algorithm

Step 1.
Set $\lambda_1 = 1$ and solve the traffic equations:

$$\lambda_j = \sum_{i=1}^{J}\lambda_i r_{ij}, \quad j = 1,\ldots,J. \tag{9.57}$$

Step 2.
Define $L_j(0) = 0$ for $j = 1,\ldots,J$.
Step 3.
For $n = 1,\ldots,N$, calculate

$$\begin{aligned} W_j(n) &= \big(1 + L_j(n-1)\big)\mathbb{E}[S_j], \quad j = 1,\ldots,J,\\ v_1(n) &= \frac{n}{\sum_{j=1}^{J}\lambda_j W_j(n)},\\ v_j(n) &= v_1(n)\lambda_j \quad j = 2,\ldots,J,\\ L_j(n) &= v_j(n)W_j(n), \quad j = 1,\ldots,J. \end{aligned} \tag{9.58}$$

Step 4.
The mean waiting time at queue *j* is given by:

$$\mathbb{E}[W_j] = W_j(N). \tag{9.59}$$

The mean number of patients at queue *j* is given by:

$$\mathbb{E}[L_j] = L_j(N). \tag{9.60}$$

□

9.2.4 Networks of Queues with General Arrival and/or Service Processes

As said, the few exact results that exist for general queues cannot be transferred to general queuing networks. However, many of the approximation results are. In this subsection we describe three types of networks that have an exact solution for the queue length distribution, namely networks with fixed routing, BCMP networks, and loss networks. We conclude with the queuing network analyzer (QNA). This is a generalization of MVA for networks of $G/G/s$ queues.

9.2.4.1 Networks with Fixed Routing

All of the queuing networks we have discussed so far employ Markovian routing. This means that after departure, patients are routed to other queues or leave the network with a certain probability. This excludes fixed routes in which patients follow a prescribed path.

Consider a network in which each patient class has its own route. The route of patient class k, $k = 1, \ldots, K$, is given by the sequence of queues to visit before leaving the system (Kelly 1979):

$$r(k,1), r(k,2), \ldots, r(k,H(k)). \tag{9.61}$$

So in stage h, $h = 1, \ldots, H(k)$, patient class k visits queue $r(k,h)$. Note that one queue may appear multiple times in the route. Using this notation enables to include patients who visit the same queue multiple times, but have a different destination depending on the times the queue has been visited. An example route for a patient class could be $3 \to 2 \to 3 \to 4$, where queue 2 is visited after the patient departs from queue 3 the first time, and queue 4 is visited after the patient departs from queue 2 the second time. This type of queuing network can be seen as a set of intertwined tandem networks (Sect. 2.3.1). Each patient class is routed through its own tandem network of queues, and different patient classes may meet each other at one of the queues.

Let γ_k denote the arrival rate of patient class k. As a consequence of fixed routes, the arrival rate of patient class k at stage h to queue $r(k,h)$ equals the arrival rate of the patient class to the network. In order to be able to determine how many patients of class k being in stage h of their route, are present at queue j, we have to record the position in the queue for each individual patient. We introduce some additional notation. Let $k_j(\ell)$ denote the class of the patient who holds position ℓ in queue j, and let $h_j(\ell)$ denote the stage the patient is currently in. Then $c_j(\ell) = [k_j(\ell), h_j(\ell)]$ gives the type of this patient. Since a patient may visit one queue several times, his type potentially gives more information than his class. The state of queue j is given by the vector $c_j = [c_j(1), \ldots, c_j(n_j)]$, and $C = (c_1, \ldots, c_J)$ gives the state of the queuing network. Now if we define the parameter $\alpha_j(k,h)$ as follows:

$$\alpha_j(k,h) = \begin{cases} v_k & \text{if} \quad r(k,h) \equiv j, \\ 0 & \text{otherwise,} \end{cases} \tag{9.62}$$

where v_j is given by $\lambda_j \mathbb{E}[S_j]$, and a_j is the load of queue j:

$$a_j = \sum_{k=1}^{K} \sum_{h=1}^{H(k)} \alpha_j(k,h), \tag{9.63}$$

then the marginal queue length distribution of the number of patients of class k, $k = 1, \ldots, K$, present at queue j, is given by:

$$\begin{aligned} P_j(c_j) &= B_j^{-1} \prod_{\ell=1}^{n_j} \alpha_j\big(k_j(\ell), h_j(\ell)\big), \quad \text{where} \\ B_j &= \sum_{n=0}^{\infty} a_j^n. \end{aligned} \tag{9.64}$$

The queue length distribution for the entire queuing network is then given by:

$$P(C) = \prod_{j=1}^{J} P_j(c_j). \tag{9.65}$$

The queue length distribution of the number of patients at the queues in the network is given by:

$$P(n_1, \ldots, n_J) = \prod_{j=1}^{J} (1 - v_j) v_j^{n_j}. \tag{9.66}$$

Note that this result does not discriminate among patient classes. Even though the notation required can be quite cumbersome, networks with fixed routing introduce substantial modeling flexibility.

9.2.4.2 BCMP Networks

If each queue j in a network of J queues is one of the following types:

1. $M/M/s$ – FCFS
2. $M/G/1$ – PS
3. $M/G/1$ – LCFS preemptive resume
4. $M/G/\infty$,

an exact solution exists and the network is a BCMP network. It is named after the authors Baskett, Chandy, Muntz, and Palacios, who described it in 1975 (Baskett et al. 1975). The network may be open or closed with multiple patient classes, and employ Markovian or fixed routing. In the case of an open network, the external arrival rates to the queues are Poisson. For notational convenience, we give the product-form solution for a BCMP network with Markovian routing and a single patient class. In this case the queue length distribution is given by:

$$P(n_1, \ldots, n_J) = B(N) \prod_{j=1}^{J} P_j(n_j), \tag{9.67}$$

where $B(N)$ is the normalization constant such that $\sum_N P(n_1, \ldots, n_J) = 1$, and $P_j(n_j)$ is the equilibrium distribution for queue j, $j = 1, \ldots, J$. If queue j is of type 1:

$$\begin{aligned} P_j(n_j) &= \frac{\rho_j^{n_j}}{m(n_j)} P_j(0), \quad \text{where} \\ m(n_j) &= \begin{cases} n_j! & \text{for } 0 \le n_j < s_j, \\ s_j^{n_j - s_j} s_j! & \text{for } n_j \ge s_j, \quad \text{and} \end{cases} \\ P_j(0) &= \left(\sum_{n_j=0}^{s_j-1} \frac{\rho_j^n}{n_j!} + \frac{\rho_j^s}{s_j!} \frac{s_j}{s_j - \rho_j} \right)^{-1}. \end{aligned} \tag{9.68}$$

If queue j is of type 2 or 3:

$$\begin{aligned} P_j(n_j) &= \rho_j^{n_j} P_j(0), \quad \text{where} \\ P_j(0) &= 1 - \rho_j. \end{aligned} \tag{9.69}$$

If queue j is of type 4:

$$\begin{aligned} P_j(n_j) &= \frac{\rho_j^{n_j}}{n_j!} P_j(0), \quad \text{where} \\ P_j(0) &= e^{-\rho_j}. \end{aligned} \tag{9.70}$$

Note that the four queue types include the service disciplines we discussed in Sect. 2.2.5. For BCMP networks the queue length distributions for these service disciplines are insensitive to the service requirement distribution, that is, only the mean service times are required to obtain the equilibrium distribution (9.67).

9.2.4.3 Loss Networks

A loss network is the multi-dimensional generalization of the Erlang loss queue (Sect. 2.2.3). In a loss network, patients simultaneously claim at least one server in at least one queue. When upon arrival at the network one of the designated queues is full, the patient is blocked and lost. Note that this kind of queuing network shows an analogy with some hospital processes. For instance, a patient who needs to be admitted to the ICU after surgery, will not be operated on when there is no ICU bed available. Thus the patient simultaneously claims an OR and an ICU bed. If either one is not available, the surgery will not commence.

For a loss network handling K patient classes, the queue length distribution of the number of patients of class k, $k = 1, \ldots, K$, is given by Kelly (1991), Zachary and Ziedins (2011):

$$\begin{aligned} P(n_1, \ldots, n_K) &= B(S)^{-1} \prod_{k=1}^{K} \frac{\rho_k^{n_k}}{n_k!}, \quad \text{where} \quad n \in S(S), \\ S(S) &= \{ n \in \mathbb{N}_0, \sum_{k=1}^{K} A_{jk} n_k \leq s_j \}, \\ B(S) &= \sum_{n \in S(S)} \prod_{k=1}^{K} \frac{\rho_k^{n_k}}{n_k!}, \quad \rho_k = \lambda_k \mathbb{E}[S_k], \end{aligned} \tag{9.71}$$

with λ_k the arrival rate to the network of patients of class k, $\mathbb{E}[S_k]$ the mean sojourn time in the network, s_j the number of servers at queue j and A_{jk} the number of servers a patient of class k claims at queue j. Loss networks are insensitive to the sojourn time distribution. Various algorithms and approximations exist to obtain blocking probabilities (Kelly 1991, Zachary and Ziedins 2011).

9.2.4.4 The Queuing Network Analyzer

Despite the fact that many real world problems do not exhibit exponential service times, open Jackson networks have been used in numerous applications, often with good results. However, to analyze networks of general queues, the queuing network analyzer (QNA) is a better alternative. The QNA was developed in 1983 by Ward Whitt (1983) for approximate analysis of open networks of $G/G/s$ queues with FCFS service discipline. There are several variations on the QNA, also known as reduction or decomposition methods (see Buzacott and Shanthikumar 1993). In this subsection we summarize the basic QNA algorithm.

QNA Algorithm

Step 1.

Calculate the aggregate arrival rates at queue j, λ_j :

$$\lambda_j = \gamma_j + \sum_{i=1}^{J} \lambda_i r_{ij}. \tag{9.72}$$

Step 2.
Calculate the load of a server at queue j, ϕ_j :

$$\phi_j = \frac{\lambda_j \mathbb{E}[S_j]}{s_j}. \tag{9.73}$$

Step 3.
Calculate the flow from queue i to queue j, λ_{ij} :

$$\lambda_{ij} = \lambda_i r_{ij}, \tag{9.74}$$

and the fraction of arrivals at queue j that come from queue i, q_{ij} :

$$q_{0j} = \frac{\gamma_j}{\lambda_j}, \quad q_{ij} = \frac{\lambda_{ij}}{\lambda_j}, \tag{9.75}$$

where q_{0j} denotes the fraction of external arrivals to queue j.
Step 4.
Calculate the scv for the arrival process at queue j, $c^2_{A,j}$:

$$\begin{aligned} c^2_{A,j} =& a_j + \sum_{i=1}^{J} c^2_{A,i} b_{ij}, \quad \text{with} \\ a_j =& 1 + w_j \left[(q_{0j} c^2_{0j} - 1) + \sum_{i=1}^{J} q_{ij}((1 - r_{ij}) + r_{ij}\phi_i^2 x_i) \right], \end{aligned} \tag{9.76}$$

where c^2_{0j} is the scv of the external arrival process at queue j, and

$$x_i = 1 + \frac{1}{\sqrt{m_i}}(\max(c^2_{S,i}, \frac{1}{5}) - 1), \tag{9.77}$$

with $c^2_{S,i}$ the scv of the service process at queue i. We have

$$\begin{aligned} b_{ij} = w_j q_{ij} r_{ij}(1 - \phi_i^2), \quad w_j = \left[(1 + 4(1 - \phi_j)^2(\eta_j - 1) \right]^{-1}, \quad \text{and} \\ \eta_j = \left[\sum_{i=0}^{J} q_{ij}^2 \right]^{-1}. \end{aligned} \tag{9.78}$$

Step 5.
The mean waiting time at queue j, $\mathbb{E}[W_j]$, is given by

$$\mathbb{E}[W_j] = \mathbb{E}[W_{M/M/s}] \frac{c^2_{A,j} + c^2_{S,j}}{2}. \tag{9.79}$$

□

The calculations involved with the QNA are usually straightforward and can be done by hand. However, when the parameters need to be changed often, we suggest using a spreadsheet program such as MS Excel. QtsPlus Software (2010) also supports the analysis of general queuing networks. Even though the QNA has proved to be very useful, other approximation methods give better results when the network is highly congested (see Buzacott and Shanthikumar 1993for further reference).

9.2.5 State of the Art in Networks of Queues

Queuing theory traces back to Erlang's historical work for telephony networks in 1909 (Brockmeyer et al. 1948). The simplicity and fundamental flavor of Erlang's famous expressions, such as his loss formula for an incoming call in a circuit switched system to be lost, see Sect. 2.2.3, has remained intriguing, and has motivated the development of results with similar elegance and expression power for various systems modeling congestion and competition over resources.

A second milestone was the step of queuing theory into queuing networks as motivated by the product-form results for manufacturing systems in the 1950s obtained by Jackson (1957). These results revealed that the queue lengths at nodes of a network, where customers route among the nodes upon service completion in equilibrium can be regarded as independent random variables, that is, the equilibrium distribution of the network of nodes factorizes over (is a product of) the marginal equilibrium distributions of the individual nodes as if in isolation, see Sect. 2.3.2. These networks are nowadays referred to as Jackson networks.

A third milestone was inspired by the rapid development of computer systems and brought the attention for service disciplines such as the PS discipline introduced by Kleinrock (1967). More complicated multi-server nodes and service disciplines such as FCFS, LCFS and PS, and their mixing within a network have led to a surge in theoretical developments and a wide applicability of queuing theory, see Sect. 2.4.2

Queuing networks have obtained their place in both theory and practice. New technological developments such as Internet and wireless communications, but also advancements in existing applications such as manufacturing and production systems, public transportation, and logistics, have triggered many theoretical and practical results. The questions arising in healthcare will no doubt again lead to a surge in the development of queuing theoretical results and applications, a fourth milestone in queuing theory.

Queuing network theory has focused on both the analysis of complex nodes, and the interaction between nodes in networks. Many textbooks and handbooks include or are devoted to queuing theory. Basic level textbooks include Taha (1997), Winston (1994), and more advanced handbooks are Gross et al. (2008), Kleinrock (1967,1976), Nelson (1995), Tijms (2003), Wolff (1989). The state of the art in the mathematical theory for queuing networks is described in the handbook (Boucherie and van Dijk 2011). Topics treated include:

- A general theory for product-form equilibrium distributions far beyond those for Jackson and BCMP networks.
- Monotonicity and comparison results that allow analytical bounds on performance measures for networks that slightly deviate from Jackson or BCMP type networks.
- Fluid and diffusion limits that aim at analyzing networks in the regimes dominated by the mean or the variances of the underlying processes such as service times and inter-arrival times.
- Computational results that are far more general than the queuing network analyzer of Sect. 2.4.4.

In the last chapter an application of networks of queues in healthcare is presented, indicating that many available theoretical results for networks of queues are waiting to be disclosed for application in healthcare.

9.3 Examples of Healthcare Applications

As we have seen in the previous section, for some queuing networks that consist of only exponential queues analytical solutions are available. When either the arrival or service process is non-exponential, approximation methods are usually required. In this section we provide several references to healthcare examples that involve queuing networks, and discuss two examples in detail. For examples that involve single queues, we refer to Green (2006).

Generally speaking, three types of healthcare networks have been studied using queuing network topologies. We distinguish between networks of healthcare facilities, networks of departments within a facility, and networks of healthcare providers within a department (see Fig. 9.9).

Using this network classification, and the distinction among exponential and general networks, the references provided in this section can be categorized as presented in Table 9.1.

9.3.1 Applications of Exponential Networks

Modeling a healthcare network with exponential queues gives a lot of insight into the structural behavior, such as bottlenecks. The modeling power of these networks is most when many of the details on patient behavior are not yet specified, but randomness is an essential part of the behavior of the system, i.e., at the strategical level of allocation of capacity, facilities, and resources.

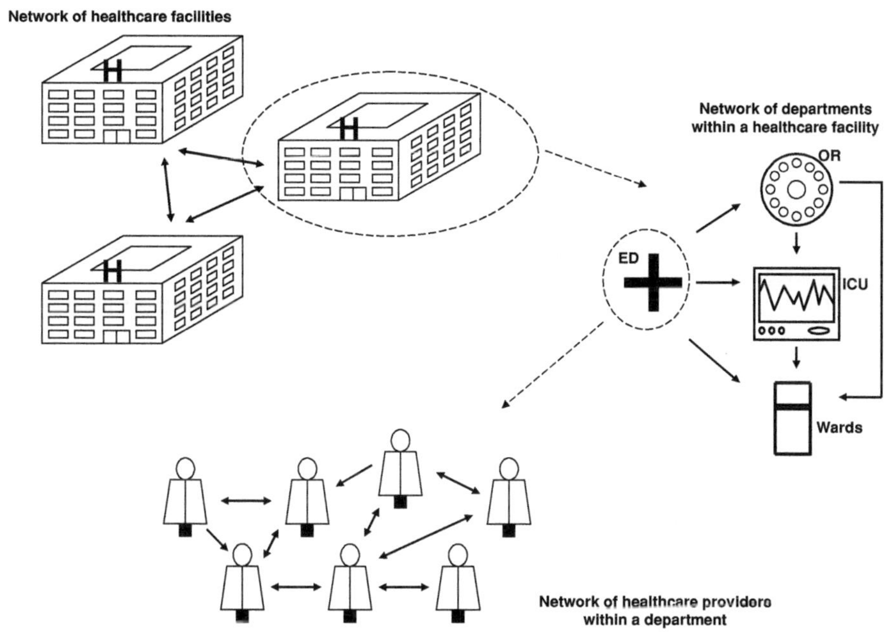

Fig. 9.9 Different types of networks in healthcare

9.3.1.1 Facility Location and Bed-Blocking Problems

One of the earliest developments in this area is given in Blair and Lawrence (1981), where a network of $M/M/s/s$ queues is combined with an algorithm to determine the optimal location of burn care facilities in the state of New York. The resulting system of equations can be solved, but due to computational difficulties only for a small number of facilities and beds. This type of network is further studied in Osorio and Bierlaire (2009). The latter paper involves an example where patients are routed through a network of operative and post-operative units (such as the OR, ICU, and nursing wards), and may experience bed-blocking when the next unit on the route operates at full capacity. Also in this model the numerical computations remain problematic when there are numerous units and beds. The relationship between the OR and bed availability on the ICU is further studied in van Dijk and Kortbeek (2009), where the authors use a loss network to determine the blocking probability for surgical patients caused by a lack of ICU beds. The bed-blocking problem is also considered in Koizumi et al. (2005), where the flow of psychiatric patients within a network of healthcare facilities is considered. A relatively simple steady-state analysis results in a product-form solution. The capacity planning problem for neonatal units (how many cots to place at each care unit) is analyzed in Asaduzzaman et al. (2010) using a loss network model. The implementation of the solution is described in Asaduzzaman et al. (2010).

Table 9.1 Categorization of references

	Exponential networks	General networks
Network of healthcare facilities	Asaduzzaman et al. (2010a); Asaduzzaman et al. (2010b); Blair and Lawrence (1981); Koizumi et al. (2005); Lee and Zenios (2009)	Aaby et al. (2006)
Network of departments within a facility	Cochran and Bharti (2006); Cochran and Bharti (2006); Osorio and Bierlaire (2009)	Creemers and Lambrecht (2011)
Network of healthcare providers within a department	-	Albin et al. (1990); Cochran and Roche (2008); Jiang and Giachetti (2007); Zonderland et al. (2009)

9.3.1.2 Patient Flow

Modeling patient flow has received limited attention (Vanberkel et al. 2010). Patient flow between different hospital departments is studied in two papers by the same author. In Cochran and Bharti (2006) the patient flow from the ED to the ICU and nursing wards is studied using an open Jackson network. The same methodology is used in Cochran and Bharti (2006) to analyze flow of obstetric patients. Patient flow within a care facility is studied from another perspective in Chaussalet et al. (2006) and Xie et al. (2007). In these papers, different phases in the care trajectory of a patient are considered. While in Chaussalet et al. (2006) a closed queuing network is used, in Xie et al. (2007) the model is extended to a semi-open queuing network with a capacity constraint (the maximum number of patients who can be admitted).

9.3.1.3 Clinical Capacity Problem

Patients with renal failure are considered in Lee and Zenios (2009). These patients either receive dialysis at a clinic, or when their condition worsens (temporarily) hospitalized. A multi-class open queuing network with two queues (the clinic and the hospital respectively) is used to determine the clinic's capacity and the maximum number of patients to be admitted into the clinic, given that patients do not use clinic resources when they are hospitalized.

9.3.2 Applications of General Networks

When a higher level of detail is required, for example when networks of healthcare providers within a department are studied, models with general queues are of more value.

9.3.2.1 Organization of Acute Care

The organization of acute care is studied in Cochran and Roche (2008) and Jiang and Giachetti (2007). In Cochran and Roche (2008) an ED is modeled with a multi-class open network of $M/G/s$ queues. The main purpose of this model is to determine the required ED capacity needed to achieve service targets such as waiting time and overflow probabilities. In Jiang and Giachetti (2007) the same kind of network is used to model an urgent care center (UCC), which is basically an outpatient clinic that delivers ambulatory urgent care to relieve pressure from the ED. The main goal of this model is to determine whether parallelization of tasks in the patient's care trajectory has a positive effect on the patient's length of stay at the UCC.

9.3.2.2 Other Applications

In Creemers and Lambrecht (2011) hospital departments and their interdepartmental relationships are modeled as a network with $G/G/s$ queues. Analysis of the network gives relevant information such as utilization rates and mean waiting times for each queue, and also allows for exploring the impact of service interruptions, aggregating patient flows, and determining the optimal number of patients in a clinic session. Another application is the recent outbreaks of viruses, such as the H1N1 influenza virus, which call for a rapid response of the authorities. In Aaby et al. (2006) the authors show how a queuing network can help to plan emergency mass dispensing and vaccination clinics. In Albin et al. (1990) an outpatient clinic is studied using the queuing network analyzer. The paper provides a nice example of how a queuing network can be of added value when performing bottleneck analysis.

9.3.3 *Example I: Distribution of Patient Classes over Nursing Wards*

This example is based on a project carried out by the authors at Leiden university medical center (LUMC), one of the eight university hospitals in the Netherlands. The LUMC admits 20,500 inpatients per year and has 14 wards with a total of 390 beds (2009 data).

9.3.3.1 The Problem

LUMC management wanted to study the distribution of patient classes over the nursing wards and the related bed requirements. We supported them by developing a loss network model that allows for an exact calculation of the fraction of patients that are blocked because the ward is full, and the mean utilization rate per ward. Of course, in practice arrival and service processes at the wards are very complex; arrivals are not homogeneously distributed over the day; patients are not always blocked when the ward is full (e.g. an extra temporary bed is created), and so on. However, for the purpose of this project, this model was a sufficient and fitting tool.

9.3.3.2 The Model

Figure 9.10 gives a simple representation of the nursing ward loss network. Patients enter the wards via the ED, the ICU, another hospital, or come from (a nursing) home. Ultimately patients leave the ward again to go home, to another hospital, or sometimes, unfortunately, die. Each patient has an attending physician from specialty i, $i = 1, \ldots, I$. We assume that patients are routed to the ward of their attending physician. Patients come in three classes k: elective short-stay patients ($k = \text{es}$), elective long-stay patients ($k = \text{el}$), and urgent patients ($k = u$), and have mean sojourn time $\mathbb{E}[S_{ik}]$. They originate from one of the four sources m: ED ($m = \text{ed}$), ICU ($m = \text{ic}$), another hospital ($m = \text{oh}$), or home ($m = \text{ho}$). Patients are admitted to one of the wards j, $j = 1, \ldots, J$, with routing probability $P_{ik,m,j}$, where $P_{ik,m,j} \in \{0, 1\}$ and $\sum_j P_{ik,m,j} = 1 \ \forall i, k, m$ (all patients should be admitted to a ward). Each ward has c_j physical beds, of which s_j are staffed and can be used to admit patients. It may occur that a ward has more physical than staffed beds, so $s_j \leq c_j$. If all staffed beds at the designated ward are full, the patient is blocked and not admitted to the ward (patients will not be admitted at another ward). The mean sojourn time, $\mathbb{E}[S_j]$, and arrival rate, λ_j, at ward j are calculated using the fraction of patients who are routed to ward j:

$$
\begin{aligned}
[B]\lambda_j &= \sum_{i=1}^{I} \sum_{k=\{\text{es,el,u}\}} \sum_{m=\{\text{ed,ic,oh,ho}\}} \lambda_{ik,m} P_{ik,m,j}, \\
\mathbb{E}[S_j] &= \sum_{i=1}^{I} \sum_{k=\{\text{es,el,u}\}} \sum_{m=\{\text{ed,ic,oh,ho}\}} \mathbb{E}[S_{ij}] P_{ik,m,j}.
\end{aligned} \tag{9.80}
$$

We assume that the departure rates from the sources m are Poisson; thus, the ward arrival rates are also Poisson. The problem we study is how the hospital should distribute the patient groups ik over the wards j. Depending on the number of staffed beds, each ward can offer a certain amount of care. The hospital should choose whether it wants to focus on achieving a blocking probability which is below a certain value, or a mean utilization rate which is above a threshold.[2] An additional benefit of a distribution that optimally uses the ward capacities is that it

---

[2] Many hospitals aim for a mean utilization of 85% and a blocking probability below 5% at the same time. This is only possible when the ward has a large (around 50) number of beds (Bruin et al. 2010).

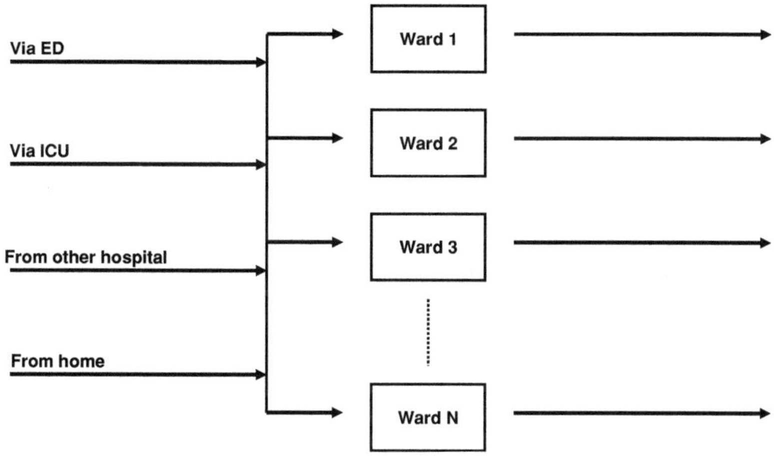

Fig. 9.10 Nursing ward loss network

might be possible to close one or more wards. Since we consider each ward j as a separate entity, the blocking probability, $\mathbb{P}_{s_j}$, is given by

$$\mathbb{P}_{s_j} = \frac{\left(\lambda_j \mathbb{E}[S_j]\right)^{s_j} / s_j!}{\sum_{l=0}^{s_j} \frac{\left(\lambda_j \mathbb{E}[S_j]\right)^l}{l!}}. \tag{9.81}$$

The utilization rate of the beds at ward j, ϕ_j, is given by

$$\phi_j = \frac{\left(1 - \mathbb{P}_{s_j}\right) \lambda_j \mathbb{E}[S_j]}{s_j}. \tag{9.82}$$

To attain the desired value of either $\mathbb{P}_{s_j}$ or ϕ_j, one can calculate the required value of $\lambda_j \mathbb{E}[S_j]$. This can be done by hand or by using spreadsheet software such as MS Excel. An easier option is to use one of the Erlang-B calculators available online [see e.g. (Patient Flow Improvement Center Amsterdam 2010)]. By amending the routing probabilities $P_{ik,m,j}$, it is possible to evaluate all kinds of patient class distributions over the wards.

During the project, we developed a practical extension to the model. We observed it was hard for hospital management to obtain a 'gut feeling' for which patient classes could be combined at a ward. We therefore printed a large map of the hospital with the locations of the wards. For each ward we printed the maximum value of $\lambda_j \mathbb{E}[S_j]$ (which depends on s_j). We also made cards that for each patient class ik had the value of $\sum_m \lambda_{ik,m} \mathbb{E}[S_{ik}]$ printed on it. Hospital management could put the cards with patient classes on the locations on the map, and explore the effect of combining various patient classes. This example shows that queuing techniques can also provide online decision support.

Using the theory of loss networks (Sect. 2.4.3), we can further improve the performance of the wards. Patient groups are still routed to a dedicated ward, but nursing staff can be shared among wards. This way, the previously unstaffed physical beds can be used as well, resulting in a lower blocking probability and a higher utilization rate. Consider for example a simple system with two wards. Ward 1 has $c_1 = 5$ physical beds, $s_1 = 3$ staffed beds, and arrival rate $\lambda_1 = 2$ patients per day. Ward 2 has $c_2 = 5$ physical beds, $s_2 = 4$ staffed beds, and arrival rate $\lambda_2 = 3$ patients per day. At both wards the mean sojourn time equals one day. If the wards would operate separately as in the example above, both wards would have a blocking probability of 21% and an utilization rate of 53% resp. 60%.

If the two wards would share nursing staff, we can formulate this example as a loss network:

$$\begin{aligned}P(n_1, n_2) =& B(S)^{-1}\frac{\rho_1^{n_1}\rho_2^{n_2}}{n_1!n_2!},\\ & n_1 \le c_1, \quad n_2 \le c_2, \quad n_1 + n_2 \le s_1 + s_2, \quad \text{and}\\ B(S) =& \sum_{n_1, n_2}\frac{\rho_1^{n_1}\rho_2^{n_2}}{n_1!n_2!},\end{aligned} \tag{9.83}$$

where n_1, n_2 denotes the number of patients present at ward 1 resp. 2. We see that in total still at most $s_1 + s_2 = 7$ patients could be present at the same time. However, now at ward 1 at most $c_1 = 5$ instead of $s_1 = 3$ patients can be admitted, and at ward 2 at most $c_2 = 5$ instead of $s_2 = 4$ patients can be admitted, as long as the total number of patients does not exceed 7. The blocking probability then decreases to 16%, while the utilization rate per staffed bed at the wards increases to 56% resp. 63%.

9.3.4 Example II: Redesign of a Preanesthesia Evaluation Clinic

This example is based on Zonderland et al. (2009).

9.3.4.1 The Problem

We consider a preanesthesia evaluation clinic (PAC). At this clinic, which is operated by the department of Anesthesiology, patients are screened before undergoing elective surgery. In the last decades most hospitals have organized this screening in an outpatient setting. Not only will a well-performed screening reduce the surgical risk for the patient, but also it reduces the number of canceled surgeries due to the physical condition of the patient (Ferschl et al. 2005). Initially, the screening process at the PAC was organized as follows. Four anesthesia care providers performed the actual screening, supported by a secretary and two clinic assistants. The screening consisted of several separate medical and administrative tasks. The majority of patients (70%) would be screened directly after their consultation at the surgeon's outpatient clinic. This direct (walk-in) screening would only be possible for non-complex patients with ASA I&II classification (American Society of Anesthesiologits 2011), patients with a more severe health status (ASA III&IV classification) would receive an appointment, since additional medical information and a longer consultation time was required. An increased staff workload, resulting from the introduction of an electronic patient data management system, led to lower job satisfaction, work stress, and prolonged patient waiting times. Although 90% of the annual 6,000 PAC patients were eligible for walk-in, one third of these patients were seen on appointment basis, due to an overcrowded waiting room when they first presented themselves at the PAC.

9.3.4.2 The Model

To identify bottlenecks in the PAC's operations, the clinic was modeled as a multi-class open queuing network (see Fig. 9.11). There were three patient classes: children, adults eligible for direct (walk-in) screening, and adults requiring an appointment because of their (more severe) health status. The PAC queuing network has three separate (connected) queues, where the employees act as servers. Patients only enter the PAC through the secretary queue, but may leave the system at any queue. The PAC queuing network was analyzed using a decomposition method, based on the QNA. This method consists of three steps. We first summarize the method and then provide a detailed description of the model with the corresponding formulas.

First, the multi-class network is reduced to a single class network. This is done by aggregating all patient flows that enter a queue. Then the workload ρ is calculated for each queue. This already gives significant and valuable information; recall that ρ is a measure for the fraction of time employees are busy. In the next step, the single class open queuing network is analyzed, where the mean contact time and scv of the joint arrival and service processes at the three queues are deduced. In the final step the mean waiting time per queue is calculated, using the variables that were derived in steps 1 and 2.

In the initial analysis of the PAC queuing network, it was found that the secretary and anesthesia care providers functioned as bottlenecks. Consequently, several alternatives were formulated together with clinic staff, in order to remove these bottlenecks. All alternatives were evaluated using the queuing network model, resulting in one alternative that outperformed the others. In this alternative, several tasks were redistributed and the patient arrival process was amended such that the arrivals were spread more equally over the day. In the year following the implementation of the alternative clinic design, patient arrivals increased (unexpectedly) by 16%. In the old situation, this would likely have resulted in even longer patient waiting times (recall Fig. 9.2) . However, the mean patient length of stay at the PAC did not increase significantly, and more patients (81%) were offered the direct screening.

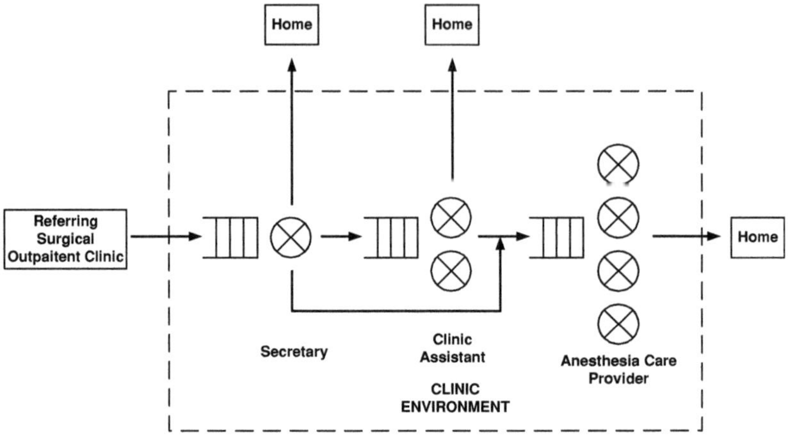

Fig. 9.11 Queuing network representation of PAC

9.3.4.3 Detailed Description of the Decomposition Method

The PAC queuing network consists of three queues. The secretary queue is a single-server queue whereas the clinic assistant and anesthesia care providers are represented by multi-server queues. Patients enter the queuing network via the secretary queue and depart the system from any of the queues. Furthermore, if upon arrival at a queue an employee is available patients are served immediately; otherwise they join the queue and are treated on FCFS basis. We use an approximate decomposition method (Bitran and Morabito 1996) that is based on the QNA to analyze the model. The model we will present here is more involved than the initial QNA formulation as given in Sect. 2.4.4. Practical situations can usually not be directly translated into an existing model. Instead, the theory has to be amended and extended to represent reality. We will describe in detail the changes we have made to the QNA algorithm.

First we introduce some notation. There are k distinct patient classes, where $k = 1$ are patients deferred to an appointment by the secretary, $k = 2$ adults with ASA I or II, $k = 3$ adults with ASA III or IV, and $k = 4$ are children. To evaluate the alternative clinic design, we also introduce $k = \{5, 6, 7\}$ to represent patients (adults with ASA I or II, adults with ASA III or IV, and children, respectively) who return for their appointment. We have j queues, $j = 1, 2, 3$, representing the secretary, clinic assistant, and anesthesia care provider.

Step 1.

The aggregated arrival rates at queue j are:

$$\lambda_1 = \sum_{k=1+d}^{4+3d} \gamma_k, \quad \lambda_2 = \sum_{k=2}^{3} \gamma_k, \quad \lambda_3 = \sum_{k=2}^{4} (1 - da_k)\gamma_k + d \sum_{k=5}^{7} \gamma_k, \tag{9.84}$$

where γ_k is the arrival rate of patient class k at queue 1, and a_k is the fraction of patients of class k who are deferred to an appointment in the alternative clinic design. Since the indices $k = \{5,6,7\}$ only exist when the alternative clinic design is evaluated, we introduce the binary variable d, which equals 1 if the alternative clinic design is evaluated and 0 otherwise.

Step 2.

The load per patient class per server for queue 1,2, and 3 is:

$$\begin{aligned}\phi_{1,k} &= \gamma_k \mathbb{E}[S_{k,1}]\frac{1}{e_1 s_1}\\ \phi_{2,k} &= \gamma_k \mathbb{E}[S_{k,2}]\frac{1}{s_2}\\ \phi_{3,k} &= \gamma_k \mathbb{E}[S_{k,3}]\frac{1}{e_3 s_3} + d(1-a_k)\gamma_k \mathbb{E}[S_{k,3}]\frac{1}{e_3 s_3}\end{aligned} \tag{9.85}$$

where $\mathbb{E}[S_{k,j}]$ is the mean service time for patient class k at queue j. Since the secretary is often consulted by other patients and co-workers while handling a patient at the reception desk, an effective capacity e_1, $0 < e_1 \leq 1$, is taken into account when calculating the mean time a patient spends at this queue. The anesthesia care provider is often disturbed, but not while treating patients and therefore the effective capacity, e_3, $0 < e_3 \leq 1$, is only used in calculating the load. These effective capacities are calculated by using direct observations and interviews with the employees. The number of servers (i.e. employees) at queue j equals s_j. Adding the load over all patient classes gives the aggregated load per server of queue j, $j = 1,2,3$:

$$\phi_1 = \sum_{k=1+d}^{4+3d} \phi_{1,k}, \quad \phi_2 = \sum_{k=2}^{3} \phi_{2,k}, \quad \phi_3 = \sum_{k=2}^{4+3d} \phi_{3,k}. \tag{9.86}$$

For stability it is required that $\phi_j < 1$ for all queues j.

Step 3.

The flow from queue 1 to queue 2 or 3 and from queue 2 to queue 3 is given by:

$$\lambda_{1,2} = \sum_{k=2}^{3} \frac{(1-da_k)\gamma_k}{\lambda_1}, \quad \lambda_{1,3} = \frac{\sum_{k=4}^{4+3d}(1-da_k)\gamma_k}{\lambda_1}, \quad \lambda_{2,3} = \sum_{k=2}^{3} \frac{(1-da_k)\gamma_k}{\lambda_2} \tag{9.87}$$

The fraction of arrivals at queue 3 that come from queue 1 or 2 is given by (note that $q_{1,2} = 1$):

$$q_{1,3} = \frac{\sum_{k=4}^{4+3d}(1-da_k)\gamma_4}{\lambda_3}, \quad q_{2,3} = \sum_{k=2}^{3} \frac{(1-da_k)\gamma_k}{\lambda_3}. \tag{9.88}$$

Step 4.

The arrival process at queue 1 has scv, $c^2_{A,1}$:

$$c^2_{A,1} = w_1 \sum_{k=1+d}^{4+3d} Q_{k,1} c^2_{A,k,1} + 1 - w_1, \tag{9.89}$$

where $c^2_{A,k,1}$ is the scv of the arrival process of patient class k at queue 1, and

$$w_1 = \left(1 + 4(1-\phi_1)^2(\eta_1 - 1)\right)^{-1}, \quad \eta_1 = \frac{\lambda_1^2}{\sum_{k=1+d}^{4+3d} \gamma_k^2}, \quad Q_{k,1} = \frac{\gamma_k}{\lambda_1}. \tag{9.90}$$

The mean service time, $\mathbb{E}[S_1]$ and scv at queue 1, $c^2_{S,1}$, are:

$$\mathbb{E}[S_1] = \frac{\sum_{k=1+d}^{4+3d} \gamma_k \mathbb{E}[S_{k,1}]}{\lambda_1}, \quad c^2_{S,1} = \frac{\sum_{k=1+d}^{4+3d} \gamma_k \mathbb{E}^2[S_{k,1}](c^2_{S,k,1} + 1)}{\lambda_1 \mathbb{E}^2[S_1]} - 1, \tag{9.91}$$

where $c^2_{S,k,j}$ is the scv of the service time for patient class k at queue j. The arrival process at queue 2 has scv, $c^2_{A,2}$:

$$c^2_{A,2} = \lambda_{1,2} c^2_{D,1} + 1 - \lambda_{1,2}, \tag{9.92}$$

where $c^2_{D,1}$ is the scv of the departure process at queue 1. Queue 2 has mean service time, $\mathbb{E}[S_2]$, and scv, $c^2_{S,2}$:

$$\mathbb{E}[S_2] = \frac{\sum_{k=2}^{3} \gamma_k \mathbb{E}[S_{k,2}]}{\lambda_2}, \quad c^2_{S,2} = \frac{\sum_{k=2}^{3} \gamma_k \mathbb{E}^2[S_{k,2}](c^2_{S,k,2} + 1)}{\lambda_2 \mathbb{E}^2[S_2]} - 1. \tag{9.93}$$

The arrival process at queue 3 has scv, $c^2_{A,3}$:

$$\begin{aligned} c^2_{A,3} &= w_3(q_{2,3} c^2_{2,3} + q_{1,3} c^2_{1,3}) + 1 - w_3, \quad \text{with} \\ w_3 &= \left(1 + 4(1-\phi_3)^2(\eta_3 - 1)\right)^{-1}, \quad \eta_3 = \left(q^2_{2,3} + q^2_{1,3}\right)^{-1}, \\ c^2_{1,3} &= \lambda_{1,3} c^2_{D,1} + 1 - \lambda_{1,3}, \quad c^2_{2,3} = (1-d) c^2_{D,2} + d(\lambda_{2,3} c^2_{D,2} + 1 - \lambda_{2,3}), \\ c^2_{D,2} &= 1 + (1-\phi_2^2)(c^2_{A,2} - 1) + \frac{\phi_2^2}{\sqrt{s_2}}(c^2_{S,2} - 1), \end{aligned} \tag{9.94}$$

where $c^2_{2,3}$ is the scv of the patient flow from queue 2 to queue 3, $c^2_{1,3}$ the scv of the patient flow from queue 1 to queue 3, and $c^2_{D,2}$ is the scv of the departure process at queue 2. Queue 3 has mean service time, $\mathbb{E}[S_3]$, and scv, $c^2_{S,3}$:

$$\mathbb{E}[S_3] = \frac{\sum_{k=2}^{4}(1-da_k)\gamma_k\mathbb{E}[S_{k,3}]}{\lambda_3} + d\sum_{k=5}^{7}\gamma_k\mathbb{E}[S_{k,3}],$$
$$c_{S,3}^2 = \frac{\sum_{k=2}^{4}(1-da_k)\gamma_k\mathbb{E}^2[S_{k,3}](c_{S,k,3}^2+1) + \sum_{k=5}^{7}\gamma_k\mathbb{E}^2[S_{k,3}](c_{S,k,3}^2+1)}{\lambda_3\mathbb{E}^2[S_3]} - 1. \tag{9.95}$$

Step 5.
We are interested in the waiting times for patients per queue and the load per employee at each queue. The latter is given by the aggregated load derived in step 1, while the mean waiting times are obtained by using the scv and mean service time calculated in step 2. The mean waiting time, $\mathbb{E}[W_j^q]$, is equal for all patient classes.

$$\begin{aligned}
\mathbb{E}[W_1^q] &= \frac{c_{A,1}^2 + c_{S,1}^2}{2}\frac{\phi_1}{1-\phi_1}\frac{\mathbb{E}[S_1]}{e_1},\\
\mathbb{E}[W_j^q] &= \frac{c_{A,j}^2 + c_{S,j}^2}{2}\mathbb{E}[W_{j(M/M/s)}^q], \quad \text{where}\\
\mathbb{E}[W_{j(M/M/s)}^q] &= G_j^{-1}\frac{(s_j\phi_j)^{s_j}}{s_j!}\frac{\mathbb{E}[S_j]}{s_j(1-\phi_j)^2},\\
G_j &= \sum_{n=0}^{s_j-1}\frac{(s_j\phi_j)^n}{n!} + \frac{(s_j\phi_j)^{s_j}}{(1-\phi_j)s_j!} \quad \text{for} \quad j=2,3.
\end{aligned} \tag{9.96}$$

□

Patient length of stay for each patient class can now be calculated by adding the mean waiting and length of stay of all care queues the patient calls at on his visit to the PAC.

9.4 Challenges and Directions for Future Research

In the last decade the number of healthcare problems that have been studied using a queuing network approach has increased tremendously. Except for Albin et al. (1990) and Blair and Lawrence (1981), all of the references included in Sect. 9.3 were published in the years 2000–2010. In this final section we point out a few directions for future research. We distinguish between mathematical challenges: healthcare problems for which appropriate queuing network models have not yet been developed, and healthcare challenges: healthcare problems which have not been studied yet, but could be studied with the queuing techniques available in the literature.

9.4.1 Mathematical Challenges

The mathematical challenges mainly lie in the modeling aspect. One example is the development of models for networks of care providers who perform several tasks in parallel, in sequence, and sometimes even in a mixed form. Polling models (Takagi 2000) could be of interest here. Also, clinics where patients have to (re-) visit specific care providers in a network of care queues still involve modeling complications. However, re-visiting occurs often in reality (consider for example the complex network of multiple care providers in ED treatment).

The application of time inhomogeneous models that capture the time-dependent arrival patterns of patients has attained only limited attention, see for example (Green et al. 2006). Introducing time inhomogeneity in queuing networks is a tremendous challenge. Related is the development of computationally efficient methods that explicitly take into account opening hours of healthcare facilities.

9.4.2 Healthcare Challenges

Healthcare professionals in a couple of fields are familiar with the possibilities of mathematical decision support techniques in general and queuing theory in particular. As we have seen in Sect. 9.3, modeling networks of healthcare facilities, departments, and care providers has received some attention. However, capturing the complex relationships between hospital departments has proved to be quite involved. The relationship studied is usually that with a downstream department (Vanberkel et al. 2010), while that with upstream departments is not considered, even though it can be of significant influence.

Our aging population requires more and more care, which has to be delivered with limited resources. Rationing care and the consequences thereof has therefore become an important research topic. Decisions regarding which patient class will be offered what type of care are inevitable. The influence of these decisions on other patient classes, regarding accessibility and other important matters, should be studied in detail. Moreover, the dimensioning of healthcare facilities, not only in the number of beds required, but also regarding care that will be offered to certain patient classes only, will become increasingly important.

This chapter has provided a thorough theoretical background on networks of queues and examples of how networks of queues may be used to model, analyze, and solve healthcare problems. In that respect, often, the theory has to be amended or extended. We are confident that this contribution has made healthcare professionals increasingly aware of the possibilities and opportunities queueing networks have to offer to tackle the challenges they are facing, now and in the future.

References

Aaby K, Herrmann JW, Jordan CS, Treadwell M, Wood K (2006) Montgomery county's public health service uses operations research to plan emergency mass dispensing and vaccination clinics. Interfaces 36(6):569–579

Adan I, van der Wal J (2011) Mean values techniques. In: Boucherie RJ, Dijk NM (eds) Queueing networks: a fundamental approach. Springer, New York

Albin SL, Barrett J, Ito D, Mueller JE (1990) A queueing network analysis of a health center. Queueing Syst 7:51–61

American Society of Anesthesiologists (2011) www.asahq.org/For-Members/Clinical-Information/ASA-Physical-Status-Classification-System.aspx, Retrieved April 20, 2011

Asaduzzaman Md, Chaussalet TJ, Robertson NJ (2010) A loss network model with overflow for capacity planning of a neonatal unit. Ann Oper Res 178:67–76

Asaduzzaman Md, Chaussalet TJ, Adeyemi S et al (2010) Towards effective capacity planning in a perinatal network centre. Arch Dis Child Fetal Neonatal 95:F283–287

Bailey NTJ (1952) A study of queues and appointment systems in hospital out-patient departments, with special reference to waiting-times. J Royal Stat Soc, Ser B-Stat Methodol 14(2):185–199

Baskett F, Chandy KM, Muntz RR, Palacios FG (1975) Open, closed, and mixed networks of queues with different classes of customers. J Assoc Comput Mach 22(2):248–260

Bitran GR, Morabito R (1996) Survey open queueing networks: optimization and performance evaluation models for discrete manufacturing systems. Prod Oper Manag 5(2):163–193

Blair EL, Lawrence CE (1981) A queueing network approach to healthcare planning with an application to burn care in New York state. Socio-Econ Plan Sci 15(5):207–216

Boucherie RJ, van Dijk NM (2011) Queueing networks: a fundamental approach. Springer, New York

Brockmeyer E, Halström HL, Jensen A (1948) The life and works of A.K. Erlang. Translations of the Danish academy of technical sciences 2

de Bruin AM, Bekker R, van Zanten L, Koole GM (2010) Dimensioning hospital wards using the Erlang loss model. Ann Oper Res 178(1):23–43

Burke PJ (1956) The output of a queuing system. Oper Res 4(6):699–704

Buzacott JA, Shanthikumar JG (1993) Stochastic models of manufacturing systems. Prentice Hall, Englewood Cliffs

Buzen JP (1973) Computational algorithms for closed queueing networks with exponential servers. Commun ACM 16(9):527–531

Chaussalet TJ, Xie H, Millard P (2006) A closed queueing network approach to the analysis of patient flow in healthcare systems. Methods Info Med 45(5):492–497

Cochran JK, Bharti A (2006) A multi-stage stochastic methodology for whole hospital bed planning under peak loading. Int J Ind Syst Eng 1(1-2):8–36

Cochran JK, Bharti A (2006) Stochastic bed balancing of an obstetrics hospital. Health Care Manag Sci 9(1):31–45

Cochran JK, Roche KT (2008) A multi-class queueing network analysis methodology for improving hospital emergency department performance. Comput Oper Res 36(5):1497–1512

Cohen JW (1982) The single server queue, 8th edn. North-Holland Publishing Company, Amsterdam

Creemers S, Lambrecht M Modeling a hospital queueing network. In: Boucherie RJ, Dijk NM (eds) Queueing networks: a fundamental approach. Springer, New York (2011)

Fackrell M (2009) Modelling healthcare systems with phase-type distributions. Health Care Manag Sci 12(1):11–26

Ferschl MB, Tung A, Sweitzer B, Huo D, Glick DB (2005) Preoperative clinic visits reduce operating room cancellations and delays. Anesthesiology 103(4):855–859

Free University, Department of Mathematics, Erlang-C calculator, www.few.vu.nl/koole/ccmath/ErlangC/

Gordon WJ, Newell GF (1967) Closed queuing systems with exponential servers. Oper Res 15(2):254–265
Green LV, Kolesar PJ, Soares J (2001) Improving the SIPP approach for staffing service systems that have cyclic demands. Oper Res 49(4):549–564
Green LV (2006) Queueing analysis in healthcare. In: Hall RW (eds) Patient flow: reducing delay in healthcare delivery. Springer, New York
Green LV, Soares J, Giglio JF, Green RA (2006) Using queueing theory to increase the effectiveness of emergency department provider staffing. Acad Emerg Med 13(1):61–68
Gross D, Shortle JF, Harris CM (2008) Fundamentals of queueing theory, 4th edn. Wiley, Hoboken
Jackson JR (1957) Networks of waiting lines. Oper Res 5(4):518–521
Jiang L, Giachetti RE (2007) A queueing network model to analyze the impact of parallelization of care on patient cycle time. Health Care Manag Sci 11(3):248–261
Kelly FP (1979) Reversibility and stochastic networks. Available online via www.statslab.cam.ac.uk/frank/rsn.html
Kelly FP (1991) Loss networks. Ann Appl Probab 1(3):319–378
Kleinrock L (1967) Queuing systems: theory, vol 1. Wiley, New York
Kleinrock L (1976) Queueing systems: computer applications, vol 2. Wiley, New York
Koizumi N, Kuno E, Smith TE (2005) Modeling patient flows using a queueing network with blocking. Health Care Manag Sci 8(1):49–60
Latouche G, Ramaswami V (1999) Introduction to matrix analytic methods in stochastic modeling. American Statistical Association and the Society for Industrial and Applied Mathematics, USA
Latouche G, Taylor P (2002) Matrix-analytic methods: theory and applications. In: Proceedings of the fourth international conference, Adelaide. Imperial College Press, London
Law AM, Kelton WD (1991) Simulation modeling and analysis. McGraw-Hill, New York
Lee DKK, Zenios SA (2009) Optimal capacity overbooking for the regular treatment of chronic conditions. Oper Res 57(4):852–865
Little JDC (1961) A proof for the queuing formula $L = \lambda W$. Oper Res 9(3):383–387
Nelson RD (1995) Probability, stochastic processes, and queueing theory: the mathematics of computer performance modelling. Springer, New York
Organisation for Economic Co-operation and Development (2011) www.oecd.org, Retrieved on April 19, 2011
Research Institute CHOIR, University of Twente, Enschede, The Netherlands (2011) ORchestra bibliography. www.utwente.nl/choir/en/orchestra/
Osorio C, Bierlaire M (2009) An analytic finite capacity queueing network model capturing the propagation of congestion and blocking. Eur J Oper Res 196(3):996–1007
Patient Flow Improvement Center Amsterdam, Erlang-B calculator www.vumc.nl/afdelingen/pica/Software/erlang_b/
QtsPlus Software, ftp://ftp.wiley.com/public/sci_tech_med/queuing_theory/
Taha HA (1997) Operations research: an introduction. Prentice Hall, Englewood Cliffs
Takagi H (2000) Analysis and application of polling models. In: Haring G, Lindemann C, Reiser M (eds) Performance evaluation: origins and directions. Lecture Notes in Computer Science 1769, Springer, Berlin
Tijms HC (2003) A first course in stochastic models. Wiley, Chichester
Vanberkel PT, Boucherie RJ, Hans EW, Hurink JL, Litvak N (2010) A survey of healthcare models that encompass multiple departments. Int J Health Manag Info 1(1):37–69
van Dijk NM, Kortbeek N (2009) Erlang loss bounds for OT–ICU systems. Queueing syst 63(1):253–280
Westbay Online Traffic Calculators, www.erlang.com/calculator
Whitt W (1983) The queueing network analyzer. Bell Syst Tech J 62(9):2779–2815
Winston WL (1994) Operations research: applications and algorithms, 3rd edn. Duxbury Press, Belmont
Wolff RW (1989) Stochastic modeling and the theory of queues. Prentice Hall, Englewood Cliffs

Xie H, Chaussalet T, Rees M (2007) A semi-open queueing network approach to the analysis of patient flow in healthcare systems. IEEE proceedings twentieth IEEE international symposium on computer-based medical systems, pp 719–724

Zachary S, Ziedins I (2011) Loss networks. In: Boucherie RJ, Dijk NM (eds) Queueing networks: a fundamental approach. Springer, New York

Zeng G (2003) Two common properties of the Erlang-B function, Erlang-C function, and Engset blocking function. Math Comput Model 37(12–13):1287–1296

Zonderland ME, Boer F, Boucherie RJ, de Roode A, van Kleef JW (2009) Redesign of a university hospital preanesthesia evaluation clinic using a queuing theory approach. Anesthesia Analg 109(5):1612–1621

Zonderland ME, Boucherie RJ, Litvak N, Vleggeert-Lankamp LCAM (2010) Planning and scheduling of semi-urgent surgeries. Health Care Manag Sci 13(3):256–267

Chapter 10
Medical Supply Logistics

Manuel D. Rossetti, Nebil Buyurgan and Edward Pohl

Abstract This chapter focuses on medical supply logistics from the perspective of materials management and technology. It covers the structure of the medical supply chain and illustrates many of the issues that make the management of medical supply chains unique, complex, and challenging. Then, a review of inventory management practices and current research for medical supplies is provided. As an example, the management of blood supply is illustrated. Finally, key technological enablers such as electronic data exchange, automatic data capture technologies, and their importance within medical logistics are discussed. Future areas for research are suggested.

10.1 Introduction

Medical supply logistics encompasses purchasing, materials planning and scheduling, inventory control, material handling and physical distribution of medical supplies, and supporting services. Medical supply logistics involves both inter-facility (between locations) and intra-facility (within the facility) management of the flow of supplies and resources to enable patient care. Many different functions

M. D. Rossetti (✉) · N. Buyurgan · E. Pohl
Department of Industrial Engineering, University of Arkansas, Fayetteville, AR 72701, USA
e-mail: rossetti@uark.edu

N. Buyurgan
e-mail: nebilb@uark.edu

E. Pohl
e-mail: epohl@uark.edu

R. Hall (ed.), *Handbook of Healthcare System Scheduling*,
International Series in Operations Research & Management Science 168,
DOI: 10.1007/978-1-4614-1734-7_10,

are utilized during this process, including information systems, warehousing, inventory, packaging, and transportation.

Since logistics can be conceptualized as “inventory in motion”, this chapter will focus on medical supply logistics from the perspective of materials management. In fact, within many health care organizations, medical supply logistics is typically within a department of materials management. Industry-wide coverage of the professional and educational aspects of medical supply logistics can be found through the Association for Health care Resource and Materials Management (AHRMM). This association is a valuable resource for understanding materials management within the health care industry and learning about practical methods for improving its function.

Medical supply materials management is critical in ensuring the safety, availability, and affordability of supplies. A critical component of ensuring patient safety is ensuring that the right supplies are used on the right patients at the right time. The first responsibility of a health care materials manager is to ensure that the products purchased for clinical use are of good quality. This involves ensuring that the product's safety and clinical effectiveness are considered in addition to the cost. The building of a team of clinicians and logistics professionals to evaluate and select appropriate items for inclusion in the procurement functions of the provider is critical to the success of this process.

Besides ensuring that the right products are used within the system (given safety and effectiveness), materials management must ensure that the items are properly stored and controlled. This must not only control the availability of the item, but also ensure that its efficacy over time is monitored. For example, among other things, this involves ensuring the proper packaging, storage, and access control of items. Items that are controlled substances, hazardous, etc. require specialized management techniques that are not found within other industries. The rotation and usage of expiring items is just one such issue that a medical supply professional must consider. Finally, the management of recalled items and their prior use on patients must be handled through systematic processes and procedures. Many regulatory issues, management structures, and objectives (e.g. saving lives) make the materials management function within health care significantly different than that found in many other industries (e.g. retail).

As one can see, materials management is essential to the proper functioning of a health care system. However, it is beyond the scope of this chapter to cover all of the aspects of material supply logistics. To limit the scope, this chapter will focus on the controlling of inventories of medicines, medical supplies, blood, and other specialized items to ensure availability and cost. That is, we assume that the aspects of patient safety have already been adequately managed. For additional information concerning the importance of patient safety, please see Kohn et al. (2000). Therefore, this chapter concentrates on viewing the aspects, techniques, and technologies of medical supply logistics that ensure that the item will be available at the right time for the lowest cost.

Indeed, reducing the cost of supply is an increasingly important focus area for health care providers. According to Ozcan, in a typical hospital budget 25–30%

goes for medical supplies and their handling. The supply chain now represents the second largest cost center after personnel cost, and it is estimated to be approximately 15–30% of overall hospital net revenue (Williams 2004). Some industry experts are even suggesting that at current rates of growth, supply costs may eventually exceed personnel costs (Moore 2010) President and CEO resource optimization & innovation (ROi) an operating division of the Sisters of Mercy Health, personal communication). Because of the opportunities within and importance of inventory within the materials management system, this chapter will focus on aspects of inventory management within health care.

A roundtable discussion at the MIT Center for Transportation and Logistics (Meyer and Meyer 2006) highlighted some of the important issues in health care, particularly in supply chains. Some of the problems and constraints discussed included the high cost of health care, wasteful behaviors, and complex requirements and regulations. The solutions focused on making supply chains more demand driven, increasing collaboration between the various parties involved, increasing visibility of practices and inventories, and implementing more and better standards. In a survey released by HFMA (Anonymous 2002), executives and supply chain leaders of health care organizations identified ways to improve care and reduce cost. These included standardizing supplies, central purchasing, reducing inventory, improving demand forecasts, reducing labor costs through automation, improved collaboration with vendors, online purchasing, and more. These important issues motivate the importance of looking at the health care supply chain from an integrated perspective.

The next section reviews the medical supply chain and some of the complexities that make the management of inventories more challenging within a health care system. Then, Sect. 10.3 describes the management science aspects of inventory management required within a health care setting. Some of the current industry practices will be reviewed. In addition, a review of relevant literature and its application (or potential application) is discussed. Specialized models for blood supply management will be used as an illustration of some of the unique challenges faced by health care providers in Sect. 10.4. Finally, Sect. 10.5 discusses enabling information systems and technologies that are critical to ensuring the proper functioning of the materials management system.

The final section will present some thoughts for the future of medical supply logistics.

10.2 Medical Supply Chains

A typical health care supply chain is a complex network consisting of many different parties at various stages of the value chain. According to Burns (2002), the three major types of players are: Producers (product manufacturers), Purchasers (group purchasing organizations, or GPOs, and wholesalers/distributors), and health care providers (hospital systems and integrated delivery networks, or IDNs). This chain is shown in Fig. 10.1.

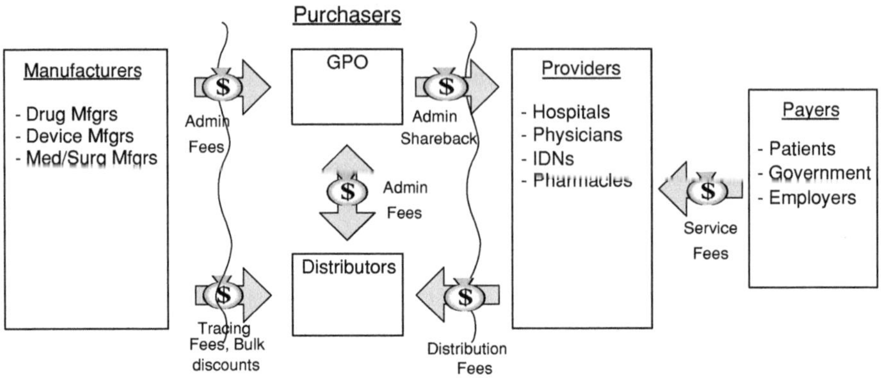

Fig. 10.1 Health care value chain [adapted from Moore (Moore V (2010)) and Burns (2002)]

Manufacturers make the products; GPOs and distributors aggregate a large number of hospitals in an attempt to leverage the economies of scale while funding their operations through administration fees and distribution fees; the provider, such as hospitals, consume the products while providing patient care; and finally the payers, such as the individual patient and his employer, pay for the services of the provider. Within the health care value chain, the products (drugs, devices, supplies, etc.) are transported, stored, and eventually transformed into health care services for the patient. A more detailed discussion of the roles and players within the health care value chain can be found in Burns (2002), Burn and Pauly (2002), Schneller and Smeltzer (2006), and Burns and Lee (2008). A summary of the product, information, and dollar flows related to the health care supply chain can be found in Schwartz (2011).

During 1990s, vertical and horizontal integration, managed care pressures, changes in federal reimbursement, the rise of e-commerce, and the passage of the Health Insurance Portability and Accountability Act (HIPAA) in 1996 all contributed to structural and operational changes within health care supply chains. Provider organizations such as hospitals and hospital systems vertically integrated into the health insurance business, such as starting up their own Health Maintenance Organizations (HMOs) and ambulatory care practices, in the process of developing Integrated Delivery Networks or IDNs. Many such attempts were unproductive and providers had to integrate upstream with the wholesalers and distributors to improve their financial position. Burns and Pauly (2002) discuss their skepticism of the trend in health care toward increasing consolidation, such as having primary care physicians or HMOs in the same organization as hospitals. They assert that the horizontal and vertical integration that health care organizations are trying to achieve are often counterproductive, and that the economies of scale of a larger organization fail to compensate for the increased bureaucracy and typically poor restructuring. Also, almost every major player along the health care value chain considered horizontally consolidation to form larger organizations.

Hospitals merged to form hospital systems or joined other systems. GPOs started catering to different systems and distributors started building warehouses where demands from various systems are consolidated.

An example of a health care system that has benefited from streamlining and integrating their inventory and distribution process is the Sisters of Mercy Health System. The St. Louis based Mercy Health System created a new supply chain division called Resource Optimization and Innovation (ROi) to establish the supply chain as an area of value for the business. ROi has simplified the health care supply chain by reducing its dependence on third-party intermediaries, such as GPOs and distributors. The ROi created its own GPO, which purchases products directly from suppliers for all products, eliminating the need for third-party GPOs. The ROi also receives products directly from suppliers to its warehouse and ships them directly to its hospitals, eliminating the need for third-party distributors. The result is a new model that has more closely linked the makers and users of health care products in a way that provides greater value for the essential trading parties. ROi converted Mercy's supply chain from a cost center to revenue center. ROi currently produces revenue in excess of $153 million. ROi also produces an annual value to the Mercy hospitals of over $16 million in net benefit.

In a traditional distribution model, suppliers ship their products to distributors. At the distributor's warehouse, the products are packed into pallets and shipped to each hospital's warehouse. The hospital warehouse then receives the pallets, breaks them down into smaller quantities, and stores the products until they are needed by the hospital. Sometimes items are also ordered directly from suppliers. Figure 10.2 shows this model. In this traditional model, there is a large amount of inventory in the system. This keeps the number of deliveries relatively low, which keeps transportation and ordering costs low. But there is a high cost in both holding inventory and the significant amount of material handling required.

In the newer model used by Mercy, a centralized warehouse system replaces the distributor and the need for a hospital warehouse is greatly reduced. In this model, the suppliers ship directly to the central warehouse called the central service center (CSC). The CSC breaks down the shipments into smaller units and repackages them for use in the hospitals. The materials are then shipped directly to the hospitals, called strategic service units (SSU). The Mercy network consists of approximately ten hospitals across four states. If the hospitals are not close enough to the CSC, the materials are cross-docked in an intermediate location. Figure 10.3 illustrates this model.

In this newer model, the CSC takes full responsibility of material handling and inventory management. The CSC receives shipments from the suppliers, which are then broken down, repackaged, bar coded, and stored. The CSC receives the orders for the next day's demand through the central server every evening. These orders show up on the pick list and are picked, sorted, packed based on their destination, and shipped early in the morning. The trucks return back to the CSC at the end of the day.

The Mercy model offers many improvements over the traditional model. No third parties between the suppliers and hospitals are used, increasing efficiency and

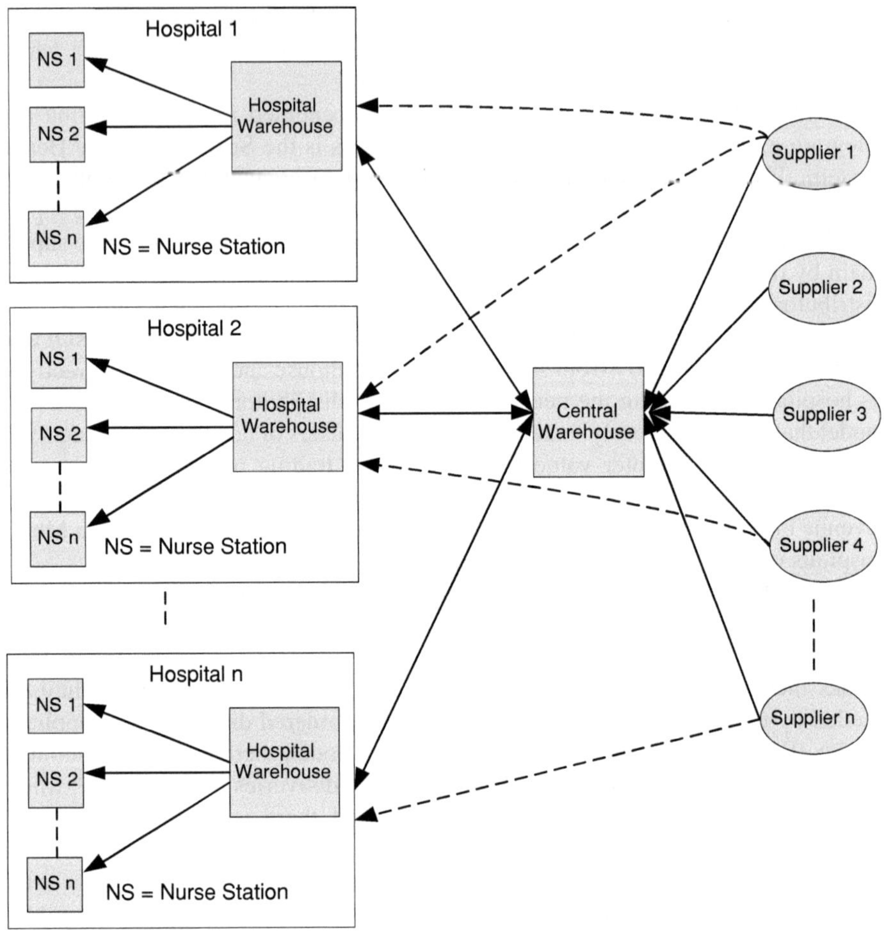

Fig. 10.2 Traditional supply chain

eliminating third-party mark-up fees. Mercy even owns its own trucking fleet, in order to further reduce cost. Inventory holding costs and material handling costs, which make up a large portion of total costs, are greatly reduced over a traditional system. The CSCs large warehouse, which stores products for all its hospitals, allows for bulk purchasing discounts to further reduce costs. In this new system, 3,000 nursing level stock-outs per week were eliminated over Mercy's old system and next day, first time, fill rates improved from 85–90% to 99% (Moore 2010). Since the CSC uses automatic repackaging equipment to repackage products into smaller, bar coded containers, the inventory management system is also greatly improved. The improved inventory management system included medicine cabinets, which automatically pick the medicines for the nurses, and a bed-side scanning system which verifies the medication by scanning the nurse's badge,

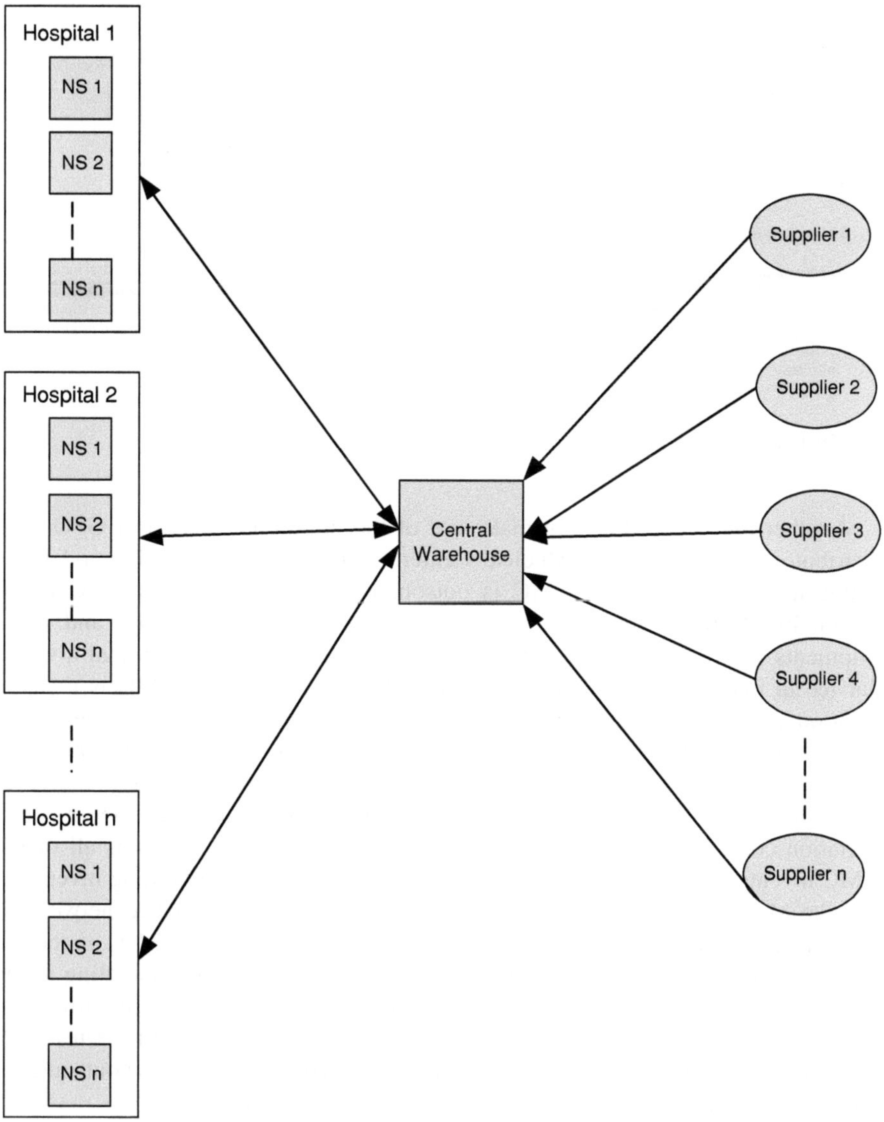

Fig. 10.3 Newer model used by Mercy

the patient's arm band, and the medication. This annually eliminated more than 178,000 medication errors such as giving medication to the wrong patient or giving the patient the wrong dosage. In addition, the CSC polls all the medicine cabinets each night and automatically downloads replenishment orders for needed medicines.

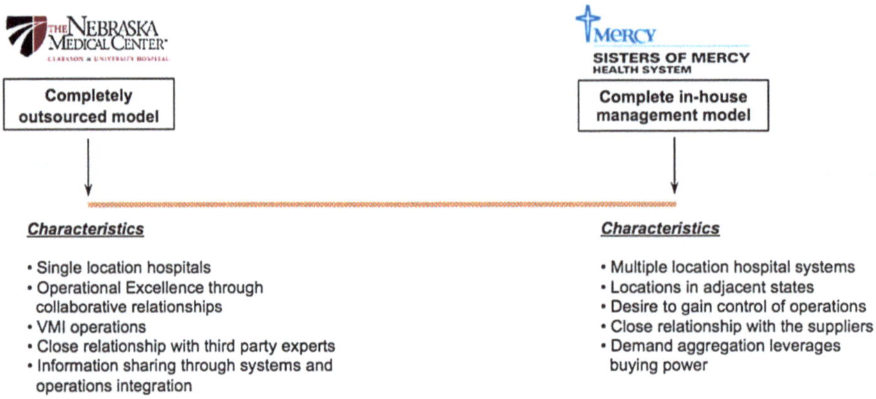

Fig. 10.4 Health care value chain spectrum

Another place that does not make use of the traditional system of GPOs and distributors is the Nebraska Medical Center (NMC). In the Nebraska model, the entire supply chain of the NMC is outsourced to a single company, Cardinal Health Inc. Cardinal has a warehouse in the same city, Omaha NE, and sends shipments to the hospital four times per week. The NMC pays Cardinal a single flat fee to manage the hospital's inventory. Unlike Mercy, the NMC is a single location hospital, which cannot easily leverage economies of scale to create a more efficient supply chain system. Also, by outsourcing its inventory management system, the NMC is able to use the comparatively small amount of capital it has to focus on patient care. Not only does the NMC not need to worry about transportation costs, material handling costs, etc., but since Cardinal owns all of the NMC inventory, the NMC does not need to tie up its capital on holding inventory.

Like Mercy, the NMC does not directly rely on the complicated network of GPOs and distributors to meet its inventory needs. Neither system relies on the use of a large warehouse at the hospital, and both minimize material handling at the hospital. Also, like Mercy, the NMC has frequent shipments to minimize the inventory needed at the hospital while keeping stock-outs low and fill rates high. Both the Mercy system and the NMC system represent two ends of the outsourcing spectrum for the health care value chain as illustrated in Fig. 10.4.

10.2.1 Healthcare Provider Supply Chains

Each health care supply chain player performs specific processes with the essential goal of assuring product availability for health care services for the patient (i.e. consumption of products at the provider while providing patient care). From the provider perspective, the supply chain processes can be classified in three main groups: external, internal, and bedside administration.

The external supply chain processes include transactions with other players upstream in the supply chain: distributors, manufacturers, and GPOs. These transactions are typically related to contract management, ordering, shipping and payment, administration fee, rebates, and sales tracing among others.

The role of a GPO in the supply chain has already been discussed; however, it is beneficial to understand information, money, and product flow in greater detail. GPOs in general negotiate contracts with manufacturers on behalf of hospitals making products available at lower prices. The contracts consist of different pricing tiers and the baseline tier is available to all GPO members (health care providers). However, based on the amount of used products, the manufacturer decides the pricing tier for GPO members. In some cases, the pricing tiers are documented via Letter of Commitment/Participation (LOC/LOP) from the provider. The contract information is shared across the supply chain to ensure accurate pricing for each provider. The distributor performs sales tracing for each provider. The sales tracing is passed to the manufacturer who estimates the administration fee based on the sales. The administration fee is sent to the GPO and the GPO sends a portion to the provider.

A typical health care provider has numerous internal clinical locations (units/floors/PAR locations) replenished by direct shipment from the supplier or replenished internally from a centralized distribution center. The direct shipments to these internal locations as well as shipments to the centralized distribution center of the provider and other models of external replenishment are achieved through three modes of purchasing. The purchase order (PO) is generated and sent to the supplier (manufacturer or distributor), the supplier processes the order and the product is delivered to the hospital receiving dock. The PO can be sent to: (1) the manufacturer; both products and invoice are received from the manufacturer (this scenario is also known as direct shipment) (2) the distributors; both products and invoice are received from the distributor (this scenario is known as indirect shipment), or (3) the distributor and in the event of stock out at distributor POs are sent to the manufacturer; products are received from the manufacturer and invoice is received from distributor (this scenario is known as drop shipment).

Internal supply chain processes are performed within the health care provider and include product and information flow from receiving the product at the dock to replenishing the internal clinical locations. The main internal supply chain processes for stocked items are warehouse/storeroom receiving, put away, storage, cart count, picking, and floor replenishment. Meanwhile, non-stocked items are received and sent directly to replenish the clinical location. The level of automation of the processes and their integration with the Materials Management Information System (MMIS) can vary. However, the handling of patient billable items is usually automated via Automatic Dispensing Cabinets (ADC) whereas non-billable items are typically stored on the open shelves in utility rooms. In the case of the use of ADCs, replenishment requisitioning and generating pick tickets are typically automated. On the other hand, open shelf items require cart count processes where the inventory is counted. In this case requisitioning is generally a

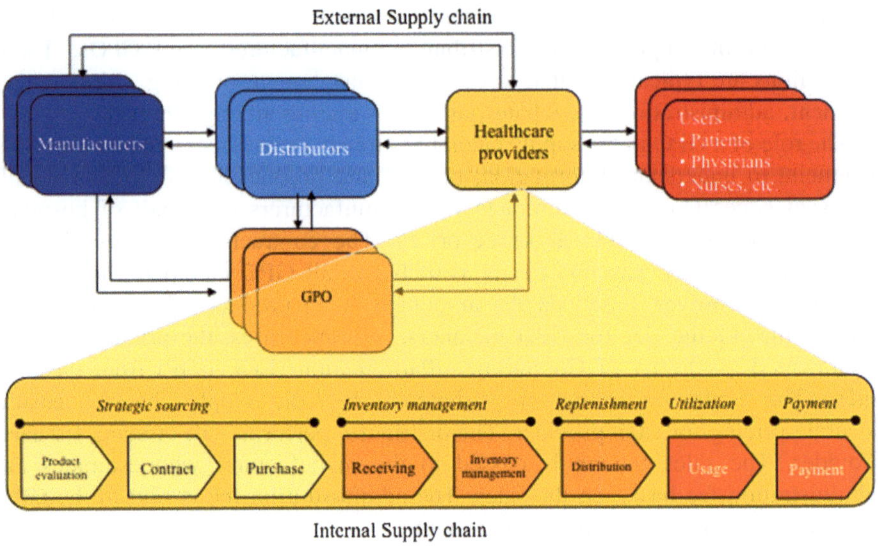

Fig. 10.5 External and internal supply chain processes (adapted from Smoker 2005)

manual process and generating pick tickets may be automated. Both the external and internal processes are depicted in Fig. 10.5.

Bedside administration processes are related to the final stage of product delivery in which the product is administered to the patient. The processes at the bedside may include verification and validation of the products to be administered, recall and outdates management, notification to patient billing, and clinical records systems. The automatic identification of product via technologies such as barcode or RFID, improves the efficiency of bedside processes.

Even with strategic reorganizations of the health care value chain and processes, supply costs have continued to increase. This has motivated the need for focused research and best practice applications for managing and reducing inventory and supply costs within the health care value chain through better inventory management.

10.3 Inventory Management in Healthcare

Inventory management encompasses all materials related activities including purchasing, transportation, logistics, production control, and inventory control. When managing inventory, there is a trade-off between the availability of the items and the cost of providing the items. The main goal of inventory management activities within health care organizations is to reduce the cost associated with the materials and supply costs of health care delivery without sacrificing service and

Table 10.1 Forms of inventory policies

Continuous Review	Periodic Review
(s, S)	(R, s, S)
(r, Q)	(R, r, Q)
	(R, S)

quality of care. This comes down to answering two fundamental questions: When to order and how much to order? No matter how complex the inventory control situation, the answers of these fundamental questions based on the state of the inventory system, as well as demand and cost factors associated with keeping and ordering inventory must be determined. These questions are addressed with the use of inventory models.

10.3.1 Overview of Inventory Modeling

Inventory modeling is predicated on describing the state of inventory over time. The state of the inventory system can be best summarized in the key state variable, *inventory position.* Inventory position reflects the inventory on hand, pending orders, and backorders. If it is shown as a formula,

Inventory position = stock on hand + pending orders minus; backorders.

Inventory can be managed by periodic or continuous review processes. In a continuous review system, a decision is made to order (or not order) a replenishment quantity whenever the value of inventory position changes. Typically, an order is placed whenever the inventory position reaches a target level (or reorders point). In a periodic-review system, the state of the inventory system (either in the form of the inventory position or inventory level) is checked at regularly scheduled times (e.g. every week). The review period is the time interval between reviews. Periodic review generally is used with slow-moving items. On the other hand, continuous review is typically utilized for fast moving items or when very inexpensive processes exist for checking the state of the inventory.

There are two common inventory ordering policies, and these policies are (r, Q) and (s, S) policies. When they are combined with periodic and continuous review, a number of fundamental inventory policies are available. These inventory policies are shown in Table 10.1.

The reorder point, order quantity (r, Q) system is a continuous review policy and the order quantity is constant. When the inventory position is on or under the reorder point (r), the order is placed for order quantity (Q). The advantage of this inventory policy is that it is quite simple and easy to understand due to its easy implementation using a two-bin system. In a two-bin system, the inventory on hand is divided into two-bins. The second bin holds r items. The first bin holds the rest of the items. Whenever a demand occurs, the required items are taken from the first bin. When there are no items left in the first bin, r has been reached, and it is time to reorder Q items. Thus, the second bin holds the safety stock, designed to hold enough inventory to last until the replenishment arrives. After the replenishment order is placed, the bins are swapped, i.e. the second bin becomes the 1st bin (where items are taken), and the original first bin becomes the second bin waiting for the replenishment of Q items. When the reorder for Q arrives, the second bin is filled with r items, and any extra are placed in the first bin. Then the process repeats. In the case of lumpy demand, an (r, NQ) policy can be used. In this case, orders for size Q are repeated until the inventory position gets above the reorder point. In addition, it can be shown theoretically that the (r, Q) policy will not have the lowest policy cost, when compared under the same assumptions as the (s, S) policy.

The reorder point, order-up-to (s, S) system uses continuous review like a (r, Q) policy. The reorder point is indicated by s, and if the inventory position decreases to or below s, the order is placed up to maximum stock level of S. Because of this, the amount ordered will be $(S - I(t))$, where $I(t)$ is the current inventory on hand at time t. Thus, the amount ordered will not be constant. A disadvantage of this system is the variable order quantity. In addition, it is more difficult to synchronize shipment quantities when the size of the order varies. However, this policy can be shown to be a theoretically optimal policy under certain conditions.

The periodic review, order-up-to-level (R, S) system is also known as a replenishment cycle policy. The control procedure is that the inventory level is checked every R units of time and an order will be placed to make the inventory level up to S. The order quantity is not constant. Due to the periodic-review feature, it is widely used in practice since it allows combining different orders in R units of time for shipment consolidation. The biggest disadvantage of this system is that it causes more stock on hand than the systems using continuous review. Within the health care industry, this system is referred to as a "par-level" system. The value of S is the par level. The idea is to bring the inventory up to par. It is by far the dominant inventory control method used to manage stock within hospitals.

The (R, s, S) system is the combination of (s, S) and (R, S) systems. The control procedure is to check inventory position every R units of time. If the inventory position is under the reorder point, the order is placed to complete the inventory level up to S. The (s, S) is the special case where R = 0, and (R, S) is a special case where s = S − 1. The disadvantage of this system is that the calculation of three parameters of the system at optimal levels is more difficult.

The (R, r, Q) system is the application of the (r, Q) system at periodic intervals. The control procedure is to check the inventory position every R time units. If the inventory position is equal to or under the reorder point, then an order for Q items is placed. This policy is often confused with the (r, Q) policy in practice. In many cases, even if the inventory position is checked continuously, the company will only place an order at the "end of the day". Thus, their review period is in fact one day. Unfortunately, the analysis often ignores this period and assumes a continuous review policy, which can make a difference in policy setting procedures.

In these models, the reorder point answers when to order and the reorder quantity, Q, provides how much to order. The calculation of the optimal order quantity has been investigated under a number of different approaches for constant, time-varying and stochastic demand. The classic economic order quantity (EOQ) developed by F.W. Harris in 1913 can be used to calculate the order quantity, under some assumptions, such as (1) demand is constant and deterministic, (2) lead time is zero, (3) no shortage is allowed, and (4) constant unit cost and it does not depend on the replenishment quantity. The EOQ is the optimal order quantity that minimizes the total inventory cost including holding and ordering cost. Even when the assumptions for the EOQ are not readily met it is used as an approximation for the optimal amount to order. The reorder point represents the safety stock necessary to cover the demand that might occur during a lead time. If the inventory policy with periodic review is used, the lead time and review period are considered together to set up the reorder point. If continuous review is used, only the lead needs to be considered. Different techniques are considered to determine the reorder point when demand is stochastic. First, the reorder point can be calculated by modeling demand using a stochastic model. Customer demand can be characterized by two components: (1) the time between demands, and (2) the amount of the demand. The amount of demand can be modeled with a discrete random variable. The time between demand occurrences is often modeled with a renewal process governed by a continuous random variable. This can be used to approximate the demand during lead-time distribution. After deciding the lead-time demand distribution, the distribution function will be used to define a reorder point that achieves a desired level of service or minimizes total cost.

Inventory management is a challenging topic in supply chains with thousands of items even though all items are located in the same echelon. The challenges of managing inventory are much bigger when items are stored in distinct echelons, such as the CSC and hospitals within the Mercy network. The typical multi-echelon network includes suppliers, regional distribution centers, distribution centers, and hospitals, etc. When an item is moving through more than one echelon before reaching the end users, a "multi-echelon" inventory system can be conceptualized. It is difficult to determine the reorder point including safety stock within a multi-echelon structure because of the interactions between the levels. Two additional questions need to be answered: how much total safety stock is needed and how to keep the stock in the different echelons.

The Clark–Scarf model is one of the best-known techniques for determining the safety stock within the multi-echelon inventory system (Clark and Scarf 1960). The technique is based on decomposition. First, the most downstream echelons meet customer demand. Shortage at the next echelon leads to stochastic delay having an additional cost. This additional cost affects the process of determining the optimal policy for the next upstream installation. For stochastic multi-echelon inventory systems, the seminal paper by Sherbrooke (1968) presents a model for determining the optimal stock levels at the bases (warehouse) and the depots (hospitals) in order to minimize the total number of outstanding backorders at the hospital level for a given amount of investment. Deuermeyer and Schwarz developed analytical models to approximate the service level of multi-echelon supply chain network by assuming (r, Q) policies with stationary Poisson demand. The model was applied to a system consisting of one warehouse that supplies *N* retailers to obtain the expected service level including fill rate and backorders.

While it is beyond the scope of this chapter to fully describe the methods of multi-echelon inventory systems, a key insight for health care supply chains is the impact of the pooling effect. The pooling effect shows up in multi-echelon inventory systems as more units of inventory are moved up to a supporting echelon, allowing less units of inventory to be held locally. This can reduce the total amount of inventory within the system while still maintaining the necessary service levels. The pooling effect is a key factor that enables the reorganized supply chain used by Mercy to be able to reduce supply chain costs.

The following section overviews some of the latest research trends in the application of advanced inventory modeling methods within medical supply contexts.

10.3.2 A Review of Inventory Modeling in Medical Supply Contexts

Enormous pressure has been brought on the health care industry to reduce inventory investment and labor costs. Many studies have been conducted to start to improve health care costs as well as external and internal customer satisfaction. Even with the awareness to improve the health care supply chain and the studies addressing inventory management, inventory management in health care is still an active and extremely large topic. In its traditional form, health care supply chains have not paid adequate attention to inventory management. See also Kelle et al. (2009).

The purpose of this section is to provide an overview of recent research into inventory modeling within health care supply chains in order to raise the awareness of this important topic. Many of the papers discussed in this section provide general techniques for reducing cost, while others go into more depth by discussing one or two specific techniques. The review proceeds more or less within a chronological framework within each section. The main ideas discussed in this section will focus on reducing inventories, better inventory management practices, and making health care supply chains more demand driven.

Multi-Item Single Location Inventory Applications

Although there are many studies of single-echelon applications for industrial companies, the research in this area within health care area is limited. VanderLinde provides a discussion of the implementation of a computerized ABC/EOQ inventory model in a 146 bed nonprofit community hospital with the goal of maximizing inventory performance involving turnover, month-end inventory cost, and inventory cost per patient, as well as a number of other measures. The results from ABC/EOQ inventory model were compared to the current situation within the hospital, and the improvements noted, such as turnover increasing from 3–4 annual turns to 9–27 annual turns. In addition, inventory cost was reduced by 28.4%.

The theme of applying inventory models to items within hospitals occurs in a variety of papers. For example, Satir and Cengiz provide a discussion of inventory control within a university health center for 47 different medicines by a stochastic, periodic-review model with a stock-out objective and budgetary constraints. Also, Prashant presents a systematic approach for optimization of inventory functions. This study provides solutions for some issues in the inventory management, which include the amount of excess and slow movement inventory, stock-out rate, and par level to manage inventory. For excess and no movement inventory, the inventory can be classified based on the age of inventory as a report to monitor the inventory level continuously and to take action proactively. For eliminating and reducing stock-outs, the author concludes that communication is the key practice. Strong communication between material management and the hospital staff enable better on-time delivery. In this application, the safety stock level and the number of stock-out situations decreased. PAR-level evaluation caused inventory reduction at the nursing units. The primary methods of this approach were based on a data driven analysis and decision making as a group.

Dellaert and van de Poel extended a new and simple inventory rule from EOQ to support a purchasing department at a university hospital in the Netherlands. This new inventory rule is called (R, s, c, S) model, where R is the periodic-review period, S is the maximum stock level, s is the minimum stock level, and c is the can-order level. After the (R, s, c, S) model is defined, some theoretical and more sophisticated alternatives are presented to compare the total cost of each model. The (R, s, c, S) model provided many beneficial results, such as reduced holding cost and total cost, increased service level, and decreased total number of orders to suppliers.

Woosley and Wiley-Patton examined a local hospital's policies, applied two quantitative inventory models for the inventory control process, and offered a decision support tool for hospital managers to make the inventory process easy-manageable. Three quantitative models were developed, but Model 1 was not used due to its complexity. Model 1 was a general multi-product (s, S) model with space constraints. The purpose of the model was to minimize the total cost including holding, ordering, and shortage costs with space constraint. Model 2 was designed to determine an optimal allocation of supplies based on ordering and holding costs by minimizing total cost with fill rate and space constraints. The last model was based on determining the optimal allocation based on ordering cost with the objective of minimizing the total number of expected orders with fill rate and space constraints. This research showed a 70–80 % cost reduction when models 2 and 3 are implemented. Even though the research results are outstanding, this does not include the reaction of the health care stakeholders for this new decision support system. Therefore, the health care stakeholder's reaction toward this decision support system is an unanswered question, and it can be a future research topic. This study is a good illustration of single-echelon inventory management by using quantitative models.

Just-In-Time and Stockless Applications

Kim et al. (1993) compare the conventional, just-in-time (JIT), and stockless material management systems in the health care industry. The authors sent survey questionnaires to randomly selected health care institutions from the database of the Health Care Material Management Society and collected data from the 66 responses. The authors then used statistical methods to compare conventional, JIT, and stockless systems based on 32 problem variables given in the questionnaire. The results of a stockless system compared to a conventional system included both psychological benefits, such as reduced employee resistance to major changes and management more willing to delegate tasks, and inventory related benefits such as fewer problems managing large inventories and better responsiveness to demand fluctuations. The study also found that there was not a significant difference between JIT and stockless systems, and that implementing either a JIT or a stockless system in a hospital that currently operates a conventional material management system would significantly improve the effectiveness of the operation.

Egbelu et al. (1998) proposed a cost model for different hospital material management systems and compared the costs via a case study using data from a hospital that operates currently under the conventional mode of material management with large bulk deliveries. An analysis was performed to determine if it would be profitable for the hospital to operate under JIT or Stockless systems. Three scenarios were analyzed in the study. First, the hospital operates in the JIT mode with less inventory at the central stores and frequent bulk deliveries. Second, the hospital operates in the stockless mode where the distributor delivers items in units of "eaches" to the receiving dock and the hospital does its own internal material transfer from the receiving dock to nurses' stations. Third, the distributor delivers in eaches directly to the nurses' stations under the stockless mode. The authors concluded that there are various factors that need to be taken into account before deciding on the system. Parameters such as the inventory levels at the nurses' stations and central stores, the number of full time equivalent workers, the amount of warehouse space, and the potential service charges from distributors that affect the total annual cost. This model is a good starting point for analyzing and comparing various material management systems in the health care industry based on total annual cost. A simulation study of various systems, concentrating on the inventory analysis and distribution, with the use of the cost model could give better insight into the implications of changing a hospital's material management system.

Rivard-Royer et al. (2002) discuss the adoption of a hybrid version of the stockless replenishment system, combining the stockless method with the conventional approach to patient care unit replenishment. The medical supply distributor supplied high-volume products for the patient care unit in case quantities, leaving the central stores to break down bulk purchases of low volume products into point-of-use format. The study revealed marginal benefits from the hybrid method for both the institution and the distributor. The experiment conducted at a health care institution in the province of Quebec (Canada), focused on a single patient care unit. The result indicated that the total cost of replenishment was reduced by a negligible amount. Although the results for this form of hybrid stockless system have not been conclusive, other alternatives may be examined. The study opens the door for wider discussions and experiments in the future for reducing total costs via examination of stocking policy and inventory location.

Outsourcing and Multi-Echelon Applications

Kamani (2004) talks about the issues involved in upgrading the inventory management system of a hospital in the context of outsourcing to a third party. Some of the important points the author makes include eliminating poor quality data about products and vendors, analyzing spending patterns of the hospital, using a good classification system of the medical supplies, and enhancing product entries with relevant data, such as whether or not gloves are latex or latex-free. In a similar study, Rosser (2006) describes the improvements to cost savings and patient care in hospitals in London, Ontario brought about by the 1997 creation of the Health Care Materials Management Services (HMMS). The HMMS consolidated a number of different departments of the area hospitals and standardized the supplies, procedures, and policies of those hospitals.

Nicholson et al. (2004) developed sophisticated multi-echelon optimization models to study and analyze the impact of outsourcing of inventory management decisions to third-party provider that offers inventory management in health care. They compare the inventory costs and service levels of non-critical inventory items of an in-house three-echelon distribution network to an outsourced two-echelon distribution network. They try to evaluate the cost savings associated with switching from an in-house network to the outsourced network. In addition, they compare the service levels for each department within the hospital under the two scenarios. They studied a hospital network in Florida with seven hospitals and approximately 20 patient departments within each hospital. They conclude that the outsourced network dominates the in-house network in terms of total cost. The service levels of both the systems were comparable.

Logistics Coordination and Scheduling

Lapierre and Ruiz (2007) present an approach for improving hospital logistics by focusing on scheduling decisions and a supply chain approach rather than the more common multi-echelon inventory management. In an inventory management model, products for a care unit are ordered from central storage based on a certain minimum stock level known as the reorder point. The central storage also makes orders from suppliers based on reorder points. However, this model does not take into account the reality that orders for items are placed together at set times. Secondly, this model may not take into account the time-expensive "hot-picks," or unscheduled picks from stock-outs at care units, which may occur as a result of this model. And thirdly, this model may not take into account the limited amount of storage capacity in both the care units and the central storage.

In a supply chain approach, all the operations involving a significant amount of labor associated with ordering are taken into account, such as the replenishment decisions, order picking, delivery of products, purchasing activities, and handling of supplies at the reception docks. Additionally, in this approach some items may be delivered directly to care units instead of the central storage. The authors use the supply chain approach in their two models, both of which focus on making decisions for the optimal time to buy and deliver products to each care unit and also decisions for employee management such as work shift and task assignments. The first model seeks primarily to minimize inventory costs, and the second model seeks primarily to balance workload among the days of the week. Since both models were complex, heuristic methods were used to solve the models. Eventually, a version of the second model was used and applied to the satisfaction of a hospital in Montreal, Canada.

The drawbacks of this approach concern the fact that models used in this paper are much more complex than traditional inventory models. Furthermore, optimal solutions could not be found due to the use of heuristics. However, given the improvements in cost, labor, organization, and stock control, this type of research, which focuses on scheduling, may warrant further study.

Vries (2010) focused on the reshaping a hospital inventory system of medicines by conducting a case study that had three phases. In the first phase, the inventory system was analyzed to address the main strengths and weakness of inventory systems. In the second phase of the project, further discussion was made to redesign the inventory system. In the third phase, the new inventory system was partly implemented. The objective of the project was to analyze and improve inventory systems containing pharmaceuticals at the provider level. In the study, a qualitative exploratory case study was conducted since the case study approach allowed an in depth analysis and allowed detailed data to be gathered for the analysis process. Even though all problems were not solved, many improvements were seen in the hospital. These improvements included: partially fixing software problems, better management of rush-orders, reorganizing the communication channel, and changing the organizational structure.

Demand Management and Forecasting

O'Neill et al. (2001) examines the effect of implementing a Materials Requirement Planning (MRP) system in a health care setting. A two-part study was conducted at The University of Iowa Hospitals and Clinics (UIHC) concerning the inventory of green linens. Green linens are linens used for surgery, which for each use require laundering, material processing, and, for many items, sterilization. In the old system, more than ten thousand pounds of laundry were processed during five and a half days per week. A number of factors made managing this system difficult. Very high service levels were required, and shortages caused delays, extra cost, and unnecessary stress. Surgical schedules for the next day were not posted until 6 pm, meaning short lead times. Most green linens had to be sterilized using a 12-h process, and sterilized items had a shelf life of only 14 days. Some items were issued both separately in pre-made packs of several items. Demand was cyclical, i.e. different for each day, and small variations for each day caused large variations for laundry, material processing, and sterilization. Finally, the system was overly complicated and resulted in some days of overflowing inventory and other days of no inventory at all.

In the first part of the study, the hospital's green linen use was monitored over an 8 week period, which was then used to estimate demand. As expected, average demand for each day was different. The study proposed two alternatives to fix the system. The first alternative proposed processing only the amount of green linens needed for the day, resulting in a variable amount of labor for each day. The second alternative proposed processing a constant amount of green linens, holding stock for the days when demand was less than that amount, and using up stock when demand was greater than that amount. Both alternatives included safety stock. Ultimately, the second alternative was chosen due to lower cost of holding stock compared to paying workers overtime in every department along the supply chain.

For the new production schedule to work, the hospital needed the cycle time and total inventory of green linens. Total inventory was especially difficult to find due to losses from pilferage and the discarding of worn out linens. In the second part of the study, 49 green linen pillowcases were dyed blue and affixed with a bar code. The pillowcases were tracked as they left laundry and material processing. Average cycle time was found, and total inventory and seepage levels were estimated using statistical methods. As a result of this study, many improvements were made. An analysis of the system revealed redundant folding and inspections across several departments. A streamlined system resulted in 5 h per day of saved labor. Safety stock was reduced by 20%, inventory within packs were reduced by 40%, and five different pack types were eliminated. Additionally, an improved system resulted in fewer incidents of stock-outs and better communication among the departments.

In Apras (Applying inventory control practices within the Sisters of Mercy Health Care supply chain, unpublished MS Thesis, University of Arkansas, 2011) a systematic application of inventory management practices within the Sisters of Mercy Health System was performed. The methods take into account the practical realities of applying inventory management practices within health care settings and are demonstrated through a case study. The case study consists of three focus areas: (1) understanding and depicting the demand and inventory control system for bulk and unit dose items, (2) examining a second location, for a comparative

Table 10.2 Number of items and percentage of items in each ABC category based on usage value, demand, and unit cost

	Usage Value		Demand		Unit Cost	
	No. of items	percentage of items	No. of items	percentage of items	No. of items	percentage of items
A	160	7	267	12	238	11
B	918	42	833	38	1036	48
C	1091	50	1069	49	895	41
Total	2,169		2,169		2,169	

analysis, and (3) understanding the multi-echelon nature of the problem and the effect of inventory pooling within the supply chain.

An ABC inventory analysis was performed to select the items that would most likely have an impact in reducing costs. ABC inventory analysis is a grouping technique by the demand, average unit cost and usage value. Typically, 20 % of the items can cover approximately 80 % of the usage value (dollar value). There are three priority rankings to show importance of the category. Category A is very important, category B is important, and category C is less important Silver et al. (1998). A Pareto ABC inventory analysis was chosen based on annual usage value because the usage value gives the same importance for both demand and unit cost.

Table 10.2 tabulates the results for a selected sample of the inventory items. The majority of items are in the B and C categories for demand and unit cost. This is typical of most inventory systems but causes challenges in hospital environment because of the need to carry a wide variety of item types. This is the so-called stock keeping unit (SKU) proliferation problem. Rossetti and Liu (2009) examine this issue within the context of a health care supply chain via simulation. The SKU proliferation problem is often caused by physician preference items (PPI), in which the physician can decide which items to stock simply by choice. Not many industries allow their customers (i.e. physicians) to decide what to have on the shelves! This often creates items that have very low usage levels because they are tied to a single physician. This creates very difficult issues in forecasting demand for these items.

The literature refers to the "hard to forecast" demand scenarios as intermittent demand, lumpy demand, erratic demand, sporadic demand, and slow-moving demand. Silver et al. (1998) proposed a definition for intermittent demand as "*infrequent in the sense that the average time between consecutive transactions is considerably larger than the unit time period, the latter being the interval of forecast updating*." Syntetos et al. (2005) in their research on intermittent demand forecasting techniques, proposed a demand categorization scheme with recommendations for an appropriate cut-off value for squared coefficient of variation and mean interval between non-zero demands. Based on the mean inter-demand interval ($p = 1.32$) and the squared coefficient of the variation of the demand size ($CV^2 = 0.49$) Table 10.3 tabulates the classification for the items analyzed in

Table 10.3 Number of items in each demand class from Apras (Applying inventory control practices within the Sisters of Mercy Health Care supply chain, unpublished MS Thesis, University of Arkansas, 2011)

Demand Class	No of Items	Percentage of Items
Erratic	108	4.97
Intermittent	1,197	55.19
Lumpy	657	30.29
Smooth	207	9.54
Total	2169	

Apras (Applying inventory control practices within the Sisters of Mercy Health Care supply chain, unpublished MS Thesis, University of Arkansas, 2011). It is clear that within this health care setting the vast majority of items are "hard to forecast".

In Apras (Applying inventory control practices within the Sisters of Mercy Health Care supply chain, unpublished MS Thesis, University of Arkansas, 2011) a subset of the items were subjected to individual forecasting techniques including autoregressive moving average (ARMA), autoregressive (AR), moving average (MA), cumulative average (CA), simple exponential smoothing (SES), damped trend linear exponential smoothing (DTLES), average demand (AD), linear Holt exponential smoothing (LHES), and naïve forecasting. In naïve forecasting, the forecasted value is simply the previously observed value. The following steps were used to determine the most appropriate forecasting model: (1) plot the data, (2) interpret the results based on the information from the data plotted, (3) define demand patterns, such as trend, seasonality, and (4) fit the forecasting model while comparing some measures of accuracy, such as the measures of forecasting errors (MAE, MAPE), AIC, BIC, and R-Square, etc. MAE is the average mean absolute errors between actual and predicted demand. MAPE is mean absolute percentage errors between actual and predicted demand. AIC and BIC are measures of the goodness of fit of forecasting models. Smaller values of these criteria indicate better fit. Table 10.4 illustrates the result of this process for 70 items analyzed within Apras (Applying inventory control practices within the Sisters of Mercy Health Care supply chain, unpublished MS Thesis, University of Arkansas, 2011). Unfortunately, this sort of analysis is hardly ever done within a health care setting because of the lack of data, the lack of analysis tools, and the lack of expertise within materials management departments.

Callahan et al. (2004) discusses the importance of demand forecasting within a health care setting, including the issues involved in making good demand forecasts and the benefits of good demand forecasts for health care. The ideal health care supply chain, according to the authors, is one that automatically performs a number of operations after a medical procedure has been scheduled. These include choosing standardized products for the patient, assessing the need for backup supplies, picking necessary supplies, grouping supplies that need to be together, verifying the latest price of items based on the latest contract price, determining if

Table 10.4 Summary of selected forecasting models from Apras (Applying inventory control practices within the Sisters of Mercy Health Care supply chain, unpublished MS Thesis, University of Arkansas, 2011)

Model	Frequency	Percentage
ARMA	28	40.0
AR	16	22.9
MA	9	12.9
CA	8	11.4
SES	4	5.7
DTLES	2	2.9
AD	1	1.4
LHES	1	1.4
Naïve	1	1.4
Grand Total	70	

any products need replenishment, placing orders for those products, and recording data for predicting future demand.

An effective demand forecast, according to the authors, first requires accurate means of tracking items, such point-of-entry data entry and RFID tags. This chapter examines the use of technology in point-of-use capture in Sect. 10.5. Next, demand can be forecasted based on hospital scheduling, seasonal variation, and the preferences of the physicians. The demand forecast can then be further refined with data about the patients, such as age, weight, gender, medical conditions, and allergies. Any effective demand forecast should include all the phases of patient care, including pre-op, procedural, and recovery phases.

There are many benefits of an improved demand forecasts and a supply chain, which is responsive to these forecasts. These include lower costs for case preparation, improved fill rates and service levels, and reduced inventory. Since many products have a high risk of obsolescence, expiration, damage, or recall, keeping low inventory levels can greatly reduce cost. Additionally, good demand forecasts also help the manufacturers and distributors of the hospital or clinic in supplying the necessary products.

The health care supply chain has a number of unique aspects because of the types of structures and how they interact with patient care. The following section highlights one such component: the blood supply.

10.4 Blood Supply Management

A critical component of any health care system is its supply of blood. Having the correct type of blood, when and where it is needed is necessary to the success of a health care system. The 2007 National Blood Collection and Utilization Survey (Whitaker et al.2007) reported that 15,688,000 Whole Blood (WB) and Red Blood Cell (RBC) units were collected in the United States in 2006. This exceeded the number of transfusions by 7.8%. Despite this excess of over 1.2 Million units of blood, 6.89% of the hospitals surveyed reported cancellations of elective surgeries for one of more days because of blood shortages. The median number of days delayed for the 412 patients affected was 3.0 days. One of the contributors to this shortage is the number of units that become outdated due to their lack of use before their expiration date. For 2006, Whitaker et al. (2007) reported that 1,276,000 (4.6%) units of whole blood and all components were disposed of by blood centers and hospitals due to expiration (35 days). This perishable life saving commodity has also increased in unit cost during this period. Whitaker et al. (2007) reported that the average cost of a unit of platelets from whole blood ($84.25) increased by 32% from 2004 to 2006. Similarly the cost of red blood cells ($213.94) increased by 6.4% during the same period. Thus, as evidenced above, the efficient design and operation of the blood supply chain is a necessary component to reducing costs and delivering timely health care services.

The blood supply chain problem has attracted the attention of many operations researchers. Nahmias (1982) and Prastacos (1984) provide comprehensive reviews of perishable inventory and blood inventory management respectively, Pierskalla (2005) states that research on the management of the blood supply chain started in the 1960s, peaked in early 1980s and dropped of significantly since then. He hypothesizes that the large drop off was due to a reduction in federal funding in the area, the difficulty of the remaining problems in the area, and the shift in emphasis to blood supply safety largely due to the advent of human immunodeficiency virus (HIV) and a suspected cancer causing agent, the human T-cell lymphotropic virus (HTVL) (Jagannathan and Sen 1991).

What makes this problem interesting and challenging from an operations research perspective? Pierskalla (2005) identifies several factors that make this an interesting and challenging problem. First, whole blood can be processed into many different components (for example, plasma, platelets, cryoprecipitate, and granulocytes), each of which is perishable but at differing rates. Second, the supply of whole blood is a random variable. This is largely a function of the effort put forth by regional and community blood centers to recruit donors. In 2006, Whitaker et al. (2007) noted that community donations accounted for 87.5% of collections, while directed donations only accounted for 0.4%. Blood centers accounted for 95.3% of the donations while hospitals accounted for only 4.7% of all donations. Once collected, the blood needs to be screened for a variety of diseases and bad units eliminated which introduces more variability into the supply. Third, just as the supply of whole blood is a random variable, so is the demand for whole blood and its components. Pierskalla (2005) states that both the frequency and size of the demand for whole blood and its components need to be modeled as random variables. Finally, Pierskalla (2005) points out that the entire blood supply system can be modeled as a complex system, and as such it needs analysis at the tactical, operational and strategic level. Policies and decisions at each of these levels need to be designed such that shortages are minimized while at the same time efforts are made to reduce costs and waste of this valuable perishable resource.

The next couple of sections briefly summarize some of the key work in this area that has recently appeared in the literature. The goal is to familiarize readers with the type of work currently being performed in this area. Readers are encouraged to refer to the specific articles for modeling and analysis details.

10.4.1 The Blood Supply Chain Management Problem

Pierskalla (2005) provides an excellent strategic overview of the blood supply chain and of all of its components. The basic supply chain begins with the collection of the unit of blood from a donor at a collection center; from there the blood is sent to a regional blood center (RBC) or community blood center (CBC) for processing. Once at the centers, the blood gets processed into different blood products such as red blood cells, platelets, fresh frozen plasma, and other possible products. This is an important step because each different product has a different shelf life. The blood then gets tested for diseases, and gets thrown out if it fails any of the tests. After passing the tests, it gets stored and is ready for delivery. The blood often gets delivered in the first in, first out sequence for either routine deliveries, or emergency deliveries. The centers send the appropriate components of the original donated unit to the local hospitals based upon their demand. Once in the hospital, the blood goes into another type of storage. In the hospital, the blood is cross-matched before transfusion to determine the compatibility between the donor and recipient's blood. Another part of the transfusion process is mismatching. Mismatching refers to the fact that one type of blood is compatible with another type of blood. This is normally discouraged because it increases the risk to the patient.

In his book chapter, Pierskalla (2005) develops a number of operational procedures for blood bank management. These procedures are designed to help answer some strategic issues such as what blood bank functions should be performed, how many community blood banks one should have in a region, and how does one coordinate the supply and demand of whole blood and its products. Pierskalla (2005) provides models and analysis that shows that economies of scale exist for many of the blood bank functions. He develops algorithms that assist in allocating donor sites (including hospitals) to community blood banks and in turn to regional blood banks. Pierskalla (2005) uses simulation and time series models to help forecast average daily demand and determine appropriate inventory decisions at all levels (hospital blood banks, community blood banks, and regional blood banks). He provides a broad set of tools and techniques capable of assisting blood bank managers with many of their key strategic and operational management decisions. For details on the specific models and results see Pierskalla (2005).

10.4.2 Two-Stage Perishable Inventory Model for the Blood Supply Chain

Goh et al. (1993) present a two-stage perishable inventory system model of the blood supply chain. In their model, fresh items will be kept in the first stage and after a certain amount of days, will be transferred to the second stage. With blood, fresh blood is needed for certain types of surgeries, so blood for these surgeries would be taken from the first stage of inventory. Blood that's ten days or older will be stored in the second stage until it is used or becomes outdated. Goh et al. (1993) explore two different first in, first out policies. The first one is a restricted policy. This means that when there are requests for old blood, it can only be fulfilled from the second stage. For the second policy, they use an unrestricted policy. This means that requests for old blood can be filled from the first stage, but only when the second stage is empty. Goh et al. (1993) measure the number of shortages and the amount of outdated blood under each policy.

Three different approximations were used to analyze both of the policies. First, Goh et al. (1993) used a one-moment approximation where all of the processes were assumed to be Poisson. The restricted policy used the moment equations from the model to evaluate performance, and approximate the performance in the second stage. The unrestricted policy had to have the second stage approximated also as Poisson, along with the first stage's rate of requests. Goh et al. (1993) assumed that unsatisfied demand from the second stage was also an independent Poisson process. Next, a two-moment approximation was used. This method takes into account the different attempts, and the information associated with the number of outdates and shortages for the processes. The last approximation used by Goh et al. (1993) was the two-configuration approximation method. The first configuration assumes that there's no inventory in the second stage. This is a single-stage system and a Poisson process is used to approximate this stage. The second configuration gets used when a blood unit exceeds its expiration date in the first stage. When the second configuration get's used it is assumed that the second stage has inventory, and no shortages occur. A simulation model was used to analyze the various models. After looking at the results, it was determined that the two-moment model should be used for the restricted policy. To approximate the performance of the unrestricted policy, the two-configuration method was shown to produce the best results.

10.4.3 Delivery Strategies for the Blood Product Supplies

Hemmelmayr et al. (2009) explore cost effective ways for delivering blood for the Australian Red Cross. In this chapter, they move from the current vendee-managed inventory, first come first serve fixed route approach, to a more flexible vendor-managed inventory approach. Hemmelmayr et al. (2009) developed two different strategies for the proposed vendor-managed inventory system. The first one retains the concept of regions and the use of fixed routes while the second one combines more flexible routing decisions with a focus on delivery regularity. To figure out which one was better, they took three different solution approaches.

The first approach taken by Hemmelmayr et al. (2009) was a basic heuristic approach. Delivery routes were constructed each day based on a hospitals current inventory levels. When a hospital received a delivery, the inventory level is filled to capacity. This policy does not specifically take into account inventory holding costs or vehicle capacities. To reduce spoiling, the inventory capacity is adjusted based on previous experience with waste of blood products at the specific hospital. The second approach used integer programing. With this method, Hemmelmayr et al. (2009) still used the fixed route, but they included short cutting by skipping the hospitals that did not require a delivery. This allowed for a reduction in delivery cost, but had to be executed carefully to make sure all hospitals have a sufficient blood supply. The integer programing model was constructed based on the demand patterns to determine the actual routes over a 14-day period. The third approach used by Hemmelmayr et al. (2009) was a variable neighborhood search approach. They selected the variable neighborhood search approach by viewing the problem as a periodic vehicle routing problem with tour length constraints. In this approach, Hemmelmayr et al. (2009) select a visit combination for each hospital and solve the implied daily vehicle routing problems. The algorithm was developed to improve the flexibility in routing decisions while still achieving delivery regularity. They did this by exploring multiple neighborhoods when delivering, instead of just one when they were routing. Although these approaches resulted in a more sophisticated delivery system, they did significantly reduced delivery costs. Hemmelmayr et al. (2009) found that their approaches achieved a cost savings of about 30%.

10.4.4 Using Simulation to Improve the Blood Supply Chain

In this study, Katsaliaka and Brailsford (2007) analyze the blood supply chain for the UK National Health Service and use a simulation model to help improve it. Katsaliaka and Brailsford (2007) attempt to address some issues that have been overlooked or oversimplified in previous models of the blood supply chain. They model the entire supply chain from donor to patient including mismatching, the various types of blood products, and the shelf life for each of the unique products (for example, 35 days for adult red blood cells, 14 days for irradiated red blood cells, 5 days for platelets). The model is based on discrete event simulation. The authors use a Poisson distribution to model the arrival process for donated blood and a time dependent Poisson process to model the different types of blood requests from physicians. The size of the request is modeled using a LogNormal distribution. The quality of the system's performance was measured using the number of outdates for blood products by group in the hospital only, the number of shortages, the number of mismatches, and the number and percentage of routine/emergency deliveries to the hospital. Using the simulation model, Katsaliaka and Brailsford (2007) show that system performance can be improved by making minor adjustments to the supply chain. Examples of minor adjustments include decreasing the holding stock to four days, managing the routine deliveries better and allowing two deliveries rather than one each week, reducing the crossmatch release period, getting more accurate orders from doctors, applying multiple-crossmatching techniques, and adhering to the rules of first in, first out so less units go bad because they exceeded their expiration period.

10.4.5 Ongoing Research Opportunities

Despite all of the previous work, there still remain many open problems in this area and plenty of opportunities exist for researchers in this interesting area. Recently, Nagurney et al. (2011) presented a generalized network optimization model of the blood supply chain. Their multi-criteria model captures discarding costs associated with waste and disposal of blood products as well as costs associated with shortages. Their model accounts for the uncertainty of demand and quantifies the supply-side risk associated with procurement of blood products. Pierskalla (2005) points out that Prastacos (1984) identified several research problems that still remain open today. These open research opportunities include optimal component processing policies, distribution scheduling for multiple products, pricing of blood products and inter-regional cooperation, and finally an analysis of donor scheduling algorithms. These are but a few examples of research opportunities in this area. Pierskalla (2005) points out that since the use of blood products account for about 1% of total hospital costs in the United States, any efficiency derived from the blood supply chain may yield significant cost savings.

A critical issue in blood supply management (as well as for other classes of inventory) is the appropriate tracking of usage and coordinating the purchase/billing cycle. The use of advance information systems is becoming a key enabler for this area and is discussed in the following section.

10.5 Important Technology Advances for Medical Supply Management

The health care industry has been slower than other industries in leveraging the immense opportunities for using technologies, especially in the medical supply chain. However, there has been progress such that health care delivery is moving in the direction of becoming a series of technology-assisted activities driven by the improved productivity, cost savings and improved patient safety associated with technological innovations. The majority of health care providers transact with their main distributor or manufacturers using an Electronic Data Interchange (EDI) platform. The use of fax or e-mail is also common. The MMIS supports inventory management and is usually integrated with financial applications such as patient billing. Automatic identification and data capture technologies like barcode and RFID is in slow and growing use. Once these technologies are integrated with the MMIS there will be significant enhancement of supply chain process automation. Once the product reaches the hospital floor, it is available for patient use; the integration of product related information with patient billing and clinical applications such as Electronic Health Records (EHR) is also common. The following sections briefly discuss these technologies.

10.5.1 Electronic Data Interchange

Electronic Data Interchange (EDI) is a technology that has been used for more than twenty years in the automotive and retail industries. The EDI transactions minimize human interventions in external supply chain processes and thus ensure accuracy in product flow, especially in ordering and receiving. It is based on the concept of electronic transmission of specific information in the form of transaction sets. A typical order cycle that starts with a purchase order and ends with the payment of invoice may involve the following transaction sets: purchase order EDI 850, purchase order acknowledgment EDI 855, advanced ship notice EDI 856 and invoice EDI 810. According to a report published by HIMSS (HIMSS2010), 70% of the purchase orders generated by hospitals are sent via EDI.

10.5.2 Materials Management Information Systems and Ancillary Systems

Materials Management Information Systems (MMIS) are computer-based systems used to manage external and internal supply chain processes, which drive the product and information flows. The MMIS manages inventory related information including inventory on hand and on order, order period and quantity, corresponding PO number, product storage locations, as well as product vendor related information, which are essential to support internal supply chain processes. MMIS functionalities are integrated with financial applications, usually provided by the same vendor. Meanwhile, ancillary systems empower MMIS for complementary functionalities and include such technologies as barcode automation and Automatic Dispensing Cabinets (ADC). A current study conducted by HIGPA, CHES, GS1 US and AHRMM in 2009 (Burks 2009) reports that the MMIS market is saturated and mainly controlled by four main vendors: Lawson, McKesson, PeopleSoft, and MediTech.

10.5.3 Automatic Identification and Data Capture

Automatic identification is the broad name given to a host of technologies that are used to help systems identify assets and products and is often coupled with automatic data capture. The objective is to identify the item, capture the information related to it, and store the information electronically without manual processing and hence increasing efficiency, reducing data entry errors and freeing staff time to perform more value added functions. Some examples of automatic identification and data capture technologies are Barcode, Radio Frequency Identification (RFID), character and voice recognition systems, machine vision systems, and magnetic stripes. Prominent among them are barcode and RFID in the context of health care system. However, the level of adoption of Automatic Identification and Data Capture technologies is low at the health care provider level, as reported by a recent American Hospital Association survey. Only 16% of hospitals fully use barcode technology and 3% RFID for supply chain related activities (AHA, 2007).

10.5.4 Data Standards in Medical Supply Chain

Data standards also known as identification standards have their origin in the retail industry with the development of the Universal Product Code (UPC) in 1974. The use of identification standards in the medical supply chain was started in 1983 by the Health Industry Business Communication Council (HIBCC) and during the same time the use of barcode technology was widely promoted among hospitals. HIBCC standards were developed as specific health care standards in contrast to the Uniform Code Council (UCC) standards developed and used by several industries. Currently, medical supply chain data standards are developed and promoted by standards organizations like GS1 (formerly UCC EAN) or HIBCC.

The basic set of GS1 identification standards include Global Trade Identification Number (GTIN) for product identification, the Global Location Number (GLN) for trading partner identification, and the Global Data Synchronization Network (GDSN) that provides a synchronization mechanism for sharing accurate product information between supply chain players. HIBCC was founded in 1983 as a standards development organization for health care related issues, including medical device identification. The basic set of HIBCC standards includes Labeler Identification Code (LIC), Health Industry Number (HIN), and Health Industry Bar Code (HIBC). Parallel to industry developments the FDA has also contributed to the development of standards by setting regulations for pharmaceutical products and efforts are underway for medical products and devices.

Data standards in the medical supply chain ensure interoperability of a number of systems across the supply chain, including external and internal processes. Effective exchange of information throughout the supply chain is vital to supply chain visibility. The implementation of data standards has impacts at the process level and affects the process related accuracy measures, exception rates and staff productivity among other performance metrics. These impacts can be due to improved item and location identification, improved item and location information synchronization across the supply chain and improved item identification efficiency via automation.

In the external supply chain processes, the use of standard product and location identifiers in contract management and GPO operations streamline membership and pricing update notification processes and increases the pricing accuracy, reimbursement rebate accuracy, and administration fee accuracy. In addition, the use of identification standards in EDI transactions reduces exceptions in ordering and shipping including missed delivery or wrong delivery.

Within internal supply chain processes, increased internal supply chain visibility can be achieved through data standards streamlining inventory management processes. The data standards bring about interoperability between the MMIS system and ancillary systems. It also decreases manual checks and eliminates product re-labeling.

In bedside administration, the use of data standards drives automated authentication bedside administration and improves patient safety. Also, product identifiers for secondary information are used with outdates and recall management. The data standards enable interoperability of systems that communicates patient's health information and also improves the accuracy in patient charge capture.

10.6 Future Directions

In the report by Meyer and Meyer (2006), a number of problems and potential solutions within the health care supply chain are articulated. Three of the future research areas for the health care supply chain suggested by the report were:

- Increasing the role of the supply chain in new product development
- Forecasting and demand management
- Inventory management practices within the walls of a hospital

The emphasis on these areas is motivated largely by the rising costs within the health care supply chain. According to Haavik (2000), in some instances supply chain costs may amount to as much as 40% of the cost of providing care and that if demand and inventory are better managed a savings of 4.5% can be achieved. Chandra and Kachhal (2004) suggest, based on a study by Pricewaterhouse Coopers that the cost savings could range from 6 to 13.5%.

Some of this cost is due to the expanded used of new products and technologies. For example, a recent study by Blue Cross Blue Shield Association (Lovern 2001) indicated that 19% of health care cost can be directly traced to the use and deployment of medical technology and that new medical technology is a key reason for double-digit health care costs. Thus, there is an increasing need to understand the role of the supply chain in new product development and adoption.

The introduction of new technology (e.g. equipment and related supplies) for patient care introduces a number of logistic management and control issues within a health care supply chain. The first decision faced by hospital systems is to evaluate whether or not a new technology and its related supplies should be adopted. This traditionally involves a cost analysis as well as an evaluation of the medical effectiveness of the technology that may or may not take into account logistic issues. After adoption, new equipment and related supplies are sometimes placed within an expense category rather than an asset category because initial treatment plans are not standardized for the use of the new technology. In addition, the potential demand for the new equipment or technology is difficult to project.

Unfortunately, as the use of the new technology matures, the items often remain an expense longer than they should rather than being moved into an inventory management category where their use can be better optimized within the health care supply chain. In addition, for many new technologies the method of marketing through personal interaction between the supplier and the doctor is well entrenched. This personal marketing can bypass the traditional controls that are in place within the managed inventory items.

To address this need, a methodology for evaluating the trade-offs between the cost and the effectiveness of the new supplies/equipment needs to be developed. Such a methodology should capture the cost of the supplies/equipment in terms of inventory asset value but also the cost of managing the inventory within the supply system. This should involve the transportation, holding, and ordering costs. A unique aspect of this inventory modeling will be in characterizing (or forecasting) the demand for new items as well as the effect of technological change on the price/value of the items over time. For example, the introduction of new technology may cause the price/value of items already in inventory to change. Planning for this change over time can be an important factor in evaluating current technology versus new technology and any discounts offered by manufacturers. In addition, "where to stock" the items will be important, because inventory pooling may be a very effective strategy for high cost, low demand items. Traditional inventory models typically assume stationary demand and static item costs over an infinite planning horizon. This will clearly provide less than ideal planning for these types of items.

An ideal methodology should also evaluate the logistical performance (e.g. fill rate) for various levels of cost. The development of such a methodology should also take into account the best practices currently being used to manage new technology as well as how to take advantage of recent advances in information technology.

As indicated in the previous discussion, even for new technology, inventory management is a critical issue. To improve inventory management, the best place to start is at the beginning of the supply chain. That is, understanding and characterizing supply chain demand is critical because so much planning depends on the form of the demand. It could not be articulated any better than in the Center for

Global Development's report on improving global health through better demand forecasts:

> "One of the weakest links—and one of the most vital for achieving both short- and long-term gains in global health—is the forecasting of demand for critical medical technologies, including vaccines, medicines and diagnostic products. Demand forecasting, which may seem at first glance to be a small piece of the very large puzzle of access to medical products, is of central importance."— CGD (2007)

Some have advocated that retail-forecasting practices be adopted within the health care supply chain; however, it is not clear how these practices should be adapted to the unique aspects of the health care supply chain. One thing that is clear is that better demand management practices are imperative for achieving the potential savings that have been suggested. Callahan et al. (2004) indicate that the time may now be right for making this adaptation:

> "Having incorporated these lessons into the lore of supply chain management, we contend that our industry is now ready to develop its own set of principles that draws upon the concepts of retail demand forecasting models, but which fully accounts for the unique nature of health care—in which a failure to meet the demands of consumers (patients and clinicians) can have dire consequences."

They indicate that projecting demand is the key. That is, utilizing all automated systems to "create realistic bill of materials for procedures from the preparation phase through recovery and follow up" (Callahan et al. 2004). See also the discussion on treatment pathway profiling in Meyer and Meyer (2006). This is a key insight to replace uncertainty with information and get closer to derived demand.

Derived demand is demand that can be computed deterministically based on the requirements from other items (e.g. end items). Typical end-item demand forecasting relies on historical records to model future demand, largely treating the demand as independent. Whenever possible, it is advisable to substitute derived demand in place of typical forecasted demand. Within manufacturing settings (e.g. make-to-assembly and make-to-order) end-item demand is forecasted and the component demand is derived via the product structure (bill of materials). Because of advances in information technology, hospitals now have large quantities of data available concerning patients and their use of supplies. These systems track diagnosis, medical events, patient satisfaction, purchasing, accounts payable, reimbursements, surgical team preferences, dispensing of pharmaceutical, etc. With this sort of information, it may now be feasible to create a probabilistic "Bill of Materials" for categories of patient types and/or disease management regiments. From such a bill of materials, it may be possible to derive demand requirements for materials according to hospital scheduling, patient demographics, admission records, and seasonal demands.

For example, consider hip-replacement surgery. These types of procedures are often scheduled weeks if not months in advance. For each procedure, there are three sets of materials (1) those that are always used, (2) those that might be used, and (3) those materials that could not have been anticipated. The analysis of information on past patients should allow some analysis of sets 1 and 2. Then, a bill of material could be determined for those materials that are always used. This could allow pre-packaged kits to be developed; however, since many procedures may have common items, it is the schedule information along with the lead time to order the item, which could allow for better just-in-time management of the items. This would allow the postponement of the kit building process to the last possible moment. Thus, given a procedure schedule, the ordering, stocking, and delivering of significant amounts of material can be pre-planned. In addition, there is the possibility of creating a probabilistic bill of materials for the items that will probably be needed. Finally, with appropriate data, those materials that are being used but could not be anticipated could be forecasted and treated as independent demand items. This process could allow for significantly reduced levels of inventory, while still meeting delivery service requirements.

In some sense, the delivery of health services (in the form of procedures) to patients can be conceptually similar to something like aircraft maintenance. In order to optimize aircraft maintenance, one looks at scheduled maintenance and unscheduled maintenance. The scheduled maintenance allows derived demand to substitute for uncertainty. Then, the supply system can handle the inventory requirements for unscheduled repairs. While the analogy is not perfect, it should be apparent that some of the techniques applied to analysis and control of spare part supply networks should be applicable to the health-care supply chain.

In order to examine these ideas within the health care supply chain, there is a need to examine and document current (best) practices in regards to demand management. Then, the information requirements for analyzing and building bill of material candidates would need to be specified. Finally, the ideas would need to be modeled and compared to current methods. This would allow for a better understanding of how much benefit could be gained before committing larger resources to demand management techniques.

Acknowledgments We would like to thank a few students for their assistance in developing this chapter. In particular, Douglas Marek, Shyam Prabhu, Amit Bhonsle, Steve Sharp, Yanchao Liu, Vijith Varghese, Raja Jayaraman, Morgan Ulesich for assistance with the literature review. In addition, we would like to thank Server Apras for the data concerning forecasting and Vance Moore for allowing access to Mercy Health Systems.

References

AHA (2007) Continued progress-hospital use of information technology, American Hospital Association survey. Retrieved from www.aha.org/aha/content/2007/pdf/070227-continued progress.pdf Accessed 4/7/2011

Anonymous (2002) Resource management: the health care supply chain 2002 survey results, HFMA White Paper. http://www.hfma.org/NR/rdonlyres/B35AA31C-D1BE-4BD5-B41A-569B864F8A17/0/scsurvey.pdf. Accessed 6 Feb 2008

Axsater S (2006) Inventory control. Springer Science and Business Media, New York

Burks (2009) Putting the pieces together: driving standards in the health care supply chain. Report on the survey and assessment of MMIS readiness MMIS readiness assessment. The Association for Health care Resource & Materials Management (AHRMM) Annual conference presentation, Burks Health care Concepts, Inc. Retrieved from http://www.smisupplychain.com/datastandards/Putting%20the%20Pieces%20Together.pdf Accessed 7 Apr 2011

Burns LR (2002) The health care value chain. Jossey-Bass, Wiley, San Francisco

Burns LR, Lee RA (2008) Hospital purchasing alliances: utilization, services, and performance. Health Care Manag Rev 33:203–215

Burns LR, Pauly MV (2002) Integrated delivery networks: a detour on the road to integrated health care? Health Aff 21:128–143

Callahan TJ, Guzman DR, Sumeren MA (2004) Effective demand forecasting in the health care supply chain.www.HCTProject.com, http://jobfunctions.bnet.com/abstract.aspx?docid=100960. Accessed May 30 2008

Chandra C, Kachhal SK, (2004) Managing health care supply chain: trends, issues, and solutions from a logistics perspective. In: Proceedings of the sixteenth annual society of health systems management engineering forum, February 20-21, Orlando, Florida

Clark AJ, Scarf H (1960) Optimal policies for a multi-echelon inventory problem. Manag Sci 6:475–490

Dellaert N, van de Poel E (1996) Global inventory control in an academic hospital. Inte J Prod Econ 46–47:277–284

Deuermeyer BL, Schwarz LB (1981) A model for the analysis of system service level in warehouse – retailer distribution systems: the identical retailer case. TIMS Stud Manag Sci 16:163–193

Egbelu PJ, Harmonosky CM, Ventura JA, O'Brien WE, Sommer HJ III (1998) Cost analysis of hospital material management systems. J Soc Health Syst 5:1–10

Goh C, Greenberg B, Matsuo H (1993) Two-stage perishable inventory models. Manag Sci 39:633–649

Haavik S (2000) Building a demand-driven, vendor-managed supply chain—brief article, Health care Financial Management. http://findarticles.com/p/articles/mi_m3257/is_2_54/ai_59495187. Accessed June 4 2008

Hemmelmayr V, Doerner K, Harli R, Savelsbergh M (2009) Delivery strategies for blood products supplies. OR Spectr 31:707–725

HIMSS (2010) Hospitals embrace e-procurement for supply chain management—enterprise integration is the next challenge. White paper, Health care Information and Management Society, Retrieved from http://www.himssanalytics.org/docs/HA_GHX_White_Paper.pdf Accessed Apr 7 2011

Jagannathan R, Sen T (1991) Storing crossmatched blood: a perishable inventory model with prior allocation. Manag Sci 37:251–266

Kamani P (2004) Hospital supply chain savings 6:62–65

Katsaliaka K, Brailsford S (2007) Using simulation to improve the blood supply chain. J Oper Res Soc 58:219–227

Kelle P, Schneider H, Wiley-Patton S, Woosley J (2009) Health care supply chain management, Chapter 5. In: Jaber MY (ed) Inventory management non-classical views. CRC Press, Boca Raton

Kim GC, Schniederjans MJ (1993) Empirical comparison of just-in-time and stockless material management systems in the health care industry. Hosp Mater Manag Q 14:65–74

Kohn LT, Corrigan JM, Donaldson MS, (eds) (2000). To err is human—building a safer health system.National Academies Press. Washington, D. C.pp, 312. ISBN 978-0-309-06837-6

Lapierre SD, Ruiz AB (2007) Scheduling logistic activities to improve hospital supply systems. Comput Oper Res 34:624–641

Lovern E (2001) A scary Halloween for providers. Mod Health care 31:12–13

Meyer A, Meyer D (2006) Roundtable proceedings, transforming the health care supply chain. In: Singh M (ed) MIT Center for Transportation & Logistics, http://ctl.mit.edu/public/Health care%20Roundtable%20Proceedings%20-%20Final1.pdf. Accessed May 30 2008

Moore, V (2006) The integration of innovation and clinical need: ROi Mercy supply chain story [White paper]. Retrieved from http://cscmp.org/downloads/public/education/06innovation/ROiMercy.pdf

Moore, V (2010) President and CEO resource optimization & innovation (ROi) an operating division of the Sisters of Mercy Health, personal communication

Nagurney A, Masoumi A, Yu M (2011) Supply chain network operations management of a blood banking system with cost and risk minimization. Computational Management Science, (Forthcoming)

Nahmias S (1982) Perishable inventory theory: a review. Oper Res 30:680–708

Nicholson LA (2000) A multi-echelon inventory approach for a distribution system in the health care industry, Unpublished PhD dissertation, University of Florida

Nicholson L, Vakharia AJ, Erenguc SS (2004) Outsourcing inventory management decisions in health care: models and application. Eur J Oper Res 154:271–290

O'Neill L, Murphy M, Gray D, Stoner T (2001) An MRP system for surgical linen management at a large hospital. J Med Syst 25:63–71

Ozcan YA (2009) Quantitative methods in health care management: techniques and applications. Jossey Bass, San Francisco

Pierskalla WP (2005) Chapter 5, Supply chain management of blood banks. In: Operations research and health care, International series in Operations Research & Management Science, 70(2):103-145, Kluwer Academic Publishers, Norwell, Massachusetts

Prashant ND (1991) A systematic approach to optimization of inventory management functions". Hosp Mater Manag Q 12:34–38

Prastacos G (1984) Blood inventory management: an overview of theory and practice. Manage Sci 30:777–800

Rivard-Royer H, Landry S, Beaulieu M (2002) Hybrid stockless: a case study, lessons for health-care supply chain integration. Int J Oper Prod Manag 22:412

Rosser M (2006) Advancing health system integration through supply chain improvement. Health care Q 9:62–66

Rossetti, MD Liu, Y (2009) Simulating SKU proliferation in a health care supply chain. In: Proceedings of the 2009 winter simulation conference, Rossetti MD, Hill RR, Johansson B, Dunkin A, Ingalls RG (eds) Institute of Electrical and Electronic Engineers, Piscataway, New Jersey

Satir A, Cengiz D (1987) Medicinal inventory control in a university health centre. J Oper Res Soc 38:387–395

Schneller ES, Smeltzer LR (2006) Strategic management of the health care supply chain. Jossey Bass,Wiley, San Francisco

Schwarz LR (2011) Health care product supply chains: medical-surgical supplies, pharmaceuticals, and orthopedic devices: flows of product, information, and dollars, 45-1-15, Chapter 45. In:Yih Y (ed) CRC Press, Handbook of health care delivery systems. Taylor & Francis Group, Boca Raton

Sherbrooke CC (1968) Metric: a multi-echelon technique for recoverable item control. Oper Res 16:122–141

Silver EA, Pyke DF, Peterson R (1998) Inventory management and production planning and scheduling. Wiley, New York

Smoker JM, (2005) Strategic planning— migrating from tactical to strategic focus: a materials management case study. Association for health care resource & materials management (AHRMM) annual conference presentation. Retrieved from http://www.docstoc.com/docs/3629808/Strategic-Planning-Migrating-From-Tactical-to-Strategic-Focus-a. Accessed Apr 7 2011

Sullivan M, Cotton R, Read E, Wallace E (2007) Blood collection and transfusion in the United States in 2001. Transfusion 47:385–394

Syntetos AA, Boylan JE, Croston JD (2005) On the categorization of demand patterns. Journal of the Oper Res Soc 56:495–503

VanDer Linde LP (1983) System to maximize inventory performance in a small hospital. Am J Hosp Pharm 40:70–73

Vries JD (2010) The shaping of inventory systems in health care services: a stakeholder analysis, Inter J Prod Econ (in press)

Whitaker B, Green J, King M, Leibeg L, Mathew S, Schlumpf K, Schreiber G (2007) The 2007 national blood collection and utilization survey report, United States Department of Health and Human Services

Williams M (2004) Materials management and logistics in the emergency department. Emerg Med Clin North Am 22:195–215

Woosley JM, Wiley-Patton S (2009) Decision support in health care supply chain management and pharmaceutical inventory control. AMCIS 2009 proceedings, Paper 498. http://aisel.aisnet.org/amcis2009/498

Chapter 11
Operations Research Applications in Home Healthcare

Ashlea Bennett Milburn

Abstract The home health care industry is an important component of health care systems that have the potential to lower the system-wide costs of delivering care, and free capacity in overcrowded acute care settings such as hospitals. Demand is doubling, but resources are scarce. A nursing shortage and near-zero profit margins hinder the ability of home care agencies to meet the increasing patient demand. The effective utilization of resources is vital to the continued availability of home care services. There is tremendous opportunity for the operations research community to address the challenges faced by home care agencies to improve their ability to meet as much patient demand as possible. This chapter describes tactical and operational planning problems arising in home health care, and discusses alternative configurations of home health supply chains. Formulations for home health nurse districting, home health nurse routing and scheduling, and home health supply chain problems are presented, and the relevant literature is reviewed. Recent developments in remote monitoring technologies that could change the home health care landscape are discussed, and future research directions are proposed.

11.1 Introduction

The home health care industry is an important component of health care systems that has the potential to lower the system-wide costs of delivering care, and free capacity in overcrowded acute care settings such as hospitals. In home care,

A. B. Milburn (✉)
University of Arkansas, North Garland Avenue, Fayetteville, AR 72701, USA
e-mail: ashlea@uark.edu

R. Hall (ed.), *Handbook of Healthcare System Scheduling*,
International Series in Operations Research & Management Science 168,
DOI: 10.1007/978-1-4614-1734-7_11, © Springer Science+Business Media, LLC 2012

specialized services such as IV medications and wound care are provided to patients in their homes by licensed clinical personnel. The number of visits and specific care that each patient receives is determined by the ordering physician. Short-term services may be provided following a hospitalization, or long-term assistance with disease management may be provided for chronic conditions. The groups of patients most often receiving home care are the elderly, disabled, and chronically ill (CMS 2008).

The National Association for Home Care and Hospice estimates that there were approximately 17,700 providers of home care nationwide in 2005 with projected total annual expenditures of $53.4 billion (NAHC 2007). In 2007, over 200,000 nurses were employed in home care, and 7.6 million patients received home care services (NAHC 2007). The demand for home care is expected to double by 2030 as the trend towards shifting the delivery of care to less acute settings continues (Super 2002). Factors driving this shift include an aging population, chronic disease epidemic, rising health care costs, and technological advances that enable home-based disease management (Steven et al. 2010):

- By 2040, the number of people aged 65 and older will quadruple (US 2004),
- 50% of all American adults have at least one chronic disease (CDC 2009),
- Care is cheaper in the home at $132/day versus $1889/day in the hospital (NAHC 2007; AHRQ 2007),
- The market for home-based health technologies is expected to double from $3 billion in 2009 to $7.7 billion in 2012 (King 2010).

The resources required to accommodate this shift of delivery of care to the home setting include home health nurses, automobiles, medical supplies and equipment, agency office space, and administrative personnel. Yet, a 20% gap between the supply and demand of skilled nursing services is expected by 2030 (Buerhaus et al. 2000). Additionally, high operating costs and low reimbursement lead to near-zero profit margins for many home care agencies, and are often negative for those operating in rural areas (NAHC 2006). With such scarce resources, their effective utilization is vital to the continued availability of home care services.

There is tremendous opportunity for the operations research community to address the challenges faced by home care agencies. The resource allocation and materials management problems encountered in home health care resemble those arising in health care facilities such as hospitals, but are complicated by geographically distributed patients and resources. Additionally, routing nurses to visit patients in their homes requires solving problems similar to those encountered in the freight transportation industry, but is complicated by critical patient service considerations. While the scientific community has actively addressed such problems in hospitals and freight transportation, the studies in the literature specific to home health care are relatively few. Existing research has focused on two primary problems: the tactical problem of assigning home health nurses to geographic service districts, and the operational problem of routing and scheduling home health nurses. Recently, the home health supply chain has also begun to receive attention.

The objectives of this chapter are to describe operations research applications in the home health industry, offer formulations for specific problems encountered, survey the relevant literature, and inspire the scientific community to actively address future topics in dire need of attention. The remainder of this chapter is organized as follows. In Sect. 11.2, select planning problems encountered in home health care are described, and formulations for those problems are presented. For each problem presented, Sect. 11.3 reviews the relevant literature. In Sect. 11.4, recent developments that could change the home health care landscape are discussed. Finally, in Sect. 11.6, future research directions are proposed.

11.2 Problems and Formulations

In this section, three classes of problems arising in home health care applications are described, and their formulations are presented. First, the operational problem of routing and scheduling home health nurses is discussed in Sect. 11.2.1. Then in Sect. 11.2.2, the tactical planning problem of developing home health nurse service districts is described. Finally, in Sect. 11.2.3, an overview of home health supply chain problems is given.

11.2.1 Home Health Nurse Routing and Scheduling

Home health care workers in the United States drive 5 billion miles each year to visit patients—double the number of miles traveled by United Parcel Service (UPS) drivers annually (NAHC 2009; UPS 2009). The logistics challenges associated with deploying nurses to deliver health care to patient homes are complicated by medical constraints and patient service considerations. The research community has actively addressed routing problems arising in the freight transportation industry, and nurse scheduling problems arising in health care facilities such as hospitals and clinics. However, the studies addressing routing and scheduling applications in the home health care industry are strikingly few (Akjiratikarl et al. 2007; Begur et al. 1997; Bertels and Fahle 2006; Eveborn et al. 2006; Rich 1999; Steeg 2008; Bennett and Erera 2011).

Home health nurse routing and scheduling (HHNRS) problems are defined for a set of patients that need to be visited in their homes according to a prescribed weekly frequency for a prescribed number of consecutive weeks during a planning horizon. The weekly visits for each patient must be performed by clinical personnel that meet patient-specific requirements (e.g., appropriate skill level, language, patient preference). Additionally, the weekly visits must occur according to patient-specific day and time requirements, with visit days selected from a set of allowable visit day combinations, and visit times selected from a set of allowable appointment times or appointment windows. An allowable visit day combination for a two visit per week patient could be {Monday,Wednesday} or {Tuesday, Thursday}, and allowable appointment times could be 8:00, 8:30, 9:00, etc., if the patient requires a morning visit. Day and time requirements may be specified by the doctor providing the prescription for home care, if the service to be delivered is time-critical. An example is IV medication that must be administered at 24-h intervals throughout a 10-day period. Day and time requirements may instead be specified by the patient, if they are only available to receive in-home nurse visits on certain days and times.

A set of nurses perform patient visits, where each nurse is available for a fixed workday length on select days throughout the planning horizon. Nurses may be differentiated according to characteristics such as skill level (e.g., Registered Nurse, Nurse Practitioner) and language spoken. A solution to a home health nurse routing and scheduling problem assigns a nurse, visit day, and appointment time to each patient visit throughout the planning horizon. Each nurse begins each day at their own home, visits their assigned patients at the times specified, and returns to their own home. The solution is feasible if the route of each nurse conforms to workday length constraints and patient requirements are met. A primary objective is minimizing total nurse travel time, because of the related (and most important) objective of maximizing the number of visits performed per nurse.

When the assignments of patient visits to nurses and days are treated as exogenous decisions, the resulting problems can be modeled as multiple traveling salesman problems with soft or hard time window side constraints (*m*-TSPTW). Including nurse assignment decisions require modeling the problem as a multi-depot vehicle routing problem with time windows (MD-VRPTW) with additional side constraints that match patient requirements and/or preferences with nurse characteristics. Further expanding the scope of decisions to include the assignment of patient visits to days results in a periodic routing problem variant (PMD-VRPTW).

In addition to minimizing total nurse travel time, other important objectives in home health nurse routing and scheduling problems include maximizing nurse and visit time consistency. Nurse consistency, referred to in the health literature as continuity of care, has positive implications for care outcomes. Studies have shown a correlation between continuity of care, increased patient satisfaction, and decreased hospitalizations and emergency room visits (Cabana and Jee 2004). Consistency in visit time has also been indicated as a predictor of patient satisfaction in conversations with various home health agency personnel. When nurse and visit time consistency objectives are considered, the resulting PMD-VRPTW models must also include linking variables and constraints that require each patient to be visited by the same nurse (or set of nurses) on the same days at the same times each week. In the routing literature, such problems that enforce driver and/or time consistency have recently been referred to as *consistent* vehicle routing problems (Groer et al. 2009). Because periodic and multi-depot components are

Table 11.1 Models for HHNRS problems and the decisions each considers

Problem characteristics	*m*-TSPTW	MD-VRPTW+	PMD-VRPTW+	CPMD-VRPTW+
Visit time assignments	x	x	x	x
Time consistency				x
Visit day assignments			x	x
Visit day consistency				x
Nurse assignments		x	x	x
Nurse consistency				x

also considered when CVRP models are used for HHNRS problems, such models are referred here as CPMD-VRPTW.

Models for HHNRS problems and the decisions each considers are summarized in Table 11.1. In the table, "+" is used to denote models that include additional side constraints to match patient requirements and preferences with nurse characteristics. An "x" is used to denote decisions each model treats endogenously. It should also be noted that discussion of HHNRS problems thus far has focused on static problem variants, where patient requests are assumed to be known with certainty. In realistic applications, the set of patients to be visited varies throughout the planning horizon as patients are discharged and new patients are admitted. Visit requests corresponding to future patient admissions are not known. Thus, dynamic variants of each model in Table 11.1 result.

11.2.2 Home Health Nurse Districting

A tactical planning problem in home health care that partially determines the quality of solutions that can be obtained for home health nurse routing and scheduling problems is the home health nurse districting problem (HHND). In the HHND problem, the geographic service area of a home health care agency is divided into districts to be served by teams of nurses. The geographic location of a patient determines the nurse to which they are assigned. The capacity of each nurse team is limited, and their productivity is influenced by the size of the region in which their assigned patient requests are distributed. A large region equates to longer travel times, requiring more total time to visit the same number of patients than in a small region. Nurse consistency measures can also be influenced by district size and staffing. If demand is not properly balanced across districts, nurses may be asked to temporarily cover demand in districts to which they are not assigned.

Home health nurse districting problems are defined for a connected service region that includes a set of $\mathcal{N} = \{1, \ldots, n\}$ subunits, e.g., zip codes, where each subunit i has an area v_i and demand p_i, measured by the number of patient visits required to subunit i per day. A set of k nurses are available each day to serve patient demand within the service region, and each nurse has a target workload b. Workload can be measured in a variety of ways, for example, by the number of hours each nurse is available to work, or by the number of patient visits each nurse performs. Nurses work in teams of size $f_j \in \mathbb{Z}^+$, where the number of nurses may vary by team; thus, the target workload of team j is bf_j. The problem is to develop a set of contiguous districts, one for each team of nurses, such that each subunit is assigned to exactly one district, and the workload of each district is near the target $\beta_j = bf_j$. Possible objectives include minimizing nurse travel and workload imbalance across districts.

Two formulations appropriate for HHND problems, depending on the specific application, are location-allocation and set partitioning. Location-allocation models require that a fixed set of district centers, or finite number of potential district centers, is known. Decisions include selecting which district centers to open (if necessary), and assigning each subunit to exactly one district center, subject to additional constraints. This formulation may be useful in applications where the district center serves as a depot, at which all nurse routes within the district begin and end. Set partitioning models do not require a fixed set of district centers. Instead, the set of potential districts includes every possible combination of subunits that meet district feasibility conditions. Then, a subset of districts are selected such that each subunit is included in exactly one district. The two primary formulations are discussed in detail below.

Location-Allocation Formulation of HHND

The location-allocation formulation developed in Hess et al. (1965) for the political districting problem is adapted here for the HHND problem. Suppose there are m district centers and n subunits. Let C_{ij} represent the cost of assigning subunit i to district center j. Let p_i be the daily demand of subunit i, and let β_j be the target workload of district j. Let x_{ij} be a binary decision variable indicating whether subunit i is included in district j. Then, the location-allocation formulation of HHND is as follows:

$$\text{Minimize} \sum_{i=1}^{n} \sum_{j=1}^{m} C_{ij} x_{ij}, \tag{11.1}$$

$$\text{Subject to} \sum_{i=1}^{n} p_i x_{ij} = \beta_j \quad \text{for } j = 1, \ldots, m, \tag{11.2}$$

$$\sum_{j=1}^{m} x_{ij} = 1 \quad \text{for } i = 1, \ldots, n, \tag{11.3}$$

$$x_{ij} \in \{0, 1\} \quad \text{for } i = 1, \ldots, n, j = 1, \ldots, m. \tag{11.4}$$

Objective function (11.1) minimizes the total cost of assigning subunits to districts, constraints (11.2) require that the total demand assigned to each district is equal to the target workload, and constraints (11.3) together with binary decision variables require that each subunit is assigned to exactly one district. Because it is unlikely that the cumulative demand of subunits assigned to each district j will equate to β_j, constraints (11.2) may be replaced with upper bound inequality constraints, i.e., $\leq (1+\alpha)\beta_j$, if some maximum allowable workload should not be exceeded. Alternatively, if balancing workload across districts is desired, a set of lower and upper bound inequality constraints may be used, with limits $(1 \pm \alpha)\beta_j$.

The objective function in the location-allocation formulation of HHND may be linear or nonlinear, depending on methods used to evaluate the cost of assigning a subunit to a district. Suppose t_{ij} represents the travel time from the centroid of subunit i to district j, approximating C_{ij} as t_{ij} results in a linear objective function equal to the sum of the travel times between all subunits and their assigned district centers. While compact and contiguous districts would be preferred in optimal solutions, the sum of out and back travel times does not mimic the true application. In practice, if subunit i is assigned to district center j, a nurse leaves his/her home, visits a sequence of patients in i and other subunits assigned to j, and returns home. Thus, approximating C_{ij} as expected daily routing costs is a more realistic modeling approach, but requires a nonlinear objective function.

The capacity constraints in the location-allocation formulation of HHND may also be linear or nonlinear, depending on methods used to measure workload. If workloads are considered balanced when each nurse performs an equal number of daily visits, then approximating β_j as described in Eq. 11.5 results in linear capacity constraints:

$$\beta_j = f_j\left(\frac{\sum_{i=1}^{n} p_i}{\sum_{j=1}^{m} f_j}\right). \tag{11.5}$$

If the expected length of a patient visit varies between subunits, and workload is measured by the total amount of time spent performing patient visits, capacity constraints are again linear. Let γ_i be the average length, in hours, of visits to patients in subunit i. Then, constraints (11.2) can be replaced with:

$$\sum_{i=1}^{n} \gamma_i p_i x_{ij} = f_j\left(\frac{\sum_{i=1}^{n} \gamma_i p_i}{\sum_{j=1}^{m} f_j}\right). \tag{11.6}$$

Just as the objective function in the location-allocation formulation of HHND becomes nonlinear when expected daily routing costs are considered, nonlinear capacity constraints result when expected daily routing costs are included in workload estimation. Despite computational difficulty, this modeling approach may be desired for home health agencies whose geographic service areas include both rural and metropolitan areas. The total time required to perform patient visits and travel between them is longer in large, sparsely populated districts, than in small, densely populated districts.

An alternate formulation that allows for evaluating complex district cost and feasibility outside the core optimization problem is presented next.

Set Partitioning Formulation of HHND

The set partitioning formulation of HHND allows for evaluating complex non-linear district cost and feasibility conditions outside of the core optimization problem. Let J denote the set of all feasible districts, i.e., those that are contiguous and meet workload balance constraints. Let ρ_{ij} be equal to 1 if district j includes subunit i and 0 otherwise. Let C_j be the cost of district j, and let y_j be a binary decision variable denoting whether district j is selected in a solution to the set partitioning problem. Let m be the number of districts to be selected. Then, the set partitioning formulation for HHND is as follows:

$$\text{Minimize} \sum_{j \in J} C_j y_j, \tag{11.7}$$

$$\text{Subject to} \sum_{j \in J} \rho_{ij} y_j = 1 \quad \text{for } i = 1, \ldots, n, \tag{11.8}$$

$$\sum_{j \in J} y_j = m, \tag{11.9}$$

$$y_j \in \{0, 1\} \quad \text{for } j \in J. \tag{11.10}$$

Objective function (11.7) minimizes the total cost of the selected districts. Constraints (11.8) together with binary decision variables require that each subunit is included in exactly one selected district. Constraint (11.9) ensures that the desired number of districts are selected. Methods for evaluating district cost and feasibility discussed in "Set Partitioning Formulation of HHND" can be used to externally create feasible districts and determine C_j.

11.2.3 Home Health Supply Chain

A 2008 survey of 1381 health care supply chain professionals conducted by the Association for Health care Resource and Materials Management (AHRMM) and the Center for Innovation in Health care Logistics at the University of Arkansas (CIHL) revealed that the average health care provider responding to the survey spends 31% of their total annual operating budget on supply chain functions (Nachtmann and Pohl 2009). In a 2009 survey of 1600 nurses and nurse executives conducted by Owens and Minor, half of the respondents reported spending too

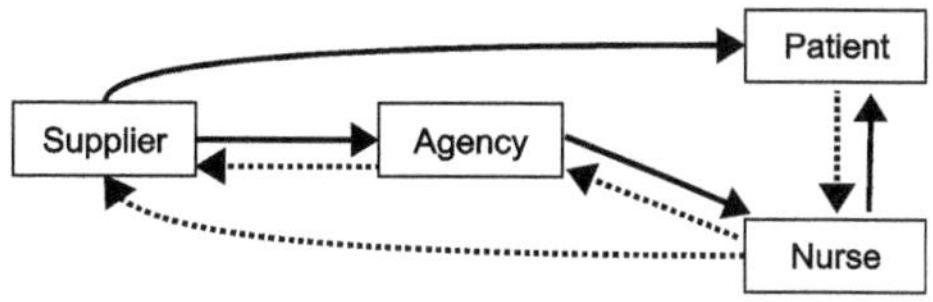

Fig. 11.1 Product and information flows in the home health supply chain

much time on supply duties (Ferenc 2010). It is not clear that home health care professionals and nurses are represented in responses to the above mentioned surveys. However, information being collected from home health care agencies regarding their supply chain practices in an ongoing CIHL project suggests that home health nurses are often assigned responsibility for portions of home health care supply chain processes as well (Bennett and Mason 2011).

The home health supply chain is distinct from hospital supply chains because care is delivered, and thus supplies are required, in geographically distributed patient homes. Patients receiving home health care are visited by a nurse one to three times per week throughout the duration of their episode of care - often a 60 day period. During each patient visit, a nurse assesses the supplies needed during the next visit to the patient, and those needed by the patient for self-use, considering the inventory of supplies the patient has available. If it is determined that a particular supply needs to be replenished, or a new supply needs to be ordered, the nurse initiates the order management process specified by the home health agency where he/she is employed. Once the order is received by the supplier, the supply distribution process agreed upon by the supplier and home health agency is executed.

Bennett and Mason (2011) have identified two frequently employed order management processes and two frequently employed channels of distribution in the health supply chain. The associated information and product flows in the home health supply chain are depicted in Fig. 11.1 using dashed and solid lines, respectively. Information received from the patient helps determine orders placed by the nurse. Depending on the policy of the home health agency, the nurse may place orders directly with the supplier, or with a supply manager at the home health agency that consolidates and relays orders to the supplier. Depending on the agreement between the home health agency and the supplier, supplies are either direct shipped to the patient, or shipped first to the home health agency for storage and subsequent nurse pickup and delivery to the patient.

When the home health agency serves as the intermediary in the supply distribution channel, nurse involvement may be required in certain supply chain functions. Examples of daily nurse routes when an agency employs a distribution channel in which they are an intermediary when they are not are depicted in Fig. 11.2 . In this simple example, the agency (A) employs two nurses, N1 and N2, and there are four patients, P1 through P4. Nurse 1 must visit P4 before visiting P3, and Nurse 2 must visit P1 before visiting P2. When supplies are stored in an inventory room at the home health agency main office, nurses begin their daily routes by traveling first to the agency before visiting patients. When supplies are shipped

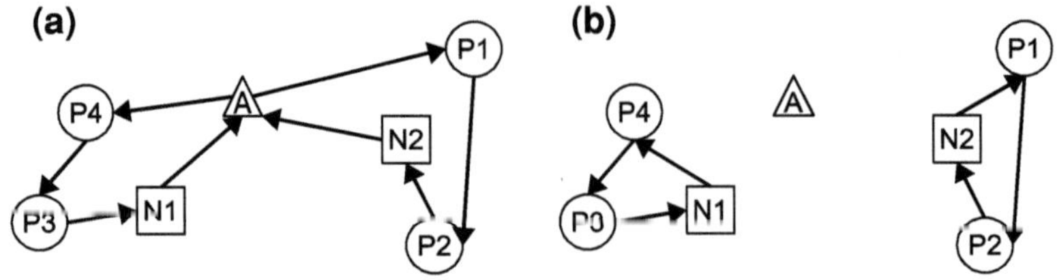

Fig. 11.2 Example of nurse routes based on supply storage and delivery policies. **a** Supplies stored at agency, **b** supplies not stored at agency

directly from the supplier to the patient, the nurse is not required to visit the agency at the beginning of each day. Letting t_{ij} represent the time required to travel from location i to location j, the difference in travel time required by the process depicted in (a) and that in (b) is:

$$t_{N1,A} + t_{A,P4} + t_{N2,A} + t_{A,P1} - t_{N1,P4} - t_{N2,P1}. \tag{11.11}$$

Assuming a complete symmetric network with travel times satisfying the triangle-inequality (a common assumption in logistics planning problems), the quantity in Eq. 11.11 is non negative. Thus, nurses spend more time traveling when supplies are stored at the agency than when they are not. The nurses may also be required to spend time picking up supplies needed for each of their patient visits, if supplies are kept in an inventory storeroom by type and no other non-clinical personnel are assigned the responsibility of picking up patient-specific supply orders.

Due to these "hidden" costs that exist in home health supply chains, models to estimate the costs associated with alternative home health care supply chain configurations are needed. Letting TC denote the total annual supply chain cost for a home health agency, a general model is defined in Eq. 11.12 that includes the following components:

- C_{n}: annual cost of nurse involvement in non-clinical supply chain duties,
- C_{d}: annual direct cost of supplies,
- C_{h}: annual holding cost of supplies,
- C_{t}: annual cost of delivering supplies to patients,
- C_{a}: annual administrative cost of supporting supply chain functions,
- C_{p}: annual penalty cost associated with stockouts,

$$TC = C_{\text{n}} + C_{\text{d}} + C_{\text{h}} + C_{\text{t}} + C_{\text{a}} + C_{\text{p}}. \tag{11.12}$$

In this model, C_{n} represents charges incurred when nurses spend time on supply chain responsibilities that they would otherwise have available for providing patient care. The per unit of time cost coefficient could thus include an hourly pay rate and/or a penalty cost associated with decreased nurse availability. Holding cost includes the cost of space for storing supplies and the opportunity cost of capital invested in inventory. Transport cost, C_t, may be modeled as a per order delivery cost, or as per mile reimbursement cost. Administrative costs can include, for example, the cost of technology and information systems used in the execution of supply chain functions, and the salaries paid to non-clinical personnel with supply chain responsibilities. Finally, penalty costs associated with not having supplies available for the patient when needed may include the cost of decreased patient satisfaction or negative care outcomes.

11.3 Prior Research

In this section, prior research corresponding to each of the problems presented in Sect. 11.2 is reviewed.

11.3.1 Home Health Nurse Routing and Scheduling

In much of the prior home health nurse routing and scheduling research, visit day combination decisions for patients are not considered. Exogenous visit day combination assignments imply, for each day, a fixed set of patients that need to be seen by one or more nurses, each of whom has a fixed limit on the number of hours they can work. Thus, the problems frequently addressed in the literature most closely resemble *m*-VRPTWs with side constraints. The problems are not periodic because visit day assignment decisions need not be made, and they are not dynamic because all patients are known in advance. Researchers instead focus on various side constraints, such as skill level requirements and patient preferences for a particular nurse. Also, in the surveyed research, nurses are assumed to be stationed at a central depot, instead of their own home locations. The approaches used and the types of decisions considered in papers that model HHNRS problems as *m*-VRPTWs with side constraints are summarized in Table 11.2. These papers are reviewed in more detail in Bennett and Erera (2011).

More recently, the scientific community has addressed the complicating dynamic and periodic aspects of HHNRS problems. For example, Steeg (2008) considers the nurse assignment, visit day combination assignment, and visit time assignment decisions. A constraint programing and large neighborhood search method is used to determine these decisions for a set of known patient requests. A tabu search algorithm is used to dynamically update routes to include newly arriving patient requests. However, consistency of provider and visit time throughout the duration of a patient's episode of care are not considered.

Bennett and Erera (2011) model the HHNRS problem as a dynamic periodic routing problem variant with fixed appointment times, where each patient visit must be assigned a precise appointment time from a fixed menu of allowable times, e.g., {8:00, 8:15, 8:30,...}. Visit day combination and appointment time

Table 11.2 HHNRS problems modeled as *m*-VRPTWs in the literature

Ref.	Objective	Decisions considered	Solution approach
Begur et al. (1997)	Minimize distance traveled	Assign nurses and visit times to patient visits; managerial considerations addressed manually	Clarke-wright savings heuristic with nearest neighbor TSP reoptimization and manual route improvement via GIS tool
Akjiratikarl et al. (2007)	Minimize distance traveled	Assign nurses and adjust exogenously specified appointment times within allowable windows	Particle swarm optimization with local route improvement
Eveborn et al. (2006)	Maximize number of patient visits and minimize distance traveled	Assign nurses based on patient preferences and skill level requirements and assign appointment times within allowable windows	Set partitioning with matching algorithm and interactive tool
Bertels and Fahle (2006)	Minimize sum of distance traveled plus penalty cost	Assign nurses based on skill levels, shift length constraints, and patient and provider preferences, and assign appointment times within allowable windows	Hybrid tabu search, simulated annealing, and constraint programming heuristic

decisions are made for each patient during the planning interval in which they arrive. To achieve visit day and time consistency, these decisions are not allowed to be changed to accommodate new requests for visits in future planning intervals. A single-nurse variant is the focus of the paper; thus, nurse assignment decisions are not treated endogenously, but perfect nurse consistency is implied. The authors develop a myopic rolling horizon planning approach that explicitly considers the capacity of the nurse's schedule (remaining time available) when making scheduling decisions for known requests, with the objective of preserving capacity for inserting future visit requests. The approach is compared to a rolling horizon planning procedure that considers only the traditional distance-based insertion criteria when scheduling known requests. Computational experiments demonstrate that the capacity-based approach is able to accommodate 4% more patient visits per day, while requiring 8.7% additional minutes of travel per visit, on average.

11.3.2 Home Health Nurse Districting

Districting problems have appeared in the literature in a variety of applications, for example: police officer territories (D'Amico et al. 2002), sales territories (Hess and

Samuels 1971; Zoltners and Sinha 1983), school districts (Caro et al. 2004), vehicle delivery districts (Haugland et al. 2007), and political districts (Bozkaya et al. 2003; Garfinkel and Nemhauser 1970; Hess et al. 1965; Hojati 1996; Mehrotra et al. 1998; Ricca and Simeone 2008). Blais et al. (2003) were the first-known researchers to study districting in home health care. In the problem they study, the service region of a community health clinic in Montreal is to be partitioned into six districts staffed by multi disciplinary teams. The selection of districts is based on five criteria: indivisibility of subunits, respect for city boundaries, contiguity of resultant districts, the ability of nurses to travel easily within the district to which they are assigned, and workload balance. The first three criteria are strictly enforced, while travel "mobility" and workload balance are addressed using a weighted objective function. Mobility is approximated by summing centroid-to-centroid travel distances between subunits assigned to each district, where travel distances are calculated as the shortest time path between centroids using public transportation and walking. The authors point out that because patients in subunits are visited on tours, this mobility measure does not accurately reflect actual distance traveled, but does serve as an adequate proxy. Workload is measured as the time spent visiting patients and traveling between patient visits, with travel between visits estimated using historical data. Districts having workloads outside an allowable range are penalized in the objective function. A tabu search procedure that considers two types of local search moves is used to solve the districting problem. To reach a new solution in a given iteration, a subunit can be moved from its current district into an adjacent district, or two subunits in adjacent districts can be swapped. The solution obtained via the tabu search procedure achieved decreased nurse transportation time for the Montreal health clinic instance, and was implemented to the health clinic's satisfaction.

Bennett (2009) studies a home health nurse districting problem, but observes that measuring nurse workload as the number of patient visits a nurse performs does not reflect the actual amount of time required to visit the patients. Longer travel times are required to visit patients in large, sparsely populated districts than in small, densely populated districts. A method is developed for approximating expected daily travel time in each district. Then, a measure for district workload is used that includes time spent performing active patient care and expected time spent traveling between patient visits. A district is feasible only if it is contiguous and the total nurse visit time and expected travel time are within lower and upper bounds on district target workload. Because the contiguity and workload balance considerations would require nonlinear constraints if handled within the core optimization problem, the authors use a set partitioning formulation, where the objective is to minimize nurse travel within the selected districts. A solution method is developed that combines ideas from column generation and heuristic local search methods. The method begins with a subset of feasible districts obtained via a clustering heuristic and solves the linear relaxation of the set partitioning formulation. Then, the dual variable values associated with the linear relaxation solution are used to guide the search for improving columns to add to the subset of feasible districts. New columns are created through the types of local search moves described in Blais et al. (2003). Solutions obtained using the hybrid approach are shown to require less nurse travel, on average, than those obtained using pure local search.

Lahrichi et al. (2006) observed that due to changes in a home health agency's patient census over time, the districting problem must be periodically solved if balanced workloads among nurses are to be preserved. Three years after the districting solution developed in Blais et al. (2003) was implemented at the Montreal health clinic, Lahrichi et al. analyzed the clinic's operation data and discovered workload imbalance (Lahrichi et al. 2006). The average number of patients seen per nurse per month was 15.3 patients in the "busiest" district, and 9.9 patients in the least busy, a 35% discrepancy. Because frequent re-solving of the districting problem presents administrative challenges, the authors suggest that a dynamic patient to nurse assignment approach that considers both the district boundaries and current nurse workload should be developed.

Lahrichi and Hertz (2009) developed such an approach to address the shortcomings, a static districting solution presents. Instead of solving a districting problem, they take a districting solution as input, and solve a patient to nurse assignment problem in which nurses are allowed to travel outside of the district to which they are assigned to visit patients. A weighted objective function is used to minimize overload (the amount by which a target is exceeded) according to three nurse workload measures: case load, visit load, and travel load. Case load is a function of the number of patients in each category assigned to a nurse, where patient categories differ according to the amount of nurse effort required. Visit load is a weighted sum of the visits a nurse must perform, where each visit is weighted by its complexity. Travel load measures the number of visits a nurse performs outside of his or her assigned district, and weighs each associated visit according to an approximation of the travel distance required. The authors formulate the multi-objective problem as a mixed integer program with nonlinear constraints and a quadratic objective. A tabu search procedure is developed where the allowable local search moves involve changing the assignments for single or multiple patients and nurses. Computational experiments suggest it is possible to reduce the case loads and visit loads of nurses if the nurses are allowed to visit patients in nearby districts. The approach is cited as an alternative to frequent re-solving of the home health nurse districting problem.

11.3.3 Home Health Supply Chain

Studies in the operations research literature that focus on the home health supply chain are few. In Chahed et al. (2000), an operations planning problem encountered in the home chemotherapy supply chain is studied. The application is relevant in the French health care system, where patients can elect to receive chemotherapy in their homes, but the drugs must be prepared in specific, licensed facilities. The drugs that are administered have short shelf-lives and are highly individualized for each patient, complicating the joint production–distribution planning problem. The authors present a model and solution approach that can be used to minimize production and delivery costs when only a single nurse route may be used to distribute and administer the drugs. They describe model extensions that incorporate various capacity constraints and patient service considerations, such as multiple nurses, patient time windows, and patient priorities corresponding to urgency of care.

Supply chain practices frequently employed by home health care agencies are characterized in Bennett and Mason (2011). In 2010, the authors administered a survey to 132 home care agencies nationwide in order to determine how product and information flow through the home health supply chain, and how various home health supply chain configurations perform. It was discovered that 50% of responding agencies act as intermediaries in the distribution channels of their respective supply chains. As described in Sect. 11.2.3, the implication is that nurses become involved in non-clinical supply chain responsibilities such as picking and delivering supplies to patients. As evidence, 40% of responding agencies report that their nurses visit the agency at least three times per week to obtain supplies.

11.4 Recent Developments

New technologies are emerging that have the potential to impact the way in which home health care is delivered. Remote monitoring devices, sometimes referred to as telehealth devices, collect biometric data from patients in their homes and transmit it to remote servers, where it can be accessed and reviewed by health care professionals. The systems can also send patient reminders and provide patient education. Thus, the devices provide continuous access to health care services, and facilitate patient communication with their caregivers via tools such as videoconferencing. These devices have been shown to increase operational efficiency and improve care outcomes. In a survey conducted by Fazzi Associates and Philips regarding the impact of telehealth in the home care industry, 49.7% of responding agencies reported a decrease in the number of in home visits performed as a result of telehealth adoption, and 88.6% reported an increase in quality outcomes (Fazzi and Ashe 2008). If telehealth videoconferences replace a number of in home visits to each patient, or to qualified patients, an agency can provide care to a larger number of patients without increasing their mobile nurse workforce. Nursing capacity must be allocated to monitoring the incoming transmissions and conducting videoconferences, but time spent traveling is eliminated. Despite the potential benefits of telehealth, reimbursement has been identified as a top barrier to implementation, according to a survey of health care decision makers conducted by Intel (Burt 2010). Many health insurance providers do not reimburse home care agencies for the devices they distribute to enrolled patients, nor the health care providers conducting the videoconferences. Developments regarding telehealth reimbursement in home health care should be closely monitored, as models presented in Sect. 11.2 do not currently incorporate the option to use such devices.

11.5 Applications and Results

In this section, applications and results found in the literature for the operational problem of routing and scheduling nurses and the tactical problem of developing home health nurse service districts are presented.

11.5.1 Home Health Nurse Routing and Scheduling

Results from the HHNRS literature summarized in Table 11.2 are described in this section. Each paper reviewed solves the daily scheduling problem of assigning visits to nurses and optimizing individual nurse routes.

The spatial decision support system developed in Begur et al. (1997) enables schedulers at home health agencies to interact with a GIS-based automatic scheduling tool to assign patient visits to nurses and develop nurse routes, with the objective of minimizing total travel. The system was implemented for a home health agency with a 2700 square mile service region, 40 patient visits per day, and seven nurses. Savings resulting from system implementation are estimated as $20,000 per year, including travel costs, nurse staffing requirements, and paperwork time and cost.

The decision support system developed in Eveborn et al. (2006) also enables users to interact with a GIS-based software tool to create daily nurse schedules. The daily scheduling problem is solved with the objective of minimizing travel time and penalty costs associated with violation of properties such as time windows and nurse continuity. The system was implemented for a home health agency with 28 employees of seven skill levels and 150 patients distributed throughout a 1.2 square mile region. The heuristic approach based on repeated matching obtains solutions in under 3 min on a standard 700 MHz PC. When compared with solutions produced manually, the software achieves 20% travel savings and reduces operational planning time by an estimated 7%.

The optimization component of an additional home health nurse scheduling software is described in Bertels and Fahle (2006). A combination of tabu search (TS), simulated annealing (SA), and constraint programing (CP) methods are used to assign nurses to visits and optimize individual routes. Results are presented for a variety of test instances with 80–200 patients, 200–600 visits per day, and 20–50 nurses that work between 5 and 9 h/day. Durations for patient visits range from 6 to 72 min, and have associated time windows up to 3 h width. The test instances are run on a Pentium III-933 PC with 512 MB RAM. Initial feasible solutions specifying routes for each nurse are obtained using CP in less than 2 min on average. When SA and TS are initialized without a feasible solution, they either produce no feasible solution, or worse solutions than CP. When SA and TS are allowed to improve an initial feasible solution from CP until a total runtime of 900 s is reached, TS terminates with an improving solution in all instances, while SA only terminates with improving solutions in 8 out of 12 sets of instances.

A particle swarm optimization (PSO) construction and improvement heuristic is used in Akjiratikarl et al. (2007) to assign visits to nurses and optimize nurse routes, such that travel is minimized and capacity and time window constraints are not violated. The authors test the heuristic on five instances with 100 visits per day, 50 patients, and 12 nurses. Test instances were run on a Pentium M processor with 1.6 GHz CPU speed and 512 MB RAM. In approximately 3.5 min on average, the PSO algorithm produces solutions that achieve 11 to 31% travel savings when compared with manually prepared solutions. The PSO algorithm also outperforms solutions produced using a previously developed proprietary software.

11.5.2 Home Health Nurse Districting

Three of the papers described in Sect. 11.3.2 present computational results for the models and corresponding solution approaches developed for HHND and related problems. The model developed in Blais et al. (2003) utilizes a weighted objective function that includes a travel-minimizing and workload-balancing component. A tabu search heuristic is used to divide a service region containing 36 subunits into 6 districts. The heuristic produces a solution in less than 300 CPU seconds on a Sun Enterprise 10000 (400 MHz). The authors compare the heuristic solution to one developed manually, and determine the distribution of workload is more uniform in the heuristic solution. The mean number of annual home visits performed per district in both solutions is 5201, while the standard deviation is 872 visits for the manual solution and 111 for the heuristic solution. The authors also report that travel time per district, expressed as a percentage of daily workload, is reduced from 18% in the manual solution to 16% in the heuristic solution.

The model developed in Bennett (2009) approximates HHND solution cost as the total expecting daily routing costs in all districts. Workload balancing is addressed through lower and upper bound constraints on time spent with patients plus expected time spent traveling in each district. A heuristic combining ideas from column generation and neighborhood search is used to divide a 5500 square mile service region comprised of 156 subunits into 32 districts, each to be staffed by a team of five nurses. Solutions are compared to those produced using a local search heuristic. When workload is constrained to be within ±10% of target expected workload, the column generation based heuristic is able to improve an initial feasible solution by 9.3%, and outperforms the local search heuristic by 4.8%. When workload bounds are relaxed, such that workload must be within ±15% of the target, expected daily routing costs are reduced by an additional 1.3%. With less strict workload balancing requirements, the column generation based heuristic again outperforms the local search heuristic, producing solutions with 5.6% lower expected daily routing costs. For both heuristics, solutions are obtained in <3 min for all instances.

The problem solved by Lahrichi and Hertz (2009) is a patient to nurse assignment problem, so the results cannot be directly compared to HHND solutions obtained in Blais et al. (2003) and Bennett (2009). A mixed integer program is used to assign patients to nurses with the objective of minimizing a weighted sum of three workload measures: case load, visit load, and travel load. A tabu search heuristic is developed to obtain solutions for a number of instances that each have two resource types and five patient types. The largest instance is comprised of 26 nurses, 36 subunits, six districts, and 1413 patients. To enable comparison of heuristic solutions with optimal values, the authors first solve instances with no case load constraints (the resulting model is linear) using CPLEX. The solutions produced by CPLEX and the tabu search heuristic are very similar, especially when travel load is heavily weighted in the objective function. An interesting insight from the computational study is that visit overload can be almost eliminated when nurses are allowed to perform visits in districts to which they are not assigned. This comes at a cost of increased travel, but the amount is difficult to quantify, because the authors measure travel load as a function of number of trips to adjacent subunits without providing actual distances. When the tabu search heuristic is used to solve instances that include case load constraints, it is observed that case load balancing can be achieved without too much expense in terms of travel load or visit load imbalance.

11.6 Future Directions

Future research directions are identified in the categories of logistics planning problems, work measurement, and design of incentive schemes.

11.6.1 Logistics Planning Problems

Of the problems presented in this chapter, the operational planning problem of home health nurse routing and scheduling has received the most attention in the literature. However, no study to date has simultaneously considered the nurse assignment and visit time assignment problems while addressing the dynamic, periodic, and consistent aspects of resulting routing problems. A possible explanation for this apparent gap in the literature is the lack of consensus among health care providers regarding how nurse and time consistency should be modeled. For example, is it preferable to minimize the *number* of different visit windows assigned to a patient throughout their duration of care, or instead to minimize the *maximum difference* between any two visit windows; i.e., which alternative in the

Table 11.3 Evaluating visit window consistency for example three-visit patient

Option	# windows assigned	Difference between windows (h)
{0800-0900, 0800-0900, 1600-1700}	2	8
{0800-0900, 0900-1000, 1000-1100}	3	2

example in Table 11.3 is preferred? And, is nurse consistency strictly preferred over time consistency, or is there an acceptable trade off between the two objectives? Posing these questions to various home care agencies may result in different answers, as the industry is highly segmented and agencies tend to be unique in their operations. For example, some agencies allow their nurses to self schedule patient visits, while others do not. In order for models and solution methods developed by the scientific community to be most applicable, the extent to which nurse and visit window consistency are prioritized must be better understood. To this end, research that surveys home health agencies and patients to determine preferences, or clinical research that determines the impact of home health nurse consistency on patient care outcomes, could be useful in guiding future research. Furthermore, a comprehensive routing and scheduling tool with the flexibility to evaluate various consistency policies and their impact on nurse efficiency would provide important information to home health planners as they develop operating policies.

11.6.2 Work Measurement

Work measurement studies are needed to describe how home health nurses spend time during the workdays. Average home health care staff productivity, as measured by visits per day, is 4.95 for Registered Nurses and 6.02 for Licensed Practical Nurses (NAHC 2007). Average visit length ranges between 30 and 60 min, depending on visit and patient characteristics (Payne et al. 1998). The remaining portion of the home health nurse workday comprises tasks such as driving, completing documentation, engaging in case management and follow-up, and performing supply chain related duties. Quantifying time per day home care nurses spend on each type of task would provide useful input for the models described in Sect. 11.2. For example, home health nurse districting models described in Sect. 11.2.2 often constrain nurse workload per district to be within allowable bounds. The total amount of time nurses spend working per day would provide a more accurate approximation of workload than simple measures such as patient visit count. Also, models for evaluating the cost of various supply chain configurations, described in Sect. 11.2.3, require an estimate of nurse time spent performing supply chain duties.

11.6.3 Design of Incentive Schemes

As a primary provider of post-acute care, home health care is uniquely positioned to engage in partnerships with hospitals and other acute care providers to coordinate care delivery. Effective incentive schemes are needed to facilitate these collaborations. In a 2010 survey sponsored by Wyatt Matas & Associates, home care providers and industry leaders were asked to choose the biggest opportunities for home care to elevate its position within the health care continuum from a list of options. Three of the most frequent selections were chronic care and disease management, reimbursement for post-episode care management, and reimbursement for telehealth (Matas 2010). Various initiatives are included in the Patient Protection and Affordable Care Act of 2010 for the creation of innovative payment models that encourage collaboration and integration across the health care continuum. Beginning in 2013, Medicare payments to hospitals with high rates of preventable readmissions for heart attack, heart failure, and pneumonia patients will be reduced (Berenson and Zuckerman 2010). Studies have shown that using home health to assist with the daily management of chronic disease decreases risk for hospitalizations (Hughes et al. 1997). Thus, hospitals may turn increasingly to home care agencies to manage post-discharge patient care in an attempt to reduce readmissions. Additionally, Centers for Medicare and Medicaid Services is piloting a bundled payment system for an episode of care that begins three days before a hospitalization and ends 30 days after discharge (Berenson and Zuckerman 2010). Research addressing the design of incentive schemes is needed to determine the appropriate sharing of revenue in bundled payment systems.

References

AHRQ (2007) National and regional estimates on hospital use for all patients from the HCUP nationwide inpatient sample (NIS): 2007 outcomes by patient and hospital characteristics for all discharges. http://hcupnet.ahrq.gov/HCUPnet.jsp. Accessed 4 November 2009

Akjiratikarl C, Yenradee P, Drake P (2007) PSO-based algorithm for home care worker scheduling in the UK. Comput Ind Eng 53:559–583

Begur S, Miller D, Weaver J (1997) An integrated spatial DSS for scheduling and routing home health care nurses. Interfaces 27:35–48

Bennett AR (2009) Home health care logistics planning. Dissertation, Georgia Institute of Technology, USA

Bennett AR, Erera A (2011) Dynamic periodic fixed appointment scheduling for home health. IIE Trans Healthc Syst Eng 1(1):6

Bennett AR, Mason S (2011) Characterizing the home health supply chain. Working paper CIHL HH 11-01, Center for Innovation in health care Logistics. University of Arkansas, USA

Berenson R, Zuckerman S (2010) How will hospitals be affected by health care reform? Timely analysis of immediate health policy issues. Robert Wood Johnson Foundation, Princeton

Bertels S, Fahle T (2006) A hybrid setup for a hybrid scenario: combining heuristics for the home health care problem. Comput Oper Res 33:2866–2890

Blais M, Lapierre S, Laporte G (2003) Solving a home care districting problem in an urban setting. J Oper Res Soc 54:1141–1147

Bozkaya B, Erkut E, Laporte G (2003) A tabu search heuristic and adaptive memory procedure for political districting. Eur J Oper Res 144:12–26

Buerhaus P, Staiger D, Auerbach D (2000) Implications of an aging registered nurse workforce. J Am Med Assoc 283:2948–2954

Burt J (2010) Intel survey shows positive impact of telehealth technology. http://www.eweek.com/c/a/Enterprise-Networking/Intel-Survey-See-Positive-Imp act-of-Teleheath-Technology-469358/. Accessed May 2010

Cabana MD, Jee SH (2004) Does continuity of care improve patient outcomes. J Fam Pract 53(12):974

Caro F, Shirabe T, Guignard M, Weintraub A (2004) School redistricting: embedding GIS tools with integer programming. J Oper Res Soc 55:836–849

CDC (2009) At a glance 2009: chronic disease—the power to prevent, the call to control. Technical report Centers for Disease Control and Prevention. National Center for Chronic Disease Prevention and Health Promotion, Atlanta

Chahed S, Marcon E, Sahin E, Feillet D, Dallery Y (2000) Exploring new operational research opportunities within the home care context : the chemotherapy at home. Health Care Manage Sci 12(2):171–191

CMS (2008) Home health quality initiatives. Technical report. Centers for Medicare and Medicaid Services, 7500 Security Boulevard, Baltimore MD, 21244

D'Amico S, Wang SJ, Batta R, Rump C (2002) A simulated annealing approach to police district design. Comput Oper Res 29:667–684

Eveborn P, Flisberg P, Ronnqvist M (2006) LAPS CARE—an operational system for staff planning of home care. Eur J Oper Res 171:962–976

Fazzi R, Ashe T (2008) National study on the future of technology and telehealth in home care. Philips and Fazzi Associates, USA

Ferenc J (2010) Time well spent? Assessing nursing supply-chain activities. Mater Manag Health Care 19(2):12–16

Garfinkel R, Nemhauser G (1970) Optimal political districting by implicit enumeration techniques. Manag Sci 16(8):B495–B508

Groer C, Golden B, Wasil E (2009) The consistent vehicle routing problem. Manuf Serv Oper Manag 11(4):630

Haugland D, Ho S, Laporte G (2007) Designing delivery districts for the vehicle routing problem with stochastic demands. Eur J Oper Res 180:997–1010

Hess SW, Samuels SA (1971) Experiences with a sales districting model: criteria and implementation. Manag Sci 18(4):41–54

Hess S, Weaver J, Siegfeldt H, Whelan J, Zitlau PA (1965) Non-partisan political redistricting by computer. Oper Res 13:998–1006

Hojati M (1996) Optimal political districting. Comput Oper Res 23(12):1147–1161

Hughes SL, Ulasevich A, Weaver FM, Henderson W, Manheim L, Kubal JD, Bonarigo F (1997) Impact of home care on hospital days: a meta analysis. Health Serv Res 32(4):415–432

King C (2010) To your health: Intel and GE's joint venture. http://www.ecommercetimes.com/. Accessed 30 August 2010

Lahrichi N, Hertz A (2009) A patient assignment algorithm for home care services. J Oper Res Soc 60(4):481–495

Lahrichi N, Lapierre S, Hertz A, Talib A, Bouvier L (2006) Analysis of a territorial approach to the delivery of nursing home care services based on historical data. J Med Syst 30(4):283

Matas (2010) Survey for envisioning the future of homecare. Technical report, Wyatt Matas and Associates, 1776 I Street NW, 9th Floor, 20006, Washington

Mehrotra A, Johnson E, Nemhauser G (1998) An optimization based heuristic for political districting. Manag Sci 44(8):1100–1114

Nachtmann H, Pohl E (2009) The state of health care logistics: cost and quality improvement opportunities. Technical report, Center for Innovation in Health care Logistics, University of Arkansas, USA

NAHC (2006) Home care profit margins update. Technical report, National Association for Home Care and Hosipce, Washington, DC

NAHC (2007) Basic statistics about home care. Technical report, National Association for Home Care and Hospice, 228 Seventh St SE, 20033, Washington

NAHC (2009) Study shows home health care workers drive nearly five billion miles to serve elderly and disabled patients. Technical report, National Association for Home Care and Hospice, 228 Seventh St SE, 2003, Washington

Payne S, Thomas C, Fitzpatrick T, Abdel-Rahman M, Kayne H (1998) Determinants of home health visit length: results of a multisite prospective study. Med Care 36(10):1500–1514

Ricca F, Simeone B (2008) Local search algorithms for political districting. Eur J Oper Res 189:1409–1426

Rich J (1999) A computational study of vehicle routing applications. PhD dissertation, Rice University, USA

Steeg JM (2008) Mathematical models and algorithms for home care services. PhD dissertation, Fraunhofer Institute for Industrial Mathematics

Steven H, Landers MD (2010) Why health care is going home. New Engl J Med 363:1690–1691

Super N (2002) Who will be there to give care? The growing gap between caregiver supply and demand. White paper, National Health Policy Forum of The George Washington University, Washington, DC

UPS (2009) UPS corporate responsibility: a commitment to safety, every day. http://responsibility.ups.com/safety/index.html. Accessed 3 November 2009

US (2004) Projected population of the united states, by age and sex. http://www.census.gov/population/www/projections/usinterimproj. Accessed 27 April 2011

Zoltners A, Sinha P (1983) Sales territory alignment: a review and model. Manag Sci 29(11):1237

Chapter 12
A Framework for Healthcare Planning and Control

Erwin W. Hans, Mark van Houdenhoven and Peter J. H. Hulshof

Abstract Rising expenditures spur health care organizations to organize their processes more efficiently and effectively. Unfortunately, health care planning and control lags behind manufacturing planning and control. We analyze the existing planning and control concepts or frameworks for health care operations management and find that they do not address various important planning and control problems. We conclude that they only focus on hospitals and are too narrow, focusing on a single managerial area, such as resource capacity planning, or ignoring hierarchical levels. We propose a modern framework for health care planning and control that integrates all managerial areas in health care delivery operations and all hierarchical levels of control, to ensure completeness and coherence of responsibilities for every managerial area. The framework can be used to structure the various planning and control functions and their interaction. It is applicable to an individual department, an entire health care organization, and to a complete supply chain of cure and care providers. The framework can be used to identify and position various types of managerial problems, to demarcate the scope of organization interventions and to facilitate a dialogue between clinical staff and managers.

E. W. Hans (✉) · P. J. H. Hulshof
Department Operational Methods for Production & Logistics, Center for Health Care Operations Improvement & Research, University of Twente, Enschede, the Netherlands
e-mail: rwhall@usc.edu

M. van Houdenhoven
Haga Ziekenhuis, Den Haag, the Netherlands

P. J. H. Hulshof
Reinier de Graaf Groep, Delft, the Netherlands

R. Hall (ed.), *Handbook of Healthcare System Scheduling*,
International Series in Operations Research & Management Science 168,
DOI: 10.1007/978-1-4614-1734-7_12,

12.1 Introduction

Planning and control in health care have received an increased amount of attention over the last 10 years, both in practice and in the literature due to an increase in demand for health care and increasing expenditures (OECD 2011). As a result, health care organizations are trying to re-organize processes for efficiency and effectiveness. It is therefore not surprising that the Operations Research/ Management Science (OR/MS) research community's interest in health care applications is rapidly increasing (Brailsford et al. 2009). In fact, the attendance in the conference of the EURO Working Group on Operational Research Applied to Health Services (ORAHS 2011) has increased from around 50 in 2002 to 150 in 2009, and involves an increasing number of countries. Within these research efforts, planning and control is a key focal area—the subject of more than 35% of the ORAHS publications (Brailsford and Vissers 2010). INFORMS recently organized the first conference on health care, presenting over 400 abstracts in a variety of OR health care topics.

Planning and control has a rich tradition in manufacturing. Graves (2002) states that "Manufacturing planning and control address decisions on the acquisition, utilization and allocation of production resources to satisfy customer requirements in the most efficient and effective way." Planning and control comprises integrated coordination of resources (staff, equipment and materials) and product flows, in such a way that the organization's objectives are realized (Anthony 1965).

health care planning and control lags behind manufacturing planning and control. Common reasons stated in the literature include:

1. Health Care organizations are professional organizations that often lack cooperation between, or commitment from, involved parties (doctors, administrators, etc.). These groups have their own, sometimes conflicting, objectives, as is nicely illustrated by Glouberman and Mintzberg in their "four faces of health care" framework (2001a, b).
2. Due to the state of information systems in health care, crucial information required for planning and control is often not available (Carter 2002). Although Diagnosis Related Groups (DRGs) and electronic health record systems have spurred the need for *financial* and *clinical* information management systems, these systems tend to be poorly integrated with *operational* information systems. This lack of integration is impeding the advance of integrated planning and control in health care, both organization-wide and between organizations. This was recognized already by Roth and Van Dierdonck (1995), but developments until now have been slow (Khoumbati et al. 2006).
3. Since large health care providers, such as hospitals, generally consist of autonomously managed departments, managers tend not to look beyond the border of their department, and planning and control is fragmented (Roth and Van Dierdonck 1995, Porter and Teisberg 2007).
4. The Hippocratic Oath taken by doctors forces them to focus on the patient at hand, whereas planning and control addresses the entire patient population,

both within and beyond the scope of an individual doctor (Maynard 1991, 1994).

5. While health care managers are generally dedicated to provide the best possible service, they lack the knowledge and training to make the best use of the available resources (Carter 2002).
6. As health care managers often feel that investing in better administration diverts funds from direct patient care (Carter 2002), managerial functions are often ill-defined, overlooked, poorly addressed, or functionally dispersed.

In this chapter we propose and demonstrate a hierarchical framework for health care planning and control to help overcome the aforementioned problems. This framework serves as a tool to structure and break down all functions of health care planning and control. In addition, it can be used to identify planning and control problems and to demarcate the scope of organization interventions. It is applicable broadly, from an individual hospital department to an entire hospital, or to a complete supply chain of care providers. The framework facilitates a dialogue between clinical staff and managers to design the planning and control mechanisms. These mechanisms are necessary to translate the organization's objectives into effective and efficient health care delivery processes (Delesie 1998). It covers all managerial areas involved in health care delivery operations and all levels of control, to ensure completeness and coherence of responsibilities for every managerial area.

We will argue in Sect. 12.2 that while frameworks for planning and control do exist in the literature, they mostly focus on one managerial area—in particular resource capacity planning or materials planning—and mostly only focus on hospitals. The contribution of our framework is that it encompasses all managerial areas, including those typically overlooked by others. In particular, *medical planning* (i.e. decision making by clinicians) and *financial planning* should not be overlooked when health care delivery processes are to be redesigned or optimized. Another contribution of the framework is its hierarchical decomposition of managerial levels, which is an extension of the classical strategic-tactical-operational breakdown (Anthony 1965), often used in manufacturing. Finally, while most frameworks focus on hospitals, our framework can be applied to any type of health care delivery organization.

This chapter is organized as follows. Section 12.2 outlines the literature on frameworks for planning and control. Section 12.3 presents the generic framework for health care planning and control. Section 12.4 describes how to identify managerial problems with the framework, and demonstrates its application. Section 12.5 presents our conclusions. Finally, Sect. 12.6 ends this book with an outlook.

12.2 Literature on Frameworks for Planning and Control

In this section we give an overview of the state of the art in the literature of both manufacturing planning and control and health care planning and control. We also discuss the strengths and weaknesses of the existing frameworks.

Almost all well-known frameworks for manufacturing planning and control (MPC) organize planning and control functions hierarchically. It reflects the natural process of increasing disaggregation in decision making as time progresses, and more information becomes available (Zijm 2000). It also reflects the hierarchical (department) structure of most organizations (Butler et al. 1996). Many MPC frameworks use the hierarchical decomposition into a strategic, tactical, and operational level, as first done by Anthony in 1965.

The classical MPC frameworks have a specific orientation on either *production planning* (e.g. hierarchical production planning; Hax and Meal 1975), or *technological (or process) planning* (e.g. computer aided process planning; Marri et al. 1998), or *material planning* (e.g. Material Requirements Planning (MRP); Orlicky 1975). As argued by Zijm (2000), this myopic orientation to one managerial area is the main cause that these MPC frameworks are inadequate in practice. Modern MPC frameworks integrate these orientations: the frameworks of Zijm (2000) and Hans et al. (2003) are designed for integrated MPC in highly complex organizations, such as engineer-to-order manufacturers.

Various researchers have proposed frameworks for (hierarchical) planning and control in health care. In the remainder of this section, we give an overview of existing frameworks for health care planning and control.

First introduced by Rhyne and Jupp (1988), and later expanded on by Roth and Van Dierdonck (1995), two papers propose a hierarchical framework that is based on application of the Manufacturing Resource Planning (MRP-II) concept. This framework considers both resource capacity planning and material planning, and focuses specifically on hospitals. It relies on Diagnostic Related Groups (DRGs), which serve as the "bill of materials" in MRP-II, to derive the resource and material requirements of patient groups. Roth and Van Dierdonck (1995) propose to use DRGs to facilitate integrated hospital-wide planning and control. Vissers and Beech (2005) criticize this framework, and argue that although DRGs are an excellent tool to market and finance hospitals, they are not a good basis for logistical control and managing day-to-day operations.

Vissers et al. (2001) propose a framework for production control in hospitals based on the design requirements of De Vries et al. (1999). The approach assumes the common situation that a hospital is organized in relatively independent business units. It is limited to resource capacity planning, for which it distinguishes five hierarchical levels: *strategic planning*, *patient volumes planning and control*, *resources planning and control*, *patient group planning*, and *patient planning and control*. These levels address "offline" (in advance) decision making. "Online" (reactive) operational control functions such as reactive planning (for example, add-on scheduling upon arrival of an emergency case) and monitoring are not considered in their framework.

Butler et al. (1992) emphasize that due to the differing complexity and information requirements of the various decisions, organizational planning processes are commonly hierarchical in nature. The first step, on a strategic level, involves strategy formation, process layout design, and long-term capacity dimensioning. Subsequent steps relate increasingly to operational concerns, with a decreasing planning horizon and increasing information availability. The hierarchical levels of control are linked: for example long-term capacity dimensioning decisions shape the capacity restrictions for subsequent operational decision making. The performance, which is measured at an operational level, is the result of how well the various hierarchical planning activities are integrated. In another paper, Butler et al. (1996) indicate that the literature neglects cooperation between different managerial areas at the strategic level of hospital planning and control. They argue that to attain exceptional operational performance, it is important that the hospital's strategy consistently and coherently integrates operations issues from areas such as *Finance, Marketing, Operations,* and *Human Resources*.

Blake and Carter (1997) focus on an operating theatre setting, for which they propose a hierarchical framework for resource planning and appointment scheduling with three hierarchical levels: *strategic*, *administrative* (tactical), and *operational* planning.

We conclude that all existing frameworks for health care planning and control focus on hospitals, and are hierarchical in nature. However, like many MPC frameworks they also focus on just one managerial area—mostly resource capacity planning. Integration of managerial areas is neglected, as well as the reactive decision functions, which are important given the inherently stochastic nature of health care processes. Modern MPC frameworks (Zijm 2000, Hans et al. 2003), however, address multiple managerial areas as well as the three well-known hierarchical levels of control. These frameworks were designed for engineer-to-order or manufacture-to-order environments, where uniquely specified products are produced on demand. In this aspect, these environments resemble health care delivery. Therefore, these MPC frameworks offer a sound basis for our framework for health care planning and control. However, for application in health care, they require significant modification. In the following section, we introduce our generic framework.

12.3 A Generic Framework for Healthcare Planning and Control

We propose a four-by-four generic framework for health care planning and control that spans four hierarchical levels of control, and four managerial areas. We first discuss the managerial areas (Sect. 12.3.1), and then the hierarchical decomposition (Sect. 12.3.2). We then combine these two dimensions to form the framework for health care planning and control (Sect. 12.3.3). Finally, we discuss the context of the framework and how it affects the content (Sect. 12.3.4).

12.3.1 Managerial Areas

As outlined in Sect. 12.2, most existing frameworks in the literature focus on one managerial area. We propose to include multiple managerial areas for health care planning and control, specifically: *medical planning*, *resource capacity planning*, *materials planning*, and *financial planning*. We describe these areas in more detail below.

Medical Planning

The role of engineers/process planners in manufacturing is performed by clinicians in health care. We refer to health care's version of "technological planning" as *medical planning.* Medical planning comprises decision making by clinicians regarding for example medical protocols, treatments, diagnoses, and triage. It also comprises development of new medical treatments by clinicians. The more complex and unpredictable the health care processes, the more autonomy is required for clinicians. For example, activities in acute care are necessarily planned by clinicians, whereas in elective care (e.g. ambulatory surgery), standardized and predictable activities can be planned centrally by management.

Resource Capacity Planning

Resource capacity planning addresses the dimensioning, planning, scheduling, monitoring, and control of *renewable* resources. These include equipment and facilities (e.g. MRIs, physical therapy equipment, bed linen, sterile instruments, operating theatres, rehabilitation rooms), as well as staff.

Materials Planning

Materials planning addresses the acquisition, storage, distribution and retrieval of all *consumable* resources/materials, such as suture materials, prostheses, blood, bandages, food, etc. Materials planning typically encompasses functions such as warehouse design, inventory management, and purchasing.

Financial Planning

Financial planning addresses how an organization should manage its costs and revenues to achieve its objectives under current and future organizational and economic circumstances. Since health care spending has been increasing steadily (OECD 2011), market mechanisms are being introduced in many countries as an incentive to encourage cost-efficient health care delivery (e.g. Westert et al. 2009). An example is the introduction of DRGs, which enables the comparison of care products and their prices. As health care systems differ per country, so does financial planning in health care organizations. As financial planning heavily influences the way the processes are organized and managed, we include this managerial area in our framework. For example, Wachtel and Dexter (2008) argue that in the US, the tactical allocation of temporary expansions in operating theatre capacity should be based on the contribution margin of the involved surgical (sub)specialties. This criterion is not likely to be used in countries with a non-competitive health care system, such as the UK or the Netherlands. Financial planning in health care concerns functions such as investment planning, contracting (e.g. with health care insurers), budget and cost allocation, accounting, cost price calculation, and billing.

We have selected medical planning, resource capacity planning, materials planning and financial planning four managerial areas, as we consider them relevant in all our research projects that revolve around optimization of health care operations (CHOIR 2011).

12.3.2 Hierarchical Decomposition

As argued in Sect. 12.2, decision making disaggregates as time progresses and information gradually becomes available. We build upon the "classical" hierarchical decomposition often used in manufacturing planning and control, which discerns *strategic*, *tactical*, and *operational* levels of control (Anthony 1965). We extend this decomposition by discerning between *offline* and *online* on the *operational level*. This distinction reflects the difference between "in advance" decision making and "reactive" decision making. We explain the resulting four hierarchical levels below, where the tactical level is explained last. The tactical level is often considered less tangible than the strategic and operational levels, as we will further explain in Sect. 12.4. Therefore, we explain the more tangible levels first, before addressing the tactical level.

We do not explicitly state a decision horizon length for any of the hierarchical planning levels, since these depend on the specific characteristics of the application. An emergency department for example inherently has shorter planning horizons than a long-stay ward in a nursing home.

Strategic Level

Strategic planning addresses structural decision making. These decisions are the bricks and mortar of an organization (Li et al. 2002). It involves defining the organization's mission (i.e. "strategy" or "direction"), and the decision making to translate this mission into the design, dimensioning, and development of the health care delivery process. Inherently, strategic planning has a long planning horizon and is based on highly aggregated information and forecasts. Examples of strategic planning are resource capacity expansions (e.g. acquisition of MRI machines), developing and/or implementing new medical protocols, forming a purchasing consortium, a merger of nursing homes, and contracting with health insurers.

Offline Operational Level

Operational planning (both "offline" and "online") involves the short-term decision making related to the execution of the health care delivery process. There is low flexibility on this planning level, since many decisions on higher levels have demarcated the scope for the operational level decision making. The adjective "offline" reflects that this planning level concerns the *in advance* planning of operations. It comprises the detailed coordination of the activities regarding current (elective) demand. Examples of offline operational planning are: treatment selection, appointment scheduling, nurse rostering, inventory replenishment ordering, and billing.

Online Operational Level

The stochastic nature of health care processes demands *reactive* decision making. "Online" operational planning involves control mechanisms that deal with monitoring the process and reacting to unforeseen or unanticipated events. Examples of online planning functions are: triaging, add-on scheduling of emergencies, replenishing depleted inventories, rush ordering surgery instrument sterilization, handling billing complications.

Tactical Level

In between the strategic level, which sets the stage (e.g. regarding location and size), and the operational level, which addresses the execution of the processes, lies the tactical planning level. We explain tactical planning in relation to strategic and operational planning.

While strategic planning addresses structural decision making, tactical planning addresses the organization of the operations/execution of the health care delivery process (i.e. the "what, where, how, when and who"). In this way, it is similar to operational planning; however, decisions are made on a longer planning horizon. The length of this intermediate planning horizon lies somewhere between the strategic planning horizon and operational planning horizon. Following the concept of hierarchical planning, intermediate tactical planning has more flexibility than operational planning, is less detailed, and has less demand certainty. Conversely, the opposite is true when compared to strategic planning.

For example, while capacity is fixed in operational planning, temporary capacity expansions like overtime or hiring staff are possible in tactical planning. Also, while demand is largely known in operational planning, it has to be (partly) forecasted for tactical planning, based on (seasonal) demand, waiting list information, and the "downstream" demand in care pathways of patients currently under treatment. Due to this demand uncertainty, tactical planning is less detailed than operational planning (consider for example block planning vs. appointment

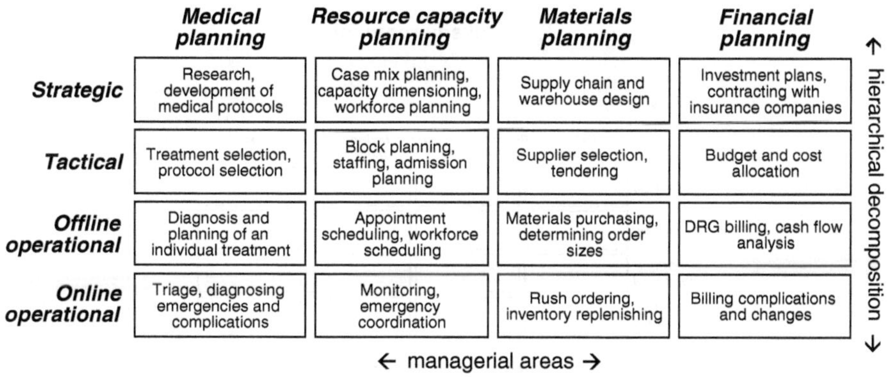

Fig. 12.1 Example application of the framework for health care planning and control to a general hospital

scheduling). Examples of tactical functions are admission planning, block planning, treatment selection, supplier selection, and budget allocation.

12.3.3 Framework for Healthcare Planning and Control

Integrating the four managerial areas and the four hierarchical levels of control shapes a four-by-four positioning framework for health care planning and control. While the dimensions of the framework are generic, the content depends on the application at hand. The framework can be applied anywhere from the department level (for example to an operating theatre department) to organization-wide, or to a complete supply chain of care providers. Depending on the context, the content of the framework may be very different. Figure 12.1 shows the content of the framework when applied to a general hospital as a whole. The inserted planning and control functions are examples, and not exclusive.

12.3.4 Context of the Framework

As argued in the previous section, the content of the framework should be accommodated to the context of the application. Regarding the context we discern the internal and external environment characteristics.

The *internal* environment characteristics are scoped by the boundaries of the organization. This involves all characteristics that affect planning and control, regarding for example patient demand (e.g. variability, complexity, arrival intensity, medical urgency, recurrence), organizational culture and structure.

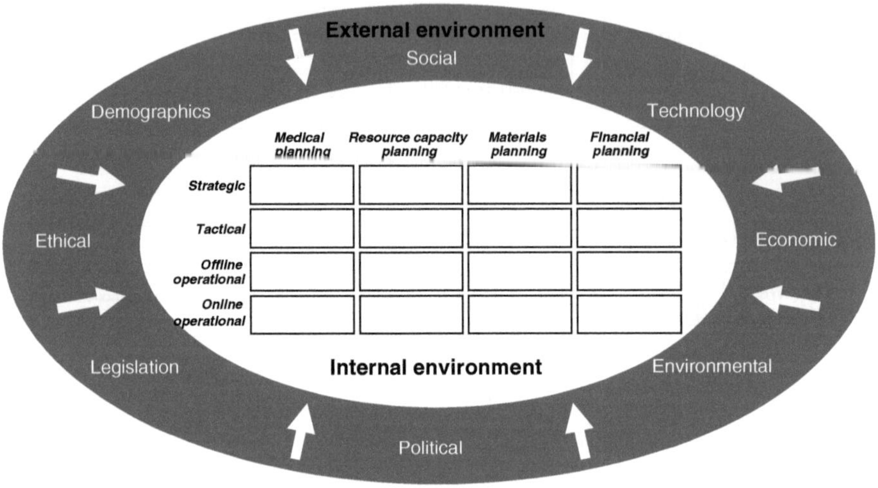

Fig. 12.2 The framework and the organization's external environment

The way health care organizations are organized is perhaps most influenced by their *external* environment. For example, a "STEEPLED" analysis (an extension of "PESTEL", see e.g. Johnson et al. 2008) can be done to identify external factors that influence health care planning and control, now or in the future. "STEEPLED" is an abbreviation for the following external environment factors:

- Social factors (e.g. education, social mobility, religious attitudes)
- Technology (e.g. medical innovation, transport infrastructure)
- Economic factors (e.g. change in health finance system)
- Environmental factors (e.g. ecological, recycling)
- Political factors (e.g. change of government policy, privatization)
- Legislation/Legal (e.g. business regulations, quality regulations)
- Ethical factors (e.g. business ethics, confidentiality, safety)
- Demographics (e.g. graying population, life expectancy, obesity)

These factors largely explain the differences amongst countries in the management approach of health care organizations. Figure 12.2 illustrates how the framework can be observed in light of the organization's external environment.

12.4 Application of the Framework

The primary objective of the framework is to structure the various planning and control functions. In this section, we give examples of how the framework can be applied. Section 12.4.1 discusses how the framework can be used to identify managerial deficiencies. Section 12.4.2 gives an example of an application of the framework to an integrated model for primary care outside office hours.

12.4.1 Identification of Managerial Deficiencies

Once the content of the framework has been established for a given application, further analysis of this content may identify managerial problems. In the remainder of this section, we discuss examples of four kinds of typical problems:

1. Deficient or lacking planning functions
2. Inappropriate planning approaches
3. Lack of coherence between planning functions
4. Planning functions that have conflicting objectives

Deficient or Absent Planning Functions

Overlooked or poorly addressed managerial functions can be encountered on all levels of control (Carter 2002), but are most often found on the tactical level of control (Roth and Van Dierdonck 1995). In fact, to many, tactical planning is less tangible than operational planning and even strategic planning. Inundated with operational problems, managers are inclined to solve problems *at hand* (i.e., on the operational level). We refer to this phenomenon as the "real-time hype" of managers. A claim for "more capacity" is the universal panacea for many health care managers. It is, however, often overlooked that instead of such drastic strategic measures, tactically allocating and organizing the available resources may be more effective and cheaper. Consider for example a "master schedule" or "block plan", which is the tactical allocation of blocks of resource time (e.g. operating theatres, or CT-scanners) to specialties and/or patient categories during a week. Such a block plan should be periodically revised to react to variations in supply and demand. However, in practice, it is more often a result of "historical development" than of analytical considerations (Vissers 1998).

An example of a deficient planning function is when autonomy is given to or assumed by the wrong staff member. We illustrate this with two examples: (1) Spurred by the Oath of Hippocrates, clinicians may try to 'cheat' the system to advance a patient. A clinician may for example admit an outpatient to a hospital bed to shorten access time for diagnostics (which is lower for inpatients). The resulting bed occupation may lead to operating room blocking. Although this may appear suboptimal from a central management point of view, it may be necessary from a medical point of view. The crux is to put the autonomy where it is actually needed. This depends on the application at hand. As argued earlier, the more complex and unpredictable the health care processes, the more the autonomy required for clinicians. Standardized and predictable activities can however be planned centrally by management, which is advantageous from an economies-of scale viewpoint. (2) Medical equipment shared by different departments is hoarded to ensure immediate availability (Dash 2009). This leads to excessive inventory (costs), which may be significantly reduced by centralizing equipment management and storage. A typical example is the hoarding of intravenous drips by wards.

Inappropriate Planning Approaches

There are many logistical paradigms, such as Just-In-Time (JIT), Kanban, Lean, Total Quality Management (TQM), and Six Sigma, all of which have reported success stories. As these paradigms are mostly developed for industry, they generally cannot be simply copied to health care without loss in fidelity. "The tendency to uncritically embrace a solution concept, developed for a rather specific manufacturing environment, as the panacea for a variety of other problems in totally different environments has led to many disappointments" (Zijm 2000). The structure provided by the framework helps to identify whether a planning approach is suitable for a planning function in a particular organizational environment. Planning approaches are only suitable if they fit the internal and external characteristics of the involved application. They have to be adapted to/designed for the characteristics that are unique for health care delivery, such as: (1) patient participation in the service process; (2) simultaneity of production and consumption; (3) perishable capacity; (4) intangibility of health care outputs; and (5) heterogeneity (Ozcan 2009).

Lack of Coherence Between Planning Functions

The effectiveness and efficiency of health care delivery is not only determined by how the various planning functions are addressed; this is also determined by how they interact. As health care providers such as hospitals are typically formed as a cluster of autonomous departments, planning is also often functionally dispersed. The framework structures planning functions, and provides insight in their horizontal (cross-management) and vertical (hierarchical) interactions. *Horizontal interaction* between managerial areas in the framework provides that required medical information and protocols, and all involved resources and materials, are brought together to enable both effective and efficient health care delivery. *Downward vertical interaction* concerns concretizing higher level objectives and decisions on a shorter planning horizon. For example, capacity dimensioning decisions on a strategic level (e.g. number of CT-scanners) impose hard restrictions on tactical and operational planning and scheduling. *Upward vertical interaction* concerns feedback about the realization of higher level objectives. For example the capacity of MRI machines is determined on the strategic level to attain a certain service level (e.g. access time). Feedback from the tactical and operational level is then needed to observe whether this objective is actually attained, and to advise to what extent the capacity is sufficient.

Planning Functions that Have Conflicting Objectives

As argued, the framework structures planning functions and their horizontal and vertical interactions. The framework can thus identify conflicting objectives between planning functions. For example, minimally invasive surgery generally results in significantly reduced length of stay in wards and improved quality of care, but results in higher costs and increased capacity consumption for the operating theatre department. These departments are often managed autonomously and independently, which leads to suboptimal decision making from both the patient's and the hospital's point of view.

Conflicting objectives also occur between two care providers in an inter-organizational care chain. For example, a nursing home's efforts to maximize occupancy may lead to bed blocking in hospitals. Aligning planning functions between health care organizations may identify and solve such problems.

12.4.2 Application of the Framework to Primary Care Outside Office Hours

In this section we give an example application of the framework. First we introduce the context: the concept of an integrated organization that provides primary care outside office hours. We then demonstrate how the framework can facilitate the discussion regarding the design of such an organization.

Introduction

The organization of primary care outside office hours, which involves telephone triage, urgent consultations, and house calls, has received increasing attention in many countries (Grol et al. 2006). In parts of Europe, general practitioners (GPs) are required by law to provide this type of care, and in some countries, GPs cooperate in primary care cooperatives (PCCs) to jointly provide primary care outside office hours. Within a PCC, the GPs can alternate who is responsible outside office hours. As a result, these GPs do not have to be available outside office hours at all times. As an alternative to the PCC, patients requiring primary care outside office hours can visit the emergency department (ED) of a hospital. Although EDs are intended for complex emergent care, they deal with a relatively large group of patients that could have been served by a GP. For example a study at King's College Hospital in the United Kingdom reports that 41% of patients visiting the ED could have been treated by a GP (Dale et al. 1996). It is more costly to serve these so-called 'self-referrals' at the ED. Therefore, methods are proposed to ensure these patients are served by GPs and do not visit an ED.

One of the proposed methods is an integrated model, where the PCC is located in close proximity to the ED, with a joint triage system. Integrated models are effective in the UK (Lattimer et al. 2005), and are also favored by the Netherlands as the appropriate system for emergency care (Van Uden et al. 2006). A survey showed that the integrated model significantly decreases the number of self-referrals in the ED, since these patients can be referred to the PCC (Van Uden et al. 2006). The integration is thus cost effective from a societal point of view (Dale et al. 1996, Van Uden et al. 2006). It is, however, under debate whether the integration is cost effective for the EDs and PCCs (Van Uden et al. 2006). For EDs, the integration decreases the number of patient visits, possibly around 50% (Grol et al. 2006). This reduces turnover, and all kinds of economies-of-scale advantages. In the Netherlands, the hourly rate for primary care outside office hours for GPs (set by government and paid by health insurers) is considered low and not profitable. Hence, GPs do not welcome the increased workload.

Application of the Framework

To successfully implement an integrated ED/PCC, the involved parties must address the aforementioned problems, and discuss how to manage the new organization's planning and control. To facilitate this discussion in a structured way, the framework can be instrumental. We mention some of the key issues per managerial area:

- *Medical planning*. How does the case of joint triage affect the role and responsibilities of the GPs, who before were considered the 'gatekeepers' of health care delivery?
- *Resource capacity planning*. What are the "24/7" resource capacity requirements? Is collaboration of ED and PCC staff possible despite the fact that they work for two independent cost centers—if so, to what extent should they collaborate?
- *Materials planning*. Should the ED and PCC jointly purchase materials? Where should inventories be kept, and who has ownership?
- *Financial planning*. Is an integration of ED and PCC cost effective for hospitals, GPs, insurance companies, society? Is it profitable for the ED to employ general practitioners for self-referrals instead of integrating with a PCC? Should hospitals, insurance companies, or the government compensate GPs for the increased workload? Should the ED and PCC be integrated into one cost center?

Based on the outcomes of the discussion around the aforementioned issues, the framework can be used further to design appropriate planning and control on all hierarchical levels and in all managerial areas. We are currently doing this for the recently integrated ED/PCC in Almelo in the Netherlands. Here, we aim to optimize the care processes within the given limited budget, focusing not only on efficiency and quality, but also on patient experience. For the latter we use a conjoint analysis to assess patient preferences in different organizational variants of the EDD/PCC. We use discrete event simulation to prospectively assess various organization interventions, which are inventoried using brainstorming sessions with the relevant stakeholders. Tactical interventions, for example, concern staffing levels during and outside office hours, patient routing, the use of an acute care and diagnostic ward, and the question whether to share the use diagnostic resources (e.g. x-ray and lab) with elective care departments in the hospital. Operational interventions for example concern patient prioritizing/scheduling in various stages of the clinical course.

12.5 Conclusions

In this chapter we propose a reference framework for health care planning and control, which hierarchically structures planning and control functions in multiple managerial areas. It offers a common language for all involved decision makers: clinical staff, managers, and experts on planning and control. This allows coherent formulation and realization of objectives on all levels and in all managerial areas (Delesie 1998). The framework is widely applicable to any type of health care provider or to specific departments within a health care organization. The contents of the framework depend on the application at hand, for example an organizational intervention, a decision making process or a health care delivery process.

While existing management and control approaches use either an "organizational unit"/vertical perspective or a "business process"/horizontal perspective, our framework accommodates both approaches. The framework facilitates a structural analysis of the planning and control functions and their interaction. Moreover, it helps to identify managerial problems regarding, for example, planning functions that are deficient or inappropriate, that lack coherence, or have conflicting objectives.

When managerial deficiencies have been identified, the framework can be used to demarcate the scope of organization interventions. In general, focusing on problems on lower hierarchical levels reduces uncertainty, as inherently the planning horizon is shorter and more information is available. However, flexibility (e.g. regarding resource expansion) is also lower. Focusing on problems on higher hierarchical levels increases the potential impact (e.g. cost savings, waiting time reduction, quality of care); however, required investments are usually also higher, and effects of interventions are felt on a longer term.

Regardless of the focal point of organization interventions, the framework emphasizes the implications from and for adjacent managerial functions. It can thus be prevented that stake holding decision makers are not involved, and that interventions like "more capacity" (the universal panacea) are not made without considering the possible effects for all underlying and related planning functions. As a result, interventions will have a higher chance of success.

As argued in Sect. 12.1, the literature regarding the application of OR/MS in health care is expanding rapidly. This framework can also be instrumental in the design of taxonomies for, for example, literature on outpatient department (appointment) planning, operating theatre planning and scheduling, and inventory management of medical supplies. Scientific papers can be positioned in the framework to illustrate the managerial area(s) they focus on, and the hierarchical level of decision making in the considered problem(s). Similarly, also algorithmic developments can be classified and positioned in the framework.

The framework can easily be extended to include other managerial areas or hierarchical levels. In particular *information management* is a managerial area that should go hand in hand with development of innovative organization-wide planning approaches. "Business-IT Alignment" addresses how companies can apply information technology to formulate and achieve their goals on the various hierarchical levels (Laudon and Laudon 2010). Another relevant managerial area that can be included is *quality and safety management*, which is involved in almost all care delivery processes, and can be decomposed hierarchically. The framework can also be expanded in the hierarchical decomposition. There may be different functions on a single hierarchical level within a managerial area, which by themselves have a natural hierarchy. For example decisions regarding the construction of a new building are of a higher level than decisions regarding the expansion of a ward, while both are strategic decisions.

12.6 Outlook

The increasing costs of health care and the introduction of (managed) competitive health care have spurred the need for improved health care management. In our experience in the Netherlands, the focus of this improvement is predominantly on the operational level, and particularly on patients with a predictable clinical course. A typical example is the widespread introduction of clinical pathways, which standardize clinical procedures. After introducing a clinical pathway, a subsequent step is often to reserve capacity for patients following such a clinical pathway. Whether this "unpooled" capacity leads to efficiency or inefficiency remains to be researched. Another example of improvement on the operational level is the introduction of logistical paradigms like lean and six sigma, which have a successful history in manufacturing industry. We believe that the selection of such a paradigm in practice is based on an enthusiastic consultant rather than on proven efficacy (Van Harten et al. 2010). Although efficiency improvements are being reported, we note that, rhetorically, a 5% improvement of a bad performance is still a bad performance.

Unfortunately, "more capacity" is wrongly regarded as the panacea for persistent performance problems in health care; this clearly contributes to rising expenditures. However, without managing the *tactical* implications of such a strategic decision (e.g. by reconsidering the tactical capacity allocation), performance problems are likely to persist. Therefore, research is needed, to assess absolute performance levels, to design new planning and control concepts on all hierarchical levels, and to prospectively assess these using mathematical (simulation) models. Tactical planning in particular deserves attention, as this level of control is underexposed in practice due to its inherent complexity. The health care planning and control framework presented in this chapter is inspired by, and designed to support, these recommendations.

In recent years, the OR/MS community has shown a rapid increase of attention to health care operations management. This book is a showcase of the developments in recent years. We believe that this field will continue to flourish in the coming decades, just like manufacturing operations management has in the last decades.

Acknowledgments This research is supported by the Dutch Technology Foundation STW, applied science division of NWO and the Technology Program of the Ministry of Economic Affairs.

References

Anthony RN (1965) Planning and control systems: a framework for analysis. Harvard Business School Division of Research, Boston

Blake JT, Carter MW (1997) Surgical process scheduling: a structured review. J Soc Health Syst 5:17–30

Brailsford SC, Vissers JMH (2010) OR in health care: a European perspective. Eur J Oper Res 212(2):223–234

Brailsford SC, Harper PR, Patel B, Pitt M (2009) An analysis of the academic literature on simulation and modeling in health care. J Simul 3:130–140

Butler TW, Karwan KR, Sweigart JR (1992) Multi-level strategic evaluation of hospital plans and decisions. J Operational Res Society 43(7):665–675

Butler TW, Keong Leong G, Everett LN (1996) The operations management role in hospital strategic planning. J Operations Manage 14:137–156

Carter M (2002) Diagnosis: mismanagement of resources. OR/MS today 29(2):26–32

CHOIR (2011) Center for health care Operations Improvement and Research at the University of Twente. http://www.utwente.nl/choir/. Accessed 12 July 2011

Dale J, Lang H, Roberts JA, Green J, Glucksmann E (1996) Cost effectiveness of treating primary care patients in accident and emergency: a comparison between general practitioners, senior house officers, and registrars. Br Med J 312:1340–1344

Dash A (2009) Lost + found: making the right choice in equipment location systems. Healthc Facility Manage 22(11):19–21

De Vries G, Bertrand JWM, Vissers JMH (1999) Design requirements for health care production control systems. Production Plan Control 10:559–569

Delesie L (1998) Bridging the gap between clinicians and health managers. Eur J Oper Res 105(2):248–256

Glouberman S, Mintzberg H (2001a) Managing the care of health and the cure of disease—part I: differentiation. Health Care Manage Rev 26:56–69

Glouberman S, Mintzberg H (2001b) Managing the care of health and the cure of disease—part II: integration. Healthc Manage Rev 26:70–84

Graves SC (2002) Manufacturing planning and control. In: Pardalos P, Resende M (eds) Handbook of applied optimization. Oxford University Press, New York, pp 728–746

Grol R, Giesen PHJ, van Uden C (2006) After-hours care in the United Kingdom, Denmark, and the Netherlands: new models. Health Aff 25(6):1733–1737

Hans EW, Herroelen WS, Leus R, Wullink G (2003) A hierarchical approach to multi-project planning under uncertainty. Omega 35(5):563–577

Hax AC, Meal HC (1975) Hierarchical integration of production planning and scheduling. In: Geisler M (ed) TIMS Studies in the management sciences: logistics. North Holland-American Elsevier, Amsterdam, pp 53–69

Johnson G, Scholes K, Whittington R (2008) Exploring corporate strategy, 8th edn. Prentice Hall, New Jersey

Khoumbati K, Themistocleous M, Irani Z (2006) Evaluating the adoption of enterprise application integration in health-care organizations. J Manage Inf Syst 22(4):69–108

Lattimer V, Turnbull J, Burgess A, Surridge H, Gerard K, Lathlean J, Smith H, George S (2005) Effect of introduction of integrated out of hours care in England: observational study. Br Med J 331(7508):81–84

Laudon KC, Laudon JP (2010) Management information systems, 11th edn. Prentice Hall, dNew Jersey

Li LX, Benton WC, Keong Leong G (2002) The impact of strategic operations management decisions on community hospital performance. J Oper Manage 20:389–408

Marri HB, Gunasekaran A, Grieve RJ (1998) Computer-aided process planning: a state of art. Int J Adv Manuf Technol 14(4):261–268

Maynard A (1991) Developing the health care market. Econ J 101(408):1277–1286

Maynard A (1994) Can competition enhance efficiency in health care? Lessons from the reform of the U.K. National Health Service. Soc Sci Med 39(10):1433–1445

OECD (2011) Data from 2011 from the website of Organisation of Economic Co-operation and Development. http://www.oecd.org/health. Accessed 12 July 2011

ORAHS (2011) Operational Research Applied to Health Services. http://orahs.di.unito.it/. Accessed 12 July 2011

Orlicky J (1975) Material requirements planning. McGraw-Hill, London

Ozcan YA (2009) Quantitative methods in health care management—techniques and applications, 2nd edn. Jossey-Bass/Wiley, San Francisco, pp 6–9

Porter ME, Teisberg EO (2007) How physicians can change the future of health care. J American Med Assoc 297:1103–1111

Rhyne D, Jupp D (1988) Health care requirements planning: a conceptual framework. Healthc Manage Rev 13(1):17–27

Roth AV, van Dierdonck R (1995) Hospital resource planning. Prod Operat Manage 4:2–29

Van Harten WH, Hans EW, Van Lent WAM (2010) Aanpak efficiency te ondoordacht (in Dutch, translation: approach to efficiency often ill-considered). Medisch Contact 6:264–267

Van Uden CJ, Ament AJ, Voss GB, Wesseling G, Winkens RA, Van Schayck OC, Crebolder HF (2006) Out-of-hours primary care. Implications of organisation on costs. BMC Family Practice 7(1):29

Vissers JMH (1998) Patient flow-based allocation of inpatient resources: a case study. Eur J Oper Res 105:356–370

Vissers JMH, Beech R (2005) Health operations management. Routledge, London

Vissers JMH, Bertrand JWM, De Vries G (2001) A framework for production control in health care organizations. Prod Plan Control 12:591–604

Wachtel RE, Dexter F (2008) Tactical increases in operating room block time for capacity planning should not be based on utilization. Anesthesia Analgesia 106(1):215–226

Westert GP, Burgers JS, Verkleij H (2009) The Netherlands: regulated competition behind the dykes? Br Med J 339:839–842

Zijm WHM (2000) Towards intelligent manufacturing planning and control systems. OR Spectrum 22:313–345

About the Authors

Bjorn Berg (Chapter 6) is a Ph.D. student in the Edward P. Fitts Department of Industrial and Systems Engineering at North Carolina State University. He received a B.A. from St. Olaf College and previously worked as a statistical programmer analyst in the Division of Health Care Policy & Research at Mayo Clinic in Rochester, MN. His research interests include methods for optimization under uncertainty with applications to health care delivery.

Richard J. Boucherie (Chapter 9) Ph.D., received M.Sc. degrees in 1988 in Applied Mathematics (stochastic operations research) and Theoretical Physics (statistical physics) from the Universiteit Leiden, and received the Ph.D. degree in Econometrics in 1992 for a thesis on Product-form in queueing networks from the Vrije Universiteit, Amsterdam. Following positions at INRIA Sophia Antipolis, CWI Amsterdam, and Universiteit van Amsterdam, since 2003 he is full professor of Stochastic Operations Research in the department of Applied Mathematics of the University of Twente. His research interests are in queueing theory with application areas including sensor networks and health care. Richard is chair of the UT Industrial Engineering research and educational programmes and co-founder of the UT research center CHOIR (Center for Health Care Operations Improvement and Research) in the area of health care logistics.

Nebil Buyurgan (Chapter 10) Ph.D., is an Associate Professor in the Industrial Engineering Department at the University of Arkansas. He received his doctorate in Engineering Management from the University of Missouri-Rolla. As the author or coauthor of over 40 technical papers, his research interests include health care systems engineering, health care logistics, health care/medical informatics, and data standards.

Murray J. Côté (Chapter 3) Ph.D., is Director of the Master of Health Administration Program and Associate Professor in the Department of Health Policy & Management at the Texas A&M Health Science Center. Dr. Côté earned

R. Hall (ed.), *Handbook of Healthcare System Scheduling*,
International Series in Operations Research & Management Science 168,
DOI: 10.1007/978-1-4614-1734-7, © Springer Science+Business Media, LLC 2012

a B.A. in Political Science and an M.B.A. from the University of Saskatchewan, Canada and a Ph.D. in Management Science from Texas A&M University. Professor Côté's primary research interests are in health care operations, including patient flow, capacity planning and management, demand forecasting, and nurse staffing and scheduling. His research findings have been published in *Decision Sciences*, the *European Journal of Operational Research, Health Care Management Science*, and *Socio-Economic Planning Sciences*, among others. In addition, his research has received awards from the Decision Sciences Institute and the Health care Financial Management Association. Professor Côté has obtained extramural funding from the Agency for Health Care Research and Quality, the Centers for Medicare and Medicaid Services, the National Science Foundation, the Department of Veterans Affairs, and the Education and Research Foundation of the American Production and Inventory Control Society. He has also consulted for a variety of health care organizations including CIGNA, the Texas Transplant Institute at Methodist Specialty and Transplant Hospital, and Shands Jacksonville.

Dr. Brian Denton (Chapter 6) Ph.D., is an Associate Professor at North Carolina State University in the Edward P. Fitts Department of Industrial & Systems Engineering. Previously he has been a Senior Associate Consultant at Mayo Clinic in the College of Medicine, and a Senior Engineer at IBM. He is currently a Fellow at the Cecil Sheps Center for Health Services Research at University of North Carolina. His primary research interests are in optimization under uncertainty and applications to health care delivery and medical decision making. He completed his Ph.D. in Management Science at McMaster University, his M.Sc. in Physics at York University, and his B.Sc. in Chemistry and Physics at McMaster University in Hamilton, Ontario, Canada.

Diwakar Gupta (Chapter 4) Ph.D., is a professor in the Industrial & Systems Engineering program and a professor of Mechanical Engineering at the University of Minnesota. He also holds a courtesy appointment as an affiliate senior member in the Health Services Research, Policy, and Administration Division of the School of Public Health. He received his Ph.D. in Management Sciences from the University of Waterloo. Before joining the University of Minnesota, Dr. Gupta held a tenured faculty appointment at the DeGroote School of Business, McMaster University, Canada. His research interests are in the areas of health care operations, state transportation agencies' operations, and supply chain management. Dr. Gupta's research has been published in *M&SOM, Management Science, Operations Research, Production and Operations Management*, and *IIE Transactions*. He has served on the editorial boards of many journals, and as editor-in-chief of the *Flexible Manufacturing and Services* journal. He currently serves as a Departmental Editor for the Health Care and Public Policy Department of the *IIE Transactions* focused issue on Operations Engineering. Dr. Gupta has been either a principal investigator or a co-investigator on 35 projects sponsored by a variety of federal and state agencies including DHHS, NSF, AHRQ, VA, MnDOT, NSERC, SSHRC, and CHSRF, as well as private companies. More information about his research projects can be found by visiting the web page of his research lab—Supply Chain and Operations Research Laboratory—at www.isye.umn.edu/labs/scorlab.

Randolph Hall (Chapters 1 and 8) Ph.D., is Vice President of Research at University of Southern California in addition to being Professor in the Epstein Department of Industrial and Systems Engineering. Dr. Hall is the author of *Queueing Methods for Services and Manufacturing* and the editor for the *Handbook of Transportation Science* and *Patient Flow: Reducing Delay in Health Care Delivery*. He has worked with health care systems throughout California to improve patient flow, in such areas as surgery, emergency departments and specialized clinics. He has also served as director for the Center for Risk and Economic Analysis of Terrorism Events and the National Center for Metropolitan Transportation Research. Dr. Hall graduated from the University of California, with a Ph.D. in Civil Engineering and a B.S. in Industrial Engineering and Operations Research.

Erwin Hans (Chapter 5) Ph.D., is a full tenured Associate Professor of Operations Management and Process Optimization in Health Care, and Director of Education within the Industrial Engineering and Management program at the University of Twente in the Netherlands. His research focuses on the area of health care process optimization using modeling and optimization techniques from operations research and management science. He co-founded the Center of Health Care Operations Improvement & Research (CHOIR—http://www.utwente.nl/choir), the Netherlands' center of expertise in health care logistics. CHOIR extensively colla-borates with the Dutch health care sector, both in operations research/ operations management research and teaching of health care professionals.

Mark Van Houdenhoven (Chapter 12) Ph.D., is member of the executive board of the HAGA teaching Hospital of Den Haag in the Netherlands. In the last 17 years he has served in several management positions in Dutch Health Care. His research focuses on the area of health care economics and health care process optimization. In 1997 he received his Ph.D. on his thesis: "Health Care Logistics: The Art of Balance".

Peter Hulshof (Chapter 12) is a Ph.D. candidate at University of Twente's Center of Health Care Operations Improvement & Research (CHOIR), the Netherlands' center of expertise in health care logistics. During his Ph.D., Mr. Hulshof collaborated with Reinier de Graaf Ziekenhuis, a hospital in Delft in the Netherlands. He is fellow initiator and one of the main contributors to ORchestra, the online bibliography of the literature in the field of operations research/ management science in health care (http://www.utwente.nl/choir/orchestra).

Laleh Kardar is a Ph.D. student of Industrial Engineering at the University of Houston (UH). She received two B.Sc. degrees in Biomedical and Industrial Engineering and an M.Sc. degree in Biomedical Engineering from Amirkabir University of Technology, Tehran, Iran in 2005, 2007 and 2008, respectively. From 2007 until 2010, she was working as a researcher in the logistics and supply chain management research group, Institute of Trade Studies and Research (ITSR), at the Iran ministry of commerce. Currently, she is serving as a secretary of INFORMS student chapter at UH. She has co-authored and edited three books in the field of Logistics and Supply Chain Management with leading publishers like Springer-Verlag, Elsevier, and IGI Global. Her current research interests concern the design of algorithms for optimization problems in health care.

J. (Joris) van de Klundert (Chapter 7) Ph.D., is Professor of Management of Health Service Organizations at the Institute of Health Policy & Management (iBMG), Erasmus University Rotterdam. From 1985 to 1991 he studied Managerial Informatics at this university. He obtained a Ph.D. (Thesis: Scheduling problems in automated manufacturing) from Maastricht University in 1996. Since then he has held various positions at Maastricht University. Before moving back to Rotterdam he served as Professor of Value Chain Optimization. He continues to work on this theme in his current positions, yet focused on the health service industry.

Gino Lim (Chapter 3) Ph.D., is an associate professor and chairman of Industrial Engineering at the University of Houston. His research interests are in optimization models and computational algorithms, especially operations research applications in health care systems, emergency planning, and logistics. He received the Pierskalla Best Paper award for his work on Gamma Knife radiotherapy optimization for brain cancer patients. His current research projects include proton radiation treatment planning optimization, hospital staff scheduling, emergency evacuation planning, and management. His research projects have been funded by various federal, state, and local funding agencies with total funding in excess of $8M USD. Besides research, he has also been an outstanding educator whose ability and talent have been well recognized with numerous teaching excellence awards by the department, the Cullen College of Engineering, and several professional organizations. Dr. Lim received both his M.S. and Ph.D. degrees in Industrial Engineering from University of Wisconsin—Madison.

Arezou Mobasher (Chapter 3) Ph.D., received her B.Sc. and M.Sc. degrees in Industrial Engineering from Sharif University of Technology (SUT), Tehran, Iran, in 2004 and 2006, respectively. She earned her Ph.D. degree from the University of Houston, Industrial Engineering department in 2011. Her research interests concern the design of algorithms for optimization problems in health care. She has developed optimization nurse scheduling models and heuristic solution algorithms to solve nurse scheduling problems in general clinics and operating suites. Her research was based on the collaboration with the University of Texas MD Anderson Cancer Center. She has been a member of INFORMS and the Industrial Engineering Research Conference since 2009 and, currently, she is serving as activity coordinator of INFORMS student chapter at the University of Houston.

Ashlea R. Milburn (Chapter 11) Ph.D., is an Assistant Professor in the Department of Industrial Engineering at the University of Arkansas. Dr. Bennett's research interests include the development and application of operations research tools and techniques for problems encountered in both health care and logistics systems. She is especially interested in home health care logistics planning. Dr. Bennett is a member of Society for Health Systems, INFORMS, Institute of Industrial Engineers, and Alpha Pi Mu.

Edward A. Pohl (Chapter 10) Ph.D., is an Associate Professor in the Department of Industrial Engineering at the University of Arkansas and serves as the Director of the Operations Management Program. Dr. Pohl received his Ph.D. in Systems and Industrial Engineering from the University of Arizona, an M.S. in Reliability Engineering from the University of Arizona, an M.S. in Systems Engineering from Air Force Institute of Technology, an M.S. in Engineering Management from the University of Dayton, and a B.S.E.E. from Boston University. His primary research interests are in risk, reliability, and their application to supply chains, decision making under uncertainty, engineering optimization, and probabilistic design. He is a senior member of Institute of Industrial Engineers, a senior member of American Society for Quality, and a senior member of IEEE. Dr. Pohl serves as an Associate Editor for the *Journal of Military Operations Research*, and the *Journal of Risk and Reliability*. He is a member of the Reliability and Maintainability Symposium (RAMS) management committee and is a two time winner of the Alan Plait award for outstanding tutorial at RAMS.

Manuel D. Rossetti (Chapter 10) Ph.D., P.E. is a Professor in the Industrial Engineering Department at the University of Arkansas. He received his Ph.D. in Industrial and Systems Engineering from The Ohio State University. Dr. Rossetti has published over 80 journal and conference articles in the areas of simulation, logistics, and health care and has been the principal investigator (PI) or Co-PI on funded research projects totaling over 3.4 million dollars. He was selected as a Lilly Teaching Fellow in 1997/98 and has been nominated three times for outstanding teaching awards. He was voted best industrial engineering (IE) teacher by IE students in 2007 and won the IE Department Outstanding Teacher Award in 2001–02, 2007–08, and 2010–11. He serves as an Associate Editor for the *International Journal of Modeling and Simulation* and is active in the Institute of Industrial Engineers, INFORMS, and American Society for Engineering Education. He was a Winter Simulation Conference (WSC) proceedings editor in 2004 and a co-editor for the 2009 WSC. He is also author of the textbook *Simulation Modeling and Arena* published by John Wiley & Sons.

P.S. (Pieter) Stepaniak (Chapter 7) Ph.D., (1967) is Director of Operating Rooms at the Catharina Hospital Eindhoven and a commercial pilot. Further, he is performing various scientific studies in optimizing operating room efficiency. He studied Econometrics and Economics at the Erasmus University Rotterdam. He has worked as a consultant at a big five consultancy firm and held various management positions in and outside the health care industry. In December, 2010, he obtained a Ph.D. at the Erasmus University (Thesis: 'Modeling and Management of Variation in the Operating Theater').

Martin Utley (Chapter 2) Ph.D., is Professor of Operational Research and Director of the Clinical Operational Research Unit at University College London, where he has worked since completing a Ph.D. in Particle Physics in 1996. Over this time, he has worked closely with clinicians in a variety of specialties, including pediatric cardiac surgery, rheumatology, thoracic surgery, and intensive care. His current research interests are in the development and use of risk models to provide clinical teams with tools to monitor their clinical outcomes, strategic and operational capacity planning in health care and the use of modeling to support health protection policy. Dr. Utley acts as scientific advisor for the National Confidential Enquiry into Patient Outcome and Death and as editor of the journal *Operations Research for Health Care*.

Peter T. Vanberkel (Chapter 5) Ph.D., graduated with a Ph.D. in Operations Research (University of Twente) in 2011 and is the first graduate from the Center of Health Care Operations Improvement & Research (CHOIR)—the Netherlands' center of expertise in health care logistics. Dr. Vanberkel also attended St. Francis Xavier University and Dalhousie University, where he earned a bachelor's degree in Industrial Engineering and a master's of Applied Science degree. He is a registered professional engineer with Engineers Nova Scotia (Canada) and has worked as an industrial engineer at IWK Health Centre and the Capital District Health Authority. As a researcher he has worked at the Netherlands Cancer Institute—Antoni van Leeuwenhoek Hospital, the British Columbia Cancer Agency, the University of British Columbia and the University of Twente.

R.A.C. (Ronald) van der Velden (Chapter 7) M.Sc., studied Econometrics at the Erasmus University Rotterdam. He graduated performing a multi-objective analysis of online and offline surgical scheduling heuristics. At the same time he worked as a student assistant, doing research on the effect of risk aversion on operating room efficiency. He is currently working as an advanced planning solutions consultant at Quintiq.

A.P.M. (Albert) Wagelmans (Chapter 7) Ph.D., is Professor of Operations Research at the Rotterdam School of Economics, Erasmus University Rotterdam. He obtained a Ph.D. (Thesis: Sensitivity analysis in combinatorial optimization) at the Erasmus University. His current research focuses on the analysis and development of models and techniques to solve planning problems in (health care) logistics and public transportation. He is currently Associate Director of Erasmus Research Institute of Management (ERIM) and Director of the bachelor–master program in Econometrics and Management Science.

Wen-Ya Wang (Chapter 4) is a Ph.D. candidate in the Industrial and Systems Engineering program at the University of Minnesota. His research interests include data-driven modeling and Industrial Engineering/Operations Research applications for health care delivery systems. Prior to joining the University of Minnesota, she received her master's degree in Applied Statistics from the University of

Michigan, Ann Arbor, and a bachelor's degree in Business Administration from the National Taiwan University.

Dave Worthington (Chapter 2) is a Senior Lecturer in Operational Research at Lancaster University Management School and has been researching and applying operations research and statistics in the health services since working in the National Health Service in the late 1970s. His health services research interests are wide ranging, and have included waiting list management, nurse workforce planning, outpatient clinic management, inpatient costing, facility location, walk-in centre design, intensive care unit planning, and accident and emergency staffing. Much of his work focuses on patient flow modeling in hospitals, quite often concerned with capacity planning. He is particularly interested in modeling health care systems which feature important time-dependent and stochastic behavior, of which there are many. A current research focus is on the challenge of managing planned and unplanned workloads in health care using a queue modeling perspective.

Maartje E. Zonderland (Chapter 9) received B.Sc. degrees in Industrial Engineering (2003) and Applied Mathematics (2006), and an M.Sc. degree in Applied Mathematics (2007) from the University of Twente, Enschede, the Netherlands. She is currently working towards completion of her Ph.D. thesis in stochastic operations research, titled *Curing the Queue*, under supervision of Professor Richard J. Boucherie and is affiliated with the UT research center CHOIR (Center for Health Care Operations Improvement and Research) in the area of health care logistics. Additionally, Ms. Zonderland has worked since 2008 as a staff consultant for Leiden University Medical Center, which is one of the eight academic hospitals in the Netherlands.

Index

R. Hall (ed.), *Handbook of Healthcare System Scheduling*,
International Series in Operations Research & Management Science 168,
DOI: 10.1007/978-1-4614-1734-7,

MIX
Papier aus verantwortungsvollen Quellen
Paper from responsible sources
FSC® C105338

If you have any concerns about our products,
you can contact us on
ProductSafety@springernature.com

In case Publisher is established outside the EU,
the EU authorized representative is:
Springer Nature Customer Service Center GmbH
Europaplatz 3, 69115 Heidelberg, Germany

Printed by Libri Plureos GmbH
in Hamburg, Germany